CW01512252

'An excellent introduction to the subject.'
Antony Beevor, author of *Russia: Revolution and Civil War 1917–1921*

'History at its best – elegantly written, rigorously researched. A wonderful weave of politics, piety, and Ash's personal journey.'
Lyse Doucet, BBC Chief International Correspondent

'I loved *The Baton and the Cross* – an engaging, well-informed and pacy survey of the profound but often overlooked impact of the Russian Orthodox Church on the formation of Putin's imperial ideology, which led 'Holy Russia' into war against Ukraine and the West. A timely and important book.'
Orlando Figes, author of *A People's Tragedy: The Russian Revolution*

'From the first page of *The Baton and the Cross*, fascinating fact after fact tumble out of this elegantly written book. Switching effortlessly between the Russian Orthodox Church's long history and disturbing present, Lucy Ash provides us with the definitive explanation of how the truly Unholy Alliance between Patriarch Kirill and Vladimir Putin was cemented with the blood of Ukraine.'
Misha Glenny, author of *McMafia: Seriously Organised Crime*

'If you want to understand why Putin thinks and acts as he does, then read this. By combining historical detail with first-hand reporting, Lucy Ash shows the hold that the Orthodox Church has over Russian power – now and in centuries past. Her erudition is leavened by her accessible style; this highly readable account casts a light onto a crucial but neglected aspect of Russian culture and politics.'
Lindsey Hilsum, International Editor, Channel 4 News

'In her thoroughly researched and beautifully written book Lucy Ash insist that if we want to grasp Putin's Russia, we should focus not on the transformation of the state, but on the transformation of the Church.'
Ivan Krastev, co-author of *The Light that Failed: A Reckoning*

'Lucy Ash has written a spellbinding book that will help you to understand how the Russian Orthodox Church became a vital force in Putin's existential war against Ukraine. This book is pure intellectual jazz, mixing the author's personal experience – starting from her first visits to the USSR in 1970s – with breath-taking analysis of Russia's convoluted religious history.'
Andrei Kurkov, author of *Death and the Penguin*

'Near the beginning of the book, there is a description of the Bassein Moskva, on the site of the former Cathedral of Christ the Saviour, a place that I remember well from my childhood. Lucy Ash's vivid storytelling transported me back in time, guiding me through the long and brutal history of Russia's relationship with religion and Christianity.

Her story is a painfully critical reflection of events in Russia today. Easily accessible and beautifully constructed, the book is essential reading for anyone looking to better understand Putin's motivations around his war in Ukraine.'
Marina Litvinenko

'Lucy Ash, a seasoned and sympathetic watcher of Russia, wrote a compelling and much needed book of how the centuries-old union between the state and the Church poisoned Russian society.'
Andrei Soldatov, co-author of *The Compatriots*

'An essential guide to understanding the often apparently contradictory and tangled truth about the Russian Orthodox Church and its political leverage, this book combines a clear historical survey with unique first-hand insight and granular analysis from the author's long experience as a journalist with specialist knowledge of Russia. It is a reliable, judicious, and deeply sobering analysis of one of the moral open sores of our world.'
Rowan Williams, former Archbishop of Canterbury

THE BATON AND THE CROSS

THE BATON AND THE CROSS

Russia's Church from Pagans to Putin

LUCY ASH

ICON

For John, Alex and Constance

Published in the UK in 2024 by
Icon Books Ltd, Omnibus Business Centre,
39–41 North Road, London N7 9DP
email: info@iconbooks.com
www.iconbooks.com

ISBN: 978-183773-183-1
eBook: 978-183773-184-8

Typeset by SJmagic DESIGN SERVICES, India

Printed and bound in the UK

CONTENTS

PROLOGUE
Christ the Saviour

The immersion ritual would fill me with dread. From the changing room, you had to edge carefully down a flight of slippery steps. Then you ducked under heavy plastic curtains, swam a few feet underwater and found yourself under the open sky. However cold it was outside, the water was the temperature of a warm bath. Such were the thick clouds of steam rising from the surface, you struggled to avoid bumping into other swimmers.

On my first visit, aged fifteen, I panicked when I lost my chaperone. Vitaly was a bespectacled professor of electrical engineering who had visited my father's laboratory in London and was keen to repay the favour by showing me around Moscow. 'I'll see you inside,' he told me at the turnstile. 'I'll be in a black swimming cap.'

I swam around the vast pool in the chlorinated fog for what seemed like hours; several men were wearing black rubber on their heads and there was no sign of Vitaly. Eventually, I heaved myself out and stood shivering on the side, trying to spot him. 'Get back in right now!' shouted a lifeguard in a fur hat. 'Are you crazy? It's minus-fifteen degrees!'

The circular outdoor pool could accommodate 20,000 swimmers per day and at one point was four metres deep. To the left, you could see the crenelated red walls and towers of the Kremlin. If the wind was blowing in the right way, sweet smells wafted across the river from the Red October chocolate factory on the opposite bank.

I had gone to Moscow on a school trip in the late 1970s, during the 'stagnation era' of Leonid Brezhnev. My visit was unexpectedly extended when Viktor and Larisa, some other engineering friends of my father's, invited me to stay in their cramped flat on the outskirts of the capital for an extra ten days. It was a formative experience. After university, in the early 1980s, I was determined to get back to Moscow and discovered that you could get a visa working as a nanny for foreign diplomats. It was the twilight of the *zastoi* – stagnation – period, presided over by two grey-faced, ailing leaders, Yuri Andropov and Konstantin Chernenko. Whenever I had time off, I went back to the open-air pool and practised my Russian, chatting to women in the showers. A decade later, back in Moscow in 1990 as a radio producer for the BBC, I grew addicted to pre-breakfast swims. In the dead of winter, I loved the surreal feeling of doing breaststroke in the clouds.

Not all Muscovites shared my affection for the *Bassein Moskva* with its rusty pipes and cracked floor tiles. They told me the place was unhygienic and contaminated with algae. No repairs were done, they said, because the Moscow authorities had other uses for such a potentially lucrative city centre site. Other friends warned me the pool attracted perverts who tried to grab your private parts underwater, their faces hidden in the steam. Some grandmothers gave it a wide berth for different reasons. They saw it as the scene of a monstrous crime and an ever-present reminder of the darkest hours in Russia's spiritual past. The pool, with its plumes of steam dominating the nearby skyline, did indeed have an extraordinarily turbulent history. I had been splashing around under the phantom Byzantine dome of the largest church ever built in Russia. This site embodied the struggle for the nation's soul after seven decades of state-imposed atheism.

On a crisp December morning in 1931, the Cathedral of Christ the Saviour was destroyed in a series of explosions. It took just an hour to bring down the mighty structure which had taken more than 40 years to build and was commissioned by Tsar Alexander I to immortalise Russia's 1812 victory over Napoleon. Some believed the cathedral was cursed from the outset. It involved the demolition of the ancient Alekseevsky Convent, built in honour of Metropolitan Alexius, a prominent fourteenth-century bishop. The nuns protested for five years but were eventually forced out. Legend has it that their abbess cursed the ground on which the cathedral was built. 'The feeling of mortal failure or perhaps even tragedy hung over the Cathedral of Christ like the sword of Damocles,' wrote one architectural historian.[1]

It took half a century to build and decorate the cathedral at a cost of 15 million roubles. In comparison, Russia sold Alaska to the US in 1867 for 7 million roubles, less than half that price. Christ the Saviour was eventually consecrated as part of Alexander III's coronation ceremony in May 1883. After the liturgy, in a tent outside the cathedral, Pyotr Tchaikovsky's 1812 overture, specially written for the occasion, was played for the first time. Alexander, a man whose party trick was bending iron pokers, adored the bellowing brass, church bells and multiple cannon shots. To him, Tchaikovsky's long descending scale symbolising the retreat of the invading French army followed by the hymn 'God Save the Tsar' was stirring and patriotic. The composer hated the piece. He confessed in a letter to his patroness that it was 'very loud and noisy, but [without] artistic merit, because I wrote it without warmth and without love'.[2]

Many artists were similarly scathing about the cathedral. It was 'ugly, bulky, and cumbersome', sniffed one art historian.[3] Alexander Herzen, the revolutionary writer, said all the churches built by the architect Konstantin Ton were 'full of hypocrisy, anachronism, and looked like five-headed cruet stands with onion domes instead of stoppers'. Ordinary people loved it. The Ukrainian art historian Konstantin Akinsha calls it probably the most successful mass-culture project of pre-revolutionary Russia. Its colourful murals provided an encyclopaedia of the Russian Orthodox world accessible to every illiterate peasant.[4]

Christ the Saviour carried on as a place of worship for several years after the October Revolution, although it was barely heated in winter and some of the murals began to go mouldy with the damp. Vasily Bellavin, a bishop, was elected Patriarch of the Russian Orthodox Church in 1917. As is the custom, he changed his name, taking the moniker Tikhon. He founded the Brotherhood of the Cathedral of Christ the Saviour in order to prevent it from being closed. He wanted to 'unite believers around this great historical monument and assist the clergy in providing for the continued spiritual evolution of Orthodox Russia'. However, its days were numbered. The Communists disliked the way the cathedral dominated the Moscow skyline – to them it was out of place in the modern age of atheism. Waves of propaganda preceded its destruction. This was 'a poisonous mushroom on the face of Moscow', a place where landlords and merchants, gendarmes and prostitutes gathered in 'the old vile world of tsarist times'.

Thousands of churches were badly damaged or destroyed in the 1920s and 1930s, at the height of Stalin's purges; but the size and prominence of Christ the Saviour gave its martyrdom a special resonance. When the decision to demolish it became public, one parishioner was moved to write a long lament which began: 'Farewell, curator of Russian glory Magnificent Cathedral of Christ, Our gold-domed Titan. Your grandeur was plain; over Moscow your gigantic crown Burned like a sun.' The poem circulated in handwritten form among Muscovites who still held it up as a shrine.[5]

The destruction began in the autumn of 1931. Specialists removed the artwork, gold, bronze, copper, mosaics of porphyry, labradorite and other precious stones. They yanked off the gold crosses from the domes with steel cables hooked to tractors. Army battalions and brigades from the Komsomol, the Communist Party youth movement, followed. A cameraman hired to film the demolition recalled paramilitary units swarming over the 'pitiful Cathedral' like a 'swarm of ants'.[6] An impatient Stalin ordered the engineers to use dynamite. It mattered little to him that the cathedral was situated in a densely populated area in the heart of Moscow.

Alexander Pasternak, brother of novelist Boris Pasternak, who lived across the road in Volkhonka Street, had a rude awakening on the morning of 5 December 1931. 'Everything suddenly trembled and shook,' he wrote in his diary, 'as if the bed wanted to jump out from under me – it felt like an earthquake.' Looking out of his window he saw 'a great red-black cloud of dust, gas, and fine rubble, which covered everything like an enormous umbrella'.[7]

The man in charge of the demolition was Lazar Kaganovich, a close associate of Stalin who built the Moscow metro. He later used some of the cathedral's Italian marble to decorate three of the city's underground stations. As the smoke cleared, Kaganovich climbed on the rubble and declared: 'Mother Russia is cast down. We have ripped away her skirts.' Kaganovich later tried to shift the blame for the decision to Vyacheslav Molotov and others, but it is clear from his account that the decision, which was backed by Stalin, was not open to debate. The cathedral was doomed.[8] It was demolished to make way for a new home for the Supreme Soviet of the USSR, supposedly a parliament but nothing more than a rubber-stamping body. With a statue of Lenin on top, the Palace of Soviets was designed to dwarf the Eiffel Tower and the Empire State Building.[9] Lenin's head was to be bigger than a five-storey house. His index finger, pointing towards a shining future, would have been six metres long.

The temple to the new secular faith was never completed. Construction came to a halt in 1941 with the German invasion of the Soviet Union. Steel used for the structure was stripped away to build tank traps and other defences.[10] Even before Hitler's troops arrived, the Palace seemed fated to be a lost cause – thanks to the soft subsoil, thousands of tons of concrete had begun slithering downhill towards the Moscow River. Engineers were brought in to help secure the foundations, but to no avail. To the faithful, the landslide seemed a form of divine retribution. Some compared the levelling of the cathedral to the crucifixion of Christ or the Bolsheviks' murder of the Russian imperial family in 1917.[11]

For more than two decades, the site was reduced to a swampy hole. It became a wasteland, frequented by drunks and prostitutes. Stalin's successor, Nikita Khrushchev, a fervent atheist, eventually covered up the unsightly spot with a massive 13,000-square-metre swimming pool. At the time of its completion in 1960, it was the largest circular pool in the world and it went into the *Guinness Book of Records*. Some elderly parishioners shed a tear as they walked past. Some performed a little shuffle with their feet, or spat over their shoulders, to stamp out the devil. One woman I met in the changing room in the early 1990s told me that if you half-closed your eyes, you could just make out the shimmering silhouette of the demolished cathedral hovering above the water. That reminded me of the legend of Kitezh, a medieval city in central Russia which suddenly disappeared. Just as the invading Mongols were on the cusp of seiz-ing it, the city was submerged beneath the waters of Lake Svetloyar, where it remains to this day. According to the *Kitezh Chronicle*, an anonymous book written in the late-eighteenth century, only the spiritually pure can glimpse it or hear the peal of its bells.

In the late 1980s, as the system began to loosen under Mikhail Gorbachev, a network of Orthodox believers began lobbying to rebuild Christ the Saviour. They met in the workshop of a sculptor, Vladimir Mokrousov, who produced an architectural replica of the cathedral from an old engraving. His model was briefly on display as part of an architectural competition in the Manezh exhibition hall near the Kremlin, although the jury denounced it as 'demagogic' and had it removed. Undeterred, the enthusiasts set up a community. They called it an *Obshchina*, a religious association of twenty or more people – under a Stalin-era law, that was the minimum num-ber needed to lease a church building. It was headed by Vladimir Soloukhin, who wrote a book about travelling around Russia in the 1960s and discovering valuable icons in the unlikeliest of places. One elderly woman was using a magnificent work depicting Palm Sunday as a cover for her barrel of salted cucumbers.[12] A priest, Georgy Dokukin, taught members of the Obshchina how to pray and suggested they registered a bank account for donations. Others on the board included ultranationalists, like the dissident mathema-tician Igor Shafarevich, who claimed that the Bolshevik revolution had been the work of an international cabal of Jews, and the com-poser Georgy Sviridov, who wrote the theme tune for the nightly news programme on Soviet TV.

At a meeting in a Moscow cinema, Sviridov said restoring the cathedral would reinstate 'the human dignity of every Russian per-son'. The dramatic blowing up of Christ the Saviour was the theme of a film called *Khram* (Cathedral), shown to a select audience on the eve of the millennium celebrations in 1988 marking a thousand years since the Eastern Slavs converted to Christianity. He said he had watched with 'terrible sorrow' the newsreel of workmen hacking the building to pieces; it was 'as if they were hammering nails into Christ himself'.[13] On 9 November 1991, *Pravda* (The Truth), the official newspaper of the Communist Party, reported that 'a well-organised column made up of an impressive number of people' set off from Lubyanka, headquarters of the KGB secret police, making its way to the spot where Christ the Saviour Cathedral once stood. 'Lenin, the national shame of Russia,' read one banner. 'We will repent,' said another. A third declared: 'Forgive us Russia for this disgrace that we suffered from 1917 until 19 August 1991.'

That year, 1991, was when everything changed. The August coup by a hardline faction failed to restore Communism. Gorbachev returned to the Kremlin, in office but out of power. The man of the moment was the leader of the Russian Federation, Boris Yeltsin. On 25 December the red flag bearing the hammer and sickle was lowered. The USSR was no more. A new future beckoned, but such was the speed of change, nobody knew what that would be. Yeltsin vowed to rebuild Christ the Saviour, to atone for the sins of the Soviet past. Russians would find 'the path to social harmony, the creation of goodness, and a life in which there will be less room for sin'.[14]

INTRODUCTION

....

Under the crack of the whip, the chanting of priests,
the Russian flock lived as slaves. The unity of Church and
State they called it.
VLADIMIR MAYAKOVSKY, 1923

....

Father Ioann Shevchenko hitches up his cassock and puffs and wheezes as we climb the narrow winding steps. He stops on a balcony halfway up to catch his breath. 'The soldiers dragged their mattresses up here where our choir sings,' he tells me. 'They slept, ate and did everything else here too, judging from the mess they left behind.' At the top of the bell tower, he shows me where Russian snipers took aim at their victims.

Russia's invasion of Ukraine reached Shevchenko's village of Bobryk, east of the capital, Kyiv, on the morning of 5 March 2022. Minutes after the congregation filed out of the Matins service, two Grad rockets smashed into the Church of the Ascension, destroying the roof and blowing out the windows. Three days later, Russian troops arrived and ordered Shevchenko at gunpoint to hand over the keys to his church. After they pulled out, the bodies of six local men were found in a basement in a neighbouring village, their hands tied behind their backs. For three weeks the people of Bobryk were terrorised by shelling. Some of the younger villagers immediately enlisted in the Ukrainian army, ready to fight for their freedom.

This war, the biggest conflict in Europe since 1945, is about territory and geostrategy. Vladimir Putin's rule has been based in grievance and a yearning to restore what he believes to be Russia's great power status. Time and again, he complained of NATO encroachment and Western political and cultural interference in his backyard. Barack Obama's dismissal of Russia as 'a regional power' enraged him. He sees himself as a twenty-first-century Peter the Great, ruling over Slav peoples united by a common language and a common faith. 'Russia is not fighting for land,' says Mykhailo Podolyak, adviser to Ukraine's president Volodymyr Zelensky. 'It is fighting for its right to live in the past.' Crucially, this war is also about religion. Putin was determined to punish Ukraine for carving its own path.

In his mission, the President has an important partner – one who shares his first name. Vladimir Gundyaev, better known as Patriarch Kirill, is head of the Russian Orthodox Church. He is a wily and ruthless politician in his own right. This book is about two men and their mutual dependency. Theirs is a marriage of convenience; one theologian describes it as 'the alliance between the missile and the incense burner'.[1] Putin found in the Church a spiritual outlet for long-held resentments and an intellectual underpinning for his expansionist foreign policy. Kirill, like his forebears, sought political patronage and access to wealth. An abusive co-dependency between church and state has perpetuated itself over the centuries. It is a toxin inside Russian society. I am devoting much of this book to history to show how this poison has worked in the past and how it has re-emerged in the present.

Few heads of state spend their summer holidays poring over history books, as Putin did in July 2021. Yet he took the time to write a 5,000-word essay entitled 'On the Historical Unity of Russians and Ukrainians'. Published eight months before the full-scale invasion, it harks back to a tenth-century homeland in which Kyiv was 'the mother of Russian cities', the place where pagan Eastern Slavs embraced Orthodox Christianity. Ukraine, he believes, is an artificial creation of the Bolsheviks, a patchwork of territories which belonged either to the mediaeval Polish-Lithuanian Commonwealth or to Russia. When the Soviet Union fell apart and Ukraine gained independence, Russia was 'robbed' of people, land and co-religionists.

In recent years, he contends, 'Ukraine was drawn into a dangerous geopolitical game. It would not be an exaggeration to say that the path of forced assimilation, the formation of an ethnically pure Ukrainian state, aggressive towards Russia, is comparable in its consequences to the use of weapons of mass destruction against us.'

In talks with President George W. Bush at a 2008 NATO summit, Putin scoffed that Ukraine was 'not even a country'. After annexing Crimea in March 2014, he described the peninsula as the 'spiritual source' of the Russian state which had 'invaluable civilisational and even sacred importance for Russia'. On 21 February 2022, three days after sending in the tanks, Putin called Ukraine 'an inalienable part of our own history, culture and spiritual space'.

Bobryk, like 12,000 other parishes in Ukraine, belonged to the Ukrainian Orthodox Church, a branch of its Russian counterpart since the seventeenth century. After the Kremlin launched its so-called 'Special Military Operation', neither Shevchenko nor his parishioners wanted anything to do with a church which answers to Moscow. They joined a rival ecclesiastical body, the Orthodox Church of Ukraine. The two churches have confusingly similar names and follow the same rituals, but they are poles apart. One is now associated with Kremlin propaganda, the other with a sovereign country seeking closer ties with Europe and the West.

The Moscow-linked church was previously the only official branch of Orthodox Christianity in Ukraine. Around 12 per cent of the world's Christians are Orthodox. There are two major branches – the Eastern Orthodox, who are largely centred in the Balkans and Eastern Europe, and a smaller branch of Oriental Orthodox based in Ethiopia and Eritrea. Many national churches are autocephalous, in other words, governed by a patriarch and his bishops. After seven decades of relentless persecution, the Eastern Orthodox Church was resurgent following the collapse of the Soviet Union. Once they had gained their independence in 1991, many Ukrainians demanded spiritual autonomy from Moscow. Infighting between rival independent churches delayed the process, but finally, in 2018, two churches in Kyiv merged to form the Orthodox Church of Ukraine. The Patriarch of Constantinople, Bartholomew I, gave it official status the following year. Although the Orthodox have no Pope, the Constantinople Patriarch, based in today's Istanbul, is the closest equivalent. Much to Moscow's chagrin, the Patriarch of Constantinople, also known as the Ecumenical Patriarch, is traditionally *primus inter pares* – first among equals and senior among all Orthodox bishops. At a ceremony in Istanbul on 5 January 2019, Bartholomew signed what is known as a *tomos*, a decree of independence, opening up the biggest rift in Christianity for centuries. Ukraine's former president, Petro Poroshenko, who had flown to Turkey for the occasion, was glowing throughout the liturgy. He had long been advocating for a self-governing Church as part of his push back against Russia. He thanked Bartholomew 'for the courage to make this historic decision'.

Humiliatingly for both Putin and Kirill, the baptismal font of their revered ancient Rus – the first East Slavic state – was located in a country which wanted no more to do with them. Ukraine's newly independent church was a slap in the face to both president and patriarch and became a *casus belli*. Kirill's Church, the biggest and the richest in the Orthodox world, stood to lose at least a fifth of its 150 million members, thousands of parishes and several hundred churches and monasteries.

At the start of the 2022 war, instead of calling for peace, Kirill branded Russia's opponents in Ukraine 'evil forces'. He suggested the invasion was part of a 'metaphysical' struggle against immoral Western values. Since then, his rhetoric has grown ever more bellicose. Many Christians, Orthodox and of other denominations, found his stance hard to fathom. Yet that was to misread him. The war gave the Patriarch a chance to reassert his authority in a post-Soviet world as he championed the twin causes of Orthodox unity and Russian imperialism.

As more and more young Russian men were sent to the front as cannon fodder, Kirill told them not to fear death on the battlefield because 'sacrifice in the course of carrying out your military duty washes away all sins'. One sermon he delivered in September 2022 echoed the Middle Ages when Europeans, waging a holy war, captured Jerusalem from the Fatimid Caliphate and slaughtered thousands of Muslims and Jews. At the start of the First Crusade in 1095, Pope Urban II had stated that those taking the cross and joining the expedition to the Holy City would receive absolution from their sins.

Ten months into the current Russo–Ukraine war, the rector of the Moscow university that trains diplomats, Father Igor Fomin, stated: 'Rulers have the right to punish, to cut off short earthly destinies and to let a person realise their mistakes even through such a terrible event as taking a life.' He was speaking on a TV channel owned by the Moscow Patriarchate – the office and headquarters of the Russian Orthodox Church. Standing in a bombed-out city in eastern Ukraine, he invoked the Old Testament Book of Deuteronomy in which God instructs the Israelites to destroy the nations living in the land of Canaan. The message was clear: Ukrainians must be sent 'into oblivion'.[2] The university priest distributed military prayer books to the soldiers. They were decorated with crosses and Kalashnikovs and inscribed with the words: 'Grant the Supreme Commander-in-Chief Vladimir, the courageous Archistratigus and God-loving Ruler of Russia, Victory.' Archistratigus is an ecclesiastical name for the Archangel Michael, the head of an army of angels: not the way most would describe Putin.

Russia is notionally a secular state. However, at the request of Kirill, the constitution was amended early in 2020 to include the word God. Christianity, Islam, Judaism and Buddhism are listed as the four 'traditional' religions, though it stresses the 'special role' of Orthodox Christianity in Russia's history and in the 'formation and development of its spirituality and culture'. Yet, just as the Church amasses ever-more powers, there are fewer churchgoers. According to Interior Ministry figures, fewer than one in twenty people regularly attend a service.

☦ ☦ ☦

To understand Putin and his patriarch, you have to understand the past – the repression, the bombast, the myths. Many contemporary themes can be traced back to different eras of Russia's history. This book is broadly chronological, moving from the pagan to the mediaeval, and to the imperial and communist eras. I have alighted upon characters who have presided over bloodshed and upheaval, and the (all too few) eras of peace and enlightenment. Russian history has both enthralled and appalled me ever since I first set foot in the country during Soviet times. My job making radio and TV documentaries for the BBC has taken me on adventures from the frozen wastes of the Yamal Peninsula to the beaches of Crimea, and from the Bering Sea to the Baltic coast. I have come to know many countries which once made up the Soviet empire, from Turkmenistan, with its North Korean-style dictatorship, to Estonia, now famous for its digital democracy. I have been intrigued by the nature of power as exercised from the Kremlin, and its relationship with ideology and faith. I have also been fascinated by Orthodoxy itself. Although I do not subscribe to any religion, I have delighted in the singing of the liturgy as voices of the choir float in the air above the congregation. I love the otherworldly beauty of Russia's churches and monasteries. Across the vast, sometimes monotonous landscape, spires and cupolas often provide the only relief for the eye. Alexander Solzhenitsyn wrote about them in his *Journeys Along the Oka:*

> They rise over ridge and hillside, descending towards wide rivers like red and white princesses, towering above the thatch and wooden huts of everyday life with their slender, ornate steeples. From far away they greet each other; from distant, unseen villages they rise towards the same sky. Wherever you may wander, over field or pasture, many miles from any homestead, you are never alone: above the wall of trees, above the hayricks, even above the very curve of the earth itself, the dome of a belfry is always beckoning to you.[3]

Beyond the granite-faced clerics preaching obedience, chastity and self-denial, Russian Orthodox traditions are rich, complex and diverse. They draw on pagan rituals connected to the landscape and changing seasons. It is a truly broad church with space for Old Believers and Holy Fools, intellectuals and charlatans, sadists and saints, totalitarian leaders and opportunistic statesmen. I differentiate between a self-serving hierarchy and the priests, monks and nuns who genuinely care for their flock. Many have often shown me kindness and inspired me. The leaders of the Church have not always lacked moral fibre or independence of mind. Metropolitan Philip denounced Ivan the Terrible's crimes and was strangled for it. Three and a half centuries later, Patriarch Tikhon excommunicated the Bolsheviks for attacking believers and was thrown into prison. Soviet-era priests and lay believers have refused to be intimidated, often paying with their lives. More recently, Alexei Navalny, Putin's most dangerous opponent, spoke in the tradition of Russia's great Christian dissidents, quoting the gospels to resist autocracy. 'Blessed are those who hunger and thirst for righteousness, for they will be satisfied,' he said during one of his courtroom trials before his murder in an Arctic prison in February 2024.

The kernel of an idea for this book began many years ago, when I met Father Christopher Hill, a down-to-earth Mancunian with a penchant for beer and black humour. He converted to Orthodoxy as a student when his university sent him to the city of Voronezh in Russia's central belt, and he began attending church services which initially struck him as 'a form of mystical theatre'. Serving at the altar and watching experienced priests, he began to feel the intricacies and the rituals, the rubrics or liturgical directions of the Church, which go back to the early Byzantine era. 'It's more complex than the Roman Catholic Church,' he told me, 'but it's like driving a car. Changing gears seems mind-bendingly difficult until you get used to it.'

I first visited Hill, his Russian wife Yelena and their three children in their flat in the south of Moscow for a 2001 radio series on Brits doing different jobs in Russia. His youngest son, Grisha, did his best to wreck the recording by crawling around the floor, singing the theme tune from *Bob the Builder* at the top of his voice. Hill serves in the busy Moscow parish of St Catherine's and has been chaplain at the City Hospice No 1 for almost three decades. His church friends include priests involved in outreach work like Father Alexei Uminsky, who established the first children's hospice and whose parish ran a charity for the homeless.

The compassion of individuals, however, is overwhelmed by the intolerance of those exercising power. Pussy Riot's protest in the Cathedral of Christ the Saviour was the most visible manifestation of that. There are countless smaller examples. Alexei Bushmakov, a lawyer from the Urals defending a young man facing a prison sentence for playing *Pokémon Go* in a Yekaterinburg church, predicted that by 2030 'Russia will be like mediaeval Spain, where the Inquisition persecuted heretics. It's terrifying to think what will happen if people are deprived of the right to choose what to believe and what not to believe in.' Colourful language, perhaps, but the concerns are real. While making a documentary on domestic abuse, I saw how the Church was not interested in protecting vulnerable people. In opposing a bill which sought to bring in restraining orders against violent partners, Kirill argued that 'any intrusion into family matters from outside carries significant negative consequences'. On interviewing a woman whose husband cut off her hands with an axe and the mother of a woman stabbed 57 times by her policeman husband, I was struck by the curious form of moral guidance in the Patriarch's assertion that 'we must protect the family first'.

I have called this book *The Baton and The Cross* to underline the role of the Church in enforcing obedience and tightening repression. Could it have been different? In the early nineties, despite the turbulence, I, like many, was driven by optimism for Russia's future. I often wonder if I was naïve or whether history could have taken a different turn had the Church leadership encouraged change and shown heartfelt repentance. By the middle of that decade, with the war in Chechnya and the rigged election for Yeltsin's second term, much of the hope had evaporated. Then, on New Year's Eve on millennium night, came Putin. A decade later, as Russia grew steadily darker, Kirill bound himself to Putin's mission and his fate. For its preservation and for the benefit of its leaders, the Church put itself at the right hand of power, as it has done for much of Russia's past millennium.

PART ONE

PAST

1. OLGA AND VLADIMIR – A CONVERT AND HER GRANDSON

Passengers who arrive by plane in the western Russian city of Pskov may not be aware that in June 2019 the airport was renamed in honour of a bloodthirsty Viking princess. The rebranding of the two-storey concrete building, a former military base, was described as 'a great historical awakening' by officials and the local bishop. Olga, also called Olha or Helga in the Scandinavian tongue of her ancestors, born in a nearby village around AD 890, is now feted as the true precursor of the Christian faith among the Eastern Slavs.

Olga was the wife of Prince Igor, a Norseman and one of the first great leaders of the medieval state called Kievan Rus. Rus derives from the old Norse word *roa,* which means to row. Over time, these formidable oarsmen, the Rus, assimilated with the indigenous population. They set off from eastern Sweden, travelling up the Neva River, where they acquired furs and slaves from the Slavs, Finnic and other tribes of the north before transporting their cargo along waterways to the south and then across the Black Sea to markets in Byzantium and the Arab caliphates.

Kievan Rus came into existence in the ninth century and was based around present-day Kyiv. Long before the rise of Moscow in the 1100s, it was the heart of Slav religion and culture. According to early chronicles, Finnic and East Slavic tribes were constantly fighting each other and incapable of self-rule. So, in 862 they invited Rurik and his fellow Scandinavian warriors to come to the city of Novgorod and impose order on the political chaos. His successor, Oleg, moved the seat of power to Kyiv in 882 and extended his domain south towards the Byzantine Empire. At its greatest extent, Kievan Rus ruled an area stretching from the White Sea in the north to the Black Sea in the south, and from the headwaters of the Vistula in the west to the Taman Peninsula in the east. The modern nations of Belarus, Russia and Ukraine all have Kievan Rus as their cultural ancestors.

Despite frequent trade with different Christian nations, Rus was officially pagan. Then one woman changed the status quo; a woman who is now venerated in churches, town squares and monasteries across the Orthodox world, even if she remains a figure of relative obscurity in Western churches.

Grand Princess Olga's path to sainthood was strewn with corpses. After her husband Igor was murdered by a rebellious forest tribe called the Drevlians, she took her revenge. Before Igor's body was cold, the head of the tribe, Prince Mal, put himself forward as Olga's new husband. Unimpressed, she buried and burned some of his emissaries alive. Then she hosted a funeral banquet for her husband and invited the Drevlian soldiers to join her at the table. Once the guests were drunk on mead, she ordered her troops to slit their throats – all 5,000 of them.

The scene is described in *The Tale of Bygone Years*. Also known as *The Primary Chronicle*, it is a detailed account of the early history of the Eastern Slavs and was compiled by three generations of Kyivan monks, using Byzantine texts, Slavonic literary sources and oral sagas. *The Chronicle* makes for a racy read, even if many details are hard to corroborate and often seem exaggerated for the sake of storytelling. Olga's final act of retribution was to burn down all of the thatched houses of the Drevlian capital, using her airborne troops – thousands of pigeons and sparrows who had rags soaked with sulphur attached to their legs.

Her tactics have won subsequent admirers. In his book on the art of public relations, Vladimir Medinsky, a culture minister under Putin, said her 'cleverness and cunning' should make her a top influencer and 'a Russian feminist icon'.[1]

Olga is better known, however, for another trip she made, thirteen years later, in 957, to Constantinople. It was here, accompanied by a large diplomatic delegation, that she embraced Christianity.

The religion had already been introduced into Kievan Rus by two monks from the Byzantine Empire in the ninth century. Saint Cyril and Saint Methodius' translation of parts of the Bible into the Old Church Slavonic language paved the way for the Christianisation of the Slavs. It is also the basis of the Russian language: Cyrillic, denoting the alphabet, is derived from Cyril, the name of one of the missionary monks.

Olga sought a grand baptism in the Patriarchal See. Emperor Constantine VII received her in one of his palaces embellished with gilded domes. She presented the emperor with gifts of sable, ermine and Drevlian slaves. Entranced, he invited her to become his second wife, but she was an expert in dodging unwanted suitors. She found a diplomatic way to refuse him by tricking him into becoming her godfather. Once she was christened, she took the name of his first wife Helena (Elena) and reminded him that according to Christian teaching a godfather cannot marry a godchild. The lovestruck old emperor had been outfoxed. Upon her return to Kyiv, Olga prayed fastidiously. *The Tale of Bygone Years* says she 'shone like the moon by night and was radiant among the infidels like a pearl in the mire, since the people were soiled, and not yet purified of their sin by holy baptism'. But she failed to impose her newfound religion on her subjects. She could not even persuade her son, Svyatoslav, to become a Christian. He feared his fellow soldiers would mock him. The task of converting the whole nation fell to her grandson.

In 988, thirty years after Olga's own conversion, Vladimir (Volodymyr to Ukrainians), now Grand Prince of Kyiv, introduced Christianity across his realm. Before that he kept 800 concubines and worshipped the god of thunder, Perun, also venerated by the Scandinavians. Why did he abandon his pagan beliefs, follow his grandmother's lead and choose the Eastern Orthodox Church? According to *The Primary Chronicle*, he was visited by the followers of four religions: Islam, Judaism, Catholicism and Greek Christianity. Then he sent out envoys on fact-finding missions. He was tempted by the Muslim Bulgars' promise of beautiful maidens in paradise but disgusted by the ban on alcohol. 'Drinking is the joy of all Rus – we cannot exist without it,' he said. Judaism was also rejected because he suspected that if the Jews had lost their homeland in Jerusalem, they might be forsaken by God. Latin Christianity failed to inspire him; in the gloomy churches of the Germans his emissaries saw no beauty. He was more impressed by his envoys' description of the candlelit Orthodox liturgy they had attended in the great Cathedral of Hagia Sophia in Constantinople. 'We knew not whether we were in heaven or on earth,' they told him, 'for surely there is no such splendour or beauty anywhere on earth. We only know that God dwells there among men.'

Vladimir needed a way of uniting his people – the Slavonic, Finnic and Lithuanian tribes living in territories his family had conquered – under one rule and one monotheistic faith. He ordered that a wooden statue of his former idol, Perun, be bound to a horse's tail, dragged along a stream and cast into the Dnipro River. Twelve men beat it with sticks as it slithered downhill. Everyone in the city was ordered to come for baptism in the Dnipro the following morning. Anyone who did not comply would be counted as the ruler's personal enemy.

A nineteenth-century painting by Klavdiy Lebedev depicts the mass baptism in lurid colours: Vladimir and his bride on the sandy bank as their subjects stand beneath them in the turquoise waters, some up to their armpits, others to their necks, women clutching small children in their arms. Looking towards the east, they were told to immerse themselves three times, once in the name of the Father, once in the name of the Son and finally in the name of the Holy Spirit. Vladimir is said to have lifted his eyes to heaven and extended his arms over the people, praying, 'O God, who has created heaven, earth, sea and all that is in them! Look down upon these thy new men and cause them to know Thee who are the true God, even as other Christian nations do.'

To this day, all Orthodox and Greek Catholic churches of the region regard the Kyiv baptismal font as their birthplace. Vladimir, or Volodymyr, is hailed as the founder of the Christian faith in Kievan Rus. In Putin's Russia, he has become an object of veneration – the binder of church and state. But the Ukrainian historian Yaroslav Hrytsak points out that 'calling Rus a nation state is like calling a wooden abacus the first computer'. He adds that fighting over claims to the legacy of Rus makes no more sense than debates over 'whether the Carolingian Empire was French or German'.[2]

Vladimir also had economic motives for his adoption of the faith. He needed to cement ties with his most valuable trading partner, the Byzantine Empire. Merchants loaded their boats with furs, wax, timber and slaves obtained in the north and on the Eurasian steppe. Then they sailed in convoys along rivers and across the Black Sea to Constantinople. As another friendly gesture, he pledged 7,000 warriors to put down a revolt against the Byzantine Emperor, Basil II. In return, Basil was supposed to give Vladimir the hand of his 26-year-old sister, Anna Porphyrogenita. She was horrified. Rather than marry a heathen prince, she said, 'it would be better to stay here and die'. Basil tried to back out of the deal, which prompted Vladimir to lay siege to the Byzantine town of Chersonesos in Crimea, near the modern city of Sevastopol.[3]

Anna was forced to consent to the match. Her brother told her that if the wedding could help to bring all the pagans of Kievan Rus to repentance, it was a worthy sacrifice. Vladimir replied that he would accept baptism, telling the emperor: 'I have already given some study to your religion and the Greek faith and rituals … and it has pleased me well.' *The Tale of Bygone Years* does not dwell on Vladimir's political motives but recounts how, in the spring of 988, accompanied by chanting priests carrying icons and crosses, the Grand Prince and his new wife made the return journey to Kyiv. The marriage ceremony and Vladimir's baptism took place in Chersonesos, in a temple whose basilica and baptismal font hold the same importance for Rus as Jerusalem does for the entire Christian world. After the annexation of Crimea, Putin's most trusted monk, Metropolitan Tikhon Shevkunov, was given the job of turning the site into an archaeological theme park with a museum of Christianity, souvenir shops, cafes and large car park. The reconstruction is being carried out by the Ministry of Defence.

Early Church history is vitally connected to Putin's war in Ukraine. Both the president and the Russian Orthodox Church claim ownership of the nation's foundation, but Kievan Rus is, inconveniently for them, located in a different and sovereign country. One would have little sense of that from the way senior clerics from the Moscow Patriarchate present the mass baptism of 988 in Kyiv. In a recent television film,[4] Metropolitan Hilarion of Volokolamsk, a bishop close to the Patriarch, delivers a piece to camera on the same bank of the river. 'A new Christian people was born in these waters,' he tells viewers, his golden cross bouncing on his chest as he strides along. 'A new civilisation began its existence, which united the peoples of Great Russia, Little Russia and White Russia thanks to the common faith of the One Church.'

As the February 2022 invasion showed, Putin views Ukraine as 'Little Russia', not an independent country. Ukrainians argue Volodymyr the Great is their legendary hero and that his successor is their Volodymyr, Zelensky. A statue of the Kyivan prince, built in 1853, towers over the Dnipro. After the full-scale invasion, it was surrounded by scaffolding and wrapped in canvas to protect it from Russian missiles. Early on in his rule, Putin saw the political potential of his own adoption of Vladimir. In 2006, on the eve of the Defenders of the Fatherland Day, came Vladimir the cartoon. Lavishly funded, *Prince Vladimir* tells a romanticised version of the country's shift from paganism and polytheism to monotheism. Like Disney's adaptation of the Book of Exodus, *The Prince of Egypt*, it did exceptionally well at the Russian box office.[5]

After his annexation of Crimea in 2014, Putin erected an even bigger statue of his early Christian namesake in Moscow, which was just a patch of empty marshland in the tenth century when Vladimir was on his throne in Kyiv. Putin was determined to portray the Grand Prince as a key figure in a unified Russian state (including Ukraine), which 'unites different peoples, languages, cultures and religions into one big family', as he put it at the unveiling ceremony. The Russian Vladimir the Great stands just outside the Kremlin, eighteen metres high. It was supposed to be even taller until UNESCO intervened.

Vladimir is used to provide an imprimatur to Putin's land grab in Ukraine. Nikolai Svanidze, a historian and member of the President's self-proclaimed Human Rights Council, declared: 'Prince Vladimir was baptised in Crimea and Putin returned Crimea to Russia – this parallel should enhance the president's standing in the eyes of his contemporaries and descendants, as well as bless Crimea's merger with Russia.'[6]

☦ ☦ ☦

When Vladimir died in 1015, a power struggle broke out between his sons. The eldest, Sviatopolk the Accursed, murdered two of his younger brothers because he wanted to snatch their lands. But he was eventually defeated by another of Vladimir's sons, who ruled from 1019 until his death in 1054 and was known as Yaroslav the Wise. Yaroslav presided over the golden age of Rus and built the magnificent Saint Sophia Cathedral in the centre of Kyiv, with a library and a school attached where he encouraged the translation of Greek texts into Church Slavonic. Modern Russian shares some vocabulary and grammar with the Church Slavonic, an early version of Bulgarian, as it was spoken from the ninth to the eleventh century. Essentially it is a Southern Slavic language, closer to Serbian, while modern Ukrainian is a Central Slavic language, which has more in common with Belarusian and Polish. Yaroslav also compiled a book of laws which, among other things, established primogeniture in the hope of avoiding future fratricide. The Pravda Yaroslava, or Justice of Yaroslav, became the basis for the legal code of Kievan Rus and future Rus principalities during the times of feudal division.

All these achievements took place during a period of great spiritual turmoil. Less than a century after Rus converted from paganism, and in the very year that Yaroslav died, the Christian world split apart. The Great Schism of 1054 divided Christianity into two competing branches, one in the west, based in Rome, and the other in the east, based in Byzantium. The city at the mouth of the Bosphorus was renamed Constantinople in AD 330 after Emperor Constantine – the first Roman emperor to embrace Christianity. His conversion began earlier, on a battlefield near Rome, when according to his biographer Eusebius, Constantine and his forces saw a cross of light in the sky, along with the Greek words for 'In this sign, thou shalt conquer'.

The breakup of the Roman Empire was one of the main causes of the Great Schism. It had become so large that it was ungovernable, and in 285, Emperor Diocletian divided it in two. Gradually the two halves – the Western Roman Empire and the Byzantine Empire – moved apart. Their churches conflicted on religious doctrine and used different rites. Tension built up in a series of 'little schisms' in the fourth, fifth and sixth centuries before the Great Schism occurred. When some churches in Constantinople began following Catholic rites instead of Eastern traditions, the city's Ecumenical Patriarch, Michael Cerularius, closed them down. The Pope in Rome sent a delegation in April 1054 to reason with Cerularius, but he refused to meet the delegates or recognise their authority. Eventually the envoys from Rome entered the Cathedral of Hagia Sophia in the middle of a service and dumped a papal bull on the altar. It was a letter of excommunication from the Pope. Cerularius promptly burned it. At the time, few imagined how long this row would endure. Just 150 years later, the siege of Constantinople and the looting and burning of the city during the Fourth Crusade only deepened the animosity between the Eastern and Western Christians. A millennium of separation has entrenched their differences.

Almost twice as old as the Catholic–Protestant division in the west, the legacy of the Great Schism lingers. In her book on Orthodoxy, *Why Angels Fall,* Victoria Clark calls it 'Europe's oldest political faultline'[7] – one that existed long before the Iron Curtain and the Warsaw Pact. Orthodox Europe stretches from the Balkans in the south to Arkhangelsk in the north, across Russia's Ural Mountains and beyond. Everything east of this line which bisects the continent is not just the heartland of another type of Christianity, but another very different culture.

Divisions between the two turned deadly in the Yugoslav wars of the 1990s, when Catholic Croats fought Orthodox Serbs. Today, with some notable exceptions, the split between Orthodoxy and Western Christendom is reflected in the chasm between the countries inside and outside the European Union and NATO. With plenty of caveats, Clark suggests that if the West relies on reason and worldliness, the

East is driven by otherworldliness and mysticism, and that the two branches of the Church are dangerously unbalanced without one another. 'To put it baldly and at the risk of oversimplifying,' she writes, 'western Christendom can be said to have lost its heart, eastern Christendom its mind.'

If Eastern theology is rooted in Greek philosophy, much of Western theology is based on Roman law. The language barrier may have exacerbated the growing lack of understanding between the two. One single Latin sentence in the Nicene Creed, the profession of Christian faith adopted at the Council of Nicaea in AD 325, proved extraordinarily divisive. The row was about whether the Holy Spirit came from the Father alone or from the Father and the Son together. Catholics and Protestants give credit to both the Father and the Son, but inserting these few words – the so-called Filioque clause – into the Nicene Creed is anathema to the Eastern Orthodox. They argue there is no scriptural evidence for it and that it jeopardises the harmony of the Holy Trinity.

Many Western theologians fail to understand the Orthodox Church. There is a widespread belief that it fell behind and remained in the dark ages because it never went through a Reformation. But most Orthodox have no desire to 'catch up'. Preserving the status quo is a sacred duty. Scientific progress and the freedom of the individual are either irrelevant or secondary. They see all the developments in Western Europe, the Renaissance, the Reformation and the Counter Reformation as deviations. In Russian the Orthodox are called *Pravoslavnye* – that is, Slavs belonging to the 'right' or 'true' faith. To the outsider, some sticking points between East and West seem minor, such as whether the bread used in the Eucharist should be leavened or unleavened. The Orthodox use the former and dip it into the wine – a practice condemned by the Roman Catholic Church. More importantly, Orthodox priests who do not aspire to the highest offices in the church can have wives and families, unlike their Catholic counterparts.

The two churches disagree about the order in which Jesus was followed by his disciples. According to the gospels of Matthew, Mark and Luke, Simon Peter is the leading apostle. When he recognises Jesus Christ as God's anointed son, he is told: 'You are

Peter, and on this rock, I will build my church'. Rome is the city where Saint Peter settled, served as bishop, and was crucified by Emperor Nero. Ever since, it has been the home of the Catholic Church. But the Eastern Orthodox Church relies more on the gospel of John, which states that Peter's brother, Andrew, was the first to identify Jesus as the Messiah and thus honours him with the name Protokletos, Greek for 'the first called'. Since he preached in ancient Scythia along the Black Sea and further north, he became the patron saint of Russia.

The Pope in Rome claims universal supremacy over his whole church. He is the earthly father of all the world's Catholics. By contrast, the churches that make up Eastern Orthodoxy are autocephalous, or self-governing. The highest church official in each is the patriarch, and the Ecumenical Patriarch in Constantinople, today Istanbul, has the status of 'first among equals'.

Alongside the enduring rift between Rome and Constantinople, there are new divisions inside the Orthodox world. The Kremlin's 2014 decision to annex Crimea and back separatists in eastern Ukraine opened a chasm between clerics in Moscow and Kyiv. For many, the establishment of the Orthodox Church of Ukraine (OCU) four years later seemed logical and inevitable. Throughout the Orthodox world, 'one country, one church' is an accepted premise and virtually every Orthodox majority country in the world (and indeed most countries with any Orthodox Christian minority) have their own autocephalous church. Russia's Patriarch Kirill was livid, calling those who followed the OCU schismatics, since, in his view, the only legitimate church was the Ukrainian Orthodox Church (UOC), historically linked to the Moscow Patriarchate.

He bent the ear of Justin Welby over the issue when the Archbishop of Canterbury visited Moscow in 2017. Kirill's office was full of Russian TV crews when Welby arrived. After the official niceties, without any prompting, the Patriarch suddenly handed a big dossier of Ukraine documents to his bemused guest. He accused Russia's neighbour of weakening the Orthodox Brotherhood. 'It was a furious rant', said the journalist Michael Binyon, who was inside the room accompanying the Archbishop on his visit. 'But once the television cameras left, he didn't say another word about it.' The visiting

Brits assumed the diatribe was for domestic consumption. Yet later on, at a sumptuous banquet at the Danilovsky Monastery, Kirill returned to the theme, talking of 'young hotheads' in Ukraine who were behaving like mobs, trying to steal churches from the Moscow Patriarchate.[8]

Today there are seventeen autocephalous or self-governing Orthodox churches, which are recognised to varying degrees by different council members. Matters relating to faith are decided by ecumenical councils in which all member churches of Eastern Orthodoxy are supposed to participate. Decisions about whether to recognise Ukraine's autonomous church have split the Orthodox world – even as far away as in Sub-Saharan Africa – and caused upheavals in Ukraine too, as we will see later on.

2. THE MEDIEVAL MAKING OF
MUSCOVY

The Cathedral of St Michael the Archangel is one of the more sinister parts of the Kremlin. Visitors wander around a dimly lit necropolis containing the tombs of almost all of Muscovy's rulers from the fourteenth to the seventeenth century. At the foot of the southern wall stands the oldest of them, Grand Prince of Moscow Ivan I. He erected the church in 1333 to commemorate the end of the Great Famine, which affected most of Europe.

Russian prestige and power has long been projected through churches. Ivan, who came to the throne after Russia had fallen under Mongol rule, built the Cathedral of the Assumption, the Kremlin's first stone church, a little before St Michael the Archangel. It was completed in 1327 after less than two years, lightning speed by medieval standards. Ivan's moniker was Kalita, Moneybags, because he collected taxes from other principalities on behalf of the Great Khan.

Two centuries of Mongol domination had begun when Genghis Khan, the founder of the Mongol Empire, sent his son Jochi in 1207 to conquer territory in what is now Siberia, Central Russia and Eastern Europe. In the winter of 1240, the invading Mongol army led by Batu Khan burned Kyiv to the ground and massacred most of the inhabitants. Kyiv was one of many cities captured and sacked; before long most of the Rus principalities had been absorbed into the Golden Horde – the state created by the Mongols on Slav lands in the mid-thirteenth century. Under the so-called Tatar-Mongol Yoke,

Slavs paid tribute and had limited sovereignty. When Ivan became Prince of Moscow, after the death of his older brother Yuri, Russia's future capital was barely on the map. It was a small trading outpost surrounded by forests in the principality of Vladimir-Suzdal.

Ivan preferred to purchase territories than win them on the battlefield. He was a good financier and administrator, not unlike Henry VII, England's 'accountant king', a meticulous bookkeeper who liked to count each bag of coins.[1] Instead of opposing the Tatars, Ivan collaborated with them to overcome his rivals. His now-deceased brother Yuri had already made an advantageous match, marrying the sister of the Mongol leader Uzbeg Khan. Ever the pragmatist, Ivan used these family connections to persuade his overlords to grant him the seat of Grand Prince of Vladimir. That allowed him to collect taxes from the Russian lands as a ruling prince, replacing the hated *baskaks*, the Mongol taxmen.

The arrangement brought Ivan great wealth and transformed the fortunes of Moscow from a modest trading post to Russia's holy capital. Ivan had already lured the head of the Church, Metropolitan Peter, to Moscow from the city of Vladimir in 1325. It became the ecclesiastical capital of Russia long before it became the political one. 'Moscow owes its greatness to the Khans,' wrote Russia's celebrated historian Nikolai Karamzin (1766–1826). He also pointed out that – like Ivan – the Church knew how to ingratiate itself with the horde rulers. This is a pattern which would be replicated down the centuries.

Villagers had to pay the Mongols a tithe – a tenth of everything they grew – either in kind or in currency – silver and furs. Merchants had to pay a percentage of capital they earned. Taxes were levied on everyone – from peasants to princes. Only the Church was exempt. The Uzbeg Khan wrote to Metropolitan Peter, confirming the tax breaks for the clergy and monastics, as well as all their servants. According to Karamzin, 'the Tatars understood uncommonly well the elementary truth that it is possible by arms to conquer a country but impossible to hold it with the help of arms alone. They could not fail to appreciate that the Church was putting at their disposal its influence over the faithful, and in return for this it was but natural to reward the Church with privileges.'[2]

The Church became a focal point of Russian culture during two centuries of Mongol domination. Liturgies and festivals loomed large in everyday life: they marked the changing seasons and governed the rhythm of the year. Cattle were turned out and sprinkled with holy water by a priest on 17 April because it was St Stephen's Day. Peasants ploughed on St George's Day while apples had to be gathered no earlier than Transfiguration Day in August. Faith in God was so deeply rooted that the word for peasant in Russian, *krestyanin*, is also the word for Christian.

A strong sense of medieval Russia emerges from Andrei Tarkovsky's 1966 epic *Andrei Rublev*, about the country's celebrated icon painter. While Western Europe was embarking on the Renaissance, in Russia, the enslaved peasant class, the people known as serfs, were tied to the land of their feudal lords. Rublev is Russia's first great artist, but there isn't a single shot of him with a paintbrush nor any trace of his work until the final montage, when the black and white film suddenly turns into a blaze of colour. This sequence keeps a steady gaze on the icons, much as Russians do in church when they pray with their eyes open.

For believers, icons are not just small paintings of the Virgin Mary, Christ or angels and saints – they are 'windows to the kingdom of God'. Statues, deemed 'graven images', are forbidden in Orthodoxy. Instead, churches are adorned with tempera paintings on wooden panels. Some are on the walls, some in special glass shrines and many more on a multi-tiered screen with three doors. Known as the iconostasis, this partition conceals the sanctuary from the congregation and marks the symbolic boundary between earthly and celestial realms. Only priests – and the tsar during his coronation – are permitted into the sanctuary. No woman, not even the tsarina, has ever been allowed behind the Royal Door, with the exception of elderly nuns in convents.[3]

☦ ☦ ☦

Humble monks have always been deeply respected by the Russian people. Even in Soviet times they carved out a place in the collective imagination. On my first ever trip to Russia, I went in search of a fourteenth-century character who became the prototype of the *starets*, or elder, a special figure in Russian Orthodoxy who inspired Tolstoy, Dostoevsky and many others.

On a spring morning in 1977, a few days after my visit to the swimming pool on the current site of the Cathedral of Christ the Saviour, I drove with my Russian hosts to the town of Zagorsk, north-east of Moscow. The journey took nearly two hours in their spluttering Zhiguli, but now takes half the time thanks to the arrival of Western cars and smooth tarmac. They put a flowery kerchief around my head, to make me look like a local. In Brezhnev's time it was forbidden to take foreigners out of the city limits without permission.

Zagorsk, then named after a prominent Bolshevik, has regained its pre-Revolutionary name of Sergiyev Posad – in honour of the saint who founded a monastery on this spot in 1337. I remember gawping at the unsmiling monks who scuttled past us in long black robes and my vain attempts to capture the majesty of the Cathedral of the Assumption with my instamatic camera. The azure-blue onion domes sprinkled with gold stars seemed a world away from the monolithic grey blocks which filled so much of Moscow.

My father's friends, Larisa and Viktor, were a modern Soviet couple. They were both engineers, party members and officially atheists, but they were respectful of the nation's most celebrated saint – Saint Sergius of Radonezh. It was Sergius who inspired the Muscovy Prince, Dmitry Donskoy, in 1380 to conquer a seemingly invincible enemy, ending two centuries of Mongol rule. One of Russia's best-known nineteenth-century historians, Vasily Klyuchevsky, describes Sergius as fostering 'the moral, then political, renaissance of the Russian people'. In the depths of the Cold War, my hosts had taken me on a pilgrimage to the Trinity St Sergius Lavra, the spiritual centre of the Orthodox Church.

Although the monastery became the richest in the land, the saint himself was renowned for his ragged clothes and his humility. He spent months in the forest as a hermit, where he built a small wooden church dedicated to the Holy Trinity. Surviving on almost no food, he devoted himself to the practice of Hesychasm, named after the Greek word for tranquillity. A Hesychast attains a divine inner peace through the contemplation of God. Alone in his small cabin in the woods, Sergius was tormented by demons. He focused his thoughts on prayer until he was no longer afraid. News of this fearless monk spread far and wide. People began flocking to the monastery, hoping to be inspired by his courage.

One such visitor was the young Prince Dmitry Donskoy, who came to power when he was only nine years old and became the first prince of Muscovy to openly challenge Mongol authority. His nickname, Donskoy, alludes to his great victory against the Tatars in the Battle of Kulikovo, by the forested banks of the River Don, south of Moscow. The story goes that just before he put on his armour, he came to ask the holy man for a blessing. 'Bravely wage war against the unbelievers, without hesitation, and you'll be victorious,' Sergius assured the prince.

On 8 September 1380, Prince Dmitry and 50,000 Russian warriors miraculously prevailed against 150,000 Tatar-Mongolian soldiers led by a formidable character called Mamai. The defeat of Mamai's troops did not prevent the Tatars from setting Moscow aflame two years later; Russia was subjugated to the Horde until the late-fifteenth century. Yet the surprising victory at Kulikovo marked the first time the Slavs fought and identified themselves as a unified force. Sergius is credited with persuading the country's medieval princes to stop their internecine fighting and focus instead on their enemies from the east. The site of the historic victory now boasts a 90-feet Orthodox cross, along with a church and museum. Every September a group of nationalists clad in chainmail and helmets re-enacts the battle.

Some historians suspect the legacy of St Sergius is being distorted to fit today's political goals. They argue that a prince in a hurry to fight a battle would have been unlikely to visit the monastery: such a detour would have taken him a minimum of two weeks. They also point out that the earliest known short chronicle of the battle, 'Slaughter on the Don', contains no mention of Sergius of Radonezh. According to historian Irina Karatsuba, Sergius embodied the best of Russia, but it is 'nonsense and political manipulation' to make out he was 'an obedient servant to the Russian state'.[4]

Linking the country's most venerable saint to Slav unity proved irresistible for Putin when he visited Sergiyev Posad for the 700th anniversary of its founder. This took place in the summer of 2014, a time of heightened international tension. Russia had enabled proxies to invade eastern Ukraine; it had annexed Crimea, and just a day before the president's tour of the spiritual site, Russian-controlled forces had shot down a Malaysian airliner as it flew over the Donetsk region of eastern Ukraine, killing all 298 passengers and crew. Putin called for an 'objective investigation' into the crash but added that 'the state over whose territory this happened bears responsibility for this terrible tragedy'.[5] Standing on a green and gold stage, next to Patriarch Kirill, he called Sergius the 'greatest ascetic and spiritual guardian of Russia', who had inspired the nation's 'patriotic, national and moral recovery'. His greatest contribution was to have built monasteries as spiritual centres and fortresses to protect Russia during 'a difficult time of foreign intervention and internal discord'.

☦ ☦ ☦

In the autumn of 2010, some curious rumours were doing the rounds in the Pskov region of north-west Russia. A blogger called Pavel Prytula claimed that Putin had banished his wife, Lyudmila Putina, to a monastery – that fail-safe method for disposing of unwanted spouses employed by Ivan the Terrible and Peter I. For two years there had been gossip about Putin's relationship with the rhythmic gymnastics champion Alina Kabaeva, including speculation about their upcoming wedding.

A spokesman for the Pskov diocese dismissed Prytula's claim as nonsense and the blogger's post was swiftly deleted. The spokesman also denied a report that Kirill had appointed Putin's wife as abbess of the Spaso-Elizarovsky Convent. 'Secular people can't be put in charge of monasteries,' he snapped. 'And Lyudmila Putina did not take monastic vows.'[6] Despite that, she had often stayed there along with her friend Lyubov Sliska, a loyal member of Putin's United Russia party. According to her own memoir, Lyudmila turned to God after a near-death experience in a car accident in her native city of Kaliningrad in the early 1990s.

Putin had already allocated 48 million roubles (roughly $1.5 million) for building works at the convent. A regional representative from the All-Russian Society for the Protection of

Monuments said money from the federal budget went directly to Spaso-Elizarovsky – an uncommon arrangement, since funds are usually channelled through the diocese. Most of this was spent on accommodation for VIPs. In total 1.14 billion roubles ($18.8 million) was spent on restoring the complex.

Spaso-Elizarovsky is hardly the most impressive monastic site in the country. Originally inhabited by monks, it was founded by a local peasant named Eleazar who built a wooden church on the site in 1447. It was later fortified, but after seven decades of Soviet neglect, the monastery was in a sorry state and converted into a nunnery. So what was it about this relatively obscure place in a forest near the Estonian border that attracted Russia's First Lady? You have to go back at least five centuries for the answer, to its mid-sixteenth century abbot, Filofei of Pskov. He is famous for promoting the notion of Russia as a unique civilisation. According to the Third Rome prophecy, the first Rome lost its prominence for various geopolitical reasons and, in Filofei's mind, it was fatally contaminated by the 'heresy' of Catholicism. The Second Rome was in Byzantium, modern-day Istanbul. It became the new epicentre of the Roman Empire in AD 330 when Constantine, the first Roman emperor to convert to Christianity, made the ancient Greek colony his capital. He called it a New Rome. Later, in his honour, this port city on the eastern Mediterranean was renamed Constantinople and it endured for more than 1,100 years as the centre of the Byzantine world. This Christian city of immense wealth and magnificent architecture would also lose its stature – and its religious control over Orthodox believers in Rus.

Until the fifteenth century the Slavs had relied on the patriarch of Constantinople to choose their supreme cleric. These ecclesiastical heads were usually Greeks. The arrangement was uncontentious until Isidore, one of the Byzantine-appointed metropolitans of Kyiv and all Rus, went to Italy. At that time, the Byzantine Empire was under threat of invasion from the Ottoman Turks. Desperate for military support from Western Europe, at a council in Medici Florence, the Greek clergy signed an agreement with Rome.

On his return to Moscow from the council, Isidore began lobbying to reunite the Eastern Orthodox and the Catholics. He brought

Latin rite crucifixes into the Kremlin and even read a prayer for the Pope. He was arrested. This was the definitive moment when the Russian Church split away from Constantinople. Russian bishops consecrated their own metropolitan, called Jonas, in 1448 and became essentially self-governing. Five years later, Constantinople fell to the Turks and the Byzantine Empire came to an end. Many Orthodox believers thought the once-proud city had been justly punished for flirting with the Catholics and abandoning its faith. From now on it would be supplanted by 'Holy Rus', the last bastion of the true church in all Christendom. In his famous epistle half a century later, Abbot Filofei wrote to his monarch, Grand Prince Vasily III: 'Observe then and take heed, O pious Prince, for all Christian realms are reduced to your realm alone. Two Romes have fallen, the third stands and a fourth there shall not be.' Muscovy was a Third Rome, with a sacred mission to redeem humanity. Shortly after, the Metropolitan was promoted to the rank of Patriarch.

Filofei's beliefs are much quoted by the man said to be Putin's confessor. In 2008, Father Tikhon Shevkunov presented a documentary, *The Fall of an Empire: The Lesson of Byzantium*,[7] which received a prime-time slot on national TV. Shevkunov argues that Byzantium was culturally and economically superior to a Europe entombed in the Dark Ages. The 'barbarian' West, according to him, became civilised and capitalist only by plundering Constantinople during the Fourth Crusade. 'Byzantium's soul, and the meaning of its existence, was Orthodoxy,' he says. It was 'the unblemished confession of Christianity, in which no dogmas had changed essentially for a thousand years'. The West, he adds, 'simply could not endure such demonstrative conservatism'. Russians, he suggests, must uphold the very existence of this Holy Rus and defend their Orthodoxy from outside corruption.

Towards the end of the film, Shevkunov informs the viewer that during the Second World War, Stalin issued a personal order to reopen an institute for Byzantine studies – academic research into this topic had been banned since the Bolshevik Revolution. 'The former seminarian, Joseph Dzhugashvili [Stalin] finally understood from whom we should be studying history.'

3. THE TYRANT AND THE POWER-CRAZY MONK

It was a curious scene. The heavily tattooed, leather-clad leader of the Night Wolves, a pro-Putin motorbike group, standing next to a black-robed priest. The cleric was armed with a small bucket of holy water. Medieval banners, nationalist emblems and the flag of Imperial Russia fluttered in the breeze over their heads. Behind them a crowd of people had come to admire a new bronze effigy of Ivan the Terrible erected in the main square of Oryol, a city 230 miles south of Moscow. He was on a horse, in battledress, grasping a sword in one hand and a cross in the other.

The sixteenth-century strongman defeated the Muslim Tatars and brought the Volga region under Orthodox control. During his reign (1547–84), Russia became an imperial power. It expanded for the first time beyond the lands occupied by Orthodox, ethnic Russians. Ivan conquered the Tatar khanate of Kazan, laying the foundations for the greatest contiguous empire on earth. Between 1500 and the Bolshevik Revolution in 1917, the Russian Empire grew at an average rate of 130 square kilometres every day.[1] At the statue's inauguration, Vadim Potomsky, the regional governor, praised Russia's first tsar for conquering new realms while defending the country and its Orthodox faith.

In Russian he is Ivan *Groznyy*, which translates as awe-inspiring or formidable rather than terrible. Ivan is known for killing his own son in a fit of rage and for creating the *Oprichniki*, the country's first secret police.² In Oryol and beyond, many were horrified when plans for the statue were announced. Kirill agreed that Ivan the Terrible should not be canonised 'because of his methods of governing' but said that as the founder of the city he deserved the bronze tribute. The Patriarch did not mention the fact that one of his predecessors, the head of the Orthodox Church in the 1560s, was suffocated in his prison cell by one of Ivan's henchmen. Metropolitan Philip was a rare cleric who stood up to tyranny. His bravery cost him his life.

Many have attributed Ivan's cruelty to his difficult childhood. His father died when he was three and his mother five years later, possibly from poisoning. Ivan was kicked around like a football between rival clans of boyars, the nobles at court. Often hidden for his protection, he grew up a lonely child who buried himself in religious books. From the age of twelve, he was taken under the wing of Metropolitan Makary, the head of the Church, who instilled in him the all-important Byzantine principle of 'symphony' between church and state. Makary choreographed Ivan's corona-tion, anointed him and put a sable-trimmed crown on his head in the Kremlin's candlelit Cathedral of the Assumption on 16 January 1547. The middle-aged Metropolitan and sixteen-year-old Tsar sat side by side on thrones on a red-carpeted dais to symbolise the unity of spiritual and secular power. The Byzantine pageantry and a sense of foreboding are powerfully captured in Sergei Eisenstein's cinematic masterpiece *Ivan the Terrible*, accompanied by Sergei Prokofiev's solemn musical score.

Tsar Ivan IV, to give him his formal title, was the first to refer to his country as 'Holy Rus', and early on he showed some signs of humility. After his coronation he married Anastasia Romanovna; the newlyweds made a penitential 40-mile pilgrimage to the Trinity Monastery, according to the Russian historian Sergey Solovyov 'the whole way on foot despite the bitter cold'.³ The young Tsar wrote poetry and music and even composed a liturgical hymn, 'Stichiron No. 1 in Honour of St. Peter'. A recording released in 1988, marking the millennium of Christianity, was the first ever Soviet-produced CD – perhaps an early piece of reputation laundering. Today's apol-ogists for Ivan say his crimes have been exaggerated and prefer to highlight his patriotism and contributions to the Church.

Around sixty monasteries were founded during Ivan's reign and scores of saints were canonised. The best-known monument of his reign is St Basil's Cathedral, close to the Kremlin, built to commemorate his victory over the Khanate of Kazan in 1552. Its multicoloured onion domes have made it a global symbol of Russia, but it was named after a man who roamed around Moscow half-naked in all weathers. Blessed Basil, credited with predicting fires and curing the blind, was a *yurodivy*, a Fool for Christ. Such men, known for their apparent, yet holy, insanity and religious zeal, were thought to possess supernatural powers. They inspired awe in nobles and peasants alike, and Ivan was no exception.

The Russia of the 1560s was reeling from famine, Tatar invasions, sea blockades and an unsuccessful attempt to secure a Baltic coastline for the Empire. One of Ivan's closest friends and advisors, Prince Andrei Kurbsky, defected to the neighbouring Lithuanian kingdom. Already resentful of the boyars who had mistreated him as a child, the Tsar grew increasingly paranoid. The death of Anastasia two years later may have pushed him over the edge. He suspected his wife had been secretly poisoned, just like his mother. Blaming traitors in the aristocracy and the clergy, Ivan left Moscow for his country residence. From there he wrote to the court to announce his abdication. Fearful of chaos, boyar envoys begged him to return to the throne. The Tsar agreed but demanded the right to condemn and execute traitors and confiscate their estates without interference from the boyar council or the Church.

Like avenging angels of the apocalypse, Ivan's 6,000-strong *Oprichniki* committed acts of pathological cruelty. They rode with dogs' heads and broomsticks attached to their horses' saddles – which symbolised their determination to bite their master's enemies and clean up the country. The rampages spread terror, including a five-week massacre in the city of Novgorod. About a third of the population were killed because Ivan believed the citizens there were too attached to sacrilegious European values and wanted to come under the rule of the Polish king. Ivan saw his henchmen as a monastic brotherhood, serving God with weapons and military deeds. In an exchange of letters with his former friend, Prince Kurbsky, he argued that the violence was ordained from on high. Citing Romans

13: 3–4, Ivan wrote that a tsar 'beareth not the sword in vain' but is 'an avenger who unleashes God's wrath on the wrongdoer'.

Ivan's religiosity increased with age – as did his cruelty. In later years, to beg God for forgiveness, he kept a book called the *Synodicon of the Disgraced*, commemorating the people he had killed and tortured personally over a lifetime. The book was sent to monasteries and churches along with generous donations. Ivan was known to repent during church services, weeping and bowing so low that he made bruises and bloody marks on his forehead. However, immediately after the end of the service, he would often return to torture, which he carried out with the same zeal as his prayers.[4]

Ivan would punish clergy for a lack of piety. Novgorod's archbishop was sewn up in a bearskin and hunted to death by a pack of hounds. Metropolitan Makary's successor survived for two years before fleeing to a monastery. The next metropolitan lasted two days. His replacement, Metropolitan Philip II, showed unflinching courage when he urged Ivan to stop the killings. 'The stones under your feet will cry out if the living refrain from accusing you and judging you,' he told the Tsar. 'It is my duty to tell you this by the will of God, even if death awaits me for doing so.'

One morning, the Tsar entered the Assumption Cathedral in the Kremlin. Philip, who was praying in front of an icon, refused him a blessing. The Metropolitan was arrested, accused of black magic and other 'crimes' and thrown into a cell. He was then sent a present, his nephew's severed head with a note from Ivan attached: 'This is your favourite relative – your sorcery couldn't help him.' Shortly after, Malyuta Skuratov, the most sadistic of Ivan's enforcers, came into Philip's cell at the Otroch Monastery in Tver and smothered him with a pillow.

Russian artists have drawn parallels between the security forces of Ivan's time and those of today. Written in 2006, Vladimir Sorokin's *Day of the Oprichnik* reads like a cross between *A Clockwork Orange* and *The Handmaid's Tale*. Their style of dress – long narrow beards and caftans – is medieval, as is the treatment of women. The *Oprichniki* attach freshly severed dog heads each morning to the hoods of their *mercedovs* (souped-up red Mercedes), watch His Majesty appear on a shining hologram and talk to each other on solid-gold *mobilos*. Futuristic technology is mashed up with the draconian codes of Ivan the Terrible, all set against a background of 'Holy Rus'. The Church in Sorokin's dystopian novel is complicit in upholding the tsar's despotism, just as it does in the real world today. Putin's Federal Security Service, the FSB, is often seen in church; its officers have taken to wearing black priest-like uniforms.

Nearly a century after he was martyred, Metropolitan Philip was canonised. There is also, however, a movement in the Patriarchate to canonise the man who ordered his murder. If Stalin can be rehabilitated, why not Saint Ivan? A year after the statue in Oryol was unveiled, at an iron ore plant in Moscow, Putin offered a revisionist spin on Ivan IV, casting doubt on the fact that he murdered his own son. The story was probably a slander cooked up by foreigners, the President told the assembled workers. Many researchers, he said, now believed this story came from a jaundiced emissary of Pope Gregory XIII. This line is often heard nowadays. Two weeks after Putin's speech, Andrei Fursov, a historian, said that Ivan the Terrible was almost 'white and fluffy'[5] compared to Henry VIII, Elizabeth I, or Spain's Philip II. He noted the tens of thousands of French Protestants slaughtered in the St Bartholomew's Massacre and other crimes committed in Western Europe. Fursov argued that Ivan, like Stalin, was a victim of 'the information war waged by the West and our liberals against the Russian state', adding: 'Russia became an empire under Ivan. Through the *Oprichnina*, he created an autocracy. It has endured for four centuries and guarantees Russia's power. No wonder it is disliked by the West.'

Two months before the statue of Ivan was erected in Oryol, Father Vsevolod Chaplin, head of the Patriarchate's Department for Cooperation between the Church and Society, was interviewed on the Echo of Moscow radio station.[6] Comparing Ivan with Stalin, Chaplin asked: 'What is wrong with destroying a certain number of internal enemies?' Then he added: 'Some people can and should be killed,' brushing off the presenter's protests that Russia no longer applied the death penalty. Quoting the final book of the New Testament, he said that God directly sanctioned the destruction of a huge number of people 'for the edification of others'. None of this surprises Russia's leading sociologist on the Church, Nikolai Mitrokhin, who believes that many rank-and-file clergy would agree with Chaplin. He claims that bishops routinely hit priests who make a mistake serving at the altar. In turn, priests sometimes slap their sacristans and subdeacons. The Church was the leading opponent of a ban on smacking children. 'So, for the Church,' concludes Mitrokhin, 'violence is the norm.'[7]

Ivan died on 17 March 1584, after collapsing over a chess board. The Church equated the game with dice and gambling, so it was formally prohibited until the seventeenth century. As he felt his life draining away, Ivan called upon witches and fortune tellers to cure him, but to no avail. Hoping to save his soul, he took monastic vows. One contemporary Russian historian, vehemently opposed to the Oryol statue, was scathing. 'The monastic robe had been laid out on the villain's stiffening corpse,' he wrote, 'but there is no doubt he is in hell, where he belongs, not on a square in one of Russia's most radiant cities.'[8]

Ivan was succeeded by his feeble-minded son, Feodor I, nicknamed the Bellringer because he was known for visiting churches and demanding that the bells ring out in his honour. His death in 1598 marked the end of the Rurikid dynasty of Kyiv and the start of what came to be known as the *Smutnoe Vremya*, the Time of Troubles – one of the most turbulent periods in Russian history. In the space of fifteen years, the crown changed hands six times. Boris Godunov, a close adviser of Ivan the Terrible, initially became the new tsar. However, soon the boyars began to plot against him. They accused him of murdering young Prince Dmitry Ivanovich, Ivan the Terrible's youngest son by his seventh wife, who had died, possibly after his throat was slashed, at the tender age of eight. A string of False Dmitrys appeared, impostors acting on behalf of Catholic Poland. They all claimed to be the Tsarevich Dmitry Ivanovich and each asserted his right to the throne.

Alongside the dynastic crisis came wars with Poland and Sweden, peasant uprisings, banditry and famine. When all seemed lost and the Poles had seized the Kremlin, the Church came to the rescue. Patriarch Hermogenes had been imprisoned for refusing to bless Władysław IV's accession to the Russian throne unless the Pole converted to Orthodoxy. From his cell in Moscow's Chudov Monastery, Hermogenes somehow managed to send letters to towns across Russia castigating citizens for abandoning the 'true faith'. He warned that unless they repented of their sins, the country would suffer the same fate as Jerusalem at the hands of the Romans.[9] A prosperous butcher and a Cossack prince from Nizhny Novgorod, a city on the River Volga, rallied to the defence of Orthodoxy. Kuzma Minin and Dmitry Pozharsky led a national liberation army to Moscow, where they defeated the Polish-Lithuanian garrison. Hermogenes blessed the volunteer force and was beaten and starved to death by the furious Poles as a result.[10] When they threatened him with execution, he stood firm: 'I fear only God. If all our enemies leave Moscow, I shall bless the Russian militia to withdraw from Moscow; but if you remain here, I shall bless all to stand against you and to die for the Orthodox Faith.' Three hundred years later, under Nicholas II, Hermogenes was finally canonised.

Every 4 November, Putin is filmed, alongside some handpicked patriots, laying flowers by the Minin and Pozharsky monument in front of St Basil's Cathedral in Red Square.[11] This ceremony has been enacted since 2005 when Putin created a new National Unity Day. Many ordinary Russians were bemused by the meaning of this autumn holiday, which was intended to replace the celebrations on 7 November, the anniversary of the Bolshevik Revolution.

Once Russia had been saved from perfidious foreigners, it needed a tsar. A *Zemsky Sobor*, a land assembly of the feudal classes, selected sixteen-year-old Mikhail Romanov as the 'God-chosen' successor. A great nephew of Ivan the Terrible through marriage, his reign established the Romanov dynasty, which ruled Russia until the February Revolution in 1917. His only son and successor, Tsar Alexis, was described as sweet-natured and pious. One religious philosopher said he was 'perhaps the only man worthy to wear the holy crown, almost a saint, with the strength of his faith, his childlike purity of heart and his thirst for the truth'.[12]

A group of senior clerics and political leaders had formed around the Tsar's confessor, Stefan Vonifatiyev, calling themselves the Zealots of Piety. Russia, they argued, had strayed from its true path during the Times of Troubles because its people had turned away from God. They were worried that Catholic clerics from western Ukraine, which was still controlled by the Polish-Lithuanian state, might corrupt Muscovy with their 'latinising' ideas. It was time for a clampdown on drunkenness and on the *skomorokhi*, travelling minstrels and harlequins who often poked fun at the pious. Tsar Alexis agreed, calling on parishioners who had indulged in such 'Satanic games' to repent.

Russia's seventh patriarch was the key figure of this era, towering over church and state. Nikita Minin was born into a peasant family with Finnish roots. He was once a popular Moscow priest and family man. But when his three children died, he underwent an existential crisis. He dispatched his wife to a convent and went to live as a hermit on an island in the White Sea, where he became a monk and took the name of Nikon. Over time, his reputation for piety and position as a leading zealot brought him to the Tsar's attention. Nikon first met Alexis when he came to the Moscow court seeking alms for the Solovetsky Monastery. Every Friday, the cleric would accost the young Tsar in his chapel with an armful of petitions from orphans, widows, prisoners and other unlucky people he had run into on his travels. Both Alexis and Patriarch Joseph were impressed with this energetic monk from the Arctic. Alexis grew somewhat obsessed with Nikon and began calling him his 'great sun' and spiritual guide.

When the old Patriarch Joseph died in 1652, Nikon was asked to become his successor. The former monk demurred, saying he was unworthy. Eventually he accepted, but on one condition: he wanted full authority over Church dogma and ritual. Alexis joyfully agreed. He was preoccupied by his struggle with the Polish-Lithuanian Commonwealth for control over territories in what is now Ukraine and Belarus. Nikon sprinkled holy water over the Tsar as he set off in 1654 to fight the Poles. A dazzling retinue carried the monarch's ensign with the motto 'Fear God and Obey the Tsar'.[13] But while Alexis was away, his subjects were told to obey Nikon instead, and they certainly grew to fear him. The distracted Tsar had invested the cleric with full sovereign powers and Nikon soon grew too big for his boots. He behaved as if his authority was superior to that of any secular ruler, including the Tsar himself. For a brief time during Nikon's fourteen-year reign, Russia was close to becoming a theocracy. He wanted to purify spiritual life and provide for the needy. But these laudable aims turned into a violent political project that polarised society. They also undermined the Orthodox Church, already weakened by Ivan the Terrible's murder of Patriarch Philip.

At first the Patriarch had the backing of many reformers and the support of the population, but he grew ever-more dictatorial. He was especially resented by parish priests who resisted efforts to centralise clerical authority. Nikon replaced court musicians with choirs of beggars and foundlings who walked around the palace chanting spiritual verses. Wine and vodka were banned at weddings; the bride, groom and their guests had to stick to non-alcoholic *kvass*, a drink made from black bread. He removed icons from homes, claiming they were painted in the wrong way.

He personally lit bonfires and took part in the burning of images that people had venerated for years. More radically, he reformed religious rites, customs and particularly liturgical books, which he had amended with the aid of Ukrainian scholars to conform more closely to Greek texts.

Some of his changes might appear inconsequential, such as using three fingers instead of two to make the sign of the cross, the spelling of Jesus' name and increasing the number of hallelujahs to be chanted during services. Nikon also decreed that Russian priests should walk around the altar counterclockwise, in the opposite direction to the movement of the sun – a relatively minor tweak to the liturgy. But many were horrified. Nikon's attempt to make the Russian Church more Greek overnight tore the country apart. Clerics who disagreed with him were exiled or excommunicated. His reforms were seen as the hijacking of religious belief by a centralised state-sponsored hierarchy. The historian Orlando Figes calls it 'a social protest in religious form'[14] and a unifying banner for popular revolts. Many priests bridled at being ordered to relearn prayers and rituals, while the masses were upset by Nikon's contempt for practices which they believed were sacrosanct. Thousands of Russians opposed his reforms, calling them the work of the Antichrist.

When Alexis returned to Moscow in 1658, he realised his once-beloved patriarch had become a liability. He was desperate for him to resign, but Nikon refused and for eight years clung to his post. Fearing damnation, Alexis was loath to get rid of him by force. Finally, in November 1666, the Tsar convened a council attended by the patriarchs of Antioch and Alexandria, at which he accused Nikon of living 'tyrannically, and not meekly as befits a prelate'.

The council banished the overweening Patriarch to a northern monastery and reduced his status to that of an ordinary monk to 'lament his sins in great silence'. Although Alexis punished Nikon's hubris, he opted to retain the Patriarch's reforms and make them his own. Asserting his authority over matters both spiritual and temporal, he legitimised the changes. Those who did not accept them would be seen as heretics and *raskolniki* – schismatics – enemies of both church and state.

The rebellion was led by another extraordinary, larger-than-life cleric, Archpriest Avvakum Petrov. A former ally of Nikon in the Zealots of Piety circle, he argued that Constantinople had fallen to the Turks precisely because the Greeks had mistakenly adopted the same heretical beliefs and practices enforced by Nikon. He and others were ignored. The reforms were ruthlessly enforced. People who resisted them were arrested, some tortured and executed. For fourteen years Avvakum was imprisoned above the Arctic Circle in a sunken hut. He wrote letters from there which were smuggled out by sympathetic guards. Apart from telling his followers to 'patiently endure whatever the Nikonians may do to us', he also railed against a new style of icon painting. He felt the medieval asceticism of Russia's religious art had been contaminated by 'sinful' Western European realism, in which the faces of saints were too fleshy and their mouths too big. Avvakum also sent defiant messages to Tsar Alexis: 'You do what you want with Russian land, but the son of God subjugated heaven and earth to me. My bare bones will be torn apart by dogs and birds of heaven and dragged over the earth so it will be good and fitting for me to lie on the earth and be clothed in light and covered by the sky.'

In the summer of 1668, lay brothers, monks, pilgrims and peasants took part in the Solovetsky Monastery Uprising, under the banner of the 'Old Faith'. Alexis' forces besieged the monastery and, after eight years, executed all the survivors. Other rebels around the country locked themselves in their churches and set themselves on fire. The historian Henri Troyat described how children of fanatical parents were told they should embrace death because in the other world they would have 'little red boots and shirts embroidered with gold thread' and they would feast on 'all the honey, nuts, and apples they wanted'. Entire families would go to the stake rather than 'bow down before the Antichrist'.[15]

Alexis was once friendly with Avvakum, so spared his life by sending him into exile. But his successor, Tsar Feodor III, had no such qualms. On 14 April 1682 the Archpriest was locked in a log cabin with other believers and burned alive.

Some dissenters sought refuge in the forests and remote parts of the country. Known as Old Believers, *starovery,* or Old Ritualists, *staroobriadtsy*, they formed self-sustaining communities and suffered persecution for centuries. Archpriest Avvakum's *Life, Written by Himself,* the first Russian autobiography, was suppressed for two centuries. The authorities feared the book could spread sectarianism and spark an uprising. Many fled to present-day Belarus and Poland, which was then run by the Catholic Grand Duchy of Lithuania. In the eighteenth century, the Old Believers were rounded up again, this time sent into permanent exile in distant Siberia. Much like the Jews, they were barred from jobs serving the state, and flourished as farmers, merchants and craftsmen.

The Revolution of 1917 led to a fresh exodus. Throughout the twentieth century, religious oppression forced them abroad, and several million are spread across the US, Canada, Australia and elsewhere. Like the Amish and Mennonites, they farm the land, adhere to strict social rules and spend much of their day in prayer. Children are taught to read Old Church Slavonic. The emphasis on large families, modest dress and traditional gender roles makes them model citizens in today's ultra-conservative Russia. In 2019, Putin granted Russian citizenship to eight leaders of Old Believer communities in the US and Brazil. Many have begun to return to the motherland under a new repatriation programme that grants them citizenship and helps with relocation to territories in Russia's underpopulated Far East.[16]

Had the Old Believers' vision prevailed, Orthodox Christianity in Russia might have taken a different path. Nikon succeeded in imposing Greek practices on the Russian Church but failed in his attempt to set the patriarch above the tsar. The schism made it easier for Alexis and future tsars to subordinate the Church and place it under the rule of the absolutist state.

4. PETER THE GREAT AND HIS REVOLUTIONARY PROCURATORS

Four months into the Ukraine war in 2022, Putin opened an exhibition in Moscow to mark the 350th anniversary of the birth of Peter the Great. He used the occasion to expound on his foreign policy and invoke history for his cause. For months, Russians had been told their troops had been sent to attack their neighbour as part of a 'special military operation' to counter 'Nazification' and NATO expansion. But on this occasion, before a handpicked audience of young entrepreneurs and engineers, Putin was comparing Peter I's Great Northern War against Sweden with his own invasion of Ukraine. Peter had 'returned' territory to Russia. 'Apparently, it is also our lot to return [what is Russia's] and strengthen,' he said.

Putin and Peter share certain similarities – including a determination to control the Church. Fiercely driven, Peter brought in a slew of reforms to modernise the country. One of these was abolishing the Patriarchate and replacing it with the Most Holy Synod. Established in 1721 in his new city of St Petersburg, in contrast to the Patriarchate in 'Holy Mother Moscow', the Synod was effectively a department of state, staffed by secular officials. It was headed by a lay chief procurator whose title in Russian, *Ober Prokuror*, sounds curiously German. That is because Peter's church reforms were partly inspired by meeting Protestants in Germany and Holland. He was also influenced by his trips to Lutheran Prussia and Anglican England, where the king was the head of the Church. The Tsar made it clear that his word trumped that of the most senior cleric. According to the historian Geoffrey Hosking, Peter spent many hours chewing the fat with Dr Gilbert Burnet, Bishop of Salisbury, who told him it was a monarch's duty to be 'a god on earth', control the church and make sure it promoted the good of the common people.[1]

Peter celebrated each military victory with a church service of thanksgiving and the hymn 'We Praise You, O God'. He had a lusty voice and enjoyed singing along with the choir during the liturgy. In 1698, on his visit to London, he opened an Orthodox chapel at the Russian Embassy. In his new capital of St Petersburg, he built the high baroque Peter and Paul Cathedral and the Alexander Nevsky Monastery to honour the thirteenth warrior saint who resisted the onslaught of Catholic Sweden and the Teutonic Knights. His approach to religion was more pragmatic than mystical. Since he wanted to attract foreigners to live in Russia to help develop the country's military and economy, he was tolerant of other faiths.

The first Russian ruler to travel widely in Europe, Peter made several trips incognito. Working as a carpenter to learn about ship-building in Dutch dockyards and visiting places like London's Royal Mint and Royal Society convinced him that Russia was lagging behind. A 1697 trip to Amsterdam, where everyone could worship whoever they pleased provided they did not challenge the established church, made a deep impression on the young Tsar. Swedish prisoners of war who settled in Russia were not forced to ditch their Lutheran faith if they married Russian women, provided their children were brought up as Orthodox. Peter was even tolerant of Old Believers if they were helpful to the state but made them pay handsomely for their facial hair.

The Church disliked Peter forcing his subjects to get rid of their beards; Russians treasured their beards as hallmarks of their Orthodox piety and symbols of their religion's superiority over Lutherans and other heretics. One British engineer, working in the south-western city of Voronezh, recalls meeting a heartbroken carpenter who kept his shorn-off beard in a pocket close to his bosom. He had told his wife to put it inside his coffin to ensure he would appear to be a God-fearing Christian in the next world.[2] Peter was unmoved by such stories. In August 1698, as soon as he returned from his Grand Embassy to

Western Europe, he armed himself with scissors and began personally snipping the hair from the faces of his noblemen and boyars.
Anyone who resisted risked having their beard pulled out by the roots.
Courtiers were ordered to swap their Byzantine robes for stockings,
breeches and wigs, and send their sons to Europe to learn navigation,
engineering and the modern sciences.

Peter grew up in an environment which had changed little since
medieval times. Noble families kept their women in a separate
upper-floor living quarters called the *terem*. Men and boys, once
they hit puberty, were denied access. Only children, girls, the master
of the house or a priest could cross the threshold. Peter found court
life stultifying and claustrophobic. He much preferred spending time
among soldiers and merchants in the more relaxed 'German Quarter'
of Moscow. It was in the north-east of the city, only a few miles from
the Preobrazhenskoe Palace, where Peter had lived with his half-sis-
ter Sophia, his regent before he came of age. Under pressure from
the Church, Alexis had forced all Catholic and Protestant foreigners
to move to this enclave to limit their influence on Orthodox believers. It was here that Peter dined with men who became some of his
closest confidants: the Scottish-born rear admiral Patrick Gordon,
the Swiss Huguenot Franz Lefort. It was also the place where he met
his long-time mistress Anna Mons, the daughter of a Westphalian
hotel owner and wine trader. He was so besotted with the German
beauty that he banished his wife Eudoxia Lopukhina to a convent
and almost made Mons his tsarina.

Naturally, the clergy disapproved. They were suspicious of
the monarch's alleged Protestant propensities. In February 1690 the
birth of Peter's first child, Alexei, was celebrated with the custom-
ary church services and bells and with cannon-fire and drumbeats.
Foreign-led infantry regiments were mustered in the Kremlin, presented with gifts and vodka to mark the occasion, much to the
disgust of the then Patriarch Joachim of Moscow. His 'Testament',
which denounced the policy of hiring foreigners, has been described
as the 'last gasp' of Old Russia:[3] 'May our sovereigns never allow any
Orthodox Christians in their realm to entertain any close friendly
relations with heretics and dissenters – with the Latins, Lutherans,
Calvinists and godless Tatars (whom our Lord abominates, and the

church of God damns for their God-abhorred guile); but let them be avoided as enemies of God and defamers of the Church.'

Such attitudes were anathema to Peter, who was forever curious and hated being told what to do. Early on, he established a drinking club called the All-Joking, All-Drunken Synod of Fools and Jesters. The purpose was to consume titanic amounts of alcohol in the company of dwarfs, clowns and courtesans and to mock the Church, especially Catholics. A pope was anointed before the party began. Holy water for bogus baptisms would magically turn into vodka for the 'infidels' who caroused until dawn, when they had to be scraped off the floor. Mock weddings were conducted where the 'newlyweds' were forced to drink out of large cups shaped like genitalia. Courtiers took on names that imitated those of real-life clerics but sounded as if they had been made up by twelve-year-old boys: Metropolitan of Great New Dick and of Great Testicles [instead of Great Novgorod and Velikie Luki], Iakov, nimble dick, motherfucker, Metropolitan of Pskov and Izborsk; Patriarch Bacchus, Archdeacon Thrust-the-Prick and so on.[4]

With his scientific mind, Peter was sceptical of superstitions, especially when he felt they were exploited by charlatans. In 1720 he heard about a miraculous icon of Mary in a St Petersburg church which shed tears during the liturgy. Peter took it off the wall and began to examine it. On closer inspection, he found pinprick perforations in her eyes and on the other side of the wooden panel a ball of wax which melted when the church was full and the temperature rose by several degrees, making the icon 'weep'. Peter was delighted by the ingenuity and kept the icon in his *Kunstkammer*, cabinet of curiosities, alongside pickled foetuses, penises and other body parts. He encouraged research into deformities – partly because they fascinated him – and partly to debunk fear of monsters and works of the devil.[5]

Peter approved of the entrepreneurial spirit of the Old Believers. Decades of persecution and isolation had fostered spiritual and economic independence in their close-knit communities across Russia. But their appetite for risk taking did not extend to what they ate. They called potatoes 'Tsar Peter's Apples', and suspected this new source of carbohydrates was a diabolical device to impoverish and corrupt the peasants by taking the place of holy bread. Peasants still say that when bread is on the table, it becomes an altar (*Khleb na stole i stol – prestol*). Given that potatoes are so central to the Russian diet and many city dwellers keep sacks of them on the balconies of their high-rise apartment blocks to get through the winter, the peasants' reaction seems quaint. But after collectivisation, when peasants were deprived of horses and ploughing implements necessary to grow grain, the Old Believers' prediction came true: for several decades most peasants were reduced to a diet of potatoes planted and dug on their own tiny plots with shovels.[6]

Peter felt his citizens were in thrall to semi-literate priests who were preventing the country from modernising. Just as he sent naval engineers to be educated in Holland, he sent clerics to theological schools in Kyiv founded by Jesuits when the city was under Polish rule. Orthodoxy remained the ideological core of the state, but Peter wanted to reform the clergy and relied heavily on those with a Western theological education. Scores of new seminaries were opened in Russia where priests had to study history, maths and physics, geography and geometry.

St Petersburg was a profoundly unorthodox, almost secular city, a characteristic noticed a century later by one of the founding fathers of Russian socialism, Alexander Herzen. 'In Petersburg one can live about two years without guessing the religion to which it adheres – here even Russian churches have taken on a certain Catholic aspect,' he writes. 'In Moscow you will know and hear Orthodoxy and its brazen voice the day after you arrive.'

Although the overweening Nikon had been removed, the Patriarchate was still a force to be reckoned with. It levied taxes on the people who lived on its estates and had authority over issues such as marriage, adultery and divorce, as well as families' wills and inheritance. Peter grew tired of lectures from Patriarch Adrian, who disapproved of his foreign friends and Western dress. The prelate also criticised the Tsar for neglecting his wife Eudoxia Lopukhina – the bride his mother chose for him when he was sixteen years old. The pious Eudoxia had little in common with Peter. After she gave birth to their ill-fated son Alexei, he left her, later divorced her and in 1698 packed her off to a convent in Suzdal. Alexei, eight years old at the time, was subsequently brought up by his aunts.

Patriarch Adrian died in 1700 while Peter was fighting the Battle of Narva against the Swedes. The Tsar was in no hurry to find a replacement. He had not forgotten Adrian's enthronement ceremony, in which the prelate repeated Nikon's doctrine of prioritising the power of the patriarch over royalty. Adrian also equated his voice to that of Jesus, claiming that whoever ignored his words 'ignores the words of our Lord God'. Peter made it clear that he saw the Church as a tool of the state. In 1708 he ordered his metropolitan to excommunicate Ivan Mazepa, the Ukrainian Cossack leader, for having the temerity to support Russia's enemy, King Charles XII of Sweden. Mazepa had been a close ally of Peter's and his decision to switch sides resonates with Ukraine's fight for independence today.

The Cossacks are an intrinsic part of the Ukrainian nation. At the end of the fifteenth century, they were groups of nomadic warriors who came down to the southern steppes in search of freedom and democratic self-rule. They survived by hunting, fishing and repelling Turkish invaders. By the seventeenth century, they had established a military organisation with an elected leader, the Hetman. The first, Bohdan Khmelnytsky (1595–1657), led an uprising against Polish rule and appealed to Alexis in Moscow for protection. At this point Nikon still had considerable influence over the Tsar and persuaded him that Bohdan's Cossacks would help him to recapture all the territories lost to the Poles. In 1654 Bohdan and Muscovite emissaries met in the city of Pereyslav, south of Kyiv, and signed an agreement pledging their allegiance to the Tsar. Although the Cossacks kept much of their independence, they promised to help Russia fight off its enemies.

But a quarter of a century later, when Peter began using the Cossacks as cannon fodder in his Northern War against Sweden and Poland, Mazepa was furious. The Cossack leader joined forces with King Charles XII instead. For him it was a question of survival. For Peter it was an act of treason. He ordered his army to raze the Hetmanate capital of Baturyn to the ground. Dead Cossacks were tied to crosses and floated down the River Dnieper. Since Peter failed to have Mazepa killed, he ensured that he was expelled from the Church instead. To this day many Russians see Mazepa as a traitor, but in Ukraine he is a national hero who sought to preserve Cossack self-determination. Peter needed well-travelled, highly educated churchmen to support his reform agenda, to help him build a secular absolutist monarchy to compete with other European states. He found most of them in Ukraine. Instead of looking for a new patriarch, Peter appointed a monk from Kyiv as a caretaker metropolitan. Stefan Yavorsky had attracted the Tsar's attention when he delivered an eloquent oration at the funeral of a boyar in Moscow. Within a short space of time, he was catapulted to high office. Another monk from Ukraine who came to Peter's attention was Feofan Prokopovich. He shared Peter's impatience with conservatives in the Church. After an Orthodox education, Prokopovich briefly became a Catholic while studying in Poland and Rome; he turned down an invitation to join the Jesuits and reverted to Orthodoxy on his return home. Well versed in thinkers such as Erasmus, Luther, Descartes, Galileo, Bacon, Machiavelli and Hobbes, Prokopovich had little in common with the average Russian bishop. Although Peter fished for talent in the Ukrainian pool of scholars, he had no qualms about destroying their language. In 1720 he issued a decree which banned the printing of the Bible and other liturgical texts in Ukrainian.

Peter surrounded himself with like-minded military officers and modernisers. He was impatient with his bookish, conservative son, Alexei, who had refused to attend his father's second wedding. Their relationship cracked for good in 1715, when Peter penned Alexei a letter bemoaning his lack of military prowess and threatening to deprive him 'of the succession as one may cut off a useless member'. Alexei agreed to become a monk, but instead of doing so, he fled for Austria, putting the Habsburg Emperor in a difficult position. Peter had several of his son's accomplices executed, fearing that Alexei was rallying forces to oppose his reform agenda. Peter's guards eventually located the terrified young man, handing him a note from the Tsar promising to forgive him for his disobedience. Alexei took him at his word and returned, only to be whipped to death in 1718. That same year, Prokopovich delivered a sermon declaring that, like the army and civil servants, churchmen must be subordinate to the state. His treatises supporting Peter's position included *A Word on the Power and the Honour of the Tsar* and *The Truth of the Monarch's Will*. To his admirers, Prokopovich used his intellectual brilliance to lay the foundations for the Russian Enlightenment. To his enemies, his scholarship was tainted by Protestantism and Dutch political theory. They saw Prokopovich as a hateful figure who pushed through reforms that proved disastrous for church and state.

Peter established the Most Holy Synod, the new organisation to run the Church. The name and the duties of this new body were borrowed from the Lutheran Church in Scandinavia and the Netherlands. The lay official in charge, the procurator, served as the 'tsar's eye' in Church affairs. Three years later, in 1723, the Patriarchate, which had been mothballed for two decades, was abolished. Prokopovich drew up a new Church constitution, outlined in the *Dukhovny Reglament*, or Spiritual Regulation. The *symphonia* of Byzantine Orthodoxy, in which church and state strive to exist in harmony, was jettisoned. The Church was no longer an equal partner. From this point on, the head of state was the supreme judge in religious matters, a system continued until the Revolution of 1917. When a group of bishops asked Peter if they could elect a new Patriarch, he waved a dagger in their faces. 'This is your spiritual Patriarch and those who object to him will get to know the Patriarch of the Sword,' he told them.[7]

The Spiritual Regulation left bishops and priests in no doubt about their duties to the state. These were enforced by the Procurator's staff, soon to be known as inquisitors. Clerics had to read decrees from the pulpit, administer oaths of loyalty and keep up-to-date registers of births, marriages and deaths. Priests were instructed to keep a record of parishioners' attendance at communion and inform the authorities if they heard anything suspicious. In a letter to Patriarch Pimen in 1972, Solzhenitsyn argued that the history of Russia would have been 'incomparably more humane and harmonious'[8] had its Church not surrendered its independence under Peter the Great.

5. CATHERINE THE GREAT AND
A REBELLIOUS BISHOP

Across the Moscow River from the headquarters of the Orthodox Church, a business innovation centre is being built next to a garish orange shopping mall. When I first came to Moscow, there was a famous factory on the site. It made Zils, the black limousines for top officials, who had their own dedicated lanes on major roads to ensure they were not inconvenienced by traffic or red lights. The special lanes endure but Zils are now museum pieces and the factory is no more.

Something else remains, however: the remnants of a fourteenth-century monastery. It was founded by St Feodor of Simonov, a disciple of St Sergius of Radonezh, the country's most revered saint. Over time it also served as a fortress, acquiring towers and strong walls. But in 1771 Catherine the Great decided the monastery was surplus to requirements and dissolved it. Later, the Bolsheviks delivered the *coup de grâce*, demolishing the fifteenth-century Dormition Cathedral and bell tower to build a palace of culture for the new car factory.

The Simonov Monastery was just one of 569 monasteries closed by Empress Catherine II – more than half of the total that were active at the start of her reign. Out of the 385 which survived secularisation, only 161 were financially supported by the government – the rest had to fend for themselves.[1] Catherine was completing the expropriation of the Church's land and wealth began by Peter the Great. Dioceses and monasteries which were used to receiving millions of roubles in rent each year were given endowments equivalent to barely a quarter of their earnings. These grants were only paid if the church could prove it was carrying out educational and charitable work – and keeping accurate lists of parishioners. Many clerics were unhappy with this state of affairs, but most kept quiet. One exception was Metropolitan Arseniy of Rostov, who blamed Catherine's foreign blood for the new regulations and suggested she was 'not firm in the faith'. He was swiftly tried for *lèse-majesté* and defrocked.[2]

Born Sophie Friederike Auguste von Anhalt-Zerbst-Dornburg, Catherine II was an unlikely candidate for Russia's throne. She arrived via a circuitous route.

Peter had died in 1725, aged 52, of bladder and kidney disease. With Alexei seen off, the crown passed first to his widow, then his niece and finally his daughter. Russia had never had a female monarch before, but women occupied the throne for much of the eighteenth century. Elizabeth was Peter's favourite child and shared his lust for life. She sought forgiveness for her hedonistic parties, which went on until dawn, by pouring money into the Church. During her two decades of rule, it regained some of its former prestige. Among the many churches she commissioned was the baroque Smolny Cathedral in St Petersburg designed by Francesco Bartolomeo Rastrelli, the Italian architect also responsible for the Winter Palace.

Elizabeth had no children, so she proclaimed her nephew, Peter, heir to the throne before looking for a suitable bride for him. Sophie, the fifteen-year-old daughter of a minor German prince from Stettin (modern-day Szczecin in Poland), seemed the perfect candidate. She had been raised a Lutheran, but before her marriage in St Petersburg converted to the Orthodox faith and changed her name to that of Elizabeth's late mother, Catherine. Under Elizabeth's watchful eye, she attended the liturgy, observed religious holidays and went on pilgrimages. She learned Russian and threw herself into her new life with gusto. Peter, raised in the Swedish court, was also a foreigner, but unlike his teenage bride, he seemed to loathe Russia.

For most of his life, Peter III remained a fanatical admirer of Frederick the Great. After ascending to the throne, he took Russia out of its war with Prussia. The army and nobility felt humiliated by the dishonourable peace, suspecting him of treason. Some of his short-lived reforms may have been laudable: the dissolution of secret police forces and forbidding landowners to kill the serfs who farmed their land. But within a short space of time, Peter had managed to make enemies almost everywhere, including inside the Church. To make matters worse, he made little attempt to hide his contempt for Orthodoxy, ordering the conscription of priests' sons into the military and the removal of all icons except for those of Jesus and the Mother of God from churches. He announced that Russians should embrace a faith akin to the Protestantism of north Germany. Sensing the outrage, and the opportunity, Catherine sprang into action. She secured the backing of the most powerful imperial regiment, while appealing to the clergy and pious masses also helped her to wrench power away from her husband.

In the Great Peterhof Palace outside St Petersburg, Russia's equivalent of Versailles, the Empress Consort is pictured sitting astride a white steed, holding a sword upright and dressed in the green uniform of the elite Preobrazhensky Guards.[3] She wears the blue ribbon of the Order of St Andrew the First-Called in honour of the first apostle of Jesus and the patron saint of Russia. (Her husband had refused to wear the Order of St Andrew and tried to replace it with the Prussian one.) Assisted by her court favourite, Count Grigory Orlov, Catherine led her troops to arrest Peter, declaring the urgent task of protecting Orthodoxy from 'the destruction of its traditions'.[4] She also suspected he might have been planning to divorce her.

She had herself immediately proclaimed empress in St Petersburg's Kazan Cathedral. It was a bloodless coup, although eight days later, the dethroned Tsar was dead. The official autopsy report claimed he died of haemorrhoids and an apoplectic stroke. Another version is that he got into a drunken brawl with a bodyguard; the most widely believed theory is that he was murdered by the younger brother of Catherine's lover, Grigory.

Senior clerics fervently supported Catherine's seizure of power hoping she would reverse Peter III's attempts to secularise Church property. Initially, she complied, revoking her dead husband's decree and granting the Church renewed possession of its land and enslaved peasants. But before long she had changed her mind, troubled by the Church's staggering wealth. In the spirit of Peter the Great, she believed that such riches should be at the disposal of the state and its citizens. She wanted the Church to play an active role in social welfare and education.

Her faith was not of the most fervent variety. She was more excited by the ideas of English and French philosophers, such as Voltaire, with whom she had a long-lasting correspondence. Catherine believed that religion was founded on ignorance and that, with the spread of enlightenment, it would gradually fade into insignificance. According to one historian, she rarely stood through the whole liturgy, especially in her old age, when her legs began to swell. She had a portable chair set up in the choir away from prying eyes, and 'evil tongues' said that up there she 'did needlework or even played solitaire'.[5] She knew, however, how to keep up appearances.

One of Catherine's most important social reforms of the 1760s was her desire to tackle one of the country's most backward institutions – serfdom. At the start of her reign the population included ten million peasants. One tenth were tied to lands owned by the Church. They were habitually mistreated; for example, torture and abuses were common at the Novospassky and Savvin-Storozhevsky monasteries. The priests of the Murom Cathedral in the Vladimir region 'beat their peasants routinely, demanded hefty bribes for permission to marry, and even raped peasant women for weeks at a time', according to one account.[6] Catherine made a public show of consulting her subjects and wrote a guide to prepare them for the meeting. Called the *Nakaz*, or Instruction, the 562-article document outlined the Empress's vision of a progressive Russian nation, including plans to abolish serfdom.

In 1762, Catherine ordered the Senate to investigate and catalogue Church assets and suggest how to share its wealth. The Senate proposed a compromise: the estates should be returned to the Church but the tax on Church peasants should be increased. Church peasants were to be freed from ecclesiastical control and put under the aegis of the state – with the Church being compensated – while clerics would become public officials on the same footing as army officers and civil servants. An imperial decree turned the Church into a state institution, and all priests became salaried employees of the state. The Church lost much of its autonomy, as well as its economic base, and hundreds of churches were forced to close. A group that once wielded immense influence over the Russian government and its people became increasingly segregated.

Most clerics reluctantly accepted the idea. Not Arseniy Matseyevich, Metropolitan of Rostov and Yaroslavl. He presided over the richest of all the church sees, which had more than 16,000 serfs. Arseniy planned to confront Catherine during her much-anticipated pilgrimage to Rostov in 1763. The bones of a newly canonised local saint were to be placed in a silver shrine in the presence of the Empress. When she postponed her visit, he was furious. He wrote to the Holy Synod, reminding it that the Empress had sworn to protect the Orthodox religion. He ridiculed the idea that the Church should teach subjects such as philosophy or mathematics or astronomy. Its job, he thundered, was to preach the word of God. If the Church were secularised, he said, bishops and priests would no longer be shepherds of their people but 'hired servants, accountable for every crust of bread'.

Arseniy was brought under guard from Rostov to a monastery in Moscow, where he was subjected to nightly interrogations in front of the Synod and the Empress. Defiant to the last, he questioned her very right to the throne. He was ritually disgraced at a public ceremony in the Kremlin, as one by one his sacerdotal garments were stripped off. Then he was sent to a monastery outside the Arctic city of Arkhangelsk. Four years later, still denouncing Catherine as a heretic and despoiler of the Church, he was dressed in peasant attire and secretly transported to the fortress of Reval – now Tallinn – in Estonia. His guards, who spoke no Russian, knew him only by the name Andrei Vral – Andrew the Liar. In solitary confinement in a dank stairwell, he sat for four years before he died in 1772. On the wall he scratched the words 'It was my fate for you to humble me, Lord'.

A month after sentence was passed on Arseniy, Catherine delivered a stern sermon to the Synod, suggesting clerics had strayed too far from the Gospel and the teachings of Christ: 'You are the successors to the apostles who were commanded by God to teach mankind to despise riches, and who were themselves poor men. How can you presume to own such riches, such vast estates? If you wish to obey the laws of your own order, if you wish to be my most faithful subjects, you will not hesitate to return to the state that which you unjustly possess.'

Having subjugated the Church, she sought to burnish her reputation as an enlightened monarch by practising a degree of tolerance towards other faiths. She established a Legislative Commission that included delegates of different social classes from across the country, including peasants, Cossacks and Tatars. The Empire's non-Christian subjects, many of whom were Muslim, had been drafted into the military during the Seven Years' War. Seats on the Legislative Commission were, in part, a reward for their loyal service. 'Orthodox sits next to heretic and Muslim,' Catherine boasted to her penfriend Voltaire. 'All three listen calmly to a heathen; and all four put their heads together to make their opinions mutually acceptable.'[7] The Orthodox leadership was not invited onto the Commission.[8]

At the same time, she used the Orthodox faith for her political ends. As her reign went on, she became less and less interested in her earlier reforms or in Voltaire's ideas about individual liberty, focusing her attention instead on conquest. The seizure of Church lands and money helped pay for Catherine's wars, which she fought under a religious banner. Peter the Great had opened Russia up to northern Europe, founding St Petersburg on the Baltic Coast. Catherine resolved to push south and east and extend the Empire to the Black Sea. She annexed much of Ukraine through wars with the Ottoman Empire and the partition of Russia's traditional rival, Poland. She declared her mission to reunify the ancient lands of Kievan Rus and preserve Orthodoxy.

In 1794 scores of Orthodox priests backed up by soldiers travelled across the Ukrainian lands annexed by the Russian Empire. They had come to wage a spiritual war against the Uniate Church. Established in the sixteenth century, it accepted Catholic dogmas while observing the Byzantine rites of the Eastern Orthodox Church. The Uniates' allegiance was to the Pope in Rome, but they kept some Eastern traditions, such as allowing clergy to marry. With 4 million adherents, it was the dominant faith in the Ukrainian and Belarusian lands of the Polish-Lithuanian Commonwealth. Catherine's priests announced that the Uniate believers should immediately convert to Orthodoxy. They demanded keys to parish churches, kicked out any priests who refused to comply and obtained signed statements of conversions. By the time of Catherine's death two years later, church and state boasted of the 'return' of 1.5 million to the Orthodox fold.

It was under Catherine that Orthodoxy became a lever of imperial expansion. She delved into history to legitimise Russia's claim to Crimea and Muslim southern borderlands, which she called Novorossiya (New Russia). She began the search for Chersonesus, the site of Prince Vladimir's baptism, which was later excavated in the nineteenth century. Catherine saw her empire as the rightful heir of Kievan Rus. By the end of her reign, most of Ukraine was occupied. It would remain under Russian control until the 1917 Revolution.

On 24 February 2022, a group of oligarchs rushed to the Kremlin, desperate to find out why Putin had launched the invasion of Ukraine in the early hours of the morning. One of them bumped into Sergei Lavrov, who admitted most officials in the Kremlin had been in the dark about the President's plans. 'He has three advisers,' Lavrov told the oligarch, 'Ivan the Terrible, Peter the Great and Catherine the Great.'[9]

6. SLAVOPHILES AND WESTERNISERS

Outside Russia, few may have heard of Olga Vasilyeva, but many teachers were appalled in the summer of 2016 when she was appointed education minister. A few years earlier, in a closed lecture for members of the ruling United Russia party, she called Stalin 'a blessing for the state'.[1] He should be congratulated, she told them, for upholding pre-revolutionary heroes, promoting the Russian language and uniting people during the Second World War. On other occasions, Vasilyeva warned about the dangers of 'blackening Soviet history' and of 'astonishing myths' peddled in the 1990s.

A historian of Russian Orthodoxy, Vasilyeva was close to Archimandrite (now Metropolitan) Tikhon Shevkunov, widely seen as Putin's spiritual father or confessor. She was also a deputy chief of the Presidential Administration's blandly titled Public Projects Directorate. Set up in the wake of street protests in 2012, its aim was to promote patriotism and reinforce the country's spiritual foundations. Vasilyeva's spiritual forefather was Sergei Uvarov, Minister for Enlightenment under Tsar Nicholas I and the man who defined Russia's national ideology in three words: orthodoxy, autocracy and nationhood.

If Peter the Great was excited by Western European technology and Catherine the Great was excited by its philosophy, Nicholas I saw in the West only danger. Count Uvarov was appointed to keep a lid on it.

This era, between the death of Catherine and the demise of the Romanovs in 1917, is defined by the battle between Slavophiles and Westernisers. It is dominated by two arch conservatives at either end of the nineteenth century, Sergei Uvarov and Konstantin Pobedonostsev, a lay head of the Church. Neither monarchs nor priests, both men were determined to ensure that Western concepts of individual liberty would never take root in Russian soil. They believed that the Church should be a part of the state and that Orthodoxy was central to the identity of the Russian Empire – even though, by this point, the Empire was multi-ethnic and multi-confessional. Russia was the only political entity in the world to be home to vast populations from the four major religions: Christianity, Islam, Judaism and Buddhism.

With his stress on Orthodoxy, Uvarov explicitly rejected the religious scepticism of the European Enlightenment. Yet he was an unlikely Russian nationalist, a European cosmopolitan from a privileged background.[2] His uncles, sons of an advisor to Catherine, had received a liberal education. Uvarov had studied in Göttingen, sparkled in elegant salons in Paris and flirted with Madame de Staël in Vienna, where he served as a young diplomat. He spoke several languages and wrote poetry in French. Even his plan for an Asiatic Academy, in which he argued that Russia should take advantage of its position straddling Europe and Asia to explore Oriental studies, was initially written in French. He also had a deep fear of social unrest, a fear that came from his childhood tutor, a cleric from Bordeaux who had fled the French Revolution.

Uvarov's career began towards the end of the reign of Alexander I (1801–25), Catherine the Great's grandson, who had seen off Napoleon Bonaparte. After the 1812 Battle of Borodino, in which Russia suffered 45,000 casualties, Napoleon marched into a deserted Moscow only to watch his prize go up in smoke. Alexander pursued Napoleon back to France and entered Paris in triumph. The Tsar believed his empire had been saved by divine intervention and that Holy Russia had come to the rescue of humanity. The burning of Moscow by French troops had 'illuminated his soul'. It was at this point, argues the historian Orlando Figes, that Russia first appeared as the champion of Christian principles against secular democracy and nationalist movements in Europe.[3]

Yet a number of officers who fought for the Tsar in the Napoleonic Wars (1812–15) began to think that much of Russian society was profoundly unchristian. Fighting alongside peasants and Cossacks, they had been impressed by the bravery and patriotism of their social inferiors. Serfdom struck them as indefensible. In his famous travelogue *A Journey from St Petersburg to Moscow*, the civil servant Alexander Radishchev had already asked in 1790: 'Can a state in which two-thirds of the citizens are deprived of civic status and are in part dead in the eyes of the law be called blessed?'[4] Attracted by the new political ideas coursing through France and other parts of Western Europe, young Russian officers began forming secret societies to regenerate and liberalise the country.

Alexander suspected people in his ranks were conspiring against him. He was especially shaken by a plot to kidnap him on his way to the Congress of Aix-la-Chapelle in 1818, where the four powers Britain, Austria, Prussia and Russia were discussing reparations against France. He grew increasingly withdrawn, believing that 'the reign of Satan' was everywhere. In the autumn of 1825 his wife was poorly, and doctors recommended a rest cure by the seaside. The royal couple travelled to the southern town of Taganrog. After a mysterious solitary visit to a monastery, Alexander caught a fever and succumbed to typhoid.

His unexpected demise, aged 47, so far from St Petersburg, led to rumours that he had not really died but had run off to become a monk in Ukraine. After all, he had made no secret of his desire to abdicate. Some said he had moved to Siberia and become a hermit named Feodor Kuzmich. The president of the Russian Graphological Society detected strong similarities between the handwriting of Alexander I and the mysterious monk. As the novelist Leo Tolstoy observed, it was not only the common people who believed the rumours about the monk, but many from the elite, including the family of Tsar Alexander III. Tolstoy was so taken with the story of the ruler who faked his own death to become a monk that he penned a fictional diary titled *Posthumous Notes of the Starets Feodor Kuzmich* and contemplated writing a short story based on the legend. One historian observed that a portrait of Kuzmich was hanging on the wall of Tsar Alexander III's office next to those of his royal predecessors.[5]

Just weeks after Alexander's apparent death, 3,000 soldiers and officers gathered on Senate Square in front of the Winter Palace in St Petersburg. Demanding a constitutional monarchy, they refused to swear allegiance to the new tsar, Alexander's brother, Nicholas I. This attempt to overthrow power marked the beginning of the revolutionary movement. Had everything gone to plan, the royal guards would have switched sides, the rebels would have stormed the Winter Palace, arrested Nicholas and declared a provisional government. But nothing went to plan. The uprising was badly organised, the nominated leader, Prince Sergei Trubetskoy, failed to appear at the crucial moment and the rebels were soon crushed. Another insurrection by the Chernigov regiment in the south was also unsuccessful. Ultimately, 289 dissenters, known as Decembrists since their rebellion took place in the last month of the year, were put on trial. Five of the ringleaders were hanged, the rest were imprisoned or banished to Siberia.

It was against this background that Nicholas I came to power, convinced that his empire was endangered by revolutionary ideas coming from the West. He believed it was his sacred duty to stamp out unrest wherever it flared up – a conviction which shaped his foreign policy. Five years after he was crowned, he suppressed a Polish revolt against Russian rule. Two decades later, France was in ferment again, with the overthrow of King Louis Philippe I and the establishment of the Second Republic. Revolutionary sentiments spread to Italy and Austria. Nicholas saw himself as the stern defender of monarchical legitimacy and offered to help conservatives suppress revolutions across the continent. In 1849 he intervened on behalf of the Habsburgs to put down an uprising in Hungary, and he urged Prussia not to accept a liberal constitution.

If he was known abroad as the 'gendarme of Europe', at home Nicholas' reputation was that of a bureaucrat and a despot. Since the officers leading the Decembrist revolt had been noblemen, Nicholas was determined to limit their power. State control was exercised over all areas of public life. The Tsar founded a secret police force, known as the Third Section, which ran a network of spies and informers.

Nicholas gave his chief ideologist, Uvarov, the job of enforcing the new regulations. Fast-tracked through the reformed state service, Uvarov served on two committees dealing with education and censorship that the Tsar had founded at the start of his reign. Not long after that, he was appointed deputy education minister, where he was tasked with raising academic standards while keeping a check on undesirable ideas. The emphasis was on theology, the classics and vocational training, while philosophy was almost eliminated from the curriculum. Uvarov unveiled his famous slogan in a report to Nicholas on his vision for Moscow university and secondary schools. Students, he told Nicholas, must have a modern education but also 'a warm faith in the genuinely Russian conservative principles of Orthodoxy, Autocracy and Nationhood, which comprise the ultimate anchor of our salvation'.[6]

Nicholas liked the tripartite formula so much – it was a deliberate riposte to the Liberty, Equality, Fraternity mantra of the French Revolution – that he promoted Uvarov to Minister of National Enlightenment in March 1833. The Tsar wanted Moscow to reflect his ideology. He dismissed Konstantin Ton, the architect appointed by Alexander I to build Christ the Saviour. He did not approve of the neoclassical style with columns, preferring instead a more Russian design with onion-shaped domes and Kokoschka arches on the façade, which evoked women's traditional headdresses. The cathedral was moved from a hilltop to a new site on the Moscow River to make an Orthodox triptych. According to this, the centre was the Kremlin, the seat of power. To the east was St Basil's, built by Ivan the Terrible to celebrate victory over Muslim Tatars; and to the west would be his new cathedral, symbolising Russia's triumph over Western Europe.

As head of the Chief Directorate of Censorship, Uvarov kept a check on writers and other members of the intelligentsia. He was not entirely comfortable in this new role, given that his brother-in-law and others from his social circle had been among the Decembrists packed off to labour camps in Siberia. But he soon grew into it. The first intellectual to earn his ire was the philosopher Pyotr Chaadaev, who attacked the Orthodox Church for failing to address the 'terrible ulcer' of serfdom. Although until the early 1800s the Catholic and Protestant churches had supported slavery and benefited from the institution, Chaadaev was inspired by the abolition campaign of William Wilberforce. Why, he asked, did the Church in Russia 'not raise her motherly voice against this disgusting violence of one part of the people over another. I do not know, but it seems to me that this alone should cause us to doubt the Orthodoxy which we boast about.'[7] Unsurprisingly, Nicholas I did not react kindly to such musings. Nor did he appreciate Chaadaev's depiction of Russia as a pariah. Under Uvarov's orders, the philosopher was declared insane, put under house arrest and constant medical supervision. This is thought to be the first recorded incident of psychiatry being used to suppress dissent in Russia.

Uvarov also put pressure on one of Chaadaev's close friends, Alexander Pushkin. According to Uvarov's biographer, the minister was jealous of the poet's literary genius. He was also irritated that the Tsar had gone over his head and asked Pushkin for advice on education. Once Uvarov found out that Pushkin's grandfather was an African slave, brought to Russia by Peter the Great, he spread gossip around town about the poet's 'dubious breeding'.[8]

Despite his professed devotion to a conservative Church, Uvarov, a married man with four children, was bisexual. He had his lover, Prince Mikhail Dondukov-Korsakov, appointed vice-president of the Academy of Sciences and, much to Pushkin's fury, chairman of the St Petersburg censorship committee. Pushkin would die two years later in a duel. Amid a mass outpouring of grief, Uvarov forbade students to attend the funeral. Mikhail Lermontov lamented his fellow poet's death, writing of a society where people crawled on their knees while 'a hungry mob gathered round the throne'. The liberal critic Vissarion Belinsky was more direct, branding Uvarov 'the Minister of Darkness and the Extinction of Enlightenment'.[9]

Despite his public rows with writers, Uvarov was no obscurantist. He successfully lobbied for better funding for schools and universities and opened higher education to the middle classes. He sponsored scholarships, voyages of exploration in Asia and created a department of Oriental Studies. Journalists who were paid agents of the tsarist police attacked Uvarov for allowing too much academic freedom. The conservative elite denigrated him for a lack of moral purpose. In a bid to save his job, Uvarov upped the rhetoric about 'an Orthodox and God favoured Russia' and reinforced Russian language teaching and divinity classes in the more remote outposts of the Empire. Such measures failed to satisfy the Tsar's appetite for repression. The university chairs of philosophy were closed. Young utopian socialists, including the future novelist Fyodor Dostoevsky, were initially sentenced to death for reading and discussing banned literature. Their sentences were commuted to Siberia exile. Nearly all foreign works were censored, bookshops were searched for prohibited material, teachers were not allowed to travel abroad, and universities were run like military barracks. This was too much even for Uvarov, who resigned in 1849 and spent the rest of his life completing a doctorate in classical studies.

Nicholas' obsession with conservative Orthodoxy was responsible for his downfall. A row over access to the birthplace of Jesus in Bethlehem was the spark which ignited the disastrous Crimean War. Russia had long controlled and maintained the holiest Christian sites in the Ottoman Empire. These were visited by many thousands of devout Russians whose co-religionists in the Greek Orthodox clergy had an agreement with the Turkish authorities. But France wanted to change the status quo. Determined to extend Catholic influence in the region, in the summer of 1852, Emperor Napoleon III sent a battleship through the Dardanelles. Diplomacy and money persuaded Sultan Abdülmecid to switch allegiances. Keys to the main door of the Church of the Nativity, previously in the hands of the Greek Orthodox Church, were given to the Catholics.

Nicholas was incensed. He saw the Sultan's decision as an insult to the millions of Orthodox Christians under his protection; he was determined to have it reversed, by force, if necessary. He had hoped for British support, only to be disappointed. When negotiations broke down, Nicholas invaded Ottoman-ruled Moldavia and Wallachia, sending other forces to advance on Constantinople. But the gendarme of Europe was no longer invincible. England, France and Sardinia sided with Turkey. The European allies sailed to the Crimean Peninsula and laid siege to the Russian naval base at Sevastopol, which fell after an agonising eleven months. A quarter of a million Russians lost their lives.

The ordeal Russia suffered in the Crimean War laid bare the weakness and backwardness of Nicholas' regime. This stiff-backed military man, who for 30 years had commanded an empire covering a sixth of the earth's surface, was shocked by the prospect of defeat. Although there were rumours that he had poisoned himself, he died of pneumonia in February 1855 after reviewing troops about to leave for the front in temperatures of minus-23 degrees. On his deathbed, he told his son Alexander he would pray for the defenders of Sevastopol in the next world. Then he raised his hand to his heir and clenched his fist. 'Hold everything like this!' he said. 'Serve Russia!'[10]

☦ ☦ ☦

The Russia that Alexander II took over was crying out for reform. The court system and local government were overhauled, universal military service was introduced, corporal punishment became less brutal, and censorship was relaxed. But the biggest change, six years into the new tsar's reign, was the emancipation of Russia's 23 million serfs. Even his father, Nicholas, had realised that depriving peasants of their human rights and tying them to nobles' estates amounted to a 'gunpowder magazine underneath the state'.

Metropolitan Philaret (Drozdov) of Moscow, who enjoyed the highest level of authority of any cleric since the seventeenth century, wrote the text of the manifesto freeing the serfs. Many hoped abolishing serfdom would promote Christian brotherhood and lead to Russia's national and spiritual rebirth. Dostoevsky compared the Tsar Liberator's Decree to Vladimir's conversion of the Eastern Slavs to Christianity in 988.[11] Even so, the Metropolitan who sanctified the emancipation did not have a liberal pedigree. The revolutionary émigré Aleksandr Herzen accused him of thanking God when Nicholas I executed the ringleaders of the Decembrists.[12]

On occasion, the Metropolitan was prepared to challenge the state. For a period in 1842 he was forced out of the Synod for having the temerity to translate the Old Testament. The procurator who banned him, Count Nikolai Protasov, a former cavalry general, had been appointed by Nicholas to bring the Church into the iron grip of the state. According to one Church historian, Protasov 'ruled over a docile Synod and truly became "a Patriarch in a soldier's uniform"'.[13]

Ever since the Napoleonic Wars, some clerics had been urging for the publication of the Bible in modern Russian. Although Church

Slavonic was used liturgically, few could read the scriptures or understand them when read out loud. Some argued it would be sacrilegious to allow ordinary people access to holy texts. Metropolitan Serafim of St Petersburg declared it would 'provoke idle minds to controversy, polemic and other aberrations'. A Russian Bible Society established in 1812 had been shut down by Nicholas I, and biblical translation was forced underground for the next 30 years. Allowed again under Alexander II's reforms, a full translation of the gospels finally appeared in 1861, and the whole Bible in 1876.[14]

Many hoped the translations would revive the piety of the Church and rescue it from the spiritual stagnation to which it had sunk after the reforms of Peter the Great. Theologian Georges Florovsky referred to this period as the 'Babylonian captivity'. The Tsar was persuaded to set up a commission, yet the real impetus came from an obscure source, a sensational book written by a provincial priest. *Description of the Rural Clergy,* published anonymously in Germany and smuggled into the Empire, circulated widely and became a cause célèbre. Its author, Ioann Belliustin, wrote scathingly about the drudgery of life in Tver, north of Moscow. He spent his days administering sacraments and ploughing fields. In much of the countryside, the priest was a subsistence farmer, just like his parishioners. It was felt necessary in some places to remind the priest to wear shoes in church when conducting the liturgy.[15]

From their salons in Moscow and St Petersburg, the upper classes praised the innate religiosity of the Russian peasant. Belliustin presented a less romantic picture, describing the 'ruinous contagion' of drunkenness which permeated village life. If the priest refused to drink vodka with his parishioners, he wrote, they would feel insulted and refuse to help him with the *pomoch*, the assistance given to local clergy at harvest time. 'At first the parishioners looked upon the sober priest with amazement, but then they all ceased to help him with his field labour. What was he to do? Somehow, he entices two or three of them and "pays his respects", that is he gulps down a few drops; at first it seems disgusting but the longer he does it the more tolerable it becomes.'[16]

Belliustin also exposed corruption and cover-ups. He complained that clerical positions were bought or inherited, regardless of vocation or ability. In schools, pupils had strict orders to bring their teachers sums of money ahead of exams. Those who underpaid were held back a year; those who gave nothing were expelled. Some parents complained, but to no avail. The corruption was exacerbated by the gulf between the so-called black and white clergy. The former, monks or nuns, made up the Church hierarchy and conducted the liturgy in monastic communities, while the latter served laypeople. Married clergymen were not eligible for promotion to a bishopric – the highest office they could reach was that of archpriest. Diocesan bishops were cut off from the secular world while their officials harassed the impoverished clergy for bribes. In a bitter aside, Belliustin compared senior clerics to American slave owners.

Although his book was published seemingly without his knowledge, Belliustin was sentenced to an Arctic exile at the Solovetsky Monastery. The Tsar, who had been alerted to the book by advisors and was sympathetic, annulled the punishment. Belliustin told his son that Alexander had saved him 'from the revenge of the monks'.[17]

Much of the ecclesiastical hierarchy saw no need for change. Alexander's interior minister, Pyotr Valuyev, thought otherwise. He accused bishops of reigning over subordinates 'like the most brutal despots'.

The government expected village clerics to provide moral guidance during the upheaval of emancipation. Many, though, were preoccupied with their own survival. Valuyev described the white clergy as 'poor and helpless' and so isolated from society that they had become almost inbred, a hereditary 'caste of Levites'. Whatever education priests managed to pick up in seminaries, much of it was forgotten amid the daily grind. Social mobility for their children was virtually non-existent.[18] Sons either became priests like their fathers or slid down the social scale and risked being drafted into the army.[19] Daughters were rarely qualified to become anything other than the wives of clergymen. This sense of a dead end made the clergy vulnerable to radicalism. 'The white clergy hates the black clergy, and spurred on by this hatred not only democratic, but even socialist strivings are beginning to spread,' Valuyev warned, 'also a certain inclination toward Protestantism, which with time could lead to a convulsion within the bosom of the Church.'

The clerical caste was formally abolished in 1869 and church schools were opened to all classes. This allowed people to pursue a genuine religious calling if they wished, but the state's ability to influence the curriculum was limited. Since the imperial treasury and the bishops baulked at the idea of providing salaries for priests, tackling poverty was difficult. Although Belliustin's book seemed to herald a new era of openness, and Valuyev had some success, resistance from the hierarchy slowed progress. Peasants gained freedom but not much else. They had to rent land at high interest rates while landowners kept the most fertile plots. In the wake of emancipation, hundreds of countryside revolts had to be suppressed by force.

To this day, the Church does not pay its priests. Instead, it takes money from them. A priest might supplement his income through teaching or helping parishioners to write letters and draw up legal documents – he was often the only literate person in his community. But most of his income came, and still comes, from donations in return for services such as baptisms, funerals and weddings. Some of the luckier clerics received a yearly stipend from a generous nobleman or bishop, but most had to rely on money or goods in kind from their parishioners to feed their families. What surplus they might have they were required to send to their already wealthy dioceses.

Despite the emancipation of the serfs, throughout the 1860s society grew increasingly polarised. Into this maelstrom strode Konstantin Pobedonostsev. The son of a university professor and grandson of an Orthodox priest, Pobedonostsev grew up in a large family with ten brothers and sisters. As a young man, he trained in civil law and was in favour of emancipation, which he once called 'a great holy thought'. Like Uvarov, his conservative early nineteenth-century predecessor, Pobedonostsev was highly educated, well-travelled and spoke several languages. Impressed by his work on restructuring the judiciary, Alexander invited him in 1861 to become the tutor in legal matters for the heir to the throne. In 1880, he appointed him Procurator of the Holy Synod, in charge of administering the Church. Pobedonostsev admired Europe's economy and wanted Russia to emulate it, but was opposed to introducing Western ideas and institutions. He loved travelling in northern Italy but refused to visit Rome because of his aversion to Catholicism.

Although he was a close friend of Fyodor Dostoevsky, his asceticism and rigidity would later alienate him from much of St Petersburg's intellectual society.

The following year, on 1 March, Alexander was returning to the Winter Palace when his carriage was attacked by the *Narodnaya Volya* (People's Will) revolutionary group. As he stepped out to help the wounded, a second bomb ripped off his legs. In one of the supreme ironies of Russian history, that very morning he had granted preliminary approval to constitutional reforms. Within days, Pobedonostsev had persuaded the new tsar, Alexander III, to ditch his father's agenda and restore an absolutist monarchy.

For a quarter of a century, Pobedonostsev put his ultra-conservative stamp on public life. As tutor and close personal adviser to both Alexander III and then his son, Nicholas II, the last tsar, he wielded enormous influence. As well as running religious affairs, he was also a member of the Council of State, the Senate and the Council of Ministers. He was allergic to any form of representative government, even consultative. Only 'half-wits, or perverted apes', he told Alexander, would be swayed by the idea that the people should have a say in how the state is run. He argued that a revolution was preferable to a constitution because the former could be suppressed and order restored throughout the land, while the latter 'is poison to the entire organism'. To him, the Russian soul was inseparably linked with the autocracy and the Church. He dismissed democracy as 'the insupportable dictatorship of the vulgar crowd'.

Pobedonostsev had a paradoxical attitude to the *narod*, the common people. Privately, he saw them as degenerates, incapable of hard work. At the same time, he publicly romanticised them as the salt of the earth, the guardians of the soul of the nation filled with basic goodness and wisdom. He suggested that, untainted by Western culture and education, the *narod* relied on Orthodox faith, which made it morally superior to the rest of society. Having killed off the constitutional reforms of Alexander II, he drafted the Manifesto of Unshakable Autocracy two months after the Tsar's assassination. It begins with a statement that it was God's will that the reign of Alexander II should culminate in 'a martyr's death', that the 'holy duty of autocratic rule' had fallen on his son and that the new tsar would be supported by the 'fervent prayers of the pious people'. Some of the language echoes Ivan the Terrible's speech at his coronation in 1547 when he declared that only absolute power can safeguard Russia.

From childhood, Orthodoxy was central to Pobedonostsev's life. He sought joy from the beauty of the services, yet his religious belief was saturated with pessimism. It was pointless, he felt, to try to change the essentially sinful nature of humankind. His outlook was not far from that of the English philosopher Thomas Hobbes, who, in his work *Leviathan,* described the life of man as 'solitary, poor, nasty, brutish, and short'. One of Pobedonostev's few pleasures was contemplating Christ's suffering while listening to the liturgy. He and his wife also enjoyed attending funerals. He wrote enthusiastically about a ceremony he had attended in a monastery near St Petersburg which seemed 'a gathering honouring life, not death'. In another letter, he described his joy at seeing a consignment of prisoners being sent to the remote island of Sakhalin with a priest on board. 'Is it not pleasant,' he asked, 'that 600 exiles are sailing the ocean and singing morning and evening prayers?'[20] An English observer drily observed that he was 'a man who would have sent his own son to Siberia'.[21] At his first meeting with Pobedonostsev in 1882, the German ambassador concluded he was more medieval monk than politician.

Beneath the cloak of sanctity, Pobedonostsev's priority in Church affairs was the preservation of a strong Russian state. He believed it essential to ensure pupils were taught obedience to the tsarist system from their earliest years. For centuries most schooling in Russia had been run by the Church. But during the Great Reforms, Pobedonostsev's predecessor was dismayed by standards in the church schools and decided to create a totally secular system run by the local authorities, the *zemstvos*. This was a trend Pobedonostsev was determined to reverse.

For him, the traditional parish school was a bastion of stability at a time of growing social unrest. He saw their real purpose less to educate than to isolate common people from any liberal or radical ideas they might get from *zemstvo* teachers or the radical intelligentsia. In a note to Nicolas II in November 1902, he wrote that 'perverted and mindless people are trying to engender depravity of thought in the *narod*'.

Like many from the official Church, Pobedonostsev was out of touch with developments on the ground. Convinced that he was the true interpreter of the *narod*, he underestimated the spiritual vitality of the Old Believers and those who rejected Orthodoxy for other creeds. In the early twentieth century, as many as a million individuals professed non-Orthodox Christian faiths. Across the empire, many evangelical groups emerged, such as the *Molokane*, from the word *moloko* (milk), who refused to stop eating dairy products during Lent. The *Doukhobors*, the name means 'spirit wrestlers', were vegetarians and radical pacifists, while the *Stundists* in southern Ukraine embraced hard work and sobriety and were influenced by German Baptists. Many other mystical sects emerged, such as the *Khlysty* and the terrifyingly puritanical *Skoptsy*. The latter thought sexual organs were the mark of Cain which had led Adam and Eve astray. They declared war on original sin by castrating men and practising female mastectomies. Understandably they were not protected by an 1883 law affording limited rights to Old Believers and some evangelical sects.

Towards the end of the century, many inside the Church thought that unless they cut ties with the state, Orthodoxy would continue to lose followers. The top-down Synodal system of Church governance was unpopular with the Slavophiles who wanted a return to grass-roots Orthodoxy. In their eyes, the collectivist peasant commune was superior to the selfish individualism of the West. Alexei Khomyakov, a philosopher and co-founder of the Slavophile movement, argued that Orthodoxy's strength lay in its spirit of *sobornost* – from the word *sobor*, which means both council and cathedral. *Sobornost* emphasised the Church as the body of Christ. He felt it should consist of all its members, including the laity, rather than a clerical hierarchy reliant on the state. In his 1864 tract, *There Is Only One Church*, Khomyakov advocated the Byzantine model of symphonic harmony where secular and spiritual forces were perfectly balanced. Russia should return to the time before Peter the Great, he argued, and to a traditional but reinvigorated Orthodoxy, which would lead the Slavs to salvation in Christ.

Pobedonostsev respected Khomyakov but reserved his greatest animosity for other intellectuals and writers, none more so than Tolstoy. He was incredulous when the novelist urged Alexander III to follow the teachings of Christ and show mercy to the revolutionaries who had killed his father. Tolstoy asked the Procurator, as head of the Church, to pass a letter to the heir apparent, pleading with him not to execute the assassins. Pobedonostsev binned the letter and instead penned one of his own. 'The Russian people are fearful that your Majesty could be swayed by these perverted thoughts,' he wrote to Alexander. 'Could it happen? No, a thousand times no!'

Pobedonostsev prevailed. On 3 April, a month after the assassination, five of the revolutionaries were hanged. The sixth, Gesya Gelfman, was spared only because she was pregnant and protest letters were sent from all over the world, including one from Victor Hugo. She died shortly after giving birth, for lack of medical treatment.[22]

Pobedonostsev wrote back to Tolstoy in June: 'I saw that your faith and that of the Church are not one. Your Christ is not our Christ. Ours is a man of truth and virtue, a healer of the sick. Yours is weak minded and in need of healing himself.' Convinced the writer was a danger to the state, Pobedonostsev did whatever he could to prevent publication of his works. Even though the Tsar had enjoyed a rehearsal of *The Power of Darkness*, Pobedonostsev cancelled all performances. He called the play, which included scenes of adultery and drunkenness, an 'abasement of art'.

Tolstoy exacted revenge in his novel *Resurrection*, which features a cold-blooded, lizard-like character named Toporov who, like Pobedonostsev, is Chief Procurator of the Most Holy Synod. In one scene, the protagonist appeals to Toporov on behalf of some sectarians who have been arrested for holding non-Orthodox prayer services. The hero, a conscience-stricken nobleman trying to make up for past misdeeds, senses that Toporov 'in the depths of his soul really believed in nothing'. Tolstoy's Procurator is a complacent nihilist who uses Orthodoxy to brainwash the masses: 'He treated the religion he supported as a poultry farmer treats the carrion with which he feeds his chickens: carrion is very unpleasant, but it's what chickens like to eat.'

In the late 1870s, despite the success of *War and Peace* and *Anna Karenina*, Tolstoy underwent an existential mid-life crisis. He was restless and filled with self-disgust over his inherited wealth and other privileges. He had already attacked a subservient Church for bolstering the aristocracy. 'The sanctification of political power by Christianity is blasphemy; it is the negation of Christianity,' he wrote in his 1866 article 'Church and State'. In search of the meaning of life, he sought solace in the countryside. Listening to peasants talk about their daily lives and their faith kept his despair at bay. By the mid-1880s, he broke with the Orthodox Church to emerge as a Christian anarchist, refusing to believe in the Virgin birth, the Holy Trinity and the sacraments. Despite his reverence for the Gospel, he saw Christ as a man rather than the Son of God. He argued that people could affirm the good in themselves through self-improvement rather than through rituals. His loathing of institutional Christianity infuses *Resurrection*, his final completed novel, published in the last year of the nineteenth century. Stripped of mystical significance, a Eucharist celebrated in a St Petersburg prison appears grotesque. He describes the priest 'wiping the children's mouths' and 'eating God's flesh and drinking His blood' as if he were observing a semi-cannibalistic cult rather than a sacred rite.

Pobedonostsev realised that neither the state nor church could prevent Tolstoy's influence on Russian society. In 1901 he formally cut ties with the 72-year-old writer. A statement signed by six metropolitans, an archbishop and seven bishops said Tolstoy, 'seduced by intellectual pride', could no longer be considered a member of the Church. The decree caused a scandal. Nobody had been excommunicated in more than a hundred years.

By this point, a new tsar had taken the throne. Perturbed by the publicity, Nicholas II accused Pobedonostsev of publishing the statement without his approval. The affair made him even more vindictive. Later in the year, when Tolstoy was seriously ill, Pobedonostsev sent instructions to governors and police chiefs that no memorial services in Tolstoy's honour were to be allowed on his death. Pobedonostsev dreamed of staging a deathbed recantation. He had prearranged for a priest to slip into the Tolstoy household and announce that in his last hour, the writer had rejoined the Orthodox Church. But the plan was foiled when the writer recovered. He survived for almost a decade until he caught a fatal dose of pneumonia at a remote railway station. By that point Pobedonostsev had been in his own grave for more than three years. Tolstoy also outmanoeuvred the procurator over the treatment of non-Orthodox Christians. He defended the pacifist *Doukhobors* who destroyed all their weapons in protest at forced conscription. As a result, the state imprisoned them or sent them to penal battalions. Using his royalties from his novel *Resurrection*, as well as contributions from English Quakers and Russian merchants, Tolstoy chartered ships to bring 7,500 *Doukhobors* to safety and to new lives in Canada.

The Church would resume its vendetta more than a century later. Sergei Stepashin, a former prime minister and director of the FSB, with close ties to the Moscow Patriarchate, could not help feeling that there was something un-Christian about its approach to Russia's best-known writer. After visiting the unmarked mound of earth where Tolstoy is buried, he felt so disturbed that he wrote to Patriarch Kirill in 2011 begging forgiveness on behalf of Tolstoy. The Patriarch's cultural secretary replied that Tolstoy had 'purposely used his great talent to destroy Russia's traditional spiritual and social order'. The ban on burning candles for Tolstoy or commemorating him in Orthodox churches remains in place to this day.

Nicholas II was intimidated by Pobedonostsev, but he was also under pressure to modernise. Four months earlier, a massacre of striking factory workers in St Petersburg sparked the 1905 Revolution. Carrying icons and led by an Orthodox priest from Ukraine, the workers marched to the square in front of the Winter Palace. They wanted to present their grievances to the Tsar, but Nicholas was not in the city. His uncle, Grand Duke Vladimir, ordered police to fire upon the unarmed demonstrators. More than a hundred were killed, many more wounded. Bloody Sunday was followed by a series of strikes in other cities, peasant uprisings in the provinces and mutinies in naval bases. The turmoil left Nicholas a choice – crack down further or reform. He took the latter option, resulting in the October Manifesto, which granted a limited constitutional government. Horrified, Pobedonostsev resigned as procurator. Throughout the turmoil, Pobedonostsev had shut himself off in his study, translating the New Testament.[23] When he died two years later, a decade before the Bolshevik Revolution, he was convinced that both Russia's church and empire were doomed to collapse.

Many Russians disagreed, and several attempts were made to kill the procurator. The first took place two weeks after Tolstoy's excommunication, when a civil servant from Samara took a few pot shots at Pobedonostsev through the window of his government residence but the bullets hit the ceiling. When police interrogated the would-be assassin, he told them he had wanted to 'eradicate the main obstacle to progress and freedom'.[24]

Pobedonostsev was feared and hated in equal measures. Fellow officials compared him to a snake or spider.[25] The artist Ilya Repin painted him in pallid, deathly tones. The normally charitable Christian philosopher Nikolai Berdyaev described him as 'a living corpse', doubting whether human blood flowed through his veins. The symbolist poet Alexander Blok depicted him as a creature of the night in a verse called Retribution.

> *In those distant, deaf years*
> *Dream and dark ruled over hearts*
> *With owl-like wings, Pobedonostsev*
> *Flew over the skies of Russia.*
> *And there was neither day, nor night,*
> *Only the shadow of those wings.*
> *He drew a magic circle around Russia,*
> *Staring her in the eyes*
> *With a glassy wizard's stare.*[26]

In the Putin era, Pobedonostsev is back in fashion, adopted by nationalists as a true Russian. In a political manifesto, *Right and Truth*, published in 2010, the Kremlin-friendly film director Nikita Mikhalkov praised his 'enlightened conservatism'. It was time to stop deceiving the *narod*: 'People are tired of declarations on political independence. They are tired of calls for individual freedoms. They don't believe in fairy tales about the wonders of the market economy. The euphoria over liberal democracy is over.'

☦ ☦ ☦

However far-fetched it might seem, Russians are encouraged to see their last tsar as a divine figure, a miracle worker, even. Virtually every Orthodox church I have visited, from Spain to Siberia, has a (usually mass-produced) icon in pride of place featuring Nicholas II, Empress Alexandra, their son Alexei and four daughters, all wearing golden haloes. Many people swear they have recovered from illness after praying to the Romanovs. The Tsar and his family were canonised in 1981 during Leonid Brezhnev's time by the Russian Orthodox Church Abroad, which at that time was separate from the Soviet Church.

Three decades later, in August 2000, nearly a decade after the collapse of communism, the Moscow Patriarchate followed suit. Only one senior cleric, Metropolitan Nikolai (Kutepov) of Nizhny Novgorod, refused to view the last tsar as a saint. 'He is a state traitor. He, one might say, sanctioned the collapse of the country. And no one will convince me otherwise,' he declared in 2000.[27] Since it could not be argued that the Tsar and his family were explicitly killed for their Orthodox faith, the Council of Bishops did not proclaim them martyrs. Officially, they are on the bottom rung of sainthood as 'passion bearers', people who accepted their imminent death at the hands of their enemies with Christian humility. A statement released by the Patriarchate's press office described them as 'meek, humble and long suffering people who sincerely sought to live by the commandments of the Gospels'.[28]

Under Putin, the veneration has gone into overdrive, as the makers of one movie found to their cost. Some Orthodox believers could not contain their fury at a costume drama about the love affair between the future tsar Nicholas II and a ballerina called Matilde Kschessinka. He was still unmarried, as was she, and after three years the heir to the throne broke off the relationship and wed his betrothed, Princess Alix of Hesse. But the trailers for *Matilda*, featuring passionate love scenes between the young prince and the half-Polish teenager, sparked outrage. One MP, Natalia Poklonskaya, renowned for her religious conservatism, campaigned to have the film banned. She insisted the depiction of a saint having sex on screen was blasphemous.

Others threatened to take the law into their own hands, inspired by white supremacists and alt-right evangelicals in the US and by radicals in the Middle East. A group calling itself Christian State Holy Rus said it had more than 300 active members and that its name deliberately echoed that of the Islamic State of Iraq, or ISIS. Its leader, Alexander Kalinin, said Russia 'should be like Iran'. The group wrote to a thousand cinemas across the country threatening to firebomb them if they screened the film. A Molotov cocktail was tossed into the director's St Petersburg film studio. Cars parked on the Moscow street in front of his lawyer's office were set alight. Leaflets with the words 'Burn for Matilda' were left on the charred wreckage. Two men tried to smash their way into a cinema in the Urals driving a truck loaded with gas canisters. Several cinemas scrapped their screenings, citing public safety or 'technical reasons'.

Poklonskaya condemned the violence but, without seeing the film, submitted a 39-page report to the prosecutor's office detailing the way it disparages 'the human dignity of Russian Orthodox believers'. Before she won her seat in the Duma, she served as a prosecutor in Crimea following the annexation of the Ukrainian peninsula in 2014. A devotee of Nicholas II, she once claimed a bust of the Tsar in the regional capital of Simferopol wept tears of myrrh on the centennial of his abdication of power. The diocese in Crimea sent a commission to check but found no trace of tears on his bronze cheeks. Nevertheless, a priest from an adjacent chapel was ordered to monitor the situation in case of signs of a myrrh flow.

Nicholas was unarguably devout, yet the decision to beatify the family was hotly debated, even inside the clergy. His weakness and narrow-mindedness brought disaster to his people and almost annihilated the Orthodox Church. He had little appetite for power and felt unfit for the role. He was horrified when his father died prematurely, aged 49 in 1894. 'What will become of Russia?' he said on hearing news of Alexander III's demise. 'I am not yet ready to be Tsar. I know nothing of the business of ruling. I don't even know how to speak to my ministers.' Throughout his childhood, he had been inculcated with the notion that the tsar's power was holy and incontestable. He was being anointed by God to steer his country into the twentieth century. This led him to become deaf to advice from pragmatic army commanders and members of his court. He prized loyalty over competence. He blundered into a war with Japan, while failing to reinforce Russia's military presence in the Far East. Advisors who urged him to avoid, or at least postpone, the naval assault were ignored.

Nicholas reigned over a vast empire which desperately needed to modernise, but he had almost no curiosity about what was going on outside his palace. Many have likened him to a country squire, at his happiest walking in the fresh air, chopping logs, attending the divine liturgy and spending time with his family.

Heavily influenced by his father and by Pobedonostsev, the Tsar had been loath to agree to any representative form of government, believing it was harmful to the people God had entrusted to his care. But his October Manifesto promised basic civil rights and established the first representative bodies of legislative power – the Imperial Duma and the upper house, the State Council. Duma deputies consisted of landowners, the industrial middle class, merchants, urban intellectuals, peasants and some clergy. Many clergy were impatient for change. Nicholas refused to allow the Church limited autonomy, to the frustration of Pobedonostsev's replacement at the Holy Synod, Alexander Obolensky. For several months in 1906, clerics and theologians worked on ideas for reform. They recommended convening a *Sobor*, a council of elected clergy and laity which would itself then elect a patriarch.

Over the following years Nicholas dug in his heels. He was bruised from his encounters with the first two Dumas, which he later dissolved by imperial decree. He had been appalled by what he saw as their radical demands for universal suffrage and land reform, and he did not want yet another forum where his subjects could air hostile opinions. He feared the *Sobor* would elect a patriarch capable, as Pobedonostsev had warned him, of rivalling his authority. The Prime Minister, Pyotr Stolypin, supported the Tsar, but for different reasons. He felt a modern industrial economy should institutionalise religious diversity by replacing the Holy Synod with a Ministry for Religious Denominations responsible for all faiths in the Empire.[29]

Even conservative churchmen became disillusioned with autocracy in the last years of tsarist rule. This was in part prompted by the growing influence on the imperial family of a self-proclaimed holy man from Siberia. History tends to mythologise Grigory Rasputin as a devilish, sex-crazed peasant with magnetic eyes and appalling table manners. His acolytes preferred to focus on his stories of travelling across Russia's vast expanse barefoot, wearing iron chains around his ankles. To them, he was a *starets* – an elder whose ascetic experiences afforded him mystical insights and a direct connection to God. Some society ladies were so entranced by him that they even collected his fingernail clippings and sewed them into their clothing as if they were holy relics.

Rasputin may never have gained admittance to the palace were it not for three-year-old Tsarevich Alexei, the royal couple's only son and the heir to the throne. He was the unlucky recipient of a chromosome condition acquired through the line of his maternal great grandmother, Britain's Queen Victoria. When the boy's umbilical cord was cut, he bled profusely, and the couple began to dread Alexei's fate. His haemophilia was kept secret for fear it could be seen as a divine punishment and destabilise Russia. Empress Alexandra's anxiety, much chronicled in Nicholas II's diary, made her vulnerable to promises of miracle cures. Rasputin's standing at court has often been put down to his ability to soothe Alexei and stop his bleeding attacks. Before long both Nicholas and his Empress had fallen under Rasputin's spell. Impressed by his great piety and wisdom, they began to trust him not just with their son's health and private spiritual matters, but also with affairs of state.

The relationship between the royals and the Siberian peasant was complicated.[30] From the outset, Nicholas valued Rasputin's guidance about how to govern Russia. Alexandra was desperate to cure her son, but she was also desperate to put some backbone into a husband who was notoriously weak and indecisive.

Rasputin first met the Tsar and Tsarina in St Petersburg during the autumn of 1905. He made it clear that Nicholas ought to heed the 'sage advice' that comes from God, not the 'stiff and formal' variety from his ministers. It reassured the Tsar that a humble peasant was telling him exactly what he wanted to hear – to believe in God, trust in miracles and have faith in himself and his reign. In his diary he described Rasputin 'as just a good, religious, simple-minded Russian', adding: 'When in trouble or assailed by doubts, I like to have a talk with him, and I invariably feel at peace with myself afterward.'

The son of a peasant farmer from a village in western Siberia, Rasputin left his wife and seven children to set off on a spiritual quest.[31] He spent several years as a *strannik*, a wanderer, visiting holy sites around the Empire. Although he was neither trained nor ordained as a priest, he gained an education of sorts on his travels and learned to read and write. His folk wisdom, psychological acumen and familiarity with the scriptures soon garnered him followers. He eventually gained access to the Romanovs thanks to some concerted networking and high society's fascination with the psychic and paranormal. Far from the bread queues and factory strikes, it seemed as if everyone was talking about hypnotism, faith healers and the supernatural, and séances were conducted in drawing rooms across St Petersburg.

Rasputin was not the first mystic the royals had consulted. Two Montenegrin princesses, Grand Duchess Militza and Grand Duchess Anastasia, dubbed the Black Crows by newspapers because of their fascination with the dark arts, introduced the Tsarina to an occultist from Lyon. They knew Alexandra was desperate to conceive a son after giving birth to four daughters. The Frenchman, Philippe Nazier-Vachot, told her he could manipulate the sex of a child in the womb. Even though he had no medical training, he told them he could make their wish come true. They believed him.

Monsieur Philippe informed the royal couple that he had fallen into a trance and received a prophecy from St Seraphim of Sarov that the Empress would soon give birth to a baby boy. Alexandra was keen to offer prayers to Seraphim, but the snag was that there was no such saint. A *starets* from the early nineteenth century, Seraphim was a hieromonk who spent 25 years living in a hut in the woods. Although he was greatly revered, he had not passed the test of saintliness, because when he died, his corpse had decomposed. Alexandra gave orders that Seraphim should nonetheless be canonised and told Nicholas to override the Holy Synod's decision. 'The Emperor can do anything,' she insisted.

A ceremony attended by 300,000 pilgrims took place in Sarov, in central Russia, in July 1903. The royal couple bathed in the Sarov River as instructed by Monsieur Philippe; within three months Alexandra was pregnant with Alexei. Nicholas agreed to distance himself from Monsieur Philippe only after countless pleas from his advisers and a warning from one of the most respected holy men of the day, Saint John of Kronstadt, who lived on a fortress island in the Gulf of Finland.

Some accounts suggest Rasputin's rise was engineered by a group of Orthodox clergymen seeking to curb the influence of foreign interlopers. Before long, Rasputin was the talk of the town. The foreign minister Sergei Sazonov told the French ambassador: 'The emperor reigns, but the empress governs, inspired by Rasputin.' As stories emerged about his heavy drinking and debauchery, the Church tried to distance itself from him. When the Tsar was away at the front, rumours spread that the Tsarina and her mystic healer were in the pay of the Germans. Alexandra's foreign birth may have fed the gossip, and some saw Rasputin's pacifism as disloyal. He tried his best to keep Russia out of the First World War. In July 1914 he was in Siberia, where he was recovering from a head wound after a botched assassination attempt. From his sick bed, he sent a desperate telegram to the palace: 'Let Papa [his nickname for Nicholas II] not plan war, for with the war will come the end of Russia and yourselves and you will lose to the last man.' A lady in waiting who delivered the telegram reported that Nicholas angrily tore it to pieces. Later, Rasputin suggested he should go to the front and bless the troops. The army's commander-in-chief, Grand Duke Nicholas Nikolaevich, vowed to have the Siberian mystic hanged if he came anywhere near the frontlines.

As Russia's position worsened on the battlefront and revolutionary fervour increased at home, conservative politicians fell into despair. 'The powers of darkness are now attacking Russia's last hope – the church,' declared a Duma member, Vladimir Purishkevich. 'The most terrible part of all is that this seems to emanate from the Throne itself. A filthy, illiterate peasant is playing his dirty tricks on our prelates. Into what abyss are we being driven?' Four years later, in the early hours of 30 December 1916, Purishkevich and a group of nobles, led by Prince Felix Yusupov, finally took action. Rasputin was lured to a midnight rendezvous at the Moika Palace with Yusupov's beautiful young wife Irina. He was led into a cellar and served cakes and Madeira wine laced with cyanide. But getting rid of Rasputin was hard work. The poison had little effect so the assassins had to beat him, riddle him with bullets and dump him in the River Neva before they could be sure that they had finished him off.

Rasputin had prophesied that he would be killed by a relative of the royal family and that, as a result, the Tsar would lose his throne and also die. By February 1917, after more than two years of war, hardship gripped Russia. Bread rationing was the final straw. At textile factories, women poured into the streets of Petrograd, as St Petersburg had been renamed, holding banners saying 'Bread' and 'Down with the Tsar'. By the end of the first day 100,000 workers were on strike. Regiments of the Petrograd garrison mutinied and joined the protest. Workers and soldiers formed revolutionary councils, or Soviets. The imperial government was forced to resign. Members of parliament who wanted to preserve the monarchy and agitators from the Petrograd Soviet compromised to form a provisional government. They agreed to seek Nicholas' removal in favour of the Tsarevich Alexei. By 15 March, Nicholas realised his position had become untenable and stepped down but insisted the crown should go to his brother rather than his frail, haemophilic son. Grand Duke Michael agreed but got cold feet when members of the provisional government said they could not guarantee his safety. He was emperor for just one day. After 304 years, the Romanov dynasty was over.

At his coronation, Nicholas had symbolically married his kingdom, so it seemed unfathomable that any tsar could abscond from this holiest of unions. When the monarchy collapsed, the Church did not come to its defence. The Synod instructed Grand Duke Michael to refuse the crown. The following month, the Synod signed a declaration calling on the nation to fully support the provisional government and the new democracy. The end of the Romanov dynasty galvanised those in the clergy who wanted more autonomy for the Church. Bishops took advantage of the revolutionary fervour to convene a council attended by delegates from across Russia. All aspects of ecclesiastical life, from church–state relations to finances, religious education and, most radically, the role of women were hotly debated. It was extraordinarily progressive; some call it the Orthodox equivalent of Vatican II convened many decades later, in the early 1960s, by Pope John XXIII, which brought the Catholic Church into the modern world by updating the liturgy, focusing more on laypeople and starting a dialogue with other religions. For eight heady months of 1917, as Russia's political structures were in flux, clerics argued over whether to restore the patriarchate or install a more collective style of leadership.

That autumn everything changed. The centre of Moscow echoed to the sound of artillery shells and machine-gun fire as Red Guards fought military cadets for control of the Kremlin. Compared to the relatively bloodless storming of the Winter Palace in Petrograd in February, the fighting lasted for several days and left hundreds dead. The Kremlin's towers and churches were freshly scarred by shelling when, on 21 November 1917, Metropolitan Tikhon was enthroned in the Assumption Cathedral. By then, the Bolsheviks had toppled the moderate provisional government and seized power. When Tikhon heard that he was to become the first Patriarch of Moscow and All Russia since the time of Peter the Great, he compared his fate to that of the prophet Ezekiel, who had to eat a scroll on which was written 'lamentation, and mourning, and woe'.

7. THERE IS NO GOD: ORTHODOXY IN THE SOVIET ERA

....

In a political system cleansed of medieval mould,
the proletariat will lead the struggle against economic slavery,
the true source of the religious humbugging of mankind.
VLADIMIR LENIN, *NEW LIFE* (1905)

....

I first visited Yekaterinburg in the winter of 1991. The smoke belching out of the chimneys seemed to freeze in the air and turn the snow grey. During shift changes at the heavy-machine building plant, tens of thousands of workers in drab coats and hats poured off buses and out of the metro station and were soon swallowed up behind factory gates. Uralmash was the noisy clanging centre of Soviet manufacturing, producing everything from T34 tanks to oil rigs. It was a city within a city, built from scratch in barely five years as a socialist paradise for its 16,500 comrades. 'The clouds will disperse over the gloomy Urals,' declared its chief engineer. 'It will wake up rich and strong, open its powerful stone chest and, waving its iron wings, will irresistibly fly forward'.[1]

Even in the final months of the Soviet Union's existence, workers told me they were proud to work in the 'factory of factories'. During a cognac-laced tea break, one of them whipped out a guitar and played a song called 'My Grandfather Built Uralmash'. 'In front of

my machine, I take my place/Our sacred labour is filled with grace,'
he sang. Then came the obligatory tribute to the war dead:

> My grandfather, in '42, took his stand
> Defending our Uralmash, on Stalingrad's land
> And as I tread the path to the factory door
> His spirit walks beside me, just as before.

I assumed this hymn was trotted out for visiting dignitaries and foreign guests. But the worker sang with such fervour, even in the 1990s,
that I wondered whether he might, still now, be filling some kind of
void. It reminded me of one of the first songs I learned in Russian,
which has a catchy melody that, try as I might, I cannot forget:

> Lenin is always alive, Lenin is always with you, in sorrow, in
> hope and joy.

> Lenin is in your spring, in every happy day, Lenin is in you
> and in me![2]

Lenin's successor declared that the new 'socialist man' was an atheist, free of the religious chains that had helped to bind him to class
oppression. At the same time, the party that had destroyed religion
realised that it needed something to put in its place. A cult was built
around 'holy' Lenin. 'Lenin Lives!' declared the banners.

On his death in January 1924, the leader of the Bolshevik
Revolution was denied a normal burial, against his wife's wishes.
His body was pumped with chemicals, put in a glass box and displayed in a specially built granite mausoleum in Red Square which
always reminds me of an art deco cigarette box. It was a grotesque
caricature of the hermit caves in Russia's most sacred monasteries
where the relics of holy men are covered in rich embroidery and
displayed in dimly lit glass coffins.

Lenin, the ascetic saint, self-denying monk, supplanted Christ in
iconography. His framed portrait replaced the shrines with icons and
candles. The *krasniy ugol*, the beautiful corner, became the *krasniy
ugolok*, the little red corner. Heaven was brought down to earth in

the shape of a 'workers' paradise'. Russian certainty about a messianic destiny had been channelled into a vision of a sunlit communist future. The religious philosopher Nikolai Berdyaev saw a continuity between Russia's vocation as guardian of Orthodox Christianity and its purpose of spreading Communism across the entire globe.

To understand the Church's relationship with power after the October Revolution there is no better place to start than Yekaterinburg – the city where Russia's last tsar and his family were murdered in the basement of a merchant's mansion. On that spot now stands the Church on the Blood, its crypt symbolically bathed in red light.

For most of their train journey from Siberia, Nicholas and Alexandra thought they were heading for Moscow, or to Crimea and eventual exile outside Russia. As their carriage approached Yekaterinburg, their hearts sank. 'I would go anywhere at all, only not to the Urals,' Nicholas is reported to have said.[3] The regional capital was reputed to be in the grip of violent revolutionaries. For centuries, dissidents and ordinary criminals had been sent from there to forced labour in the harsh climes of Siberia. The Romanovs were confined in the Ipatiev House, a mansion which belonged to an engineer responsible for a section of the Trans-Siberian railway. After the revolution, it had been confiscated by the Communists and designated 'The House of Special Purpose'. Halfway up a hill, it commanded a fine view of the city, but the Bolsheviks had built a high fence of logs and telegraph poles around it and covered all the windows with white paint.

Despite their isolation from the outside world, nuns from the nearby Novotikhvinsky Convent knew that members of the Romanov family were there and devotedly brought them fresh milk and eggs every morning. One of the first clerics to be murdered by the Bolsheviks was Archbishop Hermogenes (Dolganov), Bishop of Siberia and Tobolsk, who had led a church procession past the house where the Romanovs were imprisoned. He had stopped outside and briefly made the sign of the cross. That was enough to get him arrested and later drowned in the Tura River. Ironically, that same bishop had been persecuted by Nicholas because of his opposition to Rasputin.

On the night of 17 July 1918, after eleven weeks of imprisonment, Nicholas, Alexandra, their children Olga, Tatiana, Maria, Anastasia and Alexei, and their physician and three servants were dragged from their beds and ordered downstairs. Once in the cellar, their captors told them they were sentenced to death. An incredulous Nicholas only had time to shout, 'What? What?' before he was shot several times in the chest. The others took longer to die. Precious stones and diamonds sewn into the girls' underclothes shielded them from the first round of bullets, which horrified their panic-stricken executioners. Finally, they stabbed the teenage girls with bayonets and shot them at point-blank range in the head. The bodies were doused with acid and dumped in a mineshaft so that they would not become objects of veneration.

Shortly after the slaughter, the Ipatiev House became a Red Army officers' mess. It was later an agricultural college, then a local museum of atheism. Visitors came less for the anti-religious displays in dusty display cases upstairs than the opportunity to take photographs in the cellar. There was no signage but the bullet marks on the walls were still visible. As the sixtieth anniversary of the murders approached, the authorities became increasingly twitchy about the house becoming a place of pilgrimage for monarchist sympathisers. The KGB was also worried about the number of 'foreign specialists' visiting the site and making it 'a subject of their careful scrutiny'.[4] In 1977, the then regional Communist Party chief Boris Yeltsin was ordered by the Politburo to demolish the house, an act he later described in his memoirs as a 'piece of barbarism'.

On my 1991 trip to Yekaterinburg with a BBC colleague, we had trouble finding the site, as it was just an empty stretch of tarmac. One old woman who ran a newspaper kiosk nearby noticed our confusion. She grabbed my elbow and pointed to a small wooden cross, telling me that a steady trickle of people came to the barren spot every day to remember the Romanovs and pray for their souls.

On my next visit to the city, I was equally disorientated. On the very same spot, an enormous white Byzantine structure with five golden domes appeared before me, like a mirage. A bride and groom had just emerged from the upper church and were posing for photographs, laughing as a gust of icy wind almost robbed the young woman of her veil.

This gleaming apparition was the Church on Blood in Honour of All Saints Resplendent in the Russian Land, consecrated in 2003 on the anniversary of the executions. Patriarch Alexei II was too ill to attend the ceremony but said it marked 'a possible historic turn' for Russia and called for unity between Church, state and people. In the blood-red crypt below, glowing icons above marble plaques were dedicated to each family member. Archpriest Maxim Minyailo, a towering figure with a spade-shaped beard, proudly showed me another icon of the Royal Passion-Bearers, as the martyred family are now described. He said it had cosmic properties because it had been sent into outer space in 2007 and orbited the earth 240 times. In an adjoining room stood familiar pictures of the Tsar in his tunic and knee-high boots, the Romanov daughters wearing spotless white dresses and the twelve-year-old Tsarevich in his sailor suit.

Yekaterinburg was founded by Peter the Great and named after his second wife, Catherine I. Straddling Europe and Asia, the region is a treasure chest of resources – iron ore, precious metals and gemstones – buried beneath the Urals, one of the world's oldest mountain ranges. The city began as a garrison centred around a smelting plant. It soon attracted mining engineers and merchants, and became home to the Imperial Mint. The capital of the 'Red Urals', it was a hub of Bolshevik activity and was renamed Sverdlovsk in honour of a man praised by Lenin as 'the most perfectly complete type of professional revolutionary'.[5] Yakov Sverdlov was the Extraordinary Commissar sent from Moscow to mastermind the execution of the Imperial Family. His signature is inscribed on their death warrant.[6]

Lenin's visceral hatred of religion is well documented. In one letter he compared it to 'the most dangerous foulness, the most shameful infection' – code for venereal disease.[7] Marx's one-liner is better known, the 'opiate of the masses'. The Bolsheviks denounced all religions – Russia's rabbis, imams and Buddhist abbots came under attack – but their fiercest hostility was directed towards the Orthodox Church. With tsardom gone and the provisional government toppled, it was seen as the last remaining bastion of the old regime and a direct threat to the Bolsheviks' hold on power. Soviet propaganda used a variety of gruesome imagery. Priests were depicted as fat parasites, exploiting the peasants. One poster shows communion as a depraved feast in which a rabble of churchgoers chew off hunks of Jesus's body and drink his blood, while an old woman gobbles up his entrails. The pious grandmother, who secretly baptises babies and teaches children the Gospel at home, was especially demonised.

Within days of coming to power, the Bolsheviks declared that church weddings must be replaced by civil ceremonies. Their next move, in January 1918, was an attempt to seize the Alexander Nevsky Lavra in St Petersburg, one of Russia's holiest shrines. People travelled thousands of miles to visit this monastery where Russia's famous medieval warrior is buried. Alexandra Kollontai, the Commissar of Social Welfare, decided it would serve a higher purpose as a sanctuary for injured war veterans. But things did not go to plan. When the head of the Lavra, Bishop Prokopii, refused to surrender, the Red Guards arrested him. Thousands of believers, summoned by the monks' frantic ringing of bells, confronted them. One priest was shot and killed, and the guards were forced to leave without accomplishing their mission.

At first, the church and clergy suffered more from random rather than targeted acts of violence. Society was in upheaval: poverty was widespread, lawlessness was rampant. By the time troops returned from the front, brutalised and radicalised by four years of war, many were determined to seize whatever they could. Lenin explained to a meeting of party agitators in 1918 that they should encourage workers and peasants to 'loot the looters', to help themselves to bourgeois property. People ransacked churches, drank the communion wine and terrorised priests.

Patriarch Tikhon issued an encyclical, condemning the violence and vowing to excommunicate those responsible for inciting it. Although he did not name anyone, it was clear whom he was referring to when he denounced the 'godless rulers of darkness'. He urged 'faithful and devoted children of the Church' to defend their belief whatever the cost. 'It is better to shed one's blood and to be awarded a martyr's crown than to let enemies desecrate Orthodox faith,' he wrote in a pastoral letter. The government responded with a decree on the Separation of Church and State, denying the Church legal status and the right to own property. Religious education was banned in schools, seminaries closed, books impounded. Nevertheless, and in spite of his personal animosity towards religion, Lenin initially trod carefully. At the eighth and tenth party congresses (in 1919 and 1921) he urged giving 'no offence to religion', since to offend 'the religious susceptibilities of believers' would lead only to 'the strengthening of religious fanaticism'. He was convinced that once the Church had been disestablished, Soviet education would steadily make it irrelevant.

Once the civil war erupted in 1918, the violence against clergy became more systematic. Tikhon did not give his blessing to the anti-revolutionary forces known as the Whites fighting the Bolsheviks, also called the Reds. He declared his neutrality yet some of his clerics sympathised and collaborated with the counter-revolutionaries and foreign interventionists. They hoped for a restoration of the status quo, including the monarchy, and supported the anti-Bolshevik volunteer armies led by General Lavr Kornilov, Admiral Alexander Kolchak and General Anton Denikin. In so doing, they provided the Bolsheviks with a perfect pretext.

A few days after the attempt to seize the Alexander Nevsky Lavra, the Bolsheviks executed their first bishop outside the Monastery of the Caves in Kyiv. Before he was shot, Metropolitan Vladimir Bogoyavlensky prayed for his murderers to be forgiven. Such executions were replicated across the country. The church historian Dmitry Pospielovsky has chronicled incidents of priests being scalped, beheaded and crucified. One was brought to a cemetery and undressed, but when he tried to cross himself before being killed, a soldier chopped off his right arm. In one Cossack settlement near the Black Sea, an 80-year-old priest was forced to dress in women's clothing, brought to the village square and ordered to dance; when he refused, he was hanged.[8] Church records say that between June 1918 and January 1919, one metropolitan, 18 bishops, 102 priests, 154 deacons, and 94 monks and nuns were killed. This is almost certainly an underestimate, as almost 600 monasteries and convents had already been closed. The mass executions of monks and nuns during these liquidations are not listed.

Between the Revolution and the Second World War, tens of thousands of priests were murdered.[9] The persecution was on such a scale that it easily overtook the estimated 3,500 people thought to have died in the early centuries of Christianity, when

Emperor Diocletian threw the faithful to the lions. An estimated 85 per cent of Russian clergy and monastics were arrested, killed or forcibly removed from their posts. Of the 50,000-plus churches operating in the pre-revolutionary era, only a couple of hundred remained in 1939.

In 2017, on the centenary of the October Revolution, I was in the far north of Russia, in a small town called Kholmogory, an hour's drive from Archangel. I was there to make a radio series on an often-ignored episode, the Allied Intervention of 1918–19, in which 180,000 British, American, French and Japanese forces were dispatched to bolster the Whites' resistance to the Bolsheviks.[10] While there, I discovered what happened shortly after the foreign troops left and the Communists consolidated their power. On the orders of Mikhail Kedrov, a close confidant of Lenin, the Red Army turned the town's Convent of the Dormition, where nuns taught local children, into a death camp. Up to 8,000 people were imprisoned and killed at this picturesque spot beneath a seventeenth-century bell tower on the banks of the River Dvina. Many were White Army officers and sailors from the Kronstadt naval fortress near Finland who had rebelled against the Bolsheviks. But some were clergy and parishioners who had been labelled counter-revolutionaries.

By the time of my 2017 visit, the church had been partially rebuilt, but an oppressive atmosphere still clung to the place like the damp patches on the refectory walls. Elena Pavlova, the choir mistress, told me that the few nuns who escaped execution were required to clear up the aftermath and wash blood off the stone floors every day. The camp commander took over the priest's house and threw wild parties during which he invited his inebriated guests to machine-gun a handful of prisoners. Few of the victims were given a proper burial. Elena said locals still find skulls when digging up potatoes in the nearby fields. Priests and volunteers then collect the human remains in sacks and bury them under a marble cross. Each year they sing a requiem for the dead.

Despite such horrors, the chaos of the Civil War prevented the Communists from fully enforcing their decrees against the Church. The Bolsheviks were not winning the battle for hearts and minds as they radically reshaped society. A fresh crackdown was prompted by the famine which gripped the country in the winter of 1921–22. By this point, Orthodox Christians still far outnumbered card-carrying Communists and Tikhon remained a dissenting force to be reckoned with. In response to an appeal from the Patriarch, parishioners had pawned heirlooms and other valuable items to help the starving. Such was the scale of the disaster, Tikhon allowed church decorations and objects to be put into a state fund to buy grain from abroad. He appealed to other Christian leaders around the world to assist. In so doing, he earned the ire of the Bolsheviks, who resented him playing such a prominent role and advertising the desperate plight of their new state.

It was Leon Trotsky who came up with a plan. He decreed that agents of the state would enter churches and decide for themselves what to confiscate. Tikhon resisted, telling believers they should not surrender items consecrated for liturgical use, such as chalices for the Eucharist. The state now had a pretext for arresting anyone who disobeyed the directive. The stage was set for further conflict.

In the town of Shuya, a curious sculpture stands opposite the Resurrection Cathedral's soaring bell tower. It features a trio of martyrs: a distressed-looking small girl with plaited hair and two cler-gymen, one of whom is leaning back at a perilous 45-degree angle, resignation etched into his face. The town sits on the banks of the River Teza, five hours north-east of Moscow. A trading centre from the sixteenth century, it was best known for making Catherine the Great's favourite soap – there is even a bar of soap on the city's coat of arms.[11]

Events in Shuya marked the beginning of a more intense battle against the Church. In March 1922, thousands of parishioners, armed with wooden stakes, fought to guard their Resurrection Cathedral and resist the seizure of sacred objects. Police on horseback armed with whips were sent to disperse the crowd, but they faced serious resistance, so reinforcements were sent in. Initially, Red Army soldiers fired into the air from machine guns mounted on trucks. The walls of the cathedral were peppered with bullet marks. Then the guns were turned on the protesters. According to some accounts, the first man to die, called Nikolai Malkov, shouted, 'Orthodox People, stand up for the faith!' seconds before he was struck in the temple by a bullet.

Among those killed was a young factory worker named Anastasia, shot dead on the church steps. Mass arrests began. Four priests were charged with resisting the seizure of church valuables. Their trial was presided over by a former Orthodox priest from St Petersburg turned fanatical atheist who edited a magazine entitled *Bezbozhnik*, the Godless.

News of the Shuya affair spread quickly. Lenin sent a memorandum to Politburo colleagues, demanding that 'the trial of the Shuya rioters for resisting aid to the hungry' should lead to the 'maximum possible number of executions'. He told Vyacheslav Molotov, at the time second in command, that speed was of the essence: 'Precisely now and only now, when in the famine regions they are eating people and the roads are littered with hundreds, if not thousands, of corpses, we can (and therefore must) carry out the expropriation of church valuables with the most furious and ruthless energy to secure for ourselves a fund of several hundred million gold roubles.'[12]

Lenin was not exaggerating – cannibalism was rife in some areas. The ravages of the Civil War, crop failure and drought led to severe hunger from the Volga to the Urals, from Ukraine to Kazakhstan. The Bolsheviks railed against a 'heartless' Church unwilling to save lives by parting with its gold and silver. The priests and those killed in front of the church were canonised as New Russian Martyrs in 2000.[13]

In February 2022, Patriarch Kirill began a Sunday sermon by invoking the centenary of the 'trampled shrines' of Shuya. He said the 'terrible lines' of Lenin's memo made him 'shudder'; the 'godless builders of the new Russia' were not motivated by the concern for the starving but by 'hellish malice and hatred for the Church'. The sermon took place a few days after Putin's full-scale invasion of Ukraine, but Kirill drew no connection.

As the Communist regime consolidated its power, many churches were turned into cinemas and new-style Soviet palaces of culture. Trotsky conceded that anti-religious propaganda alone would fail to dissuade people; many ordinary Russians stuck with Orthodoxy's 'meaningless rituals' through force of habit. His next plan was to split the Church from within, handing administration to a group of priests who used covert government money to set up a rival organisation loyal to the goals of Communism. The *Obnovlentsy*,

Renovators, were a combination of careerists and idealists. A priest from Petrograd, Vladimir Krasnitsky, led the most active faction, called the Living Church. Clergy and laypersons who opposed them were arrested by the secret police.

At first, Tikhon refused to be intimidated. He accused the Bolsheviks of secretly sending gold to Germany and claimed that the valuables expropriated from his churches were being spent on the army and on fomenting world revolution. Lenin finally had had enough. The Patriarch was put on trial by military tribunal and only narrowly escaped execution by a firing squad. Fearful that his continued imprisonment would cause further instability, local party chiefs incited people to demand the death sentence for Tikhon. One such resolution, from the Zagorskaya Administrative Region outside Moscow in 1923, describes him as 'a blood-sucker in a cassock, a counter-Revolutionary and a cannibal'. It implores the central authorities to inflict upon him 'a stern and pitiless measure of punishment'.[14]

Only international pressure kept him alive; the Soviets badly needed foreign loans. Meanwhile, the Living Church movement seized church buildings across the country. The movement designed to split Orthodoxy was itself soon divided into rival factions pushing for different kinds of reforms. One group led by parish priests lobbied for more freedom in their private lives. They wanted to allow bishops and monks to marry and priests to be able to remarry and to marry widows. Another group defended traditional Orthodox practices but promised lay believers a greater voice in church affairs, while a third renovationist party, the League of Communities of the Ancient Apostolic Church, advocated Christian socialism – a synthesis of 'ethical' Communism and Christian Orthodoxy. Karl Marx ridiculed the Anglicans in Britain who had espoused the movement half a century earlier. He called Christian Socialism 'the holy water with which the priest consecrates the heart burnings of the aristocrat'.[15]

By the mid-1920s, Party ideologists had to recognise that the Living Church had been a failure. Services were poorly attended, and the movement lost more followers when the Patriarch was freed from prison in June 1923. Yet the Politburo only agreed to release him if he signed an article published in *Izvestia*, the government daily newspaper, denying he had been tortured and apologising for his 'hostility' towards the authorities.

When Tikhon died two years later, in 1925, the government refused to allow another patriarch to succeed him. Although he was a respected theologian, Metropolitan Sergius Stragorodsky quickly fell into line. The collaboration between the Church and the Communists became known as 'Sergianism'. 'Let us publicly express our gratitude to the Soviet Government for the interest it is showing in all the religious needs of the Orthodox,' he declared in his now-infamous declaration of July 1927. 'We want to be Orthodox and, at the same time, to recognise the Soviet Union as our civil motherland, whose joys and successes are also our joys and successes, whose failures are our failures. Every attack directed against the USSR is presented as being directed against ourselves.' He also praised Joseph Stalin as a 'great, God given leader of the Russian people' who had taken over after Lenin's death three years earlier in 1924.

Supporters of the Sergianist line argued that the Church had to compromise or face annihilation. Those who did not abide by the new rules were hunted down. Some were forced into hiding. An abbess in Petrograd, expelled along with her nuns, set up a convent in a private home. She referred to it in letters in 1923 as her 'secret catacomb church'.[16] The religious underground created an alternative hierarchy, with clandestine chapels and secret hideaways. More than a decade later, in 1935, a young convert to Orthodoxy called Vera Vasilievskaya described her first encounter with an underground church in Zagorsk, now Sergiyev Posad, home to the Trinity Lavra of Saint Sergius monastery that for many centuries has been the epicentre of Russian Orthodoxy. When Vasilievskaya visited the town, its famous monastery had already been closed for fifteen years: 'The pathway led to a small house; the shutters were tightly closed. Tonya rang four times, as agreed. They quickly opened the door for us. Inside it was light, warm and cosy. I felt part of some particularly harmonious life; the small kitchen was covered with icons and had such a festive appearance, as had everything else in the house.'[17]

Whatever solace they found in communal prayer, they were running huge risks. At any moment they could be informed on. During the liturgy someone was posted outside to check whether the singing could be heard from the street. In her memoirs, Vasilievskaya's cousin, a scientist called Elena Semenovna Men, writes eloquently about the double life of a believer under Communism.[18] One Passion Sunday, she is forced to go on a May Day demonstration. When anti-religious songs are sung, she is relieved when another woman in the crowd sees her face and whispers: 'I also believe in God.' Such solidarity was rare. Many from the so-called 'catacomb church' were betrayed by priests of the official Church, ending their lives as martyrs.

The war on the Church reached its zenith with the 'Atheist Five-Year Plan', launched in 1932. Stalin's goal was to eradicate religion in the USSR by 1 May 1937. His timetable was precise: all churches and prayer houses would close in the first year, all religious traditions such as the observance of holidays and fast days should be banned by 1933–34, clerics were to be defrocked or eliminated by 1935–36. In the final year, 1937, the word God would disappear from the Russian vocabulary. Tirades on loudspeakers and propaganda posters reinforced the message. One such poster shows a bedraggled Jesus being dumped out of a wheelbarrow by a muscular worker, alongside text declaring that Industrialisation Day would replace the celebration of the Transfiguration. Above the entrance to the Dormition Cathedral of the Kyiv Pechersk Lavra was a sign which read: 'Monks – Bloody Enemies of the Working Class'.

An organisation called the League of Militant Atheists was charged with stripping churches, synagogues and mosques of their remaining contents. Most church bells had already been turned into scrap metal. Alexander Solzhenitsyn wrote that their ringing for evening prayer was a cue for people 'to set aside trivial earthly matters and offer the moment to eternity'. Central planners sought to eradicate any reminders of the divine in daily life. They abolished weekends and imposed the *nepreryvka*, the continuous working week. It was five days long, with days of rest randomly staggered across the week. Officially, the aim was to boost productivity, but the main reason was to remove Fridays, Saturdays and Sundays as days of worship.

I returned to the Sverdlovsk region, along the eastern slopes of the Ural Mountains, to explore how Stalin's purges affected Orthodox believers in the *glubynka*, Russia's hinterland. The story of one church in a village outside Yekaterinburg is emblematic. It was uncovered by Alexei Mosin, a historian and academic who grew up in an ordinary Soviet family of non-believers and in later life became curious about the fate of his great-great-grandfather.

Two decades ago, Mosin came across his relative's name in a book dedicated to the victims of political repressions in the Sverdlovsk region. Determined to find out more, he began digging and in 2014 he found a 245-page file on his relative's case in the state archive at 34 Lenin Avenue, headquarters of the city's former Communist Party Committee. From the interrogation reports and witness statements, Mosin learned that there were seven defendants in the case. These included Father Alexander Kornyakov, the priest from the village of Kamennoye Ozero, where Mosin's great-great-grandfather lived.

Mosin's ancestor, Alexander Vorobyev, a peasant and member of his local church council, was arrested when he was 82 years old. Officers from the NKVD, the People's Commissariat for Internal Affairs, as the secret police were then known, arrived in a trademark black car, known as the black horse, dragged him from his bed in the dead of night and took him to Yekaterinburg. His family never saw him again. Like millions of others, they were cowed into silence. 'If you asked questions, the same thing could happen to you,' said Mosin. In 1937, the bloodiest year of the purges, the authorities murdered an average of a thousand of their own citizens per day. Every fifth adult was a victim.

Devastated by the closure of their church, the parishioners of Kamennoye Ozero sent a petition to Moscow. Their appeal could not have been more mistimed. Although the Orthodox leadership was divided after Tikhon's death, the Patriarch's encouragement of lay believers to take control of their parish communities led to a grass-roots religious revival, especially in the countryside. The Orthodox parish became a source of resistance and a threat to Communist ideas about re-educating the peasants. In 1937, a census was taken, and, at Stalin's insistence, it included a column on attitudes to faith. Some 57 per cent of those questioned said they were believers. The results were so unwelcome to the authorities that they were not published at the time. Instead, the officials who had conducted the survey were arrested. Stalin ordered a further crackdown.

Following his detention, Mosin's great-great-grandfather was accused of plotting to kill the head of the collective farm and chairman of the village council based on the seizure of a single-barrelled antique rifle in his house and 500 grams of shotgun pellets. Police also confiscated thirty holy books, which the octogenarian had taken from the church for safekeeping. One priest and six parishioners from a small village in the Urals, armed with two hunting rifles and a small bag of shotgun pellets, were branded 'church terrorists' capable of overthrowing the Soviet government. 'You could say it was funny,' Mosin told me, 'if it didn't end so tragically.'

The arrests began with the priest and continued throughout August. The cases were heard by a *troika*, the infamous courts of the Stalin era, made up of three officials who dispensed with all legal niceties and had absolute power. Four days later, at midnight on the 29 September, the death sentences were carried out. The youngest defendant, Anastasia Osintseva, was spared the death penalty because she was pregnant. She was sentenced to ten years' hard labour and gave birth in prison, but her baby didn't survive. Mosin read me the concluding words of his great-great-grandfather's case, No. 8455: 'He is accused of being a member of a counter-revolutionary fascist insurgent organisation of churchmen in the Urals since 1935. Resolved: that Aleksandr Grigorievich Vorobyov be shot. Personal property to be confiscated.'

The bodies were thrown into ditches next to the highway. Today, the spot, twelve kilometres outside Yekaterinburg, is a place of pilgrimage marked by a tall black cross and two 'masks of sorrow'. Tears, in the shape of human heads, run down the face of each bronze mask. More than 18,000 people executed in Sverdlovsk between 1937 and 1938 were dumped here, their shallow graves later covered by apple trees.

Two decades later, with Mikhail Gorbachev's policy of *glasnost*, topics which people whispered about in their kitchens began to be discussed openly at public meetings. A new independent group of historians and volunteers started investigating and exposing the crimes of the Stalin era. The group, Memorial, was founded in Moscow in 1988 but branches soon sprung up across Russia. Just as Jewish and other organisations focused on lessons associated with the Holocaust, Memorial vowed to educate society about the stories, memories and experiences of the millions who suffered under Stalin's purges. Decades of shame and fear and anger had been repressed. These emotions poured out as families began to actively seek answers about missing relatives. There was an explosion of articles, exhibitions, books and films on the gulag, show trials and the secret police. Memorial linked the totalitarian past to contemporary human rights abuses. That is one of the reasons Putin liquidated the organisation in December 2021. It had been targeted under the controversial foreign agent law for supposedly using overseas funds to sway Russian public opinion. Opening a Wall of Grief to victims on Moscow's ring road in 2017, Putin said that the Great Terror could not be 'justified by anything.' Yet his obsession with the Soviet victory in the Second World War has led to a steady rehabilitation of Stalin.

In 1990 a woman called Nina Baronova wrote to the secretariat of the KGB for the local region, begging the security police for information about her mother, Anastasia Osintseva. Mosin came across her letter when he later gained access to the archives. Anastasia was chairwoman of the church council at the same village, Kamennoye Ozero. Although she was semi-paralysed and had four young children, she was arrested and locked in a squalid cell for more than a month before she was shot. 'To this day we do not know why she was arrested and where to look for her,' wrote Nina, who was seven years old at the time. 'Please can you tell us what our mother was guilty of and where she died?'

Nina received a polite, even sympathetic reply from the head of the regional KGB. Unbeknown to her, more than two decades earlier, the prosecutor had annulled the Kamennoye Ozero case. A copy of the certificate of her mother's rehabilitation, No. 151 of 11 October 1965, was enclosed along with condolences and an admission that there was no information, as yet, about her burial place. The officer also told her that the members of the troika which had judged Anastasia had themselves been convicted of gross violations of legality and were in turn executed two years later. Although this information may not have made Nina's loss any easier, it did at least answer questions which had haunted her for half a century.

Like millions of Russians of his generation, Mosin was baptised late in life, at the age of 46. But his interest in religion began much earlier, when he was a history student on a field trip in the Ural Mountains in 1979. Off the beaten track, his group met some Old Believers, descendants of the religious dissenters who had refused to accept the liturgical reforms imposed upon the Church by Patriarch Nikon in the seventeenth century. Mosin and his friends had stumbled into a parallel universe. Some of the Old Believers they met knew nothing of the Revolution and thought they still lived in Tsarist Russia. When the students tried to describe life at their university and meetings of the *Komsomol*, Communist Youth League, their hosts had no idea what they were talking about. The focus of their lives was daily survival and communication with God. The faith of the Old Believers had a profound effect on Mosin, but he did not start going to church straight away; he could have been expelled from university. On the expedition, Mosin came across a rare copy of the first edition of the Bible in Cyrillic type produced in 1580 by the pioneering printer Ivan Fedorov. Lavishly decorated with woodcut panels, it was known as the Ostrog Bible because it was made on the estate of Prince Konstanty Wasyl in Ostroh, northern Ukraine. The Ukrainian-Lithuanian Prince had sent copies to Pope Gregory XIII and Tsar Ivan the Terrible. When asked to talk about the sixteenth-century book by a local radio station, the producer asked him in advance: '*Please* don't say the word "Bible" on air'.

The church in Kamennoye Ozero that his great-great-grandfather died trying to protect is still standing. It initially served as a collective farm workers club and was later turned into a grain storage. Over the years it became dilapidated and its frescos were damaged, so Mosin has been raising money to restore it. He also became head of the Yekaterinburg branch of Memorial, which was no easy task. Memorial plaques put up to commemorate Stalin's victims kept disappearing, sometimes just a day after their installation. Even after Memorial was banned, Mosin has soldiered on. 'Let us not be indifferent to what happened to our ancestors,' he says. 'When this memory lives in the family, this family lives with dignity.'[19]

On a rainy October morning in 2021, I drove due south out of Moscow past dreary grey tower blocks. Not far from Domodedovo

Airport, I turned off the highway and down a quiet road lined with oak trees. Master craftsmen from the local stone quarries founded a village here in the seventeenth century. Muscovites later built summer cottages in the area and wandered along paths in the woods looking for mushrooms and berries. But they stayed clear of a high green fence topped with barbed wire. It was not just the sound of gunfire that put them off, but a cloying smell lingering in the air.

Behind the fence lay Butovo, a secluded military testing site and special zone of Stalin's NKVD. It is the largest mass grave of victims of political repression in the Moscow area, where 20,762 people were killed between 1937 and 1938, at the height of the Great Terror. At least a thousand of them are known to have been martyred for their faith. Given that 230 bishops, priests, monks, nuns and laypeople murdered here were canonised in recent years, this execution site has become one of Russia's most important religious shrines. In 2007, Patriarch Alexei II called Butovo 'Russia's Golgotha' and consecrated a new church on the site.

I walked through the gate to find the museum was closed and the place pretty much deserted apart from an elderly gardener on his knees in a muddy flower bed. Outside the large white church of the Holy New Martyrs and Confessors of Russia, I came across a pensioner with a stall selling icons and candles. Alexandra Ivanova, as she gave her name, sighed noisily when I asked if she could show me around. She soon overcame her reluctance and was an enthusiastic guide. She took me first to the church crypt, where dimly lit display cases are filled with black and white photographs. Priests, students, army generals, doctors, lawyers, firemen, police officers, factory workers, circus performers, musicians, foreigners – including 50 Chinese laundrymen, an idealistic Afrikaner and dozens of Koreans – were declared enemies of the people. The oldest victim, and most senior churchman, was 82-year-old Metropolitan Chicagov from Leningrad. He was so frail he arrived on a stretcher in an ambulance and was shot the following day. The youngest known victim was a fourteen-year-old boy who stole two loaves of bread. Along with photographs of skeletons, pieces of bone and some still intact skulls, Alexandra pointed out the discarded shoes, old buttons, decaying bits of clothing and a tobacco pouch found deep inside the trenches where the corpses were buried.

On one pillar in the crypt, above a votive lamp, I spotted an icon of Bishop Arkady Ostalsky. Born in western Ukraine, he trained at the Kyiv Theological Academy and served as an army chaplain in the First World War. Alexandra said he had virtually no possessions and was renowned for his self-sacrifice. Once, knowing he was in need, some locals made him a fur coat. He put it on twice and then it suddenly disappeared. He had donated it to a poor widow with tuberculosis struggling to raise two children. On another occasion, he gave his only pair of trousers away to a peasant he met on the road. Then he sewed up the flaps of his cassock so that nobody would notice his bare legs.

Such charitable acts did not impress the authorities, who imprisoned him in Zhitomir and sent him to the Solovetsky Monastery in the White Sea. Five years after the October Revolution, Lenin had turned Russia's most remote holy citadel, on the edge of the Arctic Circle, into a labour camp. It served as a prototype for the entire gulag system. Arkady shared his barracks there with criminals as well as imprisoned clergy. Whenever possible, he performed liturgies, sometimes alongside the Solovetsky monks who had refused to leave the monastery. The prisoners held him in great respect, which irritated the camp authorities. Eventually, he was released, but he was soon rearrested and shot at Butovo in December 1937.

The martyred bishop was related to journalist friends of mine in 1990s Moscow, Dmitry and Andrei Ostalsky. He was their grandfather's cousin. For years, like thousands of others, their grandfather kept a small suitcase by the front door. 'He was afraid of being arrested at any moment because of his relationship to Bishop Arkady,' Dmitry told me.

Alexandra said local people heard the shooting at Butovo, but they assumed weapons were being tested and they didn't pay much attention. In any case, it would not have been helpful to ask questions. Now, in the summer, when services are held at the church, you can hear nightingales singing alongside the choir, she added. As we walked past the remains of fourteen trenches, all I could hear were the sounds of crows in the woods around us and the distant drone of traffic.

Father Kirill Kaleda, the archpriest of the large white church across the road and the man responsible for turning the execution site into a memorial, has researched the NKVD's operations in detail. Prisoners were brought to the spot in vans and delivery trucks marked 'meat'. The vans were unloaded, and people herded into barracks for 'disinfection'. They were then led away, one by one, to the edge of a trench and shot at point-blank range – as many as 500 people per day. A bucketful of vodka was brought out for the executioners and guards, and they were allowed to drink as much as they wanted. After they finished their work for the day, they went up to a second bucket filled with eau de cologne and doused themselves with it. They reeked so badly of blood and gunpowder that even the police dogs gave them a wide berth.

'Some of the executioners later ended up in psychiatric hospitals,' Kaleda told me. 'Others were victims of subsequent purges but there were also people like General Blokhin who shot thousands of people with his own revolver and died peacefully at home in bed. He received two awards for service in the 1960s and was buried with honours in the Donskoy Cemetery.'[20]

In two decades, across Russia, Orthodoxy had almost been wiped out. Of the more than 50,000 churches that had existed in 1917, by the start of the Second World War barely 100 were still open. Between 1931 and 1941, 600 bishops, 45,000 priests and 120,000 monks and nuns had been imprisoned or killed. Before the Revolution there were more than 1,000 monasteries and convents, but all had been closed. There were no functioning dioceses, no patriarch, no printed literature, no training for clergy.

Towards the end of the Gorbachev era and the first few years after the collapse of the Soviet system, it seemed that Russians were finally free to research and understand the horrors of the Communist era, including the persecution of believers. However, by the mid-1990s, the determination to unearth the past appeared to be waning. In 1996, the Mayor of Moscow, Yuri Luzhkov, was keen to build a housing complex on the Butovo site; he only relented after an appeal from Patriarch Alexei II. And that was before the arrival of Putin in 2000.

Not many people bother to visit Butovo now, despite all the remains buried here, despite the trauma which affected virtually every family. When I asked Alexandra, the candle seller, whether she approved of the rehabilitation of Stalin, she mumbled that he probably repented of his sins before he died. She also made sure to tell me that she had voted for Putin in the last elections, taking her cue from the Church, who had decided he was the best choice for the country. I put some money into the church collection box and thanked her for being so generous with her time.

☦ ☦ ☦

With most bishops arrested or killed, Metropolitan Sergius had to administer the remaining dioceses with the help of one deputy bishop, a secretary and a typist. On 21 June 1941, the day the Germans invaded the USSR, Sergius sent out a pastoral letter to all Orthodox Christians, calling on them to do their patriotic duty and defend the 'sacred borders of the motherland'. God would help them, he said, to 'reduce the fascist enemy to dust'.

It is one of the great ironies that the Nazis helped to save Russian Orthodoxy from extinction. Stalin spent the first few days after the invasion hunkered down in his *dacha* in an alcoholic haze and state of shock. In 1939, he had signed a secret pact with Hitler, only to be double crossed. When he sobered up and returned to the Kremlin, Stalin knew that he could not defeat the Germans without the help of the Church, the only organisation capable of inspiring people to die for their country. In a radio address eleven days later, he appealed to his 'brothers and sisters', the Orthodox form of address. He later told the US ambassador Averell Harriman that 'Russian people were fighting as they always had, for their homeland not for us'. By 'us' he meant the Communist leadership.[21]

Stalin knew the Church from the inside. Fans of counterfactual history who ask what might have happened had Hitler been accepted to Vienna's art school might also wonder about Stalin's early calling to the priesthood. The man responsible for butchering hundreds of thousands of clerics was once a model choir boy. He had such a beautiful tenor voice that people hired him to sing at weddings. The son of a violent, alcoholic cobbler, Iosif Vissarionovich Dzhugashvili, was born in the Georgian town of Gori. He spent much of his childhood in the home of an Orthodox priest, Father Charkviani, where his pious mother worked as a cleaner and laundress. She sent him to a church school and dreamed about her only son becoming a bishop. The school presented its prize pupil with David's Book of Psalms, praising his 'excellent progress, behaviour and excellent recitation and singing of the Psalter'.[22]

He won a scholarship to train as a priest at the Georgian Orthodox Seminary in the capital, Tiflis, now Tbilisi, but soon grew disillusioned. According to Trotsky, the Empire's seminaries were 'notorious for the savagery of their customs, medieval teaching, and law of the fist'. The one at Tiflis was nicknamed the Stone Sack. 'All the vices banned by the Holy Scriptures flourished in this hotbed of piety,' Trotsky said.[23] Stalin was often sent to the seminary's punishment cell for reading banned Marxist literature and Darwin's *On the Origin of Species*. By the time he left, five years later, Stalin had many reasons to loathe the clergy. One especially vindictive teacher, nicknamed the Black Spot, spied on him and regularly searched his possessions. Biographer Simon Sebag Montefiore says Black Spot taught the young Stalin 'exactly the repressive tactics – "surveillance, spying, invasion of inner life, violation of feelings", in Stalin's own words – that he would recreate in his Soviet police state'.[24]

Stalin had been general secretary of the Communist Party of the Soviet Union for thirteen years when he saw his mother, Ekatarine Geladze, for the last time on a 1935 trip to Georgia. She was still lamenting his change of career, according to Stalin's daughter Svetlana Alliluyeva: 'When father visited her not long before her death, she told him: "It's a shame that you didn't become a priest". He repeated these words of hers with delight; he liked her scorn for all he had achieved, for the earthly glory, for all the fuss.'[25]

The Nazi invasion of the USSR, the largest land offensive in modern history, was codenamed Operation Barbarossa after Frederick Barbarossa ('red beard'), a twelfth-century Holy Roman Emperor and Crusader. As Wehrmacht troops spread across Ukraine and other western parts of the Soviet Union, they began a campaign to win hearts and minds by reopening churches that had been closed down by the Communists. That included both Orthodox churches and Uniate ones, which recognised the Pope in Rome but stuck to the Eastern Byzantine liturgy. Stalin had good reason to fear that the enemy could turn the clergy and believers into a fifth column. Many people, particularly in the western reaches of the USSR, welcomed the invasion as a crusade against an atheist power. In Lviv, the head of the Uniate Church Metropolitan Szeptyckyj issued a proclamation expressing the gratitude of the Ukrainian people to the German army for liberating them.

There are no known statements or actions by the leadership of the Church regarding mass killings of Jews on Soviet soil in the war. According to one historian, the Orthodox in Russia 'have not yet learned a serious lesson from the Holocaust; the consequences of the Holocaust have not brought them closer to the Jewish people. Unlike the Western world, the Holocaust did not help them see more closely the significance and beauty of the Jewish faith. And this, in turn, prevents them from seeing the fullness of their own faith.'[26] However, a number of Orthodox priests and members of their families risked their lives to hide Jews and give them forged identity papers, and have been remembered as Righteous Among Nations at Israel's Yad Vashem Holocaust Memorial Centre. For example, in the Belarusian town of Pinsk, an Orthodox priest sold his golden cross so that the prisoners of the ghetto could pay the indemnity imposed on them. In the Crimean city of Simferopol, another priest sheltered Jewish children in his house. In 1942, an *Einsatzgruppe,* the Nazi euphemism for a mobile killing squad, executed the mayor of the eastern Ukrainian city of Kremenchuk because, together with a local priest, he helped to baptise Jews in an attempt to save them from the death camps.

In the midst of war, Stalin had other reasons for taking a more conciliatory approach to the Orthodox Church. He wanted the Allies to relieve pressure on the Red Army by opening a Second Front in Western Europe, but Franklin Roosevelt was stalling. America's president was troubled by the 'religious question in Russia'. The NKVD's initial response was to produce a coffee-table book. Lavrenty Beria, head of the secret police, presented a plan to the Politburo, and the Moscow Patriarchate duly published *The Truth About Religion in Russia.* The lavishly illustrated blue tome, embossed with gold lettering and aimed at foreigners, denied that there had ever been any persecution of believers in the USSR.[27]

The Archbishop of York, Dr Cyril Garbett, was invited to visit the USSR by the Moscow Patriarchate in late 1943. It was a clerical charm offensive, and he became the archetypal 'useful idiot', the term Lenin used to describe Westerners who were not communists but praised the workers' paradise of the USSR. Garbett was taken to a church filled with worshippers who had been specially brought in for the occasion. It was a classic case of *pokazukha*, or window-dressing. This Russian tradition goes back at least to the days of Catherine the Great, when her favourite, Grigoriy Potemkin, was supposed to have erected facades of villages to hoodwink the monarch as she travelled to her newly conquered territory of Crimea. The Church of England prelate was so impressed by the crowds, the chanting and the clouds of incense that he returned home with a glowing report about the freedom believers enjoyed under the Soviet regime.[28]

British newspapers began running positive articles about religious life in the Soviet Union and the Church's contribution to the Great Patriotic War. One British cleric, Hewlett Johnson, was so pro-Stalin that he was known as the Red Dean of Canterbury. 'Of course, the Church of the new patriarchate differs widely from the Church which fell from power with the collapse of the tsarist regime. It is more moral in its outlook,' he gushed. 'That is what rejoices my heart and uplifts my spirit for I believe the new Soviet system ... opens the gateway through which struggling, toiling humanity may find the kingdom of God on earth.'[29]

Sergius repeatedly called upon the faithful to donate to a special account in the state bank to supply armoured vehicles to the Red Army. They collected enough to create a tank division, named in honour of Dmitry Donskoy, the Moscow prince who defeated the Mongols at the Battle of Kulikovo in 1380. One of the battle-scarred tanks is still on display in the grounds of Moscow's Donskoy Monastery. The church also raised funds for a fighter squadron. It was named after Alexander Nevsky, who fought off German crusaders in the thirteenth century. The medieval hero had just been glorified in a Stalin-approved film by Sergei Eisenstein, which depicts the invaders as godless and sub-human in their sinister, horned helmets. Chaplains were also sent to the front; churches were turned into hospitals.

Stalin rewarded these efforts by inviting Sergius and two other senior clerics to the Kremlin in September 1943. He told them he was prepared to give the Church official recognition for its services to the state, including permission to elect a patriarch after an eighteen-year hiatus. He offered them the former German ambassador's residence for their office, but then turned to them with a puzzled expression. 'Where are your personnel? Where have they got to?' he asked in a tone of mock innocence. Sergius is said to have looked Stalin in the eye and replied, 'We lack personnel for several reasons, one of which is we train a man to be a priest, but he becomes a marshal of the Soviet Union.' Stalin was apparently impressed by this reference to his own days as a seminarian and, at the end of their meeting, helped the exhausted Sergius down the stairs.[30] Metropolitan Nikolai Yarushevich, one of those present, reported that the churchmen had been 'overwhelmed' by Stalin's charisma: 'Our people see in him the incarnation of everything that is best and brightest: everything which represents the holiest heritage of our Russian nation bequeathed to us by our ancestors.'[31]

Now Stalin allowed churches to reopen, ordered the release of thousands of imprisoned priests and restored church property, including the Trinity Lavra of St Sergius, the centre of Russian Orthodoxy. In 1920, the Bolsheviks had turned most of it into a college for radio engineers and other technicians. The British Communist Charles Ashleigh described a lecture he attended at the holy site in 1923, where an audience of peasants in their 'long buttoned coats, high boots and great shaggy fur caps' sang folk songs and heard a lecture on the benefits of chemical manure and machine ploughs.[32]

Four days after the Kremlin encounter with Stalin, nineteen bishops, some of whom had been dragged out of prison camps, met for a *sobor*, council, and unanimously chose Sergius for the newly restored position of patriarch. An American hieromonk named Trifon, who witnessed the enthronement ceremony, described him as 'a very sick man, who looked like he had just come out of a Nazi concentration camp'.[33] Although he had helped to loosen the Communists' vice-like grip on the church, Sergius was not fated to witness its rebirth. He died from a brain haemorrhage eight months later. A psychologist before he became an orthodox monk, Trifon rejected criticism of Sergius. Decades later, at a church conference in the US in 2003, he said he was 'amazed by callousness of those who dare speak so irreverently about this man'. While there are those who have argued that Sergius saved the Church from obliteration by collaborating, others insist he paid too high a price. They talk of the legacy of *Sergiyanstvo*, Sergianism, a pattern of servility which persists to this day.

By 1947, Sergius's successor, Patriarch Alexei I, had managed re-establish eight seminaries to train a new generation of priests, the first formal theological training anywhere in the Soviet Union. It was the first time since the Revolution that the authorities had admitted the Church might have a future.[34] But, with a few exceptions, the quality of teaching was low and so was the calibre of the students. The authorities admitted obedient young men who would limit themselves to performing rituals. According to one church historian, 'this disastrous "personnel policy" had the most painful impact on the theological schools'.[35] The Patriarch increased the clergy to 30,000, including 74 bishops, and reopened 10,000 churches along with 67 monasteries and convents. Many churches were destroyed or damaged, but some were relatively unscathed, having been repurposed as lecture halls or museums.

The Church's fundraising efforts among the faithful to buy weaponry had paid off. Its new status was clear when the top clerics were accorded the highest honour, an invitation to a sacred Soviet ritual, the Victory Parade on Red Square in June 1945. The Patriarch, a former metropolitan of Leningrad, had garnered some moral authority for remaining in the besieged city alongside his people for 900 days. During the German blockade, in which 800,000 died of hunger, Alexis lived on the edge of starvation. People in the cathedral choir were dying around him, and the choirmaster himself dropped dead in the middle of a church service. Alexei himself barely had the strength to clear a path to the cathedral through the snow. Yet he urged his congregations to donate clothes and food to the soldiers and continue the fight for the city. Later that year, Mikhail Kalinin, a Stalin ultra-loyalist and president of the USSR, presented the Patriarch with the Red Workers Banner for patriotic services in the war. 'Moscow is already the world centre of international politics,' said Kalinin. 'It must also become the spiritual nucleus.'[36]

In this post-war accommodation, the Moscow Patriarchate became an arm of the Soviet government. Under the guise of

Christianity, it spread Communist propaganda abroad, assuring the world that there was complete freedom of worship in the USSR.

After the Molotov–Ribbentrop non-aggression pact of 1939 between the Soviet Union and Nazi Germany, western Ukraine, which had been ruled variously by the Polish-Lithuanian Commonwealth, the Austro-Hungarians, the Poles and for a short period the Ukrainians themselves, was subsumed into the USSR. Moldova and then the Baltic States were also occupied and swallowed up by the Soviet Union. These regions had many Orthodox churches and monasteries, most of which escaped persecution before the Nazis invaded in June 1941. Clergy were sent from there to Russia to replenish the stock. At the same time, Russian clergy were sent west to help destroy any vestiges of Ukrainian nationalism in areas that had been annexed.

It could be said that the Russian Orthodox Church 'had a good war'. It had acquired several million believers from well-organised and active parishes in the newly annexed territories. It also gained tens of thousands of unwilling converts: the Uniate or Greek Catholic Church that existed in western Ukraine was suppressed and forcibly 'reunited' with the churches governed by Moscow. Religious life was strictly controlled by a new department, overseen by the secret police, called the Council for the Affairs of the Russian Orthodox Church. The officer in charge, Grigory Karpov, a colonel in the NKVD, had a role similar to that of the Procurator of the Synod in the tsarist era. His nickname was Narkomopium, an abbreviation of the People's Commissar for Opium and a play on Marx's view of the role of religion.

☦ ☦ ☦

After Stalin's death in 1953, thousands of people arrested for their political and religious beliefs began returning from the camps, including many from the clergy. The new era, which began with Nikita Khrushchev's 1956 denunciation of Stalin's crimes, saw censorship relaxed and literature blossom. But the Thaw did not extend to the Church. At first Stalin's truce with the Patriarchate did not unduly bother the new Soviet leader, although he thought religion stood in the way of Communism. Everything changed with the exposure of the so-called 'anti-party group' – a collection of die-hard Stalinists who tried to depose Khrushchev in 1957. The group, which included wartime foreign minister Vyacheslav Molotov and former premier Georgiy Malenkov, was part of Stalin's scheme to make the Church answerable to the secret police. After Stalin's death, these hardliners argued that Orthodoxy was popular, so it made little sense to attack it. Far better, they said, to use the Church to strengthen the state.

Khrushchev was understandably hostile to the views of those trying to usurp him. I spoke to his granddaughter, Nina Khrushcheva, a journalist and academic. She told me that his misgivings about a Church in the grip of the security services were prescient. 'Today we see that he was right because the FSB, Putin and the church are inseparable,' she said. 'They punish non-believers now as communists used to punish believers back then.'[37]

Having denounced Stalin's murderous personality cult, Khrushchev sought to overhaul ideology and inspire people with a renewed faith in Communism. He promised higher living standards, mass housing, better food and a plentiful supply of consumer goods. 'What sort of Communist society has no sausage?' he asked. He vowed that the economy would overtake that of the West within a decade. Such confidence soared with the 1957 launch of Sputnik, the first man-made satellite to orbit the Earth. Obsolete religion would give way to science. Leonid Ilyichov, Khrushchev's favourite ideologist, wrote: 'It is imperative to oppose religion with militant, progressive scientific-atheistic propaganda.'[38]

One of the posters celebrating Yuri Gagarin's 1961 flight featured the cosmonaut floating above church spires among the stars with the slogan 'There is no God'. The press gleefully reported that Gagarin's Soyuz flight had given believers a 'headache'. 'He flew right through the heavenly mansions and did not run into anyone,' proclaimed the government newspaper *Izvestia*. 'Not the almighty, nor Archangel Gabriel nor the angels of heaven: it seems then that the sky is empty.'[39] Gagarin supposedly said that he 'looked and looked' and saw no sign of divinity in space, but these words were later contextualised. Gagarin's friend, the pilot-cosmonaut Alexei Leonov, told a Church magazine that the first man in space was not an atheist:

'After all, he was baptised, like me by the way, but the party was so all controlling that it was almost impossible to openly profess your belief. Yet, many of us had enough mind and soul to feel that there was something out there.'[40]

The first woman in space is often filmed in church these days. With a scarf over her beehive hairdo, the octogenarian Valentina Tereshkova, a cosmonaut turned Duma deputy, has posed for pictures with Patriarch Kirill. She is a staunchly loyal member of the pro-Kremlin United Russia party and was one of those in 2020 who put forward a constitutional amendment extending Putin's term of office, potentially until 2036. The opposition politician Alexei Navalny retweeted a post at the time: 'Tereshkova – the first woman who bravely travelled into cosmic cold and darkness, and then brought the entire country there.'[41]

Under Khrushchev, apostate clergy were feted in the media. One priest, Nikolai Rusanov, told the party journal *Kommunist* that he had broken with the Church as a result of Gagarin's flight. There is no point waiting for a heavenly paradise which does not exist, he said. People should put their faith instead in 'an earthly paradise which will be built within the next fifteen to twenty years, here in our godless, Soviet country. The name of this paradise is Communism.'

When talking to foreigners, Khrushchev was careful to say that faith was a matter of conscience and not something to be regulated by the state. He may have hoped that under the bright glare of scientific enlightenment, belief in God would just shrivel away. But the trend was going the other way. Dmitri Shepilov, editor of *Pravda*, told the Soviet leader that in 1954 his reporters estimated the Soviet Union had 18,000 functional churches, mosques and synagogues in the USSR and a similar number of registered clerics. Government figures showed an increase in church income, attendance and rites. Applications to theological schools were also rising, especially among 18- to 22-year-olds. Many had university degrees, and, to the authorities' consternation, some were even members of the Komsomol, the Communist Party's youth wing.

Khrushchev was becoming increasingly frustrated, despite his reputation abroad as a liberaliser. Officials were told to only allow students with poor academic records into the seminaries. Others were called up for military service before they could embark on their studies. The Foundations of Scientific Atheism became a mandatory course in all higher education establishments. The Komsomol declared that 'no parent should be allowed to cripple a child spiritually', as 'freedom of conscience does not apply to children'.[42]

In 1961, priests were removed from the executive body in their parishes. A new Council for the Affairs of the Orthodox Church appointed atheists to replace them. Most of the churches which had been reopened during and immediately after the war were forced to shut again. New financial penalties were levied. The ban on the ringing of bells, lifted in 1941, was reimposed in the late 1950s, especially from May to October, when it was thought they might distract collective farm workers.

An Anglican priest, the Reverend Canon Michael Bourdeaux, first visited Moscow in 1959 as an exchange student. He was spellbound by the Orthodox liturgy but repelled by the official deceit surrounding the Church. Walking around the capital, he discovered that only 41 churches were still holding services out of the 1,600 which operated before the Revolution. Angered by the clampdown and the lies peddled to the outside world, on his return to the UK Bourdeaux founded the Keston Institute, which monitored religious persecution in Eastern Europe. According to Oleg Gordievsky, the Soviet double agent who escaped to the UK in the boot of a car, Keston was second, after Amnesty International, in the list of Western organisations hated by the KGB.[43]

On another trip to Moscow, in 1964, Bourdeaux discovered that the Transfiguration Church of St Peter and St Paul in the north-east of the capital had been closed; shortly afterwards it was blown up, even though it was ringed by crowds of distraught protestors. Some people broke through police cordons and refused to leave, clutching copies of the Soviet constitution, which officially guaranteed religious freedom. The church was detonated at 4am on 18 July 1964. Parishioners and onlookers wept and gathered bricks as keepsakes. By the time Bourdeaux arrived a few weeks later, all that remained was a pile of rubble surrounded by a hastily erected wooden fence.[44]

The most prominent of the thousands of churches closed under Khrushchev was the Kyiv Pechersk Lavra, also known as the

Monastery of the Caves, in the Ukrainian capital. The second most holy place in Ukraine, the Pochaiv Monastery, a stunning baroque complex perched on a hill in the western Volyn region, had somehow managed to stay open despite exorbitant taxes being levied on it, as well as other forms of intimidation. Bourdeaux gained access to documents written by a group of lay Orthodox believers living nearby. They claimed that elderly monks were being forcibly removed to mental hospitals while younger ones were drafted into the army.[45] Pilgrims were arrested, their donations to the monks confiscated. Surrounding guest houses were closed, forcing visitors to sleep on the stone floors of the churches. As a final disincentive, a building next to the main cathedral was turned into an asylum for the mentally ill, whose screams drowned out the liturgy.[46]

Pilgrimages and feast days were also targeted; it was suggested that such holidays threatened agricultural production targets because they gave farm workers an excuse to drink and skive off work. None of it seemed to work. Officialdom struggled to understand why religion remained such a force in daily life. In the winter of 1956, several hundred people descended on a quiet street in Kuibyshev, present-day Samara in south-western Russia. They had come to gawp at the remains of a young woman supposedly punished for blasphemy. Tired of waiting for her boyfriend to collect her for a local dance, she had grabbed an icon of St Nicholas the Miracle-Worker from the wall and begun spinning around with it, saying, 'If there is a God, let him punish me!' Lightning and thunder allegedly followed her taunt and when the smoke cleared all that was left of young Zoya was a pillar of stone. The local Communist party called it a 'preposterous fable', but the Kuibyshev affair received so much attention that it went all the way up to the Central Committee in Moscow.[47]

However strong the classroom propaganda, anti-religious campaigners realised that their efforts to mould the next generation of Communists faced one formidable challenge – the Russian *babushka*. Families still rely on grandmothers to raise children while both parents are at work. The Soviet utopia promised free pre-school education for everyone, but in reality, state-run nurseries could not keep up with demand. As the Soviet Union urbanised, a constant stream of grandmothers left their villages to settle with their children in the city, bringing their faith with them. Posters portrayed them as foolish peasants or witches dragging the young into dark rooms to worship icons instead of playing with other young pioneers outside in the sunlight.[48]

The Khrushchev authorities reacted far more vehemently, with near hysteria, to the growth of Russian Protestants – Evangelical Christian Baptists, Pentecostals and Seventh-day Adventists. At the height of the Cold War and the Cuban Missile Crisis, state media accused 'sectarians' of spreading fear of an apocalypse. In one popular anti-religious film from 1960, *Tuchi nad Borskom* (Clouds Over Borsk),[49] a lonely young girl in a Siberian town falls into the hands of a cult thanks to a boy in her class. She gives her widowed father a heart attack when she announces she is leaving the *Komsomol*, the Communist Party's youth organisation. In the closing scenes, demonic Pentecostals attempt to crucify the schoolgirl in the village barn. She is rescued in the nick of time by the locals, led by an upstanding young Communist.

The Bolsheviks created a secular bureaucracy to take over the recording of births, marriages and deaths from religious institutions. It was known as the ZAGS, an acronym for *Zapis Aktov Grahzdanskogo Sostoaniya* – the Office for the Registration of Acts of Civil Status. There was nothing fancy about these registry offices at first, but the authorities realised people needed a meaningful way of marking the key events in their lives. In the early days under Stalin, 'red rituals' were devised, ceremonies organised by the party or Komsomol in factories and collective farms. These became objects of satire, even in the party newspaper *Pravda*. Under Khrushchev, the ZAGS was revamped. Readers of *Izvestia* were offered prizes for a secular, and cool, version of baptisms; requests were made to come up with more modern coming-of-age ceremonies and marriage rituals. In 1959 the first palace of weddings opened its doors in a converted eighteenth-century mansion in Leningrad, overlooking the River Neva. Soon these palaces sprung up everywhere. Demand quickly outstripped supply; six-month waiting lists to get hitched were not uncommon.

Death also required a Soviet makeover. The Decree on Funerals and Cemeteries issued just after the Revolution in 1918 stated the need for new 'non-religious' funeral practices, the nationalisation of the private death care industry and guarantees for any working person to be buried at the state's expense. Cremation, the 'fiery burial', was seen as the best solution both ideologically and aesthetically.[50] But for years after the Second World War, cremation was associated with Nazi war crimes, as well as a makeshift crematorium used during the 900-day Leningrad Siege, so that method of disposing of bodies did not feature much during Khrushchev's atheist campaigns. A shortage of fuel for Soviet crematoriums before major oil and gas fields were discovered in Siberia in the late 1960s meant they did not become widespread until Leonid Brezhnev's time (1964–82).[51] In the countryside, most people were still buried in the ground in ceremonies conducted by priests.

Khrushchev was removed by the Politburo after eleven years in power, his rule deemed too quixotic and too accommodating of the West. In her book about her grandfather, Nina Khrushcheva wrote that some old women whispered about divine powers spiriting the bald-headed atheist out of office: 'I have heard more than once that Khrushchev's resignation on 14 October (1964) was no coincidence. It was the day of the Intercession of the Blessed Virgin Mary and believers thought she had covered them with a miraculous blanket and saved them from the assertive First Secretary. I do not share such superstitions, but I admit that Khrushchev's time was not the best for the church.'[52]

Still, the persecution of believers carried on into the era of the next general secretary, Leonid Brezhnev. Legislation in 1968 allowed the state to remove children from unfit parents, anyone deemed to be abusive, neglectful, immoral, alcoholic, drug-addicted – or who taught religion to their children.[53] Another law passed that year made it a crime to invite a child to a church.

Harassment such as this continued well into the 1980s. In 1983, I had been invited to stay with the poet Yevgeny Yevtushenko and his English wife Jan at their home in the writers' colony of Peredelkino, a twenty-minute train ride from Moscow. When I tried to attend an Easter service, men with red armbands blocked my entry into the church. These were the *druzhinniki*, the voluntary militia who helped the police arrest drunks and deal with social nuisances. 'What do you want to go in there for? It's full of old crones,' drawled one of the men, looking me up and down. He recommended watching a film instead. Over Easter blockbuster movies from the West were widely shown to deter young people from going to church with their grandparents.

The Brezhnev years came to be known as the era of stagnation. The Soviet Union fell behind the West in economic growth, technology and the development of ideas. Illegal books, newspapers and films smuggled in from abroad made Russians increasingly aware of the yawning gap. A growing number of young intellectuals were looking for alternatives to the official ideology; some of them were turning to the Church. A couple of brave Moscow priests, Gleb Yakunin and Nicholas Eshliman, wrote two open letters, to Patriarch Alexei I and to the head of the government, Nikolai Podgorny, in 1965, attacking apologists from the Church hierarchy for fostering a 'spirit of indifference, servility, and pharisaism'.[54] They accused the Council for Russian Orthodox Church Affairs of making a mockery of the religious freedom much proclaimed outside the USSR and of violating Lenin's principle of the separation of church and state.[55] News of the letter spread like wildfire.

The Patriarch responded by suspending the two priests for ten years. Eshliman never returned to the priesthood but Yakunin did, after surviving for a decade on a series of badly paid odd jobs. Occasionally, he was hired to read psalms in Moscow churches. Despite the hardships he endured, he was undeterred. Once he was allowed to serve again, he created the Christian Committee for the Defence of Believers' Rights to draw attention to abuses of the rights of the faithful of all denominations, not just Orthodox. In 1979, he was sent to a labour camp for slander. His trial attracted worldwide press coverage. It was the first time a Russian Orthodox priest had been put in the dock since the USSR had signed the Helsinki Accords in 1975. That agreement required other nations to respect the inviolability of borders – de facto recognition of the Soviet Union's control over the Warsaw Pact states of Eastern Europe. In exchange, the Soviets had pledged to defend human rights and fundamental freedoms, including the freedom of thought, conscience, religion and belief.[56]

Many felt the priests' letters in 1965 marked a turning point. The Anglican priest Michael Bourdeaux argued they heralded the emergence of a civic consciousness which eventually became a factor in destabilising the Soviet Union. The atmosphere in churches began to change, as did the average age of congregations. Under the grey lid of the Brezhnev era, fresh ideas were bubbling up. Many young priests felt it was not enough to celebrate the liturgy and perform rites. They wanted a church more rooted in human rights and prepared to play a far more active role in contemporary life.

☦ ☦ ☦

One of those inspired by Yakunin was Zoya Krakhmalnikova, a literary critic who came to Orthodoxy in her early forties. When she was baptised, she was sacked from her job at a prestigious magazine and thrown out of the Union of Writers, which meant that she could no longer publish her work. Instead, she devoted herself to the underground distribution of forbidden texts, known as *samizdat*. Eventually, she was arrested and sent into exile. She bore her suffering with remarkable resilience, but one of her most trusted mentors was broken by the KGB.

On my last visit to Russia, a few months before the 2022 invasion of Ukraine, I dropped in on Krakhmalnikova's daughter, the journalist and human rights activist Zoya Svetova. Her home off Moscow's Boulevard Ring was crammed with icons and moody black and white photographs. Four years earlier, in February 2017, the FSB spent ten hours searching the apartment. They did not like the fact that Zoya was a regular visitor to some of Russia's worst prisons and that she reported on the conditions there. Rifling through her desk and bookshelves, they asked her why she was so keen to see the 'terrorists and spies' behind bars. Didn't she have anything better to do? As a member of an official committee, Prison Watch, Zoya had gained access to some of the country's most notorious detention centres, including Lefortovo in Moscow, where her mother had been imprisoned 40 years earlier. As we sat in the kitchen drinking tea and eating freshly baked gingerbread, she told me her mother's story.

Krakhmalnikova was born in 1929 in the Ukrainian city of Kharkiv and witnessed her stepfather's arrest when she was seven years old. He never returned home. Although she was marked by this early trauma, she did well at school, and despite her background as a daughter of an 'enemy of the people' she gained a place at the graduate school of the Institute of World Literature. Before long she had landed a job at the Soviet Writer publishing house and contributed to magazines such as *Knowledge*, *Young Guard* and *New World*. She also wrote novels and became a researcher at the Academy of Sciences.

She was active in the Church as well. Together with her husband, the writer Felix Svetov, Zoya often made long journeys outside Moscow to attend services conducted by inspirational priests who had been banished to remote parishes. Father Dmitry Dudko, who baptised Krakhmalnikova, was a mentor for many intellectuals in the 1970s, including the nuclear physicist and Nobel Prize laureate Andrei Sakharov. Dudko served at the Church of St Nicholas on Preobrazhenka in Moscow, where he accepted written questions from his congregation and replied to them in his next sermon. His discussions about Christianity and the meaning of faith attracted growing numbers of curious young people. He also shared his experiences of forced labour in the gulag. One morning, he had to tell his congregation that there would be no sermon this week. The Patriarch had forbidden him to preach until he had held 'talks with him'. All of Father Dmitry's attempts to meet Patriarch Pimen were rebuffed. Instead, he was appointed to a parish in the outskirts of the capital and later sent to a church in the village of Grebnevo, even further away from Moscow. His acolytes still flocked to his services and he conducted some prayer services privately at home.

After Krakhmalnikova was dismissed from her job in 1974, she began circulating Dudko's pastoral addresses, religious texts by other priests and some of her own work in a typewritten journal which she edited and compiled, called *Nadezhda*, Hope. It was based on a pre-Revolutionary series, *Khristianskoe Chtenie* (Christian Readings), published in Russia from 1821 to 1917. One priest credits her as having almost single-handedly 'resurrected Russia's religious memory, so desperately needed by her people'.[57] *Nadezhda* was not overtly political, although it did tell the stories of 'new martyrs', clergy and believers who had fallen victim to Communist rule. Most *samizdat* editors published anonymously, for understandable reasons of self-protection, but Krakhmalnikova proudly put her name on each issue. The typescript was initially passed from hand to hand, but later sent to a publishing house in Frankfurt, and copies were then smuggled back into the USSR. Her devotional almanacs were in such huge demand that they were passed from person to person until the bindings fell apart.

In January 1980, Dudko was arrested, under the pretext of handing 'slanderous materials' to foreign journalists. Under interrogation, his resolve started to crumble. He had already served an eight-and-a-half-year prison sentence for writing poetry about the desecration of Russia's holy places. Stalin-era prosecutors decided his wartime verse was riddled with anti-government propaganda. Later on, he was constantly hounded by the security services. He suffered two broken legs after a lorry crashed into his car when he was driving to visit his mother – an accident many blamed on the KGB – and he was vilified in the Soviet press.

Six months after his arrest, he recanted on television, looking deathly pale and reading from a written statement. He told viewers that he repudiated his actions and wanted to apologise. 'I assess my so-called struggle against godlessness as a struggle against Soviet power,' he said. Dudko's supporters were stunned. Some thought he must have been drugged; many felt betrayed. None more so than Zoya Krakhmalnikova, who would later be arrested herself thanks to the priest's testimony. 'He informed on my mother,' said Zoya Svetova. 'It was all absurd, but somehow he was frightened. The investigators put so much pressure on him.' She was being tried, among other things, for signing a letter in the priest's defence and for giving his book to her son as a gift.

Plainclothes officers barged into Krakhmalnikova's dacha outside Moscow just before dawn in August 1982. They took her to Lefortovo, the KGB's chief interrogation centre for political prisoners. Years later, in her memoir *Listen, Prison* she recalled the sound of the prison gates clanging shut and her fear that she may have left a familiar world behind for ever: 'A world where I left my daughter crying ... a world where my beloved four-month-old grandson Filip attentively watched the man searching his room, the unfamiliar black shape bending over his cot.'[58] The police search had been exhaustive. They even checked under the baby's mattress for banned books. Krakhmalnikova described 'hollow prison corridors filled with acrid, unusual smells resembling some expensive eau de cologne which is poured over corpses to kill the putrid stench' and she remembered the smell of her interrogators: 'tobacco, clean pressed shirts and sleek hair'. She had to rely on her nose and her ears to navigate her surroundings because she could see so little. The tiny window of her cell, where she spent a year, was smeared with white paint. Sometimes she could hear the faint tolling of church bells.

Sitting in her cell, she reflected on how Dudko, her former spiritual father, had walked the same corridors and been stripped of his robes and his pectoral cross, as well as his belt and shoelaces. 'I must understand him, forgive him and help him,' she wrote. It was a tall order. By the time Dudko attended her trial, he was wearing his vestments and cross again. But Krakhmalnikova observed that these outward signs of godliness 'did not prevent him from lying'. From the dock she stretched out her hands and asked for his blessing. He made the sign of the cross over her but told the court that 'he read nothing, he saw nothing, he knew nothing' and went on to give politically expedient 'false evidence' that nobody believed.[59]

The prison bosses tried to get Krakhmalnikova to incriminate herself by confessing to various anti-Soviet plots. One day she was invited into a comfortable room in the prison and offered coffee and sweets, as well as a little chat with a fellow writer who introduced himself as a 'sociologist'. He was Nikolai Yakovlev, an academic recruited by the KGB to conduct ideological operations and write books such as *The CIA Against the USSR*.[60] Krakhmalnikova refused the refreshments and the offer to cooperate. After a year in Lefortovo, she was sentenced to five years of internal exile in Siberia. She was packed off to the Altai Republic, 72 hours on the train from Moscow, near the Mongolian border. She rented a small room in the village of Ust'-Koksa and was allowed to receive food parcels and family visits. The locals were nonplussed to find this bookish woman in her late fifties in their midst. When she bumped into the captain of the local militia in the square, he asked her, 'How did this happen to you?' adding 'Are you Orthodox? No way!'[61] There was no chance of seeing a priest or attending a liturgy in such an isolated place. The Altai region has a mixture of shamanist and Orthodox believers, but there were no functioning churches anywhere near her village in the 1980s, which was why the security services had sent her there.

Three years after Krakhmalnikova's arrest, her husband Felix was also detained. He too had been expelled from the Writers' Union for supporting others persecuted by the regime, and for his religious works such as a novel about a Russian Jew converting to Orthodoxy called *Open to Me the Gates*.[62] The day the KGB turned the family's Moscow flat inside out, Krakhmalnikova's daughter Zoya went into labour. When she came back from the maternity hospital with her second son, Timofei, her father had gone. Neighbours said he had been driven away and taken to the notorious Interior Ministry prison, Matrosskaya Tishina, or Seaman's Silence.

From exile, Krakhmalnikova wrote to Patriarch Pimen, urging him to use his influence and help to free her 57-year-old husband, who was in poor health. 'I hope that your spiritual experience will help you to distinguish between truth and slander, that it will remind you that the first "political criminal" was our Lord Jesus Christ who was accused of stirring up the people, of being Caesar's enemy (John 19:12).' The Patriarch did not reply. After a year in prison, Felix was sentenced to five years' exile but was allowed to go to the Altai to join his wife. Hauled before the court ten months after Mikhail Gorbachev took over as Soviet leader, Felix was one of the Soviet Union's last religious dissidents. In her memoir, Krakhmalnikova described how she and her husband, living together in exile in January 1987, were summoned to the local prosecutor's office. He told them they would be allowed to return to Moscow, to be reunited with their children and grandchildren, if they repented of their earlier actions. The couple refused. They had broken no laws and felt that accepting the offer would be to sell their souls for an early release. A no-strings pardon was issued a few months later.

Zoya heard they had been freed as she was returning home from the maternity hospital after the birth of her third son. She and her husband decided the baby boy should be called Tikhon, after the ancient Greek goddess of luck, Tyche. The name can also mean liberator.

Before I leave, Zoya shows me one particular photograph from the 1980s. She had taken her children to see their grandparents in Siberia. Sitting on a tree trunk with the mountains in the distance, her mother is smiling serenely as the toddler Timofei wriggles in her lap and her other arm is wrapped around little Filip. These tousled-haired boys, Filip, Timofei – and the yet-to-be-born Tikhon – would become some of the best-known opposition journalists of the Putin era.

8. RESURRECTION AMIDST CHAOS – THE APOTHEOSIS OF HOPE

Dressed in ragged jeans and beaded necklaces, the twelve singing apostles swarmed around their Messiah. He wore a black leather jacket and made a dramatic exit on a motorbike borrowed from the Moscow militia. In the Russian capital in the early 1990s, *Jesus Christ Superstar* was playing to packed houses every night.

The show, which had opened on Broadway in 1971 and follows Jesus in the final days leading up to his crucifixion, became an underground hit in the USSR. In the Brezhnev era, all but the most anodyne Western pop was banned; bootleg rock tapes were hot items on the black market. A rock opera featuring a hippie called Jesus who rejects dogma and challenges earthly authority was doubly subversive. Nevertheless, two enterprising journalists managed to stage some of the songs as early as the mid-1970s. They were senior editors from the Communist Party newspaper *Pravda*, but they had worked in the United States and developed a taste for musicals. Their version, *Rock and Roll at Dawn*, was disguised as a morality play about American students, evil Pentagon generals and the Vietnam War. But, in a cunning subplot, the students rehearse an amateur production of *Superstar* and perform its most popular tunes.

Such cultural subterfuge was no longer required under Mikhail Gorbachev. The first official production in Russia, in February 1990 at the Leningrad Palace of Culture, starred a former sailor from the Baltic Fleet. He received a blessing from the Orthodox Church to play the lead role and was baptised soon afterwards. When the show later opened in Moscow, I noticed the effect it had on some of the audience. One girl was humming loudly in the queue for the cloakroom. 'Mary Magdalene gave me goosebumps,' she said. 'What a voice. And the dancing was fantastic.' An elderly man sitting next to me said he was so troubled by the relationship between Jesus and Judas that he wanted to start reading the Bible to understand it better. The blond-haired actor playing Jesus had attracted a bevy of devoted fans. One besotted girl came to almost every performance. Then, suddenly, she disappeared. Her friends told the actor that she had been so spiritually awakened by his performance, she had entered a convent.[1] A young architect helping to restore frescoes in a seventeenth-century church said he discovered religion thanks to a pirated copy of *Superstar*. Now, three decades later, he is a priest in a Russian Orthodox parish in New Zealand.

It seems far-fetched to suggest Andrew Lloyd Webber played a role in Russia's Christian renaissance. But his musical reached the Soviet Union at a time when any belief in a bright Communist future had evaporated. Alongside a revival of interest in religion, *Superstar* provided a crash course in the Gospels for a generation which had not gone to church or opened a Bible. Many of my own Russian friends had gleaned what knowledge they had about the life of Christ from Mikhail Bulgakov's satirical masterpiece *The Master and Margarita*. Written in the Stalin era, the novel contains an unforgettable confrontation between Jesus and Pontius Pilate.

Church weddings, christenings and Orthodox schools became fashionable; services were no longer the sole preserve of grannies in headscarves. Religion even smelt of teenage rebellion. Across the country, young men and women embarked on *bogoiskatelstvo*, a quest to find God. To overcome the cynicism of their parents, they turned inward. 'Hamburgers will never satisfy us,' one woman told me while I was interviewing people queuing outside Russia's first branch of McDonald's, in Pushkin Square on New Year's Eve in 1990. 'Our hunger is of a spiritual kind.'

In the 1980s, when the era of 'stagnation' was at its height and the Soviet Union was falling ever further behind the West, many citizens developed a fascination with mysticism and Eastern religions. In search of greater spiritual meaning, they began to dabble in the 'alternative' teachings of yoga, crystal therapy, mindfulness or Buddhism. They also began to re-engage with Orthodoxy.

Oleg Rumantsyev, a member of parliament who helped write Russia's post-Communist constitution, rang me excitedly one spring morning in 1991. We met often because he had become a regular interviewee on the BBC. 'Lucy,' he said breathlessly, 'are you busy tomorrow morning?' He wanted to invite me to his baptism. Rumantsyev, now an investment consultant, told me he was the first Russian to be baptised in the Kremlin's Uspensky Sobor in the post-Soviet era. The cathedral, a museum for decades, had just been returned to the Church. He asked two fellow deputies, who were also priests, to perform the ceremony. These days he feels alienated from the Church and attends services rarely. But he recalled how he felt after the baptism more than three decades ago. 'Afterwards I went back to the parliament and in the lift up to my office, people asked me: "What has happened to you? You seem to be glowing from the inside."'

According to Metropolitan Hilarion, one of the Church's most senior clerics, in the late 1980s and early 1990s, clerics were rushed off their feet. While he was teaching dogmatics and Byzantine Greek at the city's theological academy, the average Moscow priest would baptise two or three hundred people a day. By the evening, he would 'simply collapse from exhaustion'. The trouble was there was very little time for catechism: 'Many people received baptism and called themselves Christians knowing next to nothing about their religion.' Months before the collapse of the USSR in 1991, a nationwide survey asked people which figures would have 'a major influence' a decade later. Some 58 per cent named Jesus Christ. Lenin was cited by 36 per cent, according to the results of the poll published in the weekly paper *Moskovskie Novosti*. Barely a quarter mentioned Gorbachev.

If *Superstar* was playing night after night in the Mossovet State Academic Theatre, it was largely thanks to Gorbachev. Yet when he came to power in 1985, there were few signs that this new Soviet leader, greeted in the West as a liberal and a reformer, would be any more tolerant of believers than his predecessors. A year into the job, he called in a speech for renewed atheist propaganda alongside a 'firm and uncompromising struggle against religious phenomena'. Gorbachev authorised a package of secret resolutions on fighting 'religious sectarianism', the 'reactionary influence of the Islamic clergy', as well as 'limiting the impact of Catholicism' and 'stronger measures to counteract Orthodoxy'.

No matter how many KGB-sponsored Orthodox clerics flew to international conferences to promote Soviet foreign policy objectives, most party ideologists treated the Church as a nuisance or an enemy. Gorbachev's policy of *glasnost* (openness) did not at the outset extend to religion. When the poet Vladimir Soloukhin described the dynamiting of Christ the Saviour in 1931 as a crime during a TV debate, his microphone was promptly cut off.[2]

In April 1988, three years into Gorbachev's rule, it all changed. Under the vaulted ceiling of St Catherine Hall, a smiling party leader welcomed Patriarch Pimen and acknowledged the state's historic 'mistakes' towards the Church. He told him 'we have a common history, common motherland and a common future'. The sight of the Patriarch being warmly welcomed into the Kremlin, and on national television, sent a powerful signal. The last such meeting was during the Second World War, when Stalin summoned hierarchs to mobilise support against the German invasion. Pimen replied to Gorbachev: 'Esteemed Mikhail Sergeyevich, I pledge support to you, the architect of perestroika and the herald of new political thinking. We pray for the success of this process and are doing everything we can to promote it.' Although much of the conversation was bland, the Patriarch let slip that 'not all the problems of Church life are being resolved or duly attended to'. The comment, though brief, was unprecedented, as senior clerics routinely denied that any troubles existed.

Gorbachev always insisted he was an atheist, as did his wife Raisa who, at one time, taught Marxist–Leninist philosophy. It would be strange for anyone with political ambition to profess otherwise. Yet the Soviet leader admitted on an official visit to France in July 1989 that he had been secretly baptised as a baby in the southern village of Privolnoye by his Ukrainian mother, Maria Panteleyevna. The daughter of a collective farm boss, she was a devout churchgoer until her death in 1995. Her parents hid their icons behind portraits of Lenin and Stalin. Raisa confessed she had also been christened as a child in Siberia but that she and her husband had not baptised their daughter Irina, because 'times have changed'.[3]

Times were changing again, and Gorbachev was a pragmatist. After Ronald Reagan launched his Strategic Defence Initiative programme, better known as Star Wars, the Soviet Union was struggling to keep up. Saddled with a failing economy, Gorbachev was more interested in disarmament than the West. He told his foreign minister, Edward Shevardnadze, that it was 'necessary to seek a common language with the Americans at any cost'. In 1986, human rights campaigners such as Natan Sharansky and Andrei Sakharov were released. The following year, another 200 prisoners were freed, including the religious dissidents Zoya Krakhmalnikova and her husband Felix. But for Reagan, who famously branded the USSR an 'evil empire' in a speech to evangelicals in Florida in 1983, such concessions were not enough. Throughout his presidency, he attacked the USSR for preventing millions from 'the joy of knowing God'. He wanted to go down in history as a man who helped to liberate Soviet people from 'totalitarian darkness'.

To win him over and push forward with disarmament negotiations, Gorbachev made a radical change in religious policy.[4] He alighted on a convenient historical pretext. In the spring of 1988, preparations were underway to mark the thousandth anniversary of the Eastern Slavs' conversion to Christianity, when the Grand Prince of Kyiv, Volodymyr, baptised his subjects in the River Dnipro. The Central Committee had wanted celebrations to be muted. It drafted a proposal stressing that everything possible should be done 'not to attract special attention to this event'.[5] Instead, Gorbachev put on a lavish show to proclaim his newfound tolerance and demonstrate an emboldened Church. Foreign prelates, homegrown clerics and secular party bosses flocked to the celebrations. All over the country, dilapidated churches were repaired: more than 500 were opened in that one year, compared with just 16 in 1987. Within just two years, 3,000 parish churches were returned, and more than 20 new monasteries opened.

During their visit to Moscow, Ronald Reagan and his wife Nancy watched teams of monks and craftsmen restore icons and buildings of the Danilovsky Monastery. In Soviet times, the monastery, founded in 1282, had been converted into an umbrella factory, then a refrigerator plant and a prison for the children of the enemies of the people. Now, behind the high crenelated walls, the compound was being transformed into the seat of the patriarchate in Moscow – the Orthodox Church's equivalent of the Vatican complete with dormitories, dining halls, a hotel, office buildings and a quartet of refurbished churches. Inside there was also a palace for Patriarch Pimen himself, who was to move from his headquarters at the St Sergius Monastery, an hour's drive north of Moscow.

Patriarch Pimen (Sergei Izvekov), born in 1910 just east of Moscow, became a monk aged seventeen. His biography contains some curious blank spots. He was first arrested by the OGPU, Stalin's secret police during Lent, in 1932, on suspicion of spying for the Chinese. Later on, he fought in the Red Army, joined the Communist Party and rose quickly through the ranks. According to one version he suffered from shell shock and was cared for by some nuns in Moscow after leaving hospital. Some church historians believe he was an army deserter, living on fake documents, for which he was court-martialled in January 1945, stripped of his military rank and given a ten-year prison sentence. He wound up in Vorkuta, a coal-mining gulag above the Arctic Circle. I visited the town in the winter of 1992 when it was 30 degrees below zero and some of the prison watchtowers were still intact. Somehow, Pimen only served eight months in this hellhole. A former employee of the Moscow Patriarchate came to the conclusion that he was 'released after being recruited' by the security services, 'like everyone else who managed to survive in that era'. According to former intelligence officers, his file was most likely removed from the KGB archive after he was elected patriarch and transferred directly to the Central Committee.[6] Perhaps these experiences account for Pimen's reputation for weakness. A CIA report from 1987 described him as 'obsequiously receptive to government and party guidance'.[7] The dissident novelist Alexander Solzhenitsyn accused him in 1972 of having 'forsaken the flock' by allowing the authorities to make the Church a tool of the state. Moreover, by the glasnost era he was frail and suffering from diabetes. Some urged him to stand down to make way for a younger bishop.

Yet Pimen led the liturgy to open the millennium celebrations on 5 June at the Patriarchal Cathedral of the Epiphany in Moscow. Two days later, the festivities moved on to Ukraine, where the Kyiv Pechersk Lavra, confiscated under Nikita Khrushchev, was returned to the Church. Many Ukrainians argued that the celebrations should have started in their capital, since Kyiv, not Moscow, is the true birthplace of Slav Orthodoxy.

The loudest protests came from further west, where the Ukrainian Catholic, or Uniate Church, was driven underground by Stalin in 1946. It was forcibly dissolved, and its parishes were closed or merged into the Russian Orthodox Church. Most of Ukraine's 5 million Catholics live on land which was once part of Poland, until the Soviet Union swallowed it up after the Second World War. These Eastern Rite Catholics follow the Orthodox liturgy but profess allegiance to Rome. So, not surprisingly, when Gorbachev visited the Vatican a year after the millennium celebrations, the Polish-born Pope played hardball. He made clear he would accept a return invitation to Moscow only after Gorbachev had improved the status of Soviet Catholics, especially those in Ukraine.

Since his April 1988 meeting with Pimen, Gorbachev had talked up a forthcoming bill that would end repression of believers. He suggested that all religions in the multi-confessional Soviet Union were to enjoy the same legal standing and property privileges as the Orthodox Church. Pressure from faith groups was rising, including from Lithuanian Catholics and Muslims in southern Russia and Central Asia. Finally, in September 1990, parliament passed a law banning state control of religion and assuring freedom of conscience for all believers.

Orthodox Christians were no longer punished or stigmatised for attending services and no longer needed to baptise their children in secret. More couples opted for church weddings as young people joined monasteries and convents. On 7 January 1990, Christmas midnight mass was broadcast live on television for the first time. The printing and importing of Bibles and other texts was permitted again, as was charitable work and religious teaching.

The impetus for religious freedoms did not just come from abroad, however. Alexei, Metropolitan of Tallinn and Estonia, and future patriarch, sensed that the Soviet leader was dismayed by apathy to his programme of perestroika, social and economic restructuring reforms. He wrote to Gorbachev early on, assuring him that the Church could prove an indispensable ally. It would fight decisively 'against various vices and diseases in society, not only against drunkenness, but also against moral dereliction, callousness and selfishness' to 'strengthen the Soviet family as the most important unit of society'. His letter struck a chord with Gorbachev. For example, he had embarked on an anti-alcohol campaign two months after coming into office, ripping up vineyards and wrecking the economies of wine-producing areas in Moldavia, Armenia and Georgia. Ridiculed as the *mineral'nyi sekretar* (mineral-water drinking secretary) rather than *general'nyi sekretar* (general secretary), he was forced to abandon his crusade after two disastrous years. One viniculturalist, who ran a famous winery in Crimea and created 50 new varieties of grapes, committed suicide in 1986 after failing to persuade Gorbachev to preserve his life's work.[8] The restrictions led to a spate of fatal poisonings from bad vodka sold on the black market and other alcohol surrogates like eau de cologne. Drug addiction rose dramatically as well.

In the perestroika era, some clergy had a chance to make their voices heard by running for office in the new parliament, the Congress of People's Deputies. One of the priests elected, Father Gleb Yakunin, said Gorbachev might be 'a real atheist' but he was also 'a real reformer'. The outspoken Yakunin had been defrocked and exiled to Siberia for criticising the Church two decades earlier. Now he was welcomed back into the fold, but one Moscow bishop warned him to 'be reasonable' and watch his tongue if he wanted to get a parish. 'For our bishops, perestroika is like a knife to the throat,' Yakunin told a news conference, shortly after he was reinstated. 'Because if Perestroika starts, they will be replaced by people who are more active.'[9]

Aleksander Men was one of the most active priests. His little wooden church in Novaya Derevnya, north-west of Moscow, was not one of those showcased in the millennium celebrations. His sermons and talks, erudite and accessible, attracted large crowds of people who had not shown any interest in religion before. A skilled media communicator, he was keen to introduce the faith to the widest possible audience, urging openness to secular culture, to science, to other churches and, significantly, to non-Christian religions. Born Jewish, Men was baptised into the Orthodox faith as a baby along with his mother, who had become a member of the underground catacomb church. He wrote his first book in his early teens, entitled *What Does the Bible Tell Us?*, by which time he had already decided to become a priest. Although his superiors noticed his promise early on, he was not given a large parish because he refused to cooperate with the authorities. Instead, throughout the Brezhnev years, Men was the star guest at 'gatherings' in an assortment of Moscow flats. Amidst the rattling teacups, crying babies and kitchen bustle, he taught secret Bible classes in front of audiences sitting cross-legged on the floor. He catechised and baptised thousands of people. Once Gorbachev's reforms allowed it, he visited classrooms and factory floors. He started an Orthodox Open University and the first post-Communist Sunday school.

He was undoubtedly, as Patriarch Alexei later put it, 'a talented preacher of the word of God'. Others called him a modern-day apostle and the architect of religious renewal in Russia. His activities were not restricted to the faithful. Men believed that the Church should reach out beyond its own walls and tackle social problems. In 1989, with the help of the Church of the Sacred Martyrs Kosma and Damian, which ran one of Moscow's first soup kitchens, he founded a remarkable charity group at a children's hospital. It raised money for equipment and medical treatment but also invited clowns and magicians onto the wards to divert the suffering of the young patients.

Men's life was cut short when he was 55. I had been in Russia for only a month, when, one Sunday afternoon, I heard some chilling news: Men had been on his way to church the morning of 9 September 1990 when somebody hiding in the birch trees along his path to the station jumped out and struck him on the head. The priest stumbled back home, realising he had been badly injured, but collapsed in front of the fence next to his front door. By the time his wife called an ambulance, it was too late.

Some blamed the priest's murder on a group called *Pamyat*, Memory, a nationalist movement infamous for anti-Semitism.

Pamyat began as a film club for history buffs at Moscow's Aviation Ministry in the late 1970s and celebrated famous Russian victories such as the Kulikovo battle of 1380 against the Tatars. Led by the actor Dmitri Vasiliev, *Pamyat*'s members dressed in black shirts reminiscent of the pre-revolutionary anti-Semitic organisation the Black Hundreds. Others pointed the finger at the KGB, the police or conservative zealots in the Patriarchate. Fazil Iskander, a novelist from Abkhazia, a breakaway region of Georgia, was a close friend of the murdered priest: 'He was the light of our Homeland and if darkness envelops our country again, we will understand that from where that darkness came, the killer came too.'[10]

Men's work inspired many other priests. In 1990, Russia's first charitable hospital in over 70 years had just opened in the grounds of the Leningrad Theological Academy. After conducting a service for the new staff, the rector, Father Vladimir Sorokin, denounced the inhumane treatment of elderly patients. Although Soviet hospitals were theoretically free of charge, it was virtually impossible to get seen without giving the doctor some sort of 'present'. Nurses and auxiliaries also needed incentives to administer drugs or even provide bedpans. 'So many people in our society are alone and we want to create a good family atmosphere for them,' Sorokin said. Too many of Leningrad's citizens were both indifferent to religion and to each other. They had been 'spiritually dormant' throughout the Communist era. Now it was 'time for them to wake up'; the hospital would set 'a good example'.

Speaking three decades later from St Petersburg, where he still serves as an archpriest, Sorokin told me his proposal had initially been blocked. 'The Soviet Health Ministry was sceptical that we could run a hospital,' he said. 'Our people's way of thinking was that everything must be done by the state. And as a priest, I felt it was bad that they had no sense of responsibility. At that time, we didn't realise the Communist era would end and we were trying to make socialism more Christian.'

When the Church started to reclaim its property, following a 1993 decree from President Yeltsin, it was accused by some of heartlessness and philistinism. Museum directors forced out of their premises worried the Church lacked the expertise to care for precious artefacts. 'If the 1920s saw the fate of the Church shaped by mobs led by commissars, does that mean the fate of our culture is again at the mercy of the mob?' asked the chairman of the Association of Russian Restorers. 'I have spent twenty years restoring icons with my own hands,' he added. 'I am, therefore, entitled to speak out on behalf of this culture which has been preserved.' A prominent academician was furious that staff at the Sergiyev Posad Museum, north of Moscow, would be dismissed and the premises handed back to the Church. 'Nobody, not even the President, has the right to take what belongs to the cultural heritage of the entire country and give it away to various social organisations and non-state bodies,' he fumed.[11] But Patriarch Alexei insisted on the restitution. 'Places of worship first, museums second,' said his spokesman.

In St Petersburg, Archpriest Sorokin wanted to conduct services in the five-domed Feodorovsky Cathedral. But he had a fight on his hands. In the 1960s it had been turned into a dairy factory. The plant manager had no intention of handing the building back to the Church. He told Sorokin that a priest should know better than to deprive small children of cheese and other products. Sorokin protested: 'But this church was built for prayer, not for milk.' Attempts to privatise and sell the building off were eventually foiled with the help of a local radio engineer called Boris Gryzlov, who remembered visiting the church as a child.[12] Today, Gryzlov is Russia's ambassador to Belarus and a staunch Putin loyalist.

Within a short time, the Church became Russia's most important non-governmental organisation, the one body capable of unifying a vast country spread across eleven time zones. In some parishes, it began taking over from the state in supporting hospices, orphanages and drug rehabilitation centres.

For 75 years, priests had been banned from visiting prisoners. The clergy could conduct services and hear confessions in prisons and labour camps only if they too were inmates. All manifestations of religiosity were stamped out; wearing a cross could lead to beatings or a punishment cell. But after the 1990 law allowed religious groups to engage in charity work, Orthodox and Catholic priests, Protestant chaplains and Islamic mullahs were allowed, even encouraged, to set up prison ministries.

Sergiyev Posad is renowned for its monastery complex, the Trinity Lavra of Saint Sergius, for centuries the headquarters of the Orthodox Church. The town is less famous for its 'prison castle', the hulking pre-trial Detention Centre Number 8 of the Federal Penitentiary Service of the Moscow region. Father Nikodim and two fellow priests from the Trinity monastery, Fathers Bonifat and Trifon, were among the first to visit inmates. They conducted services in a communal cell converted into a small, freshly whitewashed chapel. The black-robed trio, accompanied through the narrow prison corridors by guards and Alsatian dogs, joked that they were the 'Father, Son and Holy Ghost'. One snowy March day in 1992, they arrived with a coachload of missionaries from the US and UK bearing copies of the New Testament translated into Russian. Nikodim said that the priests were softening the stone hearts of the inmates and extracting the 'poison' from their souls.[13]

The most significant Orthodox pioneer of prison ministry work at the time was Father Gleb Kaleda. His own father, Vladimir, was one of many priests killed during Stalin's Great Terror at Butovo. Gleb was a professor of geology, but for nearly two decades he had led a double life as a secret priest. He ministered to a small, clandestine congregation from his Moscow apartment, which was consecrated as the Church of All Saints. His son Kirill, now archpriest of the church at Butovo, remembers having to hide all the icons in cupboards if visitors came over. But in the perestroika era, Father Gleb started wearing a cassock and openly serving at the Church of the Prophet Elias in central Moscow. He was also elected rector at the newly established St Tikhon's Orthodox University and head of the religious education sector of the Moscow Patriarchate. One day, a parishioner asked if he would join him on a visit to Butyrka, a pre-trial detention centre. The parishioner had persuaded the guards to let him in to meet inmates. He helped their families stay in touch with them by dispatching letters and parcels to their onward places of incarceration.

Kaleda was initially nervous about going inside the notorious red brick building that dates back to the time of Catherine the Great. Butyrka's eighteenth-century architect designed a church with a belfry in the centre of the cross-shaped prison complex. The Church of the Intercession of the Blessed Virgin Mary was closed after the 1917 Revolution and turned into a hardware workshop and hospital. It was reopened for worship in 1991 but conditions in the communal cells worsened, as Father Gleb noted in his memoirs. In 1992, on average 60 people were crowded in a cell originally designed for 36; the following year, the number rose to 110. As the prison population continued to grow, prayer and conversation were almost impossible amidst 'the constant noise and distress'. The lack of oxygen caused some prisoners to suffer heart attacks. I received permission to record inside the prison a few years later, and I will never forget the sight of men packed in, their faces waxy pale. There was almost no space to lie down or even sit; they had to sleep in shifts. The men were covered in lice, and disease was rife. I met the girlfriend of one man in his early twenties who had been arrested in a Moscow market after a row over the price of batteries for his Walkman. After a few months in an overcrowded cell, he was dead from tuberculosis.

Gleb was aware that in the 'Wild East' of the early 1990s 'new dangerous temptations' awaited men who were eventually released, such as 'laundering money obtained through blood, robbery and fraud'. He wanted them to receive spiritual guidance in halfway houses or Orthodox rehabilitation centres. He felt that many prisoners were 'talented, dynamic people who simply did not know where to direct their energy'.[14] He died in 1994 before he could put his plans into action. Few priests seemed keen to follow in his footsteps. Some thought the work too dangerous while the majority claimed they were too busy helping their own parishioners. Father Gleb protested that 'a prison is also a parish, and one parish cannot thrive at the expense of another'.

☦ ☦ ☦

On 19 August 1991, the world awoke to the news of a coup. Armoured vehicles took over Moscow's main arteries; we could see a long line of them outside our flat on the Garden Ring road. A group of eight hardliners, including the Interior Minister, Minister of Defence and head of the KGB, formed a State Emergency Committee.

Alarmed at Gorbachev's *glasnost* and perestroika reforms, at growing pro-independence and anti-Communist movements in other republics, they announced they were 'assuming supreme power in the USSR'. Gorbachev had been arrested at his holiday villa in Crimea. By this point, the country had two power bases – the existing Soviet power structures and those of the increasingly powerful Russian Federation, led by Boris Yeltsin.

It was Yeltsin who led the resistance to the putsch and who would ultimately profit from its failure. Although most Muscovites kept their heads down and went about their business as usual that morning, a sizeable number began gathering around the Russian parliament building, known as the White House, and erecting barricades. Around lunchtime, Yeltsin climbed atop a tank in front of the White House and addressed the troops through a megaphone. He urged them not to turn against their own people and condemned the coup as a 'new reign of terror'. Surprisingly, the soldiers backed off, some of them choosing to join the resistance. There were cheers from the crowd when ten tanks defected. Paratroopers from the Alpha Unit refused to storm the building. A clandestine radio station began broadcasts, while journalists from banned newspapers printed and handed out leaflets to keep people informed.

Later that afternoon, the plotters struggled to justify their actions at a televised press conference. Gennady Yanayev, the new figurehead president, looked thoroughly miserable. His hands were shaking from nerves and too much vodka. A few others on the podium with him also appeared to be drunk. A young journalist had the nerve to stand up and ask them: 'Could you please say whether or not you understand that last night you carried out a *coup d'état*?' The whole performance was so bizarre that the wife of the British ambassador christened it 'The Muppet Show'.[15]

Farcical it might have seemed, but nobody was sure that a bloodbath could be averted. Yeltsin made some calls to Western leaders asking for help but only received statements of concern and sympathy. Then he addressed the new Patriarch, Alexei II, on national radio, urging the Church not to stand aside at 'this moment of tragedy for our Fatherland'. He warned that the Church, which had suffered so much under totalitarian rule, may once again 'experience disorder and lawlessness'. At the end, he declared: 'All believers, the Russian nation, and all-Russia awaits your word!' It may have been part flattery, part desperation, but Yeltsin was telling him that the whole country, not just the faithful, were in need of the Patriarch's protection and guidance.

After 70 years of Communist rule, the fusion of Russian nationalism and Russian Orthodoxy was making a comeback. The Church had survived the Soviet era by deference. Now that the system was collapsing, many wondered what kind of institution would emerge. How would it reinvent itself for a new world? The turmoil gave Alexei a chance to get the population on side and reassert the moral authority of his Church.

On the first day of the coup the Patriarch said nothing. He was presiding at a liturgy for the Feast of the Transfiguration in the Kremlin's oldest church, the Uspensky Sobor. Although tanks were gathering in Red Square, a stone's throw away, he made no reference to them during the service, only offering one clue about his discomfort. Instead of commemorating the civil authorities and the army as usual, he ended by praying 'for our country protected by God and its people'. On the second day, following Yeltsin's appeal, Alexei issued an announcement from his office by fax. He questioned the legality of the State Emergency Committee, demanded that Gorbachev's voice be heard and pleaded with the army 'not to permit the shedding of fraternal blood'. The statement was carefully worded. Church historian Jane Ellis points out that the Patriarch did not call for the Soviet leader's release and made it sound as if his departure might have been voluntary. Had the coup succeeded, she argues that Alexei 'would have done or said nothing to endanger the church's position with the country's new leaders'.[16]

Neither Alexei nor any of his senior clerics risked a visit to the defenders camped outside the White House. Given that the Imam of Moscow Mosque did show up, along with Catholic priests and Protestant ministers, their absence was striking. A handful of junior Orthodox priests, including Yakunin, responded to the crisis early on. When Yeltsin first arrived, the only queue longer than the one of people waiting to talk to him was that of parliamentarians, fearful for their lives, hoping to be baptised.[17] The atmosphere was especially tense in the early hours of 21 August, when a column of military vehicles drove towards the barricades surrounding the White House. Two young protesters who tried to stop them were shot dead and a third man was crushed under a tank. In response, crowds set fire to a couple of armoured vehicles.

It was at this point that Alexei took the plunge and went live on radio. He opened his address with the words 'Brothers and Sisters', just as Stalin had done in his wartime appeal. This time, the nation was not facing foreign invaders but, said the Patriarch, 'the flames of civil war'. His tone was solemn and personal. Although he called them 'dear ones', he had a clear message for the military: 'Every person who raises arms against his neighbour, against unarmed civilians, will be taking upon his soul a very profound sin which will separate him from the Church and from God. The Church does not condone and cannot condone unlawful and violent acts and the shedding of blood.' He ended with a plea to the Most Holy Mother of God, the Protector of Moscow, 'to preserve all of us'. On hearing the Patriarch's words, some people outside the White House began crossing themselves and bowing. The army did not move in. By 3am, Vladimir Kryuchkov, one of the plotters, phoned Yeltsin and told him there would be no assault that night.

On the morning of the third day of the coup there was an almost festive atmosphere despite the drizzle. One man was strumming his guitar, sausages were sizzling on makeshift fires next to the barricades, while clerics and laymen handed out food and spiritual nourishment. Father Alexander Borisov from the Church of St Cosmas and Damian, head of the newly founded Russian Bible Society, was laden with bundles of New Testaments. He knocked on tank hatches to find out how many soldiers were inside. When nobody answered him, he asked: 'Is this a military secret? We want to give you the Gospel!' Several hands shot up and grabbed the little books. 'In my heart,' he later said, 'I believed that soldiers with New Testaments in their pockets were not going to shoot their brothers and sisters.'[18]

Even though by this point most people recognised that the coup had failed, some members of the Church were still keeping their options open. That same day, just as a plane took off to rescue Gorbachev from house arrest in Crimea, Metropolitan Pitirim

(Nechayev) visited Boris Pugo, the interior minister and one of the junta's leaders. A parliamentary inquiry into the failed putsch the following year condemned the bishop's visit as 'de facto recognition' of the coup plotters. Unlike his patriarch, Pitirim had defended the army's killing of unarmed civilians during protests earlier in the year in the Baltics. Pitrim made a bad investment. Later that day, Pugo put a gun inside his mouth and pulled the trigger.

In the twilight years of the Soviet Union and into the mid-1990s, it looked as if the Church had the potential to bring people together and provide guidance for millions of Russians. Priests played a prominent role in discussions about human rights and crimes committed in the Stalin era. Yet to date, no official reckoning has taken place to identify those in the clergy who betrayed their colleagues by informing on them to the secret police. During heated debates in the Gorbachev-era parliament, impassioned calls were made to examine past complicity and ensure a proper separation of church and state. Would Communism's downfall usher in a new era of integrity?

Events unravelled fast. Gorbachev was sidelined. Although Yeltsin gave him token support, he seemed to enjoy mocking the Soviet leader in parliament that autumn. When Ukraine voted for independence in early December, Yeltsin pounced. He invited the leaders of Ukraine and Belarus, Leonid Kravchuk and Stanislav Shushkevich, to a secret meeting. In a secluded Belarusian hunting lodge, the trio abolished the USSR and Gorbachev's job. All fifteen republics, including Russia, gradually assumed power. On 25 December 1991, as he watched the red hammer-and-sickle flag being lowered from the Kremlin and replaced with the Russian tricolour, Gorbachev put a brave face on it. Instead of mourning his job, he said: 'The threat of world war is no more.'

Communism, as a ruling ideology, had ended. The Soviet Union was dissolved, to be replaced by its fifteen constituent parts. The countries of the former Warsaw Pact had already cast out on their own. George Bush Sr crowed that by 'the grace of God, America won the Cold War'. The triumphant mood in the West was summed up by the political scientist Francis Fukuyama in his essay proclaiming 'the end of history' and the universalisation of Western liberal democracy as the final form of human government.

The sudden dissolution of the USSR left most citizens disorientated and traumatised. On the day the Soviet Union was no more, the headline in *Komsomolskaya Pravda*, a popular daily, mirrored the nation's shock: *Ya prosnulsia—zdras'te! Net sovetskoi vlasti!* ('I woke up, and hello!—Soviet power is gone!'). In amongst the uncertainty, many Russians craved something, anything, to bring back a sense of national pride and identity. As one Presbyterian pastor who lived in Russia throughout the turbulent nineties put it: 'Russians wanted to know more than ever what made Russia uniquely "Russian". Orthodoxy has offered an answer. It has told Russians that their world view is fundamentally different from the West's – as different as Orthodox onion domes are from Catholic and Protestant church steeples.'[19]

Two parallel processes were underway. Freedom of expression and other liberties flourished; entire economic structures collapsed. Within weeks, the system of state-controlled prices vanished. Annual inflation soared to 2,000 per cent. 'Shock therapy', the overnight introduction of market forces presented by Western advisers and enthusiastically introduced by young Russian ministers, impoverished millions. On street corners and outside metro stations, people sat huddled on cardboard boxes trying to sell anything they owned just to stay alive.

Highly qualified academics fed their families by moonlighting as unlicensed taxi drivers. I sometimes felt uncomfortable, even ashamed, to find out that my driver was a genetics professor or a renowned astrophysicist struggling to get by. Salaries in still-state enterprises often went unpaid. In the Altai region of western Siberia, the authorities attempted to pay teachers with toilet paper and coffins before settling on vodka. I will never forget the mortification of one elderly woman when a Japanese TV crew filmed her receiving a box of frozen chicken legs. Brought in as humanitarian food aid from the US, they were dubbed 'Bush's legs', after the president.

Yeltsin, the Communist Party boss from Yekaterinburg turned Russian president, had been the firebrand of reform, champion of democracy. But just two years after his rousing speech atop a tank, his popularity was in freefall. In 1993, the White House again found itself at the centre of a resistance movement — this time against him.

A power struggle pitted the President and pro-market reformers in his government against Communists and nationalists in the parliament. By the third week, the only plausible mediator was the Church. Again, Patriarch Alexei warned against bloodshed and civil war, but this time his words went unheeded.

Two days of talks between the opposing sides in the Danilovsky Monastery ended in failure. Gunshots rang out in the centre of Moscow and Yeltsin's tanks punched gaping holes in the facade of the parliament building. A total of 147 people were killed and 437 wounded, according to government figures. The ten-day constitutional crisis was christened Black October, the worst street violence since the October Revolution of 1917. I remember seeing people standing on the bridge over the Moscow River, only a few hundred yards from the White House, seemingly oblivious of the danger, as if they were watching a firework display. When tank shells slammed into the building some onlookers scattered – others hardly flinched.

With Russia in turmoil, a new cathedral hardly seemed a priority, but a community of believers had already registered in 1990 to agitate publicly for the restoration of Christ the Saviour. The Patriarchate was struggling with a massive repair bill for hundreds of dilapidated churches and monasteries. By rattling collection tins on the streets and in underpasses, the activists had amassed around 60 million roubles by 1993, but inflation at over 300 per cent was eating into the money.[20] Nevertheless, Alexei blessed the *Obshchina*, the community of believers, at a temporary wooden chapel erected near the swimming pool.

Everything changed once Yuri Luzhkov, the mayor of Moscow, became involved. Archpriest Leonid Kalinin, who was responsible for the decoration of the new Christ the Saviour, told me that the mayor's interest was piqued when he was visited by a devout old woman. She presented him with a copy of *The Four Gospels* which she claimed had been salvaged from the destroyed cathedral. It was time, she told him, to restore it to its rightful place in a rebuilt Christ the Saviour. Luzhkov politely thanked her for the book but told her he had no plans to build any churches. 'You might not have plans, but the Almighty does,' she retorted. With that, she swept out of his office.[21] According to Kalinin, Luzhkov got on the phone to Alexei and asked: 'Your Holiness, what do you think about the possibility of reconstructing Christ the Saviour?' The Patriarch answered that it ought to happen but was unlikely during their lifetimes. The mayor admitted he was not a believer, but he saw the Church as a potential business partner. Rebuilding Christ the Saviour would allow City Hall to regain control over a large expanse of precious municipal land, part of which had been handed over to the *Obshchina* activists for their chapel.

Above all, Luzhkov wanted to leave his mark on Russia's capital. So, he allowed the Patriarch to baptise him, and in 1994 the swimming pool was drained and the cranes moved in. The mayor had a reputation for twisting arms and getting the job done. He regularly visited the construction site, TV crews in tow, wearing his trademark leather cap which made him look a little like one of the revolutionary commissars who had destroyed the cathedral. Not everyone backed the project – even inside the Church. Archpriest Mikhail Ardov described it as morally indefensible to spend billions on a new cathedral when Russia, fast becoming a land of 'criminality, pornography, and active satanism', lacked hospitals. He reminded his ecclesiastical superiors of King Solomon's words: 'Except the Lord build the house, its builders labour in vain'.[22]

The Patriarchate insisted the restoration of Christ the Saviour was backed by a majority of Muscovites. According to one survey, 37 per cent were in favour of the project, 33 per cent thought it best to wait for better times and 17 per cent thought it was a waste of money.[23] Tamara, a teacher struggling to raise her daughter in a single-parent household, had no doubts. She received some hard currency in the 1990s by cleaning a foreigner's apartment and donated a hard-earned $100 to the new fund. 'I felt so ashamed for having swum in the pool there when I learned about the cathedral's history,' she told me. 'I didn't like the idea that I was one of those people who had degraded the place. When I saw it rise from the ground again, I was proud.'[24]

Luzhkov's deputy, Vladimir Resin, insisted that society bore moral responsibility for the destruction wrought by 'our relatives and grandfathers'. Man, he said, did not live by bread alone. In any case, he said, the project was being built 'from donations and non-budgetary sources'.[25] A torrent of TV advertisements played up the significance of the cathedral. In one clip, a little boy asked his grandfather where the heart of Russia was. The old man answered, 'Christ the Saviour!' Another featured an old woman trudging through the snow on a village road with a sharp-suited wheeler-dealer and a leather-clad biker with metal rings on each of his fingers. All were eager to donate a handful of kopecks or a fistful of dollars. Igor Ptichnikov, the fund's young director, fresh from a job in advertising, liked telling wealthy New Russians: 'A Mercedes can vanish with one explosion. *This* is an investment in the eternal.' Yet individual donors covered only a fraction of the cost. Ptichnikov admitted that 90 per cent of the 115 billion roubles already collected by the summer of 1995 was corporate money. Most companies obediently invested in the mayor's pet project. 'It's very important to have good relations with the Moscow city government, and people are not averse to paying for this,' he said. 'I'm not concerned about the motivation behind their actions, as long as the money keeps coming in.'[26] Banks, arms exporters, metal, oil and gas firms put their hands in their pockets. The biggest donors had their names engraved on plaques in the crypt, alongside those of officers and soldiers who fell in the Napoleonic Wars. They also received tax breaks, access to prime office space and markets in the capital.

Although some Russians argued against the idea of using foreign money to build the 'patriotic shrine', several multinationals chipped in. Coca-Cola gave $100,000 to help decorate the exterior with statues of Christ, the Virgin Mary and St Thomas the Apostle. The company, which had a dozen plants in Russia at the time, described the donation as 'an act of good citizenship'. McDonald's forked out a similar amount. Philips electronics provided free floodlighting at night. An Austrian firm which had made chandeliers for the Kremlin and replaced lighting in the battle-scarred White House after the 1993 crisis was later asked to recreate Christ the Saviour's pre-revolutionary chandeliers. A prototype with 43 candles was made in Vienna and airfreighted to Moscow, but it was rejected by the design team and the Austrians never got paid.[27]

The foundation stone was laid on Orthodox Christmas, 7 January 1995. It was a freezing day, recalled Archpriest Kalinin, but, suddenly, the sun came out. 'I was standing between two cameras of the main TV channels,' he said. 'When the Patriarch read a prayer, it felt as if a fire had come down from heaven. We sensed the whole project was now under God's divine protection.' Luzhkov said the cathedral would stand as 'symbolic proof of hundreds of destroyed churches and millions of lost lives'. He praised a 'great government' which offered 'not just words but prayers and deeds – prayers to God, words to the people and deeds by building for all of Russia'.

A journalist for the daily newspaper *Izvestia* saw significance in the date for a different reason. The symbol of Russia's spiritual rebirth, he noted, was blessed on the same day that Yeltsin's forces launched a massive air and artillery attack on the rebel Muslim republic of Chechnya.[28] As Russians were finding God, their army was massacring civilians. Four months later, in April, Russian troops gunned down a hundred unarmed women, children and elderly people in the Chechen village of Samashki, sparking international outrage.

While the army fought insurgents in Chechnya, Russia was becoming increasingly lawless. In several towns and cities, shootouts between rival gangs were commonplace. The homicide rate more than tripled from 1988 to 1994; by the end of the decade, it was among the highest in the world.[29] Realising that they might soon meet their maker, many bandits sought solace in God. Garish new tombstones and mausoleums appeared in cemeteries, commemorating mobsters cut down in their prime. They looked nothing like most pre-Revolutionary graves featuring wooden or stone crosses and a small icon of a saint. In Orthodox sepulchral traditions the focus is on the soul of the deceased, not his mortal flesh. But the graves of post-Soviet thugs glorify muscular bodies and pious souls. The 10-foot-high malachite tombstone of one Yekaterinburg kingpin, Mikhail Kuchin, is typical. In a photo engraving, he is pictured wearing a designer suit over an unbuttoned shirt, displaying his bejewelled baptismal cross. To the left of his head and shoulders is a raised Orthodox cross, emphasising his ties with the Church. The cross on the headstone represents his moral purification after death. In one hand he clutches the keys to his Mercedes, as if to make a quick getaway from his everlasting home.[30]

Thousands of churches stood derelict across the country, and the Patriarchate had limited funds to repair them. It was going to need some serious help, and was willing to ask few questions about the provenance of the money. For example, the Church of the Annunciation next to Patriarch Alexei's residence in Novo Peredelkino received nine newly cast bells. Along the circumference of the biggest bell, an inscription in ornate letters read *Ot Solntsevskoi Bratvy*, From the Brethren of Solntsevo. Solntsevo is a western suburb of the capital and the name of Moscow's most notorious mafia group.

When a journalist from an Orthodox website asked Alexei how he felt about this method of obtaining indulgences, the Patriarch insisted there was nothing bad about 'various rich people' helping to restore temples. He added: 'It's better if they spend their money here in the motherland than allow it to float off to offshore zones and wind up in foreign accounts.'[31] By 1995, the Solntsevskaya Bratva ran about 300 banks and large firms, and its leader Sergey Mikhailov (Mikhas) received several of the highest awards of the Orthodox Church, including the orders of Sergei Radonezhsky and that of Prince Vladimir. Alexei personally pinned these honours onto the bandit's chest. The group continues to sponsor several churches in the western suburbs of the capital. 'Many people I know decided to wash away their sins by helping the church,' said Oleg Sysuev of Alfa Bank, reminiscing several years later. 'Lots of dirty money was used in the construction of churches. People have a primitive idea of their religious duty.'[32]

One of the worst gangland showdowns took place around a gold ingot factory five hours' drive east of Moscow. The Soviet authorities chose Kasimov, a picturesque town on the River Oka, to build the Prioksky non-ferrous metals plant. It was tightly guarded by a whole battalion of Interior Ministry troops. But plenty of stolen gold found its way into the town. Bullion bars were hidden in the cistern of the men's toilet and smuggled out. Soldiers and security guards were given wads of banknotes and new Zhiguli cars to look the other way. Factory employees who refused to play by these rules paid a high price. 'If you refused to take gold out of the factory or put it in a secret place, they would come after you to your home,' Natalya Suchkova told me. 'Children were kidnapped, wives were murdered – it was a scary time.'[33]

Suchkova's husband Vladimir had been in charge of the factory construction but died of cancer before the first gold was smelted there. She said he suffered from lead poisoning on an earlier job in Siberia. A successful, and some say ruthless, entrepreneur, Suchkova built her own plant nearby that recycled radio-electronic scrap from Sweden. Her products contained enough precious metal to attract the interest of men with machine guns. 'I think God was protecting me because, you know, in the end we came to an agreement,' she said. Suchkova admitted she had an earthly protector too: Alexander Korzhakov, a former KGB general who served as Yeltsin's personal bodyguard and had connections with the criminal underworld.

Whatever her business dealings, Suchkova left a positive mark on Kasimov by saving an eighteenth-century church that was on the verge of collapse. She told me it was her husband's deathbed wish. 'Back in the late 1980s and early 90s, a lot of people wanted to do this,' she said. 'We were educated as atheists but somehow Orthodoxy is implanted in our genes and in our subconscious.' The Babino-Bulygino Church of the Transfiguration had lost all its windows and was exposed to the elements. Trees were growing inside it when she came to the rescue. She built a new roof, repaired the crumbling masonry, installed golden domes and restored the main iconostasis. Suchkova told me she also rebuilt eleven more churches and helped to rebuild a monastery.

Back in Moscow, the PR machine went into overdrive at Christ the Saviour. The pace of the reconstruction was frenetic, with 1,500 workers on shifts around the clock. Luzhkov wanted the domes to be gilded in time for Easter of 1996, but there was a more important deadline in June that year, elections designed to keep the president in power. The vodka-loving Yeltsin, who was famously 'too tired' to get out of a plane while on a visit to Dublin and was increasingly a liability at official events, was facing stiff competition from the Communists. Luzhkov was also facing his own mayoral elections. He plastered Moscow with billboards which read: 'Cathedral of Christ the Saviour – Symbol of Russia's Renaissance'.

It was not faith in God or Yeltsin which saw off the Communists, but money. Much of it came from a select group of oligarchs – the men who had gained control over Russia's vast natural resources in the notorious loans-for-shares auctions at the start of the decade. Their media empires heaped praise on the President and screened nightmarish films about the totalitarian past to discredit the Communist opposition. They spent millions on political adverts and rallies, small change for the billions they had already been granted. All the while, the West watched, convincing itself of the merits of manipulation for a good cause.

Alexander Smolensky was one of the so-called *semibankirsh-china*, the seven business tycoons who banded together in 1996 to save Yeltsin's re-election campaign. He founded Stolichny, the first private bank in the USSR, which later became SBS-Agro, Russia's largest commercial retail bank. Smolensky donated 53 kilograms of gold to the cathedral and received a medal from Alexei, the order of Holy Prince Daniil of Moscow, the youngest son of Alexander Nevsky and forefather of all princes of Moscow. He received an earthly reward too – the right to manage lucrative accounts of the Moscow Patriarchate.[34]

Neither the Patriarch nor Holy Prince Daniil were much help three years later when the rouble crashed and SBS-Agro was declared bankrupt. Hundreds of depositors lost their entire savings. Soon afterwards, Smolensky was charged with the illegal transfer of $32 million to Austrian banks. He fled to Vienna and the trial never took place; the warrant for his arrest was withdrawn shortly afterwards, on 20 April 1999. When I approached his villa on the outskirts of the city more than two decades later, a voice on the intercom said the banker was in Moscow. Smolensky did not reply to my written request for an interview either.

Smolensky's gold was a generous gift, but only 20 kilograms of it were used to gild the cathedral's domes, instead of the 312 kilograms used on the pre-revolutionary cupolas.[35] These savings were made by spraying golden lacquer between a base layer of titanium nitrate and a protective film of graphite. Luzhkov went to the Patriarch with two pieces of golden metal, asking him which one looked authentic. The Patriarch chose the cheap version. 'See! Even you can't tell the difference,' exclaimed the delighted mayor. He explained that the lacquer was more resistant to ageing and scratching by birds. Crucially, a director from *Mospromstroy,* the construction company, had warned that cladding the roofs with real gold leaf would have taken five to six years – far too long in an electoral year.[36] The ersatz gold was typical for the whole project. Bricks were replaced by concrete enclosed in a thin marble membrane. Artists were essentially told to paint by numbers, colouring in computer-outlined frescos. The art historian Konstantin Akinsha observed that the new Christ the Saviour seemed inspired by Las Vegas.[37]

With help from the oligarchs, Yeltsin secured his second term. Work on the cathedral continued. Yakunin, the parliamentarian and outspoken priest, felt the building symbolised everything that was wrong with post-Soviet Russia. Beneath the marble-clad structure was an underground shopping mall with souvenir and jewellery shops, conference halls and restaurants. Yakunin asked why the building needed a garage with space for 600 cars and 28 lifts, including one for VIPs that went straight up to the altar. 'It is clear that this project has nothing in common with the Cathedral of Christ the Saviour, blown up in 1931,' he wrote in his pamphlet, *The True Face of the Moscow Patriarchate*. 'But this does not embarrass the politicians and Chekists in cassocks.'[38] He was referring to the Cheka, an acronym of Emergency Commission set up by Lenin, which was the first of a succession of Soviet secret police organisations.

Throughout the construction process, Luzhkov, rather than the Patriarch, called the shots. The first architect produced historically accurate designs that went against the vision of the city hall; he was dismissed. Contracts were dished out to the mayor's friends and business partners. The sculptor Zurab Tsereteli, who created several eyesores in the capital, including a gargantuan statue of Peter the Great looming over the Moscow River, designed the cathedral's crosses as well as paintings inside and bronze and plastic figures around the facade. The sacked architect said the bas reliefs made the saints look like 'caricatures or dolls'. The job of producing fourteen new bells was given to the near-bankrupt car factory ZiL, a company under the city administration. An Orthodox Sunday school was originally supposed to be beneath the cathedral, but in a sign of the times, the space was taken by a high-tech media centre to broadcast official ceremonies.[39]

When pressed, officials said the cathedral would cost $250 million. But in 2021, Luzhkov's deputy Resin, later put in charge of Moscow's church building programme, admitted that the expenditure over five years had ballooned to more than $1 billion. Much of the money came from the federal budget at a time of deep economic turbulence.[40] In 1998, the year the rouble collapsed and citizens' savings were wiped out, the government spent nearly $12 million buying icons for Christ the Saviour. Most came from foreign collections and some experts believe the Church paid well over the odds for them. One fifteenth-century icon valued at $150,000 by a respected London dealer was sold to the patriarchal collection for triple the price, at $550,000.[41]

These 'gifts' from taxpayers were sanctioned by Prime Minister Viktor Chernomyrdin and not made public until several members of the Duma, the lower house of parliament, got wind of it. Tamara Gudima, who sat on the culture committee, was furious. 'It is very rare for the government to allocate funds like this because the Church is a separate entity from the state,' she said. 'Thanks to the budget crisis, we have hardly any funding for culture and Russian culture consists of a great deal more than just the Church. So, I am far from indifferent about how this vast sum of state money was spent.'[42] Yakunin, the perennial thorn in the side of the Church, once said it was far easier for him to get hold of the army budget than that of the Moscow Patriarchate. It was especially hard to find out how much was being spent on Christ the Saviour.

The last mural inside the cathedral was completed in late 1999. By this point, Yeltsin had lost all grip on power. The key decisions were being taken by 'the family', a small clique of businessmen and his daughter and son-in-law. Their key task was to find a successor who would restore authority in the country without disturbing the oligarchs' sources of wealth and guaranteeing the Yeltsin family immunity from prosecution. They believed that, in a diminutive former KGB operative from St Petersburg, they had found their man.

On New Year's Eve, Yeltsin went on television to announce that he was stepping down from power. By this point most Russians were pleased to see him go. Both capitalism and democracy, which Russians dubbed *dermokratiya*, or shitocracy, had been largely discredited. The standard of living for all but the super-rich had plummeted, as had life expectancy. Yeltsin asked the country's forgiveness, almost like a penitent seeking absolution. He apologised for 'failing to justify the hopes' of those who believed it would be possible to suddenly 'leap from the grey, stagnating totalitarian past into a bright, prosperous and civilised future'.

Russia may have grown impoverished and lawless, but the Church had emerged stronger. The Moscow Patriarchate had reopened churches and monasteries across the country. It had sent hundreds of chaplains into the army and even worked its way into Russia's nuclear forces. Pilots of strategic bombers had started consecrating their planes before combat sorties and taking icons of patron saints into their cockpit.

On the very last day of 1999, the day of the political transition, Patriarch Alexei performed a small consecration of Christ the Saviour. Then he was invited to the Kremlin for the transfer of power. The new man had specifically asked for the Patriarch's blessing, the first leader to do so since Tsar Nicholas II. This was the first decision taken by Vladimir Putin, the new Vozhd, the supreme leader. The Church was back where it believed it belonged – at the right hand of power.

PART TWO

PRESENT

9. PUTIN AND SPIRITUALITY

'*Do you know who are the only God-bearing people on earth, destined to regenerate and save the world in the name of a new God, and to whom are given the keys of life and of the new world?' The answer, of course, is 'the Russian nation'.*

SHATOV IN *THE DEVILS*, FYODOR DOSTOEVSKY

Wearing nothing but a pair of tight blue swimming trunks, Vladimir Putin walked down a few steps into a specially built swimming pool in the shape of a cross. He dunked himself three times in the freezing water. Each time he emerged, he made the sign of the cross across his pale chest and only slightly flabby stomach. It was a solitary dip – TV cameras aside – to mark the Feast of Epiphany. Across the country, people cut holes in the ice of lakes and rivers and immerse themselves to celebrate the day Christ was baptised in the River Jordan. The tradition, which the President observes every January according to his press secretary, is supposed to toughen the immune system and wash away sins.

On this occasion, people were struck by the colour of the President's trunks. Why, they asked on social media, was he sporting the underwear of his nemesis? Was it some kind of sign? Two days earlier, on 17 January 2021, Alexei Navalny had flown home to Moscow after life-saving medical treatment in Germany. Russia's leading opposition figure had been poisoned with the Novichok nerve agent the previous summer and accused FSB officers of putting the toxin in the lining of his blue underwear. Navalny's supporters had taken to hanging blue boxer shorts from street signs.

But as Putin clambered out of the water, he did not look repentant; he only looked cold. As ever with his photo opportunities, he was making a point. After two decades, after repeated challenges from opposition leaders who came and went, his power was unchallenged. At his side stood the two institutions that had survived the Communist era and the so-called decade of 'chaos' under Yeltsin – the KGB (now called the FSB) and the Church.

A slang term had emerged in the 1990s: politicians who showed up at televised Christmas and Easter services but had only a superficial knowledge of the Orthodox faith were called *podsvechniki*, candlesticks. At the start of his rule, Putin knew little about Church protocol. Sergei Pugachev, a banker and former senator, said that the president asked him how to address the Patriarch before their first meeting. The President was embarrassed to learn that he should say, 'Your Holiness,' and eventually he just said, 'Hello, Alexei Mikhailovich.' The Patriarch thought better than to correct him.[1] Putin's attitude to his marriage seemed at odds with his professed Christianity. A devout Orthodox leader would be unlikely to forgo a church blessing for his marriage, especially when it no longer posed a risk to his career. Yet when Putin and his wife Lyudmila announced their divorce in 2013, he said: 'As for the religious side of the affair, there is none, because we didn't have a church wedding.'[2]

Anna Politkovskaya, one of the earliest Putin critics to be gunned down by contract killers, had long before dismissed his spiritual awakening as political theatre. She concluded that he had replaced the May Day parade with the Easter liturgy as the chief 'obligatory national ritual'. The journalist observed how the President and two of his sidekicks stood to attention in Christ the Saviour during one Easter service 'as if they were at a military parade'. She described how they 'clumsily and clownishly' crossed themselves. The Prime Minister, Dmitry Medvedev, touched his forehead then his genitals. Instead of kissing the Patriarch's hand, the politicians pumped it as if he were one of their comrades.[3] Even if he was on a steep learning curve in matters spiritual, Putin's faith has struck many of his international interlocutors as genuine.

According to his authorised biography, Putin was secretly initiated into the Orthodox faith as a baby. *From the First Person,* based on interviews shortly after becoming president, recounts how his mother christened six-month-old Vladimir with help from a devout neighbour, Baba Anya.[4] His father, a convinced Communist, would have strongly disapproved and would have lost his factory job had the truth got out. Putin added that when he went to Israel in 1993, as part of an official delegation from St Petersburg City Council, his mother gave him his baptismal cross to consecrate at the Church of the Holy Sepulchre in Jerusalem. He said he placed it on the altar as she requested then started wearing the crucifix and has not taken it off since.

Many world leaders seemed happy to buy the line. At a press conference after their first meeting, beneath the majestic Slovenian Alps in 2001, George W. Bush was asked whether Americans could trust Putin. He famously responded that he had looked him in the eye and was 'able to get a sense of his soul'.

Putin insisted that a Bible was always on the presidential plane and that his long journeys gave him ample time to read it. He shared one 'curious story' with CNN's Larry King and later with Bush. He was at his dacha near St Petersburg. Before going into the sauna, he had removed his baptismal cross and left it in the house. Then an electrical fault caused a fire. 'I jumped out with my comrades, practically naked,' he said, 'because everything happened unexpectedly but that cross was very dear to me.' Putin told the fire brigade that the only truly valuable object in the house was his christening necklace – nothing else mattered. The house was destroyed, but later on a fireman opened his hand and, lo and behold, glinting on his palm was the aluminium crucifix. It was enough to convince Bush that Putin 'seemed to believe in a higher power'.[5]

Six years later, the Arizona senator John McCain quipped that he saw something very different when he met Russia's leader: 'I looked into Mr Putin's eyes and I saw three things – a K and a G and a B.' Many years after that, with relations in deep freeze, President Joe Biden claimed he had once told Putin to his face that he didn't think he had a soul. The Russian president later said he could not recall this exchange, adding cryptically: 'When it comes to the soul,

I'm not sure what you mean. One has to think about what the soul is.'[6] Asked by *Time* magazine if he believed in a Supreme God, he snapped back: 'Do you?' before adding there were some things not to be shared with the public at large, 'because that would look like self-advertising or a political striptease'.

At the start of his rule, certainly the first five years, Western leaders held to the conviction that Putin was keen to be at the heart of the international community. Back in 1997, Russia formally joined the G7 at the invitation of Bill Clinton and Tony Blair, turning the group of industrialised nations into the G8. At first, Putin seemed to enjoy being part of the club. 'Russia is part of European culture. And I cannot imagine my own country in isolation from Europe and what we often call the civilised world,' he told the BBC right at the start, in March 2000.[7] Asked whether his country might join NATO he replied: 'I don't see why not.' He had a similar exchange ten months later with Bill Clinton, just before the US President left office.

Putin grew increasingly frustrated at what he saw as the West's double-standards and selective embrace. Despite the 1999 NATO bombing of Russia's brother nation, Serbia, in the Kosovo war, he had supported the post-9/11 invasion of Afghanistan. He had allowed the Americans to use air bases in Central Asia to drive out the Taliban. He hoped to secure backing for his military campaign in Chechnya and to make common cause with other countries battling insurgencies and Islamic terrorism. Two years later, he reluctantly acquiesced to the invasion of Iraq. To his mind, he received nothing in return. Instead, NATO was steadily moving into his backyard, while a series of ex-Soviet republics turned their backs on Russia's economic zone in a bid to join the European Union.

When young activists in the newly independent states organised uprisings against stolen elections, Putin was convinced they had been fomented and organised by hostile outside forces. Georgians may have been proud of their 2003 Rose Revolution in which ordinary citizens, armed with flowers, brought about a non-violent change of power. But Putin accused the West of using 'political technology' to get rid of the Soviet-era incumbent, Edward Shevardnadze, and install what he believed to be a pro-American puppet, Mikheil Saakashvili.

Then came the Orange Revolution. Reports that the results of Ukraine's presidential election run-off in 2004 had been rigged in favour of Moscow's favoured candidate, Viktor Yanukovych, provoked outrage and brought hundreds of thousands onto the streets of Kyiv and other Ukrainian cities.

People were clad in orange hats and scarves and waved orange flags – the colour of the rival campaign fought by the reformist Viktor Yushchenko. The protests were largely peaceful. Celebrities gave free concerts on hastily erected stages. Volunteers cooked cauldrons of soup. Pop and folk music blared from loudspeakers. One in five Ukrainians, and almost half the entire population of Kyiv, took part in the demonstrations. By early December, their efforts were rewarded. Ukraine's Supreme Court ruled that the ballot stuffing had rendered the election results null and void and ordered a revote. Yushchenko's ultimate victory and inauguration as president the following January concluded the largest civic action in Europe since the Velvet Revolution ended communist rule in Czechoslovakia in 1989.

For the first thirteen years after the collapse of the USSR, Russia and Ukraine suffered upheaval and endemic corruption. But the latter's popular uprising was a watershed which set it on a different path from that of its increasingly authoritarian neighbour. Furious that Ukrainians had spurned his candidate, Putin blamed the West. Russia had signed the Budapest Memorandum back in 1994, promising to respect the independence and territorial integrity of Ukraine. But Putin never really accepted his neighbour's status as a sovereign country. To him, international concern over Ukraine's ballot fraud looked like attempts to interfere in Russia's internal affairs.

A year after the disruption in Ukraine, a Tulip Revolution overthrew the kleptocratic president of Kyrgyzstan. Protestors in the former Central Asian republic accused President Askar Akaev of nepotism and election fraud. The Kremlin's reaction was milder than its response to rebellions in Georgia and Ukraine, mainly because small, mountainous Kyrgyzstan was not a candidate for NATO or EU expansion.

Putin's sense of betrayal began earlier than Western leaders fully appreciated and had grown steadily. In late 2004 he vented his frustrations to a group of international experts invited for a late-night discussion at his Moscow residence. It was the first meeting of the Valdai Club, a gathering of Russian and foreign journalists, politicians and academics. Sergei Karaganov, a political scientist and one of the founders, called Valdai a sign that Russia was 'becoming a normal European country'. But the conference took place three days after militants linked to the separatist insurgency in Chechnya attacked a school in the nearby Ossetian city of Beslan. When security forces stormed the building, attempting to end the hostage crisis, 330 people were killed, most of them children. At the late-night meeting with Putin, one British journalist expressed condolences. Then he asked if the Kremlin's policies towards Chechnya might have led to the tragedy. After two military invasions, thousands of dead, rigged elections and countless bomb attacks, Moscow appeared further away than ever from victory in its 'war on terror'. Putin began by acknowledging the unfair treatment of Chechens under Stalin. Patiently he explained that the question of the autonomous republic's independence from Russia had been subverted by Islamists with a bigger goal. But after a 30-minute historical treatise, he had a question for the journalist: 'Would you like it if people who shoot children in the back came to power, anywhere on this planet? If you asked yourself that, you wouldn't ask any more questions about Russian policy.'[8]

By 2007, the grievance that would go on to underpin his entire world view had become entrenched. Addressing the Munich Security Conference, he accused the United States of creating a unipolar world, of using 'an almost unrestrained, hyper use of force' and of hypocrisy over the invasion of Iraq. 'We, Russia, are constantly being taught about democracy,' he said. 'But for some reason those who teach us do not want to learn themselves.' He signalled that Russia would no longer adhere to a number of agreements on post-Cold War European security.

Alarmed by the 'colour revolutions', Putin was determined to keep the democracy virus out of Russia. Elections for regional governors were abolished in 2005 as he cracked down on civil society. Grassroots activists were dragged into court rooms; Russian NGOs which received grants from abroad were branded 'foreign agents'. This was not his first assault on political freedoms at home.

Within months of taking power in 2000 he replaced the head of the most outspoken television station, NTV. Over the next few years, he would bring all the checks on his power – media, judiciary and parliament – firmly under control.

Putin's response, whenever challenged, was a mixture of quasi-legal measures, thuggery and the beginnings of an ideology. He began praising the Soviet past, especially the Great Patriotic War, while downplaying the crimes of the Communist era. He called the demise of the USSR 'the greatest geopolitical tragedy of the century'. He later clarified his position – to a degree. 'Anyone who doesn't regret the passing of the Soviet Union has no heart,' he said. 'Anyone who wants it restored has no brains.' The West did not warm to him but there was a measure of respect. The same year that Putin chastised the Munich Security Conference, *Time* magazine made him person of the year for putting Russia 'back on the map', for choosing order before freedom and for creating 'stability in a country that has hardly seen it for 100 years'.[9]

Putin was not wistful about Communism. He was nostalgic for a more distant past – the glory days of the Tsarist Empire. To recreate this world, with twenty-first century trappings, there was one essential partner – the Orthodox Church.

To neutralise any possibility of uprisings like those seen in Ukraine and elsewhere, he needed a new organisation. The answer was a nationalist youth group, *Nashi*, Ours. I had my first glimpse of them in the winter of 2005 at a crowded cross-country ski lodge on the outskirts of Moscow. A familiar tang of boiled cabbage mixed with cigarette smoke drifted down the corridors. Groups of teenagers and twenty-somethings sat around tables with coloured pens and large sheets of white paper trying to invent catchy slogans about their feelings for their motherland. *Russia's future is in our hands! We Will Resurrect Our Country, Forward with Russia, America Can't Outshine Us!* they shouted as a wiry man in a tracksuit sprang between the tables, urging them on.

They reminded me of the Soviet-era Komsomol youth league, only more stylishly dressed. 'What we are doing here is looking for young people with leadership qualities,' said the founder, Vasily Yakemenko, a clean-cut young man with a steely gaze. 'After two days of training we'll pick out the most ambitious ones, the ones who haven't lost their hope in Russia.' Putin, he told me, was surrounded by bureaucrats and defeatists, liberals and oligarchs. To enable the President to pursue his grand plans, he needed to train a new generation of 100,000 young Russians, some of whom he claimed would soon be ready to start running the country instead of denigrating it and selling off its assets. The group became notorious for harassing opposition leaders, writers they disapproved of and even foreign diplomats. One UK ambassador who attended a conference of political opposition parties in 2006 had indignant Nashi members demonstrating outside his embassy and pounding on the bonnet of his car in traffic jams. At its peak the group had 300,000 members and 50 regional branches.[10] It was funded by pro-government businesses and direct subsidies from the Kremlin. But at the outset of Putin's third term as president in 2012, Nashi disbanded. The group was supplanted four years later by the more regimented Youth Army, a movement established under Russia's defence minister, Sergei Shoigu.

For all Yakemenko's bluster, Nashi was the brainchild of Putin's mercurial chief ideologue, Vladislav Surkov. After three years at Moscow's State Institute of Culture, where he studied theatre directing, Surkov excelled in the art of illusion. He invented the phrase 'Sovereign Democracy' – shorthand for pretending to give voters a choice while continuing Putin's authoritarian rule. Surkov is also godfather to the post-truth world. The notion that there is no such thing as the truth, only alternative truths, was the cardinal principle of Moscow's 24/7 English language TV Channel Russia Today, later rebranded RT. It went on air in April 2005, a year after the uprising in Ukraine, to compete with the likes of the BBC and CNN. Its slogan, 'Question More', was ironically created by an American public-relations consultancy; it set out to challenge what Russia's Foreign Minister Sergey Lavrov called a 'post-West world order'.

Putin may have spent the first sixteen years of his career working for an intelligence agency which promoted atheism and relentlessly persecuted believers, but his embrace of Orthodox Christianity is not as strange as it sounds. It dawned on the FSB that the Church was the only institution which still had a presence across all the former

Soviet republics. The Kremlin was no longer in charge from Kyiv to Vilnius, and in the other direction to Tbilisi. By contrast, the Moscow Patriarchate had property and prestige across the former Soviet Union – even in the majority Muslim countries of Central Asia.

The triangular relationship between Putin, the Church and the FSB was transactional – and became highly effective. For more than 70 years, the Communist Party had tried to destroy the Orthodox Church. But it survived and the party disappeared. Now it would take the place of the party and provide the ideological framework for Putinism both at home and abroad.

Filipp Bobkov was head of the KGB's 5th Directorate, responsible for combating ideological subversion, which included religious dissent. Yet in his memoirs, he recalls a wide-ranging internal discussion 'about how destructive the nihilist attitude toward religion was for the country'.[11] In a speech in 1981 to senior officials, he suggested that believers should no longer be treated as 'second class citizens' since many millions of them 'worked very hard in Communist brigades' and had defended the country during the war. He had come to the same conclusion as Stalin: atheism could not be relied on to instil patriotism.

Putin was of the same persuasion. Even before he grew disillusioned with the West, he and his KGB colleagues had begun actively courting the Church. The place which epitomises this extraordinary volte-face is just around the corner from Lubyanka Square, headquarters of the FSB and former home to the KGB. The Church of St Sofia of God's Wisdom was blessed by Patriarch Alexei in a ceremony in 2002 attended by the head of the FSB, Nikolai Patrushev. Balding and sandy haired, Patrushev is the archetypal *silovik*, the Russian term for strongman. The two men swapped icons: Patrushev presented the Patriarch with his heavenly patron, Saint Alexei, and in return received a gilt-framed image of St Nicholas. For many Russians, the consecration of the FSB church would have served as a reminder of the revelations regarding Alexei's own past as a KGB agent – something which the Church continues to deny officially, despite conclusive documentary evidence from the KGB archives.

Andrei Zubov, a theologian who was present, was struck by the airbrushing of the past. 'I expected to hear some words in memory of those millions of people who suffered, and the hundreds of thousands who died in or were sentenced to death by the Lubyanka,' he said. 'But I did not hear a single word, not a single memory of these myriad sufferers, as if they did not exist.' St Sophia is now the intelligence agency's official church. Operatives pray beneath a fresco of the warrior saints Alexander Nevsky and Dmitry Donskoi, renowned for their victories over foreign invaders.

The church, part of a monastery built in the late seventeenth century, was not always a sacred space for the secret police. For decades it had been used as a KGB storeroom and dormitory, before the Ministry of Culture turned it into a workshop to mend broken sculptures. When I visited in 1991, services had just started again. The sanctuary was still cluttered with wheelbarrows, the floor caked in clay dust and there was a fridge on one side of the altar. Yet on that rainy Sunday morning, it was so packed I could hardly squeeze inside.

I had come to a liturgy led by Father Georgy Kochetkov, a popular preacher and disciple of the murdered priest and intellectual Aleksander Men. When Kochetkov graduated from a Leningrad seminary 1983, the KGB tried to block his ordination because his sermons were so popular. Not long after my first visit, I heard that Kochetkov was in trouble again. He had tried to make the liturgy and rituals more accessible by using modern Russian instead of Old Church Slavonic. Traditionalists were livid. Nor did they appreciate the Bible discussion groups he organised outside the church – to them, these smacked of Protestantism. So, in the winter of 1994, Kochetkov's parishioners were thrown out of St Sophia by Cossacks armed with whips.

The purge was orchestrated by Kochetkov's successor, Tikhon Shevkunov, a media-savvy monk who swiftly ascended the Orthodox hierarchy. Today he is often called 'Putin's confessor', something he refuses to confirm or deny. What is beyond doubt is that the two are exceptionally close. The pair were introduced back in the 1990s by Sergey Pugachev, a banker now living in exile in France. According to Pugachev, their meeting was fortuitous; he had been working with the future president on a project connected to foreign assets and then gave him a lift into the city centre. 'I initially wanted to drop him off somewhere but in the end, I asked if he wanted to come to the monastery with me,' Pugachev said.[12] 'He had never been to a church before, and the service was in the sanctuary. It was wonderful that he got to see all of it.'

A former film school student, Shevkunov is a leading proponent of Russian exceptionalism which harks back to Filofei, the sixteenth-century monk who declared Moscow was the Third Rome. Early on Shevkunov was wary of the West. He sensed that perestroika was a dangerous force and feared its impact on the Orthodox church. Just before he was tonsured – the ceremony in which some hair is cut off as part of a monk's initiation – he wrote an article in which he argued that a democratic state 'will inevitably try to weaken the most influential Church in the country, bringing into play the ancient principle of divide and rule'.[13] Nearly two decades later, he presented a TV documentary, *Lesson of Byzantium*, which argued that Orthodox Russia had to withstand the West or sink without trace like the Byzantine Empire. For him, a church infiltrated and run by people with a strong KGB heritage was not only desirable but necessary.

Shevkunov's views echo those of Ivan Ilyin, an early twentieth-century religious thinker who was deported by Lenin after the October Revolution. He left on one of the so-called philosophers' steamships, along with more than 200 intellectuals, expelled to prevent their ideas from contaminating the new-born Soviet Union. In exile in Germany, Ilyin became a leading ideologue for the anti-Communist White movement. He opposed the Soviet regime not out of liberal idealism, but because it was the wrong sort of authoritarian. Russia, in his view, transcended the corrupt Western world and had a spiritual affinity with the Euro-Asiatic nations. Ideas such as democracy and individual freedom, he argued, were alien to the world's biggest country. The only way Russia could survive as a state with its ethnic and cultural diversity spread over such an immense landmass was by maintaining strong centralised power under an autocratic leadership, preferably a monarchy. Ilyin was a fan of both Mussolini and Hitler.

In 2005, Putin had the philosopher's body exhumed from a grave in Switzerland and reburied in Moscow's Donskoy Monastery. That same week, in the same cemetery, Anton Denikin, the White Army general in the Russian Civil War, was also laid to rest. His remains had been flown over from Michigan where he died in 1947. Just before he annexed Crimea in 2014, Putin instructed all his regional governors to read Ilyin's book *Our Task*. Ilyin had often argued that Russia could not call itself an empire without Ukraine.

Putin also recommended books by two other religious philosophers: *Justification of the Good* by Vladimir Solovyov and *Philosophy of Inequality* by Nikolai Berdyaev. Parts of Solovyov's work would be endorsed by human rights activists. He insisted 'the only moral norm is the principle of human dignity or of the absolute worth of each individual'. Berdyaev was also a passionate advocate of freedom. He argued that Ilyin's outlook was a perverted vision of Christianity every bit as heartless as the Bolsheviks. 'All the reactionary and revolutionary inquisitors, beginning with Torquemada down through Robespierre and [KGB founder Felix] Dzerzhinsky, esteemed themselves as bearers of goodness and not seldom also of love. They always murdered in the name of goodness and love,' he wrote.[14]

The chosen authors have very different ideas about the relationship between church and state so why did Putin bundle them together in one reading list? Perhaps it was to muddy the waters, given that Ilyin is often described as a fascist. Plausible deniability has long been a hallmark of the Kremlin. But the three writers have one thing in common – they believe in the historical uniqueness and special purpose of the Russian people. Long before the invasion of Ukraine, a new political, cultural and religious concept crept into Putin's speeches, that of the *Russkiy Mir*, Russian World.

‡ ‡ ‡

The notion of a great culture with a holy mission appeals to those yearning for superpower status after a loss of empire. The *Russkiy Mir* concept infuses nationalism with a sense of a larger destiny. It resonates at home and abroad, including among the 30 million Russian compatriots now living outside the Russian Federation. It is invoked when members of this diaspora, the third largest in the world, complain of discrimination against Russian speakers, 'unfair' requirements for citizenship, or 'disrespect' for Soviet war memorials.

After spending a decade in prison, the oligarch Mikhail Khodorkovsky, now exiled in London, established Open Russia – one of many Russian organisations abroad that seeks to counter the

Kremlin narrative. One of Putin's fiercest critics, he says the Kremlin bankrolls the Orthodox Church and supports it as the main unifying force in the country. 'In return,' Khodorkovsky says, 'the church has been the key promoter of a "Russian World" concept that casts the Kremlin as a defender of Russians outside of Russia.'[15] When Putin created the *Russkiy Mir* foundation in 2007, officials presented it as a soft power outfit with similar aims to the British Council, Alliance Française or the Goethe Institute. Its website quotes Russia's best-known female poet, Anna Akhmatova, who chronicled the darkest days of Stalin's Great Terror and the Second World War.[16]

Trustees of the foundation included Metropolitan Hilarion, then head of the Department of External Church Relations, and Vladimir Yakunin, a former KGB officer who was later boss of the Russian railways. Yakunin, a prominent Orthodox oligarch, chairs the Foundation of St Andrew the First Called, which has spent millions of dollars each year flying a holy flame from Jerusalem all over Russia as if it were an Olympic torch. He also sponsors international 'pro-family' organisations to promote Russia's geopolitical agenda. *Russkiy Mir's* stated aim is 'to promote understanding and peace in the world by supporting, enhancing and encouraging the appreciation of Russian language, heritage and culture'. In Russian, the word for world and peace are the same: *Mir*.

Russian priests have traditionally splashed holy water on weapons from muskets to ballistic missiles. A few years before the invasion of Ukraine, there was disagreement in Orthodox circles about the morality of such rituals. Some clerics were against the practice. Some thought it was fine to bless machine guns, tanks and submarines, but wanted to draw the line at weapons of mass destruction. Russia's president and patriarch seemingly have no such qualms. In 2007, Putin described Orthodoxy and nuclear weapons as 'twin elements of Russia's domestic and foreign security'. Two years before he was anointed patriarch, Metropolitan Kirill consecrated the nuclear arsenal. 'We should remember all those who laboured on the creation of Russia's nuclear shield,' he said. 'Because it prevented a third world war and spared mankind nuclear catastrophe.'

In the 1990s, after the Soviet collapse, when nuclear scientists working in closed cities were underfunded and demoralised, Kirill came to their aid, sounding more like a defence minister than a metropolitan. Addressing the government, president and parliament he warned it was 'the duty of the responsible state to prevent the collapse of Russia's nuclear weapons complex'. Kirill called nuclear weapons specialists 'outstanding people' whose capacity for sacrifice reminded him of the early Christian hermits living in caves, forests and deserts. 'In the spiritual sense, I saw in front of me Eremites,' he said. 'These people who possess colossal intellectual potential, mastering the highest technologies, who could have easily enriched themselves, have totally devoted themselves – their power, time and lives to preserving the security of our Fatherland and the security of the whole planet.'[17] These comparisons with religious ascetics may not be as far-fetched as they might sound. The birthplace of Russia's atomic bomb and the centre of its nuclear industry is in Sarov, 450 kilometres east of Moscow. In Soviet times the town was called Arzamas 16 and was impossible to find on any map.

This city, which remains closed to outsiders and is surrounded by dense pine forests, is also home to one of Orthodoxy's greatest saints. Seraphim of Sarov, born in the late-eighteenth century, was a renowned mystic and healer. He greeted those who came to see him as 'My Joy' and taught them how to attain the Holy Spirit through love. His best-known saying is: 'Acquire a peaceful spirit, and around you, thousands will be saved.' The Church made him patron saint of Russia's nuclear arsenal. In October 2023, Kirill credited the work of scientists from Sarov with saving Russia. 'By the ineffable providence of God, these weapons were created in the monastery of St Seraphim,' he said. Were it not for their work, he added, 'it is difficult to say if our country would still exist'.

Since the seventeenth century, a system called *dedovshchina* (literally rule of the grandfathers) has subjected army recruits to grossly abusive treatment at the hands of more senior conscripts. Dozens are murdered every year, thousands are traumatised. As some of the more egregious cases surfaced in the media in the late 1990s, Kirill pushed for a revival of military clergy. 'Where there is an active pastor in a military unit, the moral climate improves,' explained Archpriest Dmitry Smirnov, who chaired the Patriarchate's Department for Co-operation with the army and law enforcement. 'Suicides and escapes will be reduced, hazing will practically disappear, and servicemen will be filled with spiritual motivation to carry out their military duty.'[18]

A new generation of ideologues has sought to combine the traditional spiritual values of the tsarist empire with twenty-first century military might. Following in the footsteps of Ilyin, the philosopher Alexander Dugin argued in ultra-nationalist publications in the early 1990s the case for Russian exceptionalism. His book *The Foundations of Geopolitics* urged Russia to rebuild its influence over the former Soviet territory through alliances and annexations. Ukraine, in his opinion, had 'no geopolitical meaning' and 'no ethnic exclusiveness as a state'.

In 2008, after two terms as president, Putin was required by the constitution to step down. He endorsed First Deputy Prime Minister Dmitry Medvedev as president and stayed on as prime minister. Few doubted who was in charge, but Putin maintained the trappings of democracy. In Russia and abroad, some people tried to take the new president's talk about the rule of law at face value. Medvedev lambasted citizens for bribing police officers and stealing intellectual property while government officials dipped into state coffers and interfered in the decisions of court judges. In September 2011, he announced he would not run again and would swap jobs again with Putin. In theory, the transition needed voters' approval, but opposition parties were hobbled. Anger over suspected electoral fraud in the December 2011 parliamentary election triggered the biggest anti-government rallies in Moscow since the fall of the Soviet Union. Tens of thousands gathered to condemn alleged ballot-rigging and demand a rerun. More than a thousand people were arrested, and protest leaders like the anti-corruption campaigner Alexei Navalny were jailed.

Two years later came the caesura which put Europe onto the path of war. Ukraine's president, Yanukovych, abruptly ditched plans to sign a historic pact with Brussels – the long-awaited EU association agreement. Although it was mainly an economic document setting up a free trade area, it had political and strategic ramifications for Ukraine and other post-Soviet countries, like Georgia and Moldova, keen to move out of Moscow's orbit. Under pressure from Putin, who offered cheap gas and credit lines, Yanukovych did a U-turn and signed a rival agreement with Russia instead. As soon as the news hit Kyiv, protests broke out on *Maidan Nezalezhnosti*, Independence Square. Over the winter months, the demonstrations grew. On 20 February 2014, more than a hundred protesters were shot dead by the Berkut, an elite paramilitary force loyal to Yanukovych. Many were taking cover behind improvised shields when they were targeted by masked riflemen. As the bodies piled up, the crowd's outrage reached boiling point. The President lost his nerve and fled the country in a helicopter. Putin was furious at this turn of events but, ever the master tactician, he exploited the chaos to annex Crimea and foment war in the Donbas region of eastern Ukraine.

These events became milestones in Putin's ideological journey.

In 2016 he took with him a retinue of priests, officials and businessmen to Mount Athos to celebrate 1,000 years of Russian monks' presence on the Holy Mountain in northern Greece. He attended a service in the St Panteleimon Monastery, which is dominated by Russians. At one point, a deacon with a gravelly baritone voice bowed his head to Putin and intoned a prayer for 'our revered President Vladimir Vladimirovich, the government, and army of our God-protected fatherland'.[19] Putin thanked the hierarchs from twenty monasteries for lending holy relics to Russia, including the Cincture of the Theotokos, the Virgin Mary's belt, adding that 11,000 Russian pilgrims visited the Holy Mountain each year. He said his countrymen sought closer bonds with Athos to reaffirm 'spiritual traditions and common values'.

The ultra-nationalist philosopher Dugin, who sees Russia and Orthodoxy as inseparable, was part of the delegation. 'Our culture and our morals are baptised in Christianity,' he declared. 'You saw that even in communism. Collectivism was a secularised form of the Russian Orthodox community spirit. Likewise, I see individualism in the West as a secularised form of Protestantism.'[20] Dugin's presence was to be expected. It was more surprising that Vladislav Surkov, the mastermind behind *Nashi*, also tagged along. He was not often seen in church. Instead of icons, Surkov had a portrait of Tupac Shakur in his office and was known to idolise the American rapper. He also wrote a post-modernist novel, *Almost Zero*, a thinly disguised autobiography which savagely mocks the Orthodox faith. The hero, a corrupt PR guru called Yegor, launders the reputations of various gangsters. His biggest and richest client has a church as well as a massive sauna in his gated complex and dreams of having his own live-in bishop. Surkov's presence suggested that paying respect to the Orthodox faith, whatever your own beliefs, had become imperative for anyone in Putin's circle.

Visiting Athos and donating money to restore monasteries and churches was one way of proving Orthodox credentials. Joining the Izborsk Club was another. Founded by the novelist and ultra-nationalist newspaper editor Alexander Prokhanov, it was named after an ancient fortress near the Estonian border. Members are high-ranking clerics and officials, including Putin's supposed confessor Metropolitan Tikhon Shevkunov. Its mission is to be 'an imperial front that opposes the manipulations of foreign centres of influence'. Early on it lobbied for the return of Crimea, insisting that the peninsula was part of Russia's Christian heritage. Putin picked up on that theme in a speech justifying the annexation: 'The territory itself is strategically important because it is here that the spiritual source of the diverse, but monolithic Russian nation is located.' Crimea, he said, where Grand Prince Vladimir converted to Orthodoxy, had 'enormous civilizational and sacred significance', just like the Temple Mount in Jerusalem.

The Izborsk Club was like a seed bed. In this fertile ground, Orthodox and nationalist ideas sprouted and flourished. It received grants from the presidential administration to develop its 'Doctrine of the Russian World'. Published in 2016, it advocated 'the formation of Russian spheres of interest' to compete with the West in the Balkans and the Black Sea, and argued that Russians in Ukraine were victims of the 'Russophobia' of a Ukrainian government that had fallen under the influence of 'neo-Nazis'. The doctrine maintains an unbreakable bond between the Slavic peoples – Russians, Ukrainians and Belarussians, united by a single 'Orthodox Civilisation'. Through its local branch in the eastern Ukrainian city of Donetsk, the Izborsk Club cultivated the separatist movements. One of its members, a journalist and spin doctor, Valery Korovin, presented his book entitled *The End of the Ukraine Project*. It argued that Ukraine was an 'artificial entity created by Lenin', incapable of becoming a state in its own right. By now this was a standard view. It would reach its apogee when Putin spent his summer in 2021 writing an extraordinarily detailed essay on the impossibility of Ukrainian nationhood, which would serve as his supposed intellectual justification for the full-scale invasion of Russia's neighbour in February 2022.

✝ ✝ ✝

Kirill took over as patriarch in 2009, at a time when Putin had all but given up on the West. The head of the Church had long been intrigued by the thesis set out in 1992 by Samuel Huntington in his 'Clash of Civilisations'. Huntington argued that religious and cultural identities, rather than rival ideological systems based on economics, would be the primary source of conflict in the post-Cold War world. Kirill cleaved to the idea of a distinctly 'Orthodox' civilisation, governed by Russia and comprising much of the former Soviet Union, Eastern Europe, Cyprus and Greece.[21] Putin agreed with both, but for him the key driver was the return of *derzhavnost,* great power status.

Everywhere Putin looked, Moscow had lost ground. Its former vassals in Eastern and Central Europe had severed or loosened ties, most of them now members of both the European Union and NATO. Few of the fifteen ex-Soviet republics, apart from Belarus and some of the authoritarians in Central Asia, could be relied upon to provide support. The same applied further afield. According to several accounts, Putin was haunted by footage of the inglorious end of Libya's Muammar Gaddafi in 2011; he played the blurry video again and again of the dictator being seized from a drainage pipe full of rubbish and lynched.[22] Putin told a news conference that 'his corpse was shown on all global television channels, it was impossible to watch without disgust'. Notionally only the prime minister at the time, Putin was furious with the then supposed president, Dmitry Medvedev, for not helping Gaddafi.

The wave of uprisings that swept across the Arab world was triggered when a fruit stall vendor in Tunisia set himself on fire in protest at police harassment. Soon after, in January 2011, Tunisia's president, Zine El Abidine Ben Ali, became the first leader of an Arab nation to be pushed out by a popular uprising. The Arab Spring, as it became known, quickly spread and toppled President Hosni Mubarak of Egypt, who had been in power for 30 years. By February the unrest reached Yemen, Bahrain and Libya.

The action then moved to Syria. At the beginning of March, a dozen teenagers in the southern town of Dee'ra, southern Syria, tagged the wall of their school with the words 'Your turn, doctor', referring to President Bashar al-Assad, a trained ophthalmologist. When the boys were tortured in police custody, protests erupted. Rallies across the country were initially peaceful, with calls for democratic reform, but as they gained momentum, the regime turned its guns on the crowds. Soon the country descended into civil war, which also fuelled the rise of ISIS and other hardline Islamist groups. At least twice, Assad's government was on the verge of collapse, and it was saved largely by outside players, not least Putin.

Russia could ill afford to dispense with Assad, one of its last allies in the Middle East. Putin also needed to secure the naval port of Tartus in the west of the country, his forces' only access to the Mediterranean. The Kremlin feared the Arab Spring was a rerun of the 'colour revolutions' closer to home. Self-preservation and geopolitics were the chief motives for Putin's intervention, but the Church had already provided him with a useful imprimatur. At the time, Metropolitan Hilarion had put what he called 'Christianophobia' at the top of his agenda. In exchange for backing Putin's return to the presidency in 2012, he asked him to promise to protect Christian minorities in the Middle East, many of whom are Orthodox. The Moscow Patriarchate had been unnerved by the mass flight of Christians following the US invasion of Iraq. Syria's Christians, a tenth of the population, sided with their government from the outset of the civil war. They feared they would be persecuted, even wiped out, if Sunni Muslims succeeded in getting rid of Assad.

When Kirill first flew to Damascus in November 2011, the Church stressed that 'any interpretation of the patriarch's visit to Syria as support for the Assad regime is totally unfounded'. But soon after landing, he headed a street procession with his counterpart, Ignatius of Antioch, surrounded by people holding portraits of the Syrian leader. The Patriarch later went to the presidential palace to present Assad with a silver chalice, handcrafted in the Urals. All smiles, the

Syrian president reminded those present that it was from Damascus that Christianity began to spread across the world thanks to the labours of St Paul. He boasted that Syria gives 'a wonderful example of the peaceful coexistence of various religious communities'. Nobody at the meeting mentioned the mounting civilian death toll. Two years later, several hundred Syrians died in a series of chemical gas attacks.

In 2015, Russia launched airstrikes. Kirill called the use of military force, the first outside the borders of the Soviet Union since the end of the Cold War, 'a responsible decision' which would 'protect the Syrian people from the woes brought on by the tyranny of terrorists'. His spokesman praised the 'holy battle' against terrorism. It was meant to signal that Russia was back on the world stage, defeating terrorism and protecting the Christians of the Middle East who had been abandoned to their fate by the West. The Greek Catholic Archbishop of Aleppo said Putin was 'solving a problem', describing the airstrikes as a source of hope for Christians targeted by jihadi groups.[23]

Putin had assured the Duma that Russia's intervention would be limited to air power. Yet when Assad's depleted forces were about to give way, up to 5,000 Russian mercenaries came to the rescue. The Wagner Group, the shadow army set up by Putin's former chef, Yevgeny Prigozhin, was deployed overseas for the first time in Syria. One former Wagner fighter, who sought asylum in France and wrote a book about his experiences, said his fellow soldiers had beaten Syrian army deserters with sledgehammers and beheaded them.[24] These attacks were filmed to intimidate others. While such horrors were unfolding, the Church helped to justify the 'holy crusade' in Syria to citizens back home at a time of economic downturn. Russian media reduced the war to a contest between Assad and violent Salafi jihadism. Anything which did not fit this picture was ignored or vilified. It came as little surprise therefore that a poll conducted two months after the Kremlin's intervention showed a majority of people backed the war in Syria, despite the costs.

The Imperial Orthodox Society of Palestine was founded by Tsar Alexander III to strengthen Orthodoxy in the Holy Land and support Russian pilgrims. It was the brainchild of Konstantin Pobedonostsev, the reactionary procurator of the late-nineteenth century, and revived in 1992 under a new head, Sergey Stepashin, the first FSB chief under Yeltsin. The former counterintelligence chief visited Israel in 2008 to discuss Russia's property claims and stressed the geopolitical as well as real-estate gains. 'A Russian flag in the centre of Jerusalem, in such close proximity to the Holy Sepulchre, is invaluable,' he said.[25] The society's members include senior Kremlin officials as well as Orthodox oligarchs such as Konstantin Malofeev, owner of Tsargrad TV, a channel modelled on America's Fox News, ultra-conservative and with slick production values. Malofeev has described Putin as 'the best and the only leader who is trying to make Russia a state where Christians can live and can save their souls for eternal life'.

Another member, Sergei Gavrilov, is a Communist deputy who chairs a parliamentary group on civic and religious organisations. One of Russia's richest MPs, he paid for a monumental statue of Christ on top of the Cherubim Mountain in the Syrian city of Saidnaya in 2013. Three years later, another MP, Dmitry Sablin, rebuilt a 1,600-year-old monastery in Maaloula, in the mountains north-east of Damascus. He planned a hotel there to welcome Russian pilgrims. The town is one of the last places left on earth where Aramaic, the language of Jesus, is still spoken.

The Russian Church continues to insist that it alone can defend the Middle East's Christians, as it has done through the ages. In the eighteenth century, Catherine the Great liked to compare herself to her ancient Syrian counterpart, Queen Zenobia. She dreamed of reclaiming Constantinople for Christianity. Russians, as one of her favourite court poets put it, should 'advance through a Crusade' to the Holy Lands and 'purify the River Jordan'.

Putin claimed the credit for 'purifying' Palmyra, an architectural gem in the Syrian desert which was seized and heavily damaged by IS in 2015. Syrian government forces recaptured the ancient city from the terror group ten months later, with Russia's help. Weeks later, a 'celebratory liberation' concert was performed by St Petersburg's most famous orchestra and broadcast around the world. It took place in the same Roman amphitheatre used by IS to execute captured Syrian soldiers. Speaking live from his palace in Sochi, Putin praised the role of Russian forces in the operation. He said the concert was dedicated to the victims of 'international terrorism', which he called a 'terrible evil'. It was a piece of masterful propaganda catapulting Russia onto the world stage.

The 'Russian World' ideology draws on the Eastern Orthodox tradition of *symphonia* – an ideal harmony between church and state. In his first two terms as president, Putin had helped the loyal Patriarchate to reclaim its authority over millions of Orthodox believers around the world. In so doing, he also regained a foothold in parts of the former Soviet empire where he no longer had political power. A schism brought about by the October Revolution and the murder of the dethroned Tsar was gradually coming to an end.

The Church in Moscow controlled by the Communists was known as the Red Church. An alternative White Church, or the Russian Orthodox Church Outside Russia (ROCOR), was set up by the émigrés who fled the country with the White Army. Horrified by Metropolitan Sergius' 1927 oath of loyalty to the godless Soviet state, the émigré priests and bishops broke ties with the Moscow Patriarchate. This emigrants' church became the first globalised Russian (non-Soviet) institution, with 400 parishes spread from Europe to the US and to Australia. Initially based in Serbia, then West Germany, it moved its headquarters to New York in 1950. It attracted those who had been forced abroad, from artists to scientists, providing spiritual succour and helping them to stay in touch with their lost homeland. ROCOR was fixed on pre-revolutionary Orthodoxy as the only acceptable model for the moral future of the nation. It embodied a romantic vision of the 'other Russia' which émigrés believed had been stolen from them by the Bolsheviks. This 'other Russia' made Putin uneasy. With Communism gone, he argued that ROCOR was an anachronism. The fact that nearly half of its parishes were in the US made it doubly suspicious. He wanted one united Russia with one Orthodox Church.[26] Making this happen would not, however, be a straightforward process.

Sister Vassa Larin, a Russian-American nun, grew up in a staunchly ROCOR family. Her father Georgiy was the Orthodox

Patriarch Kirill of Moscow and All Rus with President Vladimir Putin after the liturgy in Kyiv, Ukraine, a year before the annexation of Crimea on 27 July 2013. (Shutterstock)

Vladimir Putin bathes in ice-cold water on Epiphany near the St Nilus Stolobensky Monastery on Lake Seliger in Svetlitsa, Russia, on 19 Jan 2018. (Kremlin Pool / Alamy Stock Photo)

Swimming Pool Moskva in 1980, built two decades earlier by Soviet leader Nikita Khrushchev on the site of the destroyed Christ the Saviour Cathedral. (Fmaschek, CC BY 3.0, via Wikimedia Commons)

Christ the Saviour Cathedral, built on the site of the swimming pool, is the main church, or see, of the Moscow Patriarchate. It was consecrated in 2000, the year Putin became president of Russia. (Pedro Szekely, CC BY-SA 2.0, via Wikimedia Commons)

Ivan the Terrible and his son Ivan on 16 November 1581 by Ilya Repin, one of Russia's leading nineteenth-century artists. It depicts the grief-stricken Tsar who ruled from 1547 to 1584 cradling his dying son after striking him with his sceptre in a fit of rage. (Tretyakov Gallery, Moscow)

Oryol, southern Russia, 14 October 2016: Orthodox banner-bearers at the unveiling ceremony for a new statue of Ivan the Terrible on horseback. Their black flag, decorated with bones, daggers and skulls, reads 'Orthodoxy or Death'. (Alexey Borodin / iStock)

Patriarch Nikon presents revised liturgical books to the clergy and court, which he claimed were closer to the original Greek texts. But Tsar Alexis Mikhailovich looks unimpressed, perhaps sensing Nikon's reforms will tear the Church apart. (Artist: Alexei Kivshenko, 1880)

Left: Olga of Kiev (reigned 945–62), the true precursor of Christian faith among the Eastern Slavs. Her grandson Vladimir/Volodymyr converted his subjects in Kievan Rus to Christianity in 988. This mosaic is in the new Cathedral of Russian Armed Forces outside Moscow.

Below: Archpriest Avvakum Petrov rejected the reforms of his former ally, Patriarch Nikon. He and some other Old Believers were exiled to Russia's Far North, imprisoned for 14 years and burnt alive in 1682. (Painting by Pyotr Myasoyedov, State Museum of the History of Religion, Moscow)

Feodosia Morozova, a noblewoman and famous partisan of the Old Believers movement, was arrested by supporters of Patriarch Nikon in 1671. Carried off on a sled and defiant to the last, she raises two fingers rather than three – the old way of making the sign of the cross. (*The Boyarynya Morozova* by Vasily Surikov, 1887)

Above left: Under Peter the Great, the Church was transformed into a pillar of the absolutist regime. He abolished the Moscow Patriarchate, replacing it with a Holy Synod subordinate to the state. Portrait painted by French artist Jean-Marc Nattier, during the Tsar's visit to France in 1717. (Hermitage Museum, St Petersburg)

Above right: Ivan Mazepa, the Cossack leader and Hetman of the Zaporizhian Host, angered Peter the Great by switching his allegiance to King Charles XII of Sweden. On the Tsar's orders the Church excommunicated Mazepa and all contemporary portraits of the Ukrainian commander were destroyed. (Natalia Pavlusenko created this likeness in 2017 as part of her series Heroes of Cossack Ukraine)

Above left: Konstantin Pobedonostsev was the arch conservative chief procurator of the Holy Synod, a position he held from 1880 to 1905. An inveterate pessimist, his favourite activity was attending funerals. (Portrait by Sergei Levitsky, 1902)

Above right: On 15 August 2000, the Church announced it was turning Nicholas II and his immediate family into saints. Icons depicting the seven royals with halos are now ubiquitous in churches, homes, offices and cars. (Aliksandar, CC BY-SA 3.0, via Wikimedia Commons)

Above left: Patriarch Tikhon (Bellavin), the first Patriarch of Moscow and All Russia since Peter the Great. Elected in the maelstrom of the October Revolution, he compared his fate to that of the prophet Ezekiel, who had to eat a scroll on which was written 'lamentation, and mourning, and woe'. (Courtesy of Keston Digital Archive, Baylor University, Texas)

Above right: An anti-religion poster from the Brezhnev era. The paper on the fisherman's hook is a ticket to the heavenly kingdom, but the little poem underneath mocks the idea of an afterlife and warns against lies. (Courtesy of Keston Digital Archive, Baylor University, Texas)

Throughout the enforced atheism of the Soviet era, millions of grandmothers kept the Orthodox faith alive. In this poster, the little boy longs to play with his fellow pioneers in the sunshine but his granny is trying to drag him into a dark corner to worship an icon. (Courtesy of Keston Digital Archive, Baylor University, Texas)

Nuns at a Moscow funeral in the early 1960s – possibly that of Hegumen Nikon (Vorobyev), who died on 7 September 1963. (Courtesy of Keston Digital Archive, Baylor University, Texas)

A young boy lights a candle in church. He may belong to a Russian diaspora community since the picture is marked ACER, which stands for Action Chrétienne des Etudiants Russes – a youth movement founded in France by Orthodox believers who fled the Revolution. (Courtesy of Keston Digital Archive, Baylor University, Texas)

The Christian dissident Zoya Krakhmalnikova, who was imprisoned then exiled for the underground distribution of forbidden texts, known as samizdat. She is pictured here with her baby grandson Filip, who was in his cot when police barged into their country home in the summer of 1982 to arrest her. (Courtesy of Keston Digital Archive, Baylor University, Texas)

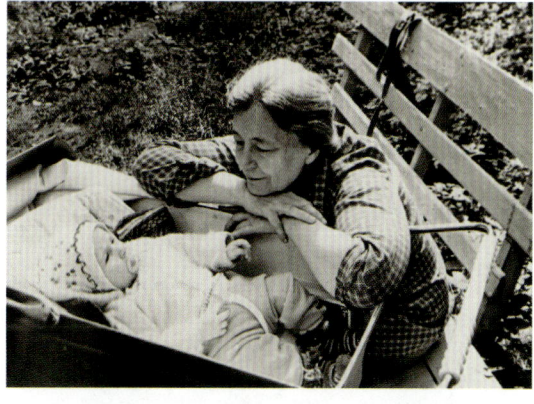

The priest and dissident Gleb Yakunin. In the mid-1960s he accused the government of lying to foreigners about the extent of religious repression in USSR. After the collapse of Communism, he investigated links between the KGB and the Church. (Courtesy of Keston Digital Archive, Baylor University, Texas)

Above left: Mikhail Gorbachev and Ronald Reagan in front of St Basil's Cathedral in 1988. The US President told Gorbachev that if he could guarantee religious tolerance, attitudes in America towards the Soviet Union would change dramatically: 'You will be a hero, and much of the feeling against your country will disappear like water in hot sun.' (National Archives Catalog)

Above right: The Main Cathedral of the Russian Armed Forces opened in 2020 in the 'military Disneyland' of Patriot Park on the outskirts of Moscow. Monumental and khaki-clad, the floors and steps are made from melted-down German tanks from the Second World War.

Icon carriers: Rejoice at the unshakeable pillar of the Church! Old lady: You'd be better off praying that they don't cut our pensions. (Drawing by the artist and activist Victoria Lomasko, from her book *Other Russias*)

Tombstones of gangsters cut down in their prime feature sharp suits, jewellery and expensive cars along with Orthodox symbols. This one is from a cemetery in Yekaterinburg, the hometown of Boris Yeltsin and the setting for some of Russia's bloodiest turf wars in the 1990s. (Amos Chapple/RFE/RL)

Above left: Archbishop Kirill of Smolensk and Kaliningrad in 1988. Kirill was born Vladimir Mikhailovich Gundyayev in Leningrad on 20 November 1946. He later claimed he was banished to Smolensk in the early 1980s as a punishment for opposing the Soviet invasion of Afghanistan. (Courtesy of Keston Digital Archive, Baylor University, Texas)

Above right: Kirill's mentor, Metropolitan Nikodim (secular name Boris Rotov) of Leningrad and Novgorod. A KGB agent assigned the codename Svyatoslav, the bishop's ecumenical activity with the Roman Catholics and the World Council of Churches served to further Soviet foreign policy. He died in his prime of a heart attack at the feet of the astonished, newly enthroned Pope Jean Paul I in the Vatican. (Courtesy of Keston Digital Archive, Baylor University, Texas)

In November 2014, Maxim Mitrofanov was ordained Flavian, Bishop of Cherepovets and Belozersk, at a ceremony presided over by Patriarch Kirill in the Cathedral of Christ the Saviour in Moscow. Mitrofanov fled Russia six years later claiming that he was being blackmailed by the FSB. (Courtesy of the Diocese of Cherepovets)

Above left: This poster reads: JOIN THE RANKS OF PUSSY RIOT! Artist Victoria Lomasko was an early chronicler of the feminist collective who sang their notorious punk prayer in the Christ the Saviour Cathedral, begging the Mother of God to rid Russia of Putin. (Victoria Lomasko)

Above right: Victoria Lomasko sat in the Tagansky District Court with her sketch pad throughout the Pussy Riot trial. The women were charged with hooliganism motivated by religious hatred. Here a priest argues that for such an act in Tsarist Russia, the defendants would have been sentenced to death. 'Quite right,' the cleric behind him says. (Victoria Lomasko)

Above left: Margarita Gracheva's husband cut off both of her hands with an axe when he suspected her of flirting with work colleagues. She had already told police about his aggressive behaviour, but officers ignored her complaints. In 2017, with the backing of the Church, Putin signed a law softening the penalties for domestic violence.

Above right: Oksana Pushkina in her office in the State Duma holding a copy of her draft legislation on domestic violence. The former parliamentary deputy was a member of Putin's United Russia party but, appalled that the penalty for wife beating was equivalent to a parking ticket, she campaigned, without success, to change the law.

Crimea's chief prosecutor Natalia Poklonskaya carried a portrait of the last Russian tsar on Victory Day celebrations in Simferopol in May 2016. Later, as a Duma deputy, she tried to ban a film about an affair between the young Nicholas II and a ballerina. She said showing saints having sex 'offends the feelings of believers'. (MAX VETROV/AFP via Getty Images)

Andrei Kormukhin, a businessman and leader of the Sorok Sorokov movement (Forty Forties, named after the number of churches in pre-Revolutionary Moscow), was fiercely opposed to introducing restraining orders for violent partners. He said the proposed law would 'lead to the genocide of the Russian family'. (Natela Sulakvelidze)

Above left: The ultra-conservative Sorok Sorokov was set up partly in response to Pussy Riot in 2013. Their website calls them 'a public movement consisting of Orthodox Christians, but open to anyone who wishes to defend their country and its traditional spiritual-moral values'. (Natela Sulakvelidze)

Above right: A knight in armour and church spires on the insignia of Sorok Sorokov. With the backing of clerics, the group formed 'Orthodox squads' to protect religious places from 'blasphemous acts' and attacked people protesting against the building of new churches in city parks. (Natela Sulakvelidze)

Putin at the Russian-dominated monastery of St Panteleimon on Mount Athos in 2016. He was accompanied by Patriarch Kirill as well as Kremlin officials and businessmen. The President said he was convinced that the Russian connection to Greece as well as to holy Mount Athos 'could only get stronger', but Greek and Russian clerics have fallen out over Ukraine. (Shutterstock)

Pope Francis kisses the pectoral cross of Metropolitan Hilarion Alfeyev, the Archbishop of Budapest and Hungary. Once seen as Kirill's successor, Hilarion was sacked from his position as the Church's foreign minister in 2022. (Independent Photo Agency Srl / Alamy Stock Photo)

Patriarch Kirill visited Moscow's Pokrovsky Convent twice in 2023. It is run by Abbess Feofaniya, an enterprising nun who persuaded the Church to turn a Soviet-era mystic into a saint. Apart from the convent, the abbess runs an Orthodox school, a farm and two hotels, but was told to give up her £100,000 Mercedes-Benz S-Class sedan in 2020 and direct donations to charity. (Photo Archive Moscow Patriarchate)

The five-day Velikoretsky procession is one of the largest pilgrimages in Russia. It is held each June to venerate the icon of St Nicholas supposedly found in the fourteenth century next to the Velikaya River. Exhausted believers rest in fields to sleep, eat and bandage blistered feet. (Nikolai Ignatiev, 1995)

Above left: Archimandrite Cyril Hovorun, a Ukrainian theologian who once worked closely with Kirill, has also been cast out by the Russian Orthodox Church and now serves Constantinople. Ostensibly defrocked for co-celebrating a liturgy with the Exarch of the Ecumenical Patriarchate in Ukraine, his outspokenness against Russia's invasion is the true cause of his dismissal.

Above right: Deacon Andrei Kuraev, theologian, missionary and perennial thorn in the side of the Church. After he was definitively defrocked by Kirill in 2023, he joined the Patriarchate of Constantinople and no longer lives in Russia.

Above left: Local carpenters Alexei Malofeev and Mihail Manovsit on the roof of the Church of the Transfiguration, which they helped to restore in the village of Turchasovo, near Lake Onega in Russia's Arkhangelsk region. August 2013. (Richard Davies – White Sea Publishing)

Above right: The Kalitinka Chapel on the verge of collapse in the Kargopol district of the Arkhangelsk region. Photographer Richard Davies travelled around the Russian north documenting the wooden churches there and people's attempts to restore them. (Richard Davies – White Sea Publishing)

Above left: Father Gerontiy Chudnevich spent 15 years behind bars for aggravated robbery. On release, he was blessed by Patriarch Kirill's own confessor to travel beyond the Arctic Circle and build churches. Chudnevich began with the reconstruction of the northernmost monastery in the world on the shores of the Barents Sea, founded in 1533 by Saint Trifon of Pechenga, himself a repentant robber. (Svetlana Stasenko)

Above right: Atrocities committed by Russian troops in Bucha on the outskirts of Kyiv at the beginning of the invasion galvanised many countries into sending weapons to Ukraine. During the occupation, the authorities had to dig a mass grave for murdered civilians behind Father Andriy Golovin's Church of St Andrew. He told me some bodies were missing arms, legs and genitals.

The Svyatohirsk Lavra, one of Ukraine's major Orthodox spiritual centres, overlooks the Siverskiy Donets River. Two monks and a nun were killed in May 2022 when Russian forces fired rockets and artillery shells at the monastery, even though it belongs to the Ukrainian Orthodox Church (Moscow Patriarchate) – UOC-MP – and conducts its sermons and official business in Russian. (André Luís Alves)

A former FSB officer, Igor Girkin, known by his *nom de guerre* Strelkov, or 'Shooter', bragged that he was under holy protection when he first led Russian 'volunteers' into battle in the Donbas region in 2014. He claimed all his personal bodyguards were monks from the Svyatohirsk Lavra. (André Luís Alves)

Above left: In 2016 a statue of Grand Prince Vladimir, patron saint of the Russian Orthodox Church, was unveiled next to the Kremlin. At the ceremony, Vladimir Putin called his namesake 'a far-sighted politician who created the foundations of a strong, unified, centralised state'. (Fotokot197 / iStock)

Above right: Ukrainians reacted with fury to Moscow's monument. They call the tenth-century prince, who converted his subjects to Christianity, the founding father of their country. Kievan Rus existed long before Moscow was on the map. A statue of St Volodymyr, as he is known in Ukraine, overlooks the River Dnieper in Kyiv where the Eastern Slavs were first baptised in 988. (André Luís Alves)

Father Georgiy Edelstein at his home in the Kostroma region. The 90-year-old priest was one of the first Russian clerics to condemn the invasion of Ukraine. 'We cannot close our eyes and call black white, evil good, and say that Abel was probably wrong and provoked his older brother,' he told his congregation.

The nineteenth-century Transfiguration Cathedral in Ukraine's Black Sea city of Odesa was destroyed in 1936 by Stalin. It was painstakingly rebuilt and reconsecrated by Patriarch Kirill in 2010. But in July 2023 Russian forces attacked it again, reducing a large part of it to rubble. (André Luís Alves)

Submarines, ballistic missiles, tanks, Soyuz space rockets and other pieces of military hardware are routinely blessed, but before the Ukraine invasion some clerics thought the practice should stop – especially for weapons of mass destruction. (Ministry of Defence of the Russian Federation)

A woman prays over an almost intact icon from the Spaso-Preobrazhensky (Transfiguration) Cathedral damaged by a Russian ballistic missile strike, Odesa, 23 July 2023. (André Luís Alves)

priest in Nyack, an enclave of exiled Russians on the banks of the Hudson River, just north of Manhattan. Christened Barbara, she and her older sisters were raised to speak Russian at home, English at school and to understand Slavonic in church. They wore long skirts and observed all the feasts and fasts of the Orthodox liturgical calendar. Her mother was very strict about behaviour in church. When she was too small to sing in the choir, Vassa had to stand for the entire liturgy facing the sanctuary. She was not allowed to turn her head to the back of the church to see if any school friends were there. The family would travel to Manhattan to picket the Russian Consulate, protesting against the treatment of dissidents in the USSR. A large portrait of Nicholas II hung in her parents' house. She remembers how it made her 'heart ache with sorrow'. At Orthodox summer camps in the Catskills, she and her sisters sang and marched to pro-monarchy songs. Echoing Count Uvarov's slogan of the early nineteenth century, they were taught three cardinal values: Faith, Tsar and Fatherland.

There were virtually no canonical differences between the churches headquartered in Moscow and New York. They abided by the same liturgical rules, Old Church Slavonic language, Julian calendar, and the pantheon of saints. The ROCOR statutes declared that it would not reunite with Moscow until the fall of 'the godless regime'. Even after the collapse of Communism, Vassa's father opposed reunification. As far as he and his compatriots were concerned, the Red Church was morally bankrupt, as it had collaborated with the Soviet authorities and was 'infested with KGB officers'. The initial approaches from Moscow were spurned. Metropolitan Laurus, who headed the White Church, refused to meet Putin at a reception in the Russian Embassy in Washington in 2001. He also turned down an invitation to visit Russia.

Two years later, though, Laurus had a change of heart, partly engineered by a German cleric. Archbishop Mark, born Michael Arndt, converted to Orthodoxy in his early twenties and later became metropolitan of Berlin and Germany. As early as the 1990s, he initiated dialogue between German dioceses of the ROCOR and the Moscow Patriarchate. By 2003 he was president of the commission on talks between the two churches. He was helped by a lay middleman.

Boris Jordan grew up in an observant Orthodox family on Long Island. His grandmother was a maid of honour to Empress Alexandra and his great uncle was Nicholas II's physician. In 1992, after graduating from university, Jordan went to Moscow. In the early days of post-Soviet capitalism, he made a fortune privatising state assets. He also funded an academy for cadets where boys were meant to be educated along the tsarist principles of 'national identity, orthodox faith, and discipline'. In April 2001, he took over NTV, the television channel, confiscated from another oligarch who was too independent. NTV had angered Putin with its lack of deference and no holds barred reports on the Second Chechen War.

Before long, the President had found another job for the young New Yorker. At a private meeting in 2001, Jordan said Putin had told him that he knew he was a religious person, before adding: 'I believe that the reunion of the churches is a very, very important thing. One of the most important things you can do is to help in the reunification of the churches, much more so than anything you're doing in television or business. This is probably the most important thing you can do in terms of your legacy.'[27]

Jordan enlisted an acquaintance, Peter Holodny, another young investment banker who was also a priest. Holodny grew up in the parish of St Seraphim of Sarov on Manhattan's Upper West Side and had talked of forging ties between the two churches. After the Revolution his grandfather, Alexander Kiselev, fled to Estonia where he served as a priest. His altar boy was the future Patriarch Alexei II. In the early 1990s, Alexei invited his former boss to Moscow and installed him in the Donskoy Monastery. ROCOR saw this as toadying up to the Moscow Patriarchate and expelled him. Despite this, Kiselev's grandson Peter was ordained in the émigrés' church in 1993 and made its treasurer. The skills he picked up at JP Morgan and Lehman Brothers came in useful. He had also worked in Moscow for the oligarch Mikhail Prokhorov.

As a ROCOR insider, Holodny pulled a few strings and helped to persuade Laurus to meet Putin at the consulate in New York. The atmosphere was tense until the Metropolitan presented the President with an icon of the last Russian empress, killed by the Bolsheviks. Putin took the hint. 'I want to assure you all that the godless regime is no longer there,' he told the priests. 'You are sitting with a president who is himself a believer.'

Holodny said he was inclined to take Putin at his word. 'I mean if it had all gone wrong, he would have looked pretty bad, right? He went to dinner in New York with these seven clerics who told him to go fly a kite. You know he wouldn't look very presidential. I think he took a pretty big risk.'[28] The émigrés' fears were partly assuaged by the fact that in 2000 the Orthodox Church had canonised Nicholas II and his family along with hundreds of clerics who became victims of Stalinist terror. Now it finally looked as if Moscow was prepared to accept some responsibility for past crimes against the Church.

Vassa recalls how hopeful she felt when Vladimir Vorobyov, head of the foundation of the St Tikhon Orthodox Theological Institute in Moscow, began researching Russia's pantheon of new martyrs in 1992. She believes that another factor may have persuaded Laurus and her father, who was stridently anti-Communist, to join forces with Moscow. 'We were completely out of union with most of Orthodoxy,' she said. 'Some of us were worried about the ROCOR turning into some kind of sect. After all, the separation from the mother church was only meant to be temporary.'

Archbishop Mark instructed Vassa to comb the archives for material which might heal the breach. Different interpretations of the Great Patriotic War were an important sticking point. A number of members of the clergy of the ROCOR had blessed General Andrei Vlasov, the Red Army commander who collaborated with the Germans and was later executed for treason. But during the war, some people in the White movement, including military officers and Orthodox clerics, felt Vlasov offered Russians the best chance of overthrowing Stalin. Nevertheless, in May 2006, after four days of debate at a conference centre in San Francisco, clergy and laity from the Church Outside Russia voted for reunification. Jordan had helped to fund the conference.

Holodny categorically denied that the ROCOR was offered any money by the Moscow Patriarchate as a sweetener. He told me the only financial benefit was that they no longer had to spend large sums on lawyers. For years, the two churches had rowed, sometimes violently, over access to sites in the Holy Land. To this day the ROCOR owns part of the Garden of Gethsemane and the Church of Alexander Nevsky, close to the Church of the Holy Sepulchre, built on the rock where Christ stood when Pilate read him his death sentence. Some were surprised that the descendants of the first wave of the émigré community were willing to trust the Moscow Patriarchate. Both Kirill and Metropolitan Tikhon Shevkunov, who helped to engineer the reunification – 'a superb steward and very charismatic', according to Holodny – were close to Putin. By 2007 it was clear that inside Russia, opposition voices were increasingly silenced and that top positions were going to present and former security agents. It was no secret that the Patriarch, along with virtually every senior cleric, had collaborated with the KGB. Yet many émigrés were impressed by the talk of spiritual renewal in the Church. Some also shared Putin's vision of Russia's greatness and uniqueness. They were stuck in the exile's time warp, treasuring memories of a glorious imperial past. It is revealing that many would enthusiastically greet the annexation of Crimea seven years later.[29] Senior clerics in the ROCOR would also refuse to condemn the full-scale invasion of Ukraine in 2022. They told their parishioners to avoid the unreliable coverage in the Western media, as it was damaging for their spiritual health.

There is another surprising element in the reunification story, the influence of Americans with no ethnic ties to Russia who have converted to the Russian Church over the last two decades. The rugged green foothills of the Appalachians in West Virginia are home to about 30 monks. At the Orthodox Monastery of the Holy Cross, the brothers support themselves by making incense and soap, which they sell online. Their animals provide them with cheese, milk, eggs and mountain honey. They have developed a unique style of Orthodox chanting based on English texts. All but one of the monks – and nine out of ten of the parishioners they serve – are American converts to the Russian Church. Most are from evangelical and Catholic backgrounds. Most are on the conservative to far-right of the political spectrum. Almost all of them admire Putin. There are two Russian Orthodox parishes in this area – the Church of St John in the nearby town of Woodford, which attracts between 30 and 50 people each Sunday, and the monastery itself, which has a handful of regular parishioners who live nearby. Alongside the Orthodox locals, the monastery attracts religious pilgrims from around the world. An anthropologist who spent several months in the area would invariably run into monks and Orthodox laypeople at the nearest supermarket.[30]

At first glance, the small community seems incongruous. In the valley below, Wayne County is a land of fast-food restaurants and Walmart stores. How were a sizable number of its citizens persuaded to pray in front of icons of Nicholas II and look to Tsarist Russia for a model? The answer lies in their disenchantment with Western democracy and their desire for closer ties between church and state. What mattered to them more than American political power was white supremacy and religiosity.[31] Putin was their ideal champion. One of the converts told the anthropologist Sarah Riccardi Swartz that he was so alarmed by the secular liberalism taking over American society, he hoped Russia would invade the US and establish a monarchy.

For most of the twentieth century, American conservatives were viscerally anti-Russian, while liberals favoured detente. The abbot of the monastery, Father Seraphim, a Benedictine monk before he converted to Orthodoxy, says today it is the other way around: 'Our country now represents anti-Christianity and Russia represents Christianity. Russia is trying with all of its might to hold up Christian morality and Christian belief and defend Christians. There's no one speaking up for persecuted Christians except for Russia. But if Putin says something, or Patriarch Kirill says something, the liberal press tears them apart.'[32]

Reunification brought one million church members in thirty countries into Moscow's orbit. In the US alone, this amounted to 323 parishes and 20 monasteries. The agreement was meant to safeguard its ownership of properties across America and Europe, where the rival churches had competed for funds and the faithful. Despite assurances that their property rights would not be affected and that they would be a self-governing branch within the Moscow Patriarchate, some were sceptical. One expert said that once ROCOR rejoined the mothership, it would enjoy as much independence as Eastern European countries did under the Soviet Union.[33]

In an instant, the enlarged Patriarchate controlled the appointments of clergy across the world. The globalised Church became a vital foreign policy instrument, acting as the Kremlin's mouthpiece in international organisations such as the UN and Council of Europe. It would go on to sanctify wars and attack universal human rights in the name of traditional Christian values.

The stage was set for a lavish reunification ceremony. Bells rang out at the Cathedral of Christ the Saviour on 17 May 2007. Patriarch Alexei was dressed in a bright green robe with red stripes and Metropolitan Laurus wore a pale blue cape over his cassock, decorated with gold embroidered crosses. Despite the splendour of their vestments, they were upstaged by the man standing between them. Tellingly, instead of first thanking God in his speech, Alexei thanked the President. The Patriarch stressed that the reunification could only have happened because the ROCOR saw in Putin 'a genuine Russian Orthodox human being'. The President replied that the split in the Church was the result of 'a deep political crisis in Russian society', and that bringing the ROCOR back into the fold would reunify the nation. Archpriest Maxim Kozlov, rector of a church at Moscow State University, called the reunion 'a genuine miracle of God'. It was, he said, as if the warring families in Verona had 'forgotten all past grievances, prayed together over the coffin of Romeo and Juliet and forever condemned the institution of the blood feud'.

Dave Brownstone tried not to panic on his Aeroflot flight when he noticed a dark blob on his shoe. He was on his way to Moscow with several plastic pouches of ink strapped to his legs and his midriff. One of them had started to leak. Sweating profusely, he made a beeline for the toilet and spent several minutes disposing of the leaking pouch and cleaning up the mess. There was a long queue when he finally emerged. When he showed his passport to the border guard at Sheremetyevo Airport, he prayed nobody would look at his feet. Brownstone had not come to Moscow to buy *matryoshka* dolls or to admire Red Square; he had been sent by a Protestant missionary group. He and his wife spent much of their free time driving around Eastern Europe, secretly delivering Bibles to remote locations at the dead of night. A thousand of the holy books fit snugly in the average camper van – it had become almost too easy. By the early 1980s, he was looking for a fresh challenge.

A group of Christians in Moscow had procured a printing press to produce Bibles in Russian, but they lacked one thing – ink. Some had tried to make their own version from melted car tires, butter and vodka, but this combination tended to jam the clandestine press. So, a succession of 'tourists' were flown in and instructed to hand the carefully packaged bags of ink to go-betweens at metro stations using a pre-arranged password. 'I knew that people were putting their life, or at least their freedom, on the line to read the Bible,' said Brownstone. 'As a committed Christian, I felt I had to help them.'

By the end of the decade, the city was awash with the holy books. A Dutchman famous for his bible-smuggling ministry had offered a gift of one million New Testaments to the Russian Orthodox Church to coincide with its millennium celebrations. Other donations flooded in and many of these free Bibles were later sold to believers, on the grounds that money was desperately needed to restore church buildings. Plenty of budding entre-preneurs also got in on the act. Russia's first private banker, Alexander Smolensky, had a job in a state printing shop. When his shift was over, he printed black market Bibles – and made a kill-ing. Evangelicals flooded in. In 1991, I watched a preacher from Virginia whip up the crowd in a packed Moscow cinema. He told them now was the time to 'win millions and millions and millions of Russian souls for Jesus Christ'. The following year, in the giant Luzhniki sports stadium, men and women of all ages were thrust-ing their arms in the air and swaying to high decibel Christian rock music. 'Everything is so hard now,' Irina, in her forties, told me at the 1992 prayer gathering. 'I'm a highly qualified engineer and I can barely feed my kids. Our country has been destroyed and we have been lied to all our lives. I need to believe in something that brings me joy and some hope.'

If Putin made the Moscow Patriarchate richer and more powerful with his reunification of the churches project, he rendered another important service almost as soon as he took office. His intelligence officers helped Orthodox clerics keep foreign faiths out of Russia. Although roughly two-thirds of the population consider themselves Orthodox, the Moscow Patriarchate does not welcome competition, especially from other Christian churches.

Legislation passed by Gorbachev revolutionised the former Soviet Union by separating religion from the state. It enshrined the freedom to follow any religion or to follow none and it allowed all faiths equal status. In the post-Communist era of Yeltsin, many people were eager to experiment, to search for the new. In terms of religious freedom, Russia was one of the most unfettered places on the planet. Whenever I boarded an internal flight or travelled by train, I would invariably bump into foreign missionaries, hungry for converts. Many were only dimly aware that these Eastern Slavs had adopted Christianity many centuries before the pilgrim fathers boarded the *Mayflower* for the New World. But they had money.

A backlash soon began. Patriarch Alexei compared the intrusions of foreign preachers to NATO's eastward expansion. He complained to the British ambassador about people exploiting vulnerable Russians who were just emerging from the horrors of Communism. Evangelical sects from America, he said, were trying to bribe his adherents with offers of humanitarian aid in exchange for attendance at prayer meetings. Alexei was particularly disparaging about Hare Krishna groups chanting their mantras along Tverskaya, Moscow's main shopping street. Astrologers, clairvoyants and witches' covens, he grumbled, were flourishing.[34]

The Patriarchate lobbied for laws banning foreigners from proselytising and demanded greater support for Russia's 'traditional confessions'. Parliament voted for the amendment in August 1993, but Yeltsin refused to sign it. With a failing economy, he relied on international support. He also noted that those in favour of restrictions were mostly the communists and nationalists who opposed him. 'It is impossible to erect a new iron curtain and legislate one's own isolation from the rest of the world,' parliamentarians were told.[35]

Four years later, a much weaker Yeltsin almost lost an election to the communists. He was rescued not just by the oligarchs but also by Alexei, who had instructed his flock on how to vote. The new law could be seen as a thank you present from the President to the Church. It turned the clock back to the Soviet era. In an impassioned speech, Metropolitan – and future Patriarch – Kirill defended it when he met a foreign delegation in January 1998. The Orthodox Church, he told them, the cornerstone of Russian identity, was like the Bolshoi Theatre, while religious minorities were 'small amateur troupes from the provinces'. Equality, he said, would be an infringement on the rights of the Church that 'would be forced to decline to exercise its thousand-year mission in Russia, consequently, to fall into sin before God and the people'.[36]

Only the four official religions – Orthodoxy, Islam, Judaism and Buddhism – would be recognised as legal entities. Other faiths, including Catholicism and Lutheranism, which had existed in Russia for hundreds of years, were downgraded to 'religious groups', stripping them of many rights. They were banned from working in schools, printing or distributing religious literature, holding public meetings or inviting foreigners to work as clergy or preachers. Nearly a third of the country's 89 regions enacted their own restrictions on the so-called subversive faiths. In some places, clerics from outcast denominations had to submit their sermons for official scrutiny. The Patriarch did not hide his animosity towards the world's largest Christian denomination – the Catholics. Polish-born John Paul II had tried several times to visit Russia, only to be rebuffed. As the first Slav Pope, he had long dreamed of a reunion with the Eastern churches that split from Roman Catholicism in 1054. But to Alexei, Christian unity under the Church of Rome was unwelcome.

Orthodox distrust goes as far back as 1448 when Isidore, Metropolitan of Kyiv and Moscow, returned from Italy and tried to promote a union with the Catholic Church. He was imprisoned in a monastery before escaping and fleeing Russia. Little has changed in modern times. In 2002, five prominent Catholic clerics were expelled after a Vatican announcement that four of its so-called apostolic administrations in Russia would be upgraded to full dioceses. One month later, four Catholic priests, including the Bishop of Irkutsk, were prevented from returning to Russia from abroad; they were told that their names were on the security services blacklist. No official explanations were provided but FSB officers hinted that the priests were suspected of espionage. Protecting Russia's religious identity has been treated as a matter of national security. The Vatican protested the priests' innocence, insisting they were merely providing pastoral services to Russia's 500,000 Catholics. Today the number has shrunk to 180,000, just 0.1 per cent of the population, as many have since died or emigrated.

The state also harasses Protestants. The story of one Baptist preacher is instructive. Towards the end of the Soviet era, Yuri found God when he was working in Norilsk, a former gulag camp and the world's biggest nickel mine. The remote Arctic city is one of the most polluted places on earth. It had a few small, stunted trees and no churches until the metallurgical factory where Yuri worked helped to build one for its workers, the Evangelical Christian Baptist Church of Reconciliation. 'It seems incredible that a Protestant Church was built by a state owned factory but we didn't make such a big distinction between Catholics, Orthodox and Protestants back then – we were just all excited about discovering Christianity,' he told me.

Yuri later became a pastor and moved to a city south of Moscow where for more than a decade he led a thriving ministry with outreach work in schools, prisons and hospitals. He was eager to help drug addicts and alcoholics. Many of his school friends had wound up dead or in prison. He told me that his church supported low-income families and took children on camping trips. But gradually more restrictions stifled the work; permission for activities outside the church premises was withdrawn. The Orthodox diocese complained of an invasion of their canonical territory. Online chat rooms asked whether the Baptists might be spies. There were rumours that anyone attending their services risked contracting measles. Yuri was twice summoned to the FSB department for combating extremism. He was repeatedly asked about sources of foreign funding. Some American Baptist friends, who had come to visit the previous dozen summers, were threatened outside their hotel by operatives posing as journalists. Screenshots of their passports were put in the local newspaper. 'If you went to ask why water or gas supplies had been cut off to the church, the first question the man or woman at the counter would ask was "Why are you not Orthodox?"' said Yuri. 'We were treated like fifth columnists, not Russian citizens.' He and his family left the country.

The authorities took an even tougher line towards other groups. In 2017, the Jehovah's Witnesses were banned as an extremist organisation. Yevgeny, a car mechanic from the textile city of Ivanovo, hosted small gatherings in his flat. He only found out that a criminal case had been opened against him when armed police wearing helmets and bulletproof vests broke down his front door. They threw him on the ground and handcuffed him. 'I was accused of organising a structural branch of the liquidated Jehovah's Witnesses centre,' he said. 'This is something I never did. I don't represent anything. I'm just a believer, like thousands of others.'[37] Since his arrest, more than 600 adherents have been charged under the extremism law, including an 89-year-old from Vladivostok who was put on a terrorism watchlist. Their homes are raided, and dozens have been jailed on sentences of up to eight years. Some allege they have been stripped to their underwear, beaten, suffocated, electrocuted and threatened with rape in custody. Their European spokesman has called their treatment 'the inquisition of the twenty-first century'.[38]

Despite the separation of church and state in the constitution, from the early 1990s, the Church lobbied to make religious education a mandatory part of the school curriculum. It did not go smoothly at first. Many parents, like Pyotr Bizyukov, a writer from Kemerovo in Siberia, worried where it might lead. 'Remember how the Church persecuted Leo Tolstoy. I don't want my children to be indoctrinated with anything at school. And I have no doubt this will be the case when I hear representatives of the Russian Orthodox Church talk,' he said.[39]

It took time, but from 2006, mandatory lessons in Orthodox culture were introduced in four regions. When the pilot scheme was rolled out across Russia, it offered six options: foundations of Orthodoxy, Buddhism, Judaism, Islam, world religious cultures and secular ethics. At first glance, the policy seemed reasonably tolerant and multi-confessional. But in practice in much of the country there was no such choice. Parents discovered that the school or regional administration had already decided what to teach. In Moscow and St Petersburg, two thirds of parents opted for secular ethics, but in smaller cities almost 100 per cent of pupils were studying Orthodox culture. One researcher investigating education in the Vladimir region found that the 'opinions of minorities were not taken seriously, and they ended up having to join the module chosen by the majority or selected by the school'.[40] Some teachers complained that while maths and other textbooks were often ragged, the Foundation of Orthodoxy course was bolstered by glossy new books and CDs.

Mainly Muslim regions like Tatarstan and Kabardino-Balkaria in the North Caucasus often lack qualified staff to teach pupils about Islam. When the Education Ministry released a 30-page description of the optional course on Orthodox culture, the chairman of Russia's Council of Muftis of Russia was alarmed. He complained that Muslims, Russia's second largest faith, had suffered even more than the Orthodox Church during the Soviet period and needed more time and resources to devise a programme for schools.

Muslim communities have also been denied permission to build mosques in a number of towns and cities. The authorities blame public opposition. According to Forum 18, a group which monitors religious repression in the former Soviet Union, the head of the Ozinsky district near the Kazakh border in south-western Russia donated construction materials for a new Orthodox church in 2005 but refused to do the same for a partly built mosque. 'Am I your servant, to be finding you roof-tiles?' he wrote to the Volga Spiritual Directorate of Muslims. 'Don't come to me with such questions again.'[41]

The Belgorod region, bordering Ukraine, was one of the first to make Foundations of Orthodox Culture mandatory. Pupils were taught to venerate the church's centuries-old alliance with state power. In every school, a list of rules explaining how to behave in church were prominently displayed, usually next to the school's coat of arms and national flag. The course was taught even in schools where 80 per cent of pupils were Muslim. To prevent rows with parents, teachers were instructed not to award low marks. When the city's Muslims asked for permission to build a mosque so their children could learn the Koran, the request was rejected.[42]

The Church's antipathy to Islam has produced some bizarre decisions. On one occasion, complaints from a popular cleric killed off a new 1,000-rouble banknote. Archpriest Pavel Ostrovsky warned the Central Bank of Russia it was 'playing with fire' because of the bill's design. 'Have you comrades completely lost your sense of fear?' he raged. 'You depict a minaret with a crescent moon, and the dome of the Orthodox church without a cross.'

He was referring to the church in the palace of Kazan, which had lost its cross in the Revolution and had since been a museum. Both it and the Söyembikä Tower are inside the Kremlin of Kazan, capital of Russia's republic of Tatarstan, home to some two million ethnic Tatars. Kamil Samigullin, their spiritual leader, pleaded for tolerance. 'We have a lot of Muslims; why can't we have both crescents and crosses?' he asked. 'It is illogical to add a cross where there is none and remove a crescent from where it stands. Hostility will lead to a ban on looking at the sky – there is a crescent moon there, too.'[43] But the Central Bank did a U-turn and two days later announced it would stop printing the notes.

Muslims and their mosques are accepted today – as long as they preach the same traditional family values as the Church, back the war in Ukraine and pose no threat to the state. Chechnya's strongman president, Ramzan Kadyrov, was given free rein to rule in his one-million-strong republic provided that he kept a lid on any stirrings of insurgency. He is thought to be behind a string of extrajudicial killings of politicians, journalists, gay Chechens and others, but his loyalty to the Kremlin is what counts. In Ukraine, his private army of so-called Kadyrovtsy has been used to brutally punish dissenting Russian soldiers, as well as intimidate civilians.

The Russian Empire and its successor, the Soviet Union, have a long and bloody history of anti-Semitism. Father Georgy Edelstein was born to a Jewish father and a Catholic mother in Ukraine in 1932. He narrowly escaped the 'Holocaust by Bullets' – the first massacre of Jews in the Second World War in a ravine on the outskirts of the Ukrainian capital. In just two days, the SS, German police units and auxiliaries killed nearly 34,000 people. 'I think that of the ten or eleven boys and girls with whom I played before 1941, only two or three survived,' he told the Russian politician and filmmaker Vladimir Kara Murza. 'I can never answer the question of why I am here, and they are all buried at Babi Yar.'[44] Edelstein converted to Orthodoxy at university and had to fight to become a priest in the 1970s. More than twenty bishops refused to ordain him. Metropolitan Gedeon of Stavropol and Baku informed him many years later that 'a baptised Jew is like a wet dog'.[45] Edelstein was dismayed but not surprised when, in front of a huge crowd,

Kirill worshipped the relics of Gabriel of Bialystok during a 2012 trip to Poland. Gabriel is worshipped as a seventeenth century child saint by some Russian and Polish Orthodox despite the anti-Semitic story associated with him. The six-year-old son of farm workers, Gabriel is supposed to have suffered a ritual murder at the hands of a Jewish landlord and bled to death while his parents were at work in the fields.

Tales about Jews murdering children to obtain Christian blood originated in England in the twelfth century. Such accusations resurfaced periodically in Germany and the Austro-Hungarian Empire, but the most notorious blood libel trial took place in the Russian Empire just before the First World War. In 1913, the state charged Mendel Beilis, a Jewish supervisor in a Kyiv brick factory, with the ritual killing of Andrei Yushchinsky, a thirteen-year-old Christian boy, in order to drain his blood for the baking of Passover matzo bread. The most likely perpetrator of the murder was a local gang leader. However, under pressure from the anti-Semitic group the Black Hundreds, the police abandoned their original investigation and reclassified the crime as a religious murder.[46] The framing of an innocent man sparked outrage around the world. Thomas Mann, Arthur Conan Doyle and the Archbishop of Canterbury were among those to denounce it. Beilis was acquitted but forced to leave his home; he eventually settled in the US. More than a century later, Yushchinsky's grave in an Orthodox cemetery in Kyiv, not far from the Babi Yar massacre site, remains a place of pilgrimage for the far-right. The court's final verdict was bizarre: it cleared Beilis of killing the boy but insisted that he had been ritually murdered, implying Jewish collective guilt. The judgment is still quoted in full on the tombstone.[47]

One Russian school textbook, first published in 2002, accused the Jews of seeking world domination and of pushing Pontius Pilate to execute Christ. After it was criticised for promoting hatred, it was toned down, but only slightly. While referring to 'brutal persecutions' of early Christians by Jews, the author, Alla Borodina, ignored pogroms of Jews by Christians. Lev Ponomaryov, a leading human rights activist, filed a lawsuit against the publisher in 2002. His complaint was dismissed by the prosecutor general. Borodina is a leader of the ultra-nationalist movement *Narodny Sobor*, the People's Council, whose stated mission is to 'unite around the idea of Russian civilization, protect it against external and internal enemies' and install it as the 'state ideology'.[48] The textbook warned pupils against the 'new sects' which allegedly cultivated 'lies and superstitions' and threatened 'psychological disorders'.

The official Church is happy to indulge strange practices of its own. In 2019, Metropolitan Savva of Tver got on a plane and dumped 70 litres of holy water as he flew over the city. It was National Sobriety Day and he wanted to save his congregation from drunkenness and fornication. However odd this may seem to some straitlaced Western Christians, in Russia, paganism and magic have generally coexisted alongside the Orthodox Church for centuries in a dual belief system known as *dvoeverie*. Folk superstitions, a belief in the miraculous healing powers of relics, parapsychology and alternative medicine became life rafts for many Russians caught up in the chaos of the 1990s. Many of these people had also started going to church.

Thousands of Russians have sought help from a former rock musician and dog handler turned exorcist. Every Saturday morning, Hieromonk Father Vladimir Gusev's church in the small village of Navesnoye in the Oryol region is filled with growls and ear-piercing screams. Busloads of people arrive for the *otchitka*, purification ceremony. After confession and the liturgy, he gets to work helping victims of witchcraft and driving out unclean spirits. He sprays people with holy water, hits them over the head with the gospel and thumps their bodies with his large gold cross. 'We must do this,' he told a wide-eyed interviewer from a local TV station. 'We must bear witness to the authority of Christ. Exorcism is the most powerful sermon of all.'[49]

Father Vladimir is no maverick – he belongs to the Orthodox establishment. His exorcism rituals have been blessed by none other than Father Iliy Nozdrin, Patriarch Kirill's confessor. The two men met at Leningrad's Theological Academy. Now in his nineties, Iliy is the archetypal mystical *starets*, or holy elder. Officially he is a schema-archimandrite, a monastic priest who has reached the highest level of spiritual knowledge. He spent a decade on Mount Athos and is now based at Optina Pustyn, the monastery which Tolstoy was heading for just before he died. The archimandrite used to carry out exorcisms himself but now provides 'healing and guidance' to senior state officials looking for career advice. One former regional official said most people believed if you wanted to bend Putin's ear, you should go through Archimandrite Iliy.[50] The elder is close to the President, who is one of his spiritual children. He helpfully referred to anti-Kremlin protests when Putin wanted to reclaim the presidency in 2011–12 as 'trash' and 'enemy acts' which 'attract dark forces from an abyss'.

What seemed extreme in the early Putin era had gone mainstream.

10. KIRILL

The church looked like a tiger that had all its fangs ripped out ... Just a big stripey pussy cat. Why keep it in a cage? Then it turned out that the teeth survived after all. What's more, they like to bite.

ARCHDEACON ANDREI KURAEV

The man on the microphone was lambasting 'the big protestant empire of the USA'. He called the 1990s a time of 'total capitulation' and thanked Putin for refocusing on 'Russia's geopolitical priorities'. But Alexander Schipkov, a Kremlin-friendly philosopher, was addressing a swathe of empty blue chairs. Few delegates had bothered to stay for his lecture, 'Church, Propaganda and the National Security of Russia'. Most were in the self-service buffet, heaping their plates with buckwheat, mashed potato, fried chicken and meat cutlets. Priests in black cassocks stood in a long line for the beer tap.

Five months before the invasion of Ukraine, I was at a health resort near Sheremetyevo Airport at the ninth biennial Word and Faith festival. The event was founded by the Moscow Patriarchate in 2004 to create a bridge between the church and the secular media, but journalists were thin on the ground. The only two I met were a reporter from a Greek newspaper and a television editor from Bosnia's Republika Srpska. They seemed nonplussed, since neither spoke Russian. Most delegates were press officers, and employees from 155 dioceses across Russia. They had come for masterclasses in TikTok, to learn how the Orthodox media should report the sudden change of a bishop and how to infuse dull church publications with a sense of fun and patriotism.

On the last day, we were promised a Q&A with Patriarch Kirill inside Christ the Saviour. Stringent security checks were in place at the entrance to the vast underbelly of the building and the Hall of Church Councils. I had prepared some questions, but the Primate appeared only on a giant screen 'due to the epidemiological situation'. A press secretary for the Patriarch informed me that the topics for conversation had in any case been selected in advance.

Looking morose, Kirill often glanced down and appeared to be reading his speech. Not once did the faintest hint of a smile appear on his lips. He began with the benefits of modern technology, which had allowed people to worship remotely during the pandemic. Then he switched to finger-wagging mode. 'Some clerics are more interested in their social media profile than their parish,' he said. 'They are obsessed with how many likes they get for a post. But beware – a careless photo can harm the image of the church.' He warned that he took a dim view of bishops who sat at their laptops and did not make the effort to visit the remote corners of their dioceses. 'Economic measures would be taken against them,' he said. One moment stayed with me. That year, a disturbed teenager had shot dead nine people at his old school in Kazan and, just weeks before the festival, a student armed with a rifle killed six people at a university in Perm. When asked about his reaction to these American-style shootings, the Patriarch described them as 'a symptom of living in a free world'. He added: 'If we talk too much about these incidents they will spread.' He might have had a point, but what struck me as odd was the lack of even the most perfunctory condolences to the families of the victims. Whether by accident or design, Kirill exudes indifference. Since the 2022 invasion of Ukraine, he has failed to express any regret for the deaths of civilians, including more than 500 children.

The Patriarch is the highest spiritual authority in the land, the man setting an example for other Orthodox Christians to follow. Yet he has seemingly turned a blind eye to rapes, summary executions and other atrocities committed by Russian troops. He not only backed the Kremlin's war in Ukraine, but he became its main cheerleader. Soon after it began, on Forgiveness Sunday, marking the start of Lent, he did not call for an end to the violence. Instead, he blamed gay pride parades in Europe for inciting it. He began his sermon talking about Ukraine's 'extermination' of Russian speakers in the breakaway eastern region of Ukraine, held since 2014 by Moscow-backed separatist groups. The full-scale invasion and bombing of civilian targets across the country did not get a look in. Instead, he explained that the war was about 'which side of God humanity will be on', in the divide between Russia and the West. Any country which wanted to join the 'happy world' of excessive consumption faced a loyalty test. 'Do you know what this test is?' he asked the congregation. 'The test is very simple and at the same time terrible – it is the Gay Pride parade.' He suggested that the pro-Russian Donbas was paying the price for its 'fundamental rejection' of such degenerate Western values.

Eight months into the war, when Russian generals were running out of cannon fodder, Putin ordered a 'partial mobilisation' draft. Aware that many men had fled the country or gone into hiding, Kirill tried to rally the troops. He promised that Russian conscripts and contract soldiers who died in battle to restore Holy Rus' would be granted eternal salvation. 'They will have sacrificed themselves for others. Therefore, we believe that this sacrifice washes away all the sins that a person has committed.' Leaving aside issues of morality, Kirill's stance is also ahistorical. Orthodoxy's most revered figures would not have endorsed such a blanket absolution. St Basil the Great, one of the leading theorists of the Christian movement back in the fourth century, taught that those who kill in war must repent for the blood they have shed. 'It might be advisable to refuse them communion for three years, on the grounds that their hands are not clean,' he wrote in one of his Canons. Yet Kirill appeared to be preaching an Orthodox version of jihad, encouraging Christians to martyr themselves in exchange for a clean conscience and a joyous afterlife.

The war stiffened the prelate's mission to sacralise Putin's power. Kirill has imposed a pyramid-shaped hierarchy on the Church that mirrors Putin's own structure of command – his vertical of power. The construct of a good tsar and bad boyars goes back centuries.

The head of state is wise and just; all the big problems must be referred upwards. Transgressions are blamed on incompetent governors or greedy bureaucrats. Clerics who have worked closely with the Patriarch tell me that they no longer recognise the man they knew. Despite his diatribes against 'the global devil' and 'gay pride parades in Europe', he once had a reputation for being too pro-Western. In the 1990s, conservative clerics were wary of his interest in ecumenism, his regular TV appearances and his modernising zeal. Kirill – or to use his secular name, Vladimir Mikhailovich Gundyaev – has been on quite some journey. His life story has crossed that of the President's in some unexpected ways.

Like Putin, Kirill was born at the end of the Second World War and raised in a cramped Leningrad apartment. While Putin's grandfather, Spiridon, was a chef who cooked meals for Lenin and Stalin, Kirill's grandfather, Vasily, was a locomotive driver turned priest. Arrested many times, he suffered for his faith and spent 18 years in exile and in camps, including a spell at the notorious Solovetsky island monastery in the White Sea. At the time, 46 archbishops and hundreds of clergy were confined at the 'special purpose camp', which became a blueprint for the gulag. Undeterred, Vasily's son Mikhail followed in his father's footsteps and became a priest. In 2016, Putin made a surprise announcement on Kirill's seventieth birthday. In a TV documentary, the President revealed that he had been dunked into the baptismal font 64 years earlier by none other than Archpriest Mikhail Gundyaev, Kirill's father. 'Such is fate!' remarked the President.[1] The film, directed by the Kazakh-born Saida Medvedeva, a Kremlin favourite, provided no documentary evidence but most baptisms were not officially registered in the Soviet era. At the time, Father Mikhail was serving at Leningrad's Transfiguration Cathedral, not far from the Putin family's home – so it is theoretically possible.

In interviews, Putin has described chasing rats with a stick in the stairwell of his parents' apartment block and getting into brawls with other boys in their communal backyard. He has claimed that he was such a 'hooligan' his school would not let him join the Communist Young Pioneers. Kirill may have come from a line of churchmen, but he also went through 'a dramatic and risky adolescence'. He did not join the Pioneers or the Komsomol, which made relations with other pupils strained. 'It was a difficult time for me, I went to school as if I were going to Golgotha,' he said.[2] In one interview, he said his early life had been marked by 'supernatural interferences involving grief, emotion and suffering'. When the interviewer asked him to elaborate, he said: 'I would prefer to keep quiet about some things, if you don't mind.'[3] It is unclear what such 'interferences' might have been.

Protodeacon Andrei Kuraev, appointed dean of theology at St Tikhon's Orthodox University by Patriarch Alexei, first met Kirill in 1990 and got to know him well. Towards the end of that decade, he helped Kirill to write the social doctrine of the Church and later campaigned for him to succeed Alexei as patriarch. Kuraev looks like your average Orthodox cleric, with his round glasses, tied-back hair, and moustache and wispy beard. But he attracted an exceptional following thanks to his colourful language and acerbic wit. He wrote several books, was one of the first clerics to use the internet, preached at music festivals and helped to convert a few drug-addicted rock stars to Orthodoxy. Kuraev suggests that the wayward young Kirill was rescued by his mentor, Nikodim, the Metropolitan of Leningrad, who went on to become his personal secretary and valet, or as they say in church language, his monastery cell attendant. Nikodim was one of the most powerful and ambiguous figures in the Church of the post-war era. He is the key to understanding Kirill. At a 2019 memorial service by his grave in the Alexander Nevsky Lavra of St Petersburg, the Patriarch called his teacher 'the great saint of the twentieth century'. Many credit him with saving the Church when a new wave of repression was unleashed by Khrushchev. Others remember him for his fascination with Catholicism – and his eager collaboration with the KGB.

Nikodim was recruited as an agent in the mid-1950s to work in the Russian spiritual mission in Jerusalem. He impressed his handlers so much that he was appointed chairman of the Department for External Church Relations of the Moscow Patriarchate in 1960, when he was only 31; at the time he was the youngest bishop in the Christian world. Nikodim made a pact with the KGB. He asked them for a little breathing space inside the country. In exchange he promised to do their bidding overseas. He would advertise the happy lives of Soviet citizens, attack American imperialism and nuclear power, promote Soviet satellites in the 'Third World' and build churches that would assist with intelligence-gathering operations. His leadership of the Church's foreign affairs department gave him access to the world. He performed well at international meetings, particularly the World Council of Churches, which the Russian Church joined in 1961. Nikodim was, of course, not unique. Virtually all senior leaders of officially recognised religious faiths were recruited by the KGB. But he was one of its most effective agents.[4]

The security services referred to Nikodim by his codename, Svyatoslav. According to material smuggled out of Russia by Vasily Mitrokhin, who defected to the UK after a 30-year career as a KGB archivist, Nikodim was especially valued for his contacts in the Catholic hierarchy. The KGB saw him as one of the top four 'influential figures' in the Church capable of sowing discord in the Vatican.[5] Ironically, he died on 5 September 1978 at the feet of the newly inaugurated John Paul I. He had flown to Rome for the enthronement ceremony, but after a fifteen-minute conversation with the new Pope, he turned pale and fell to the floor. An astonished John Paul I found himself cradling the Russian bishop in his arms, giving him last rites and absolving him of his sins.

Nikodim died of a cardiac arrest when he was only 48. He led a high-octane, stressful life and, like many clerics, he was overweight. Yet his sudden death, followed 33 days later by the death of John Paul I, also from a heart attack, gave rise to conspiracy theories. Some whispered that Nikodim met his end as the result of an unsuccessful attempt to assassinate the Pope. Others believed the bishop had been poisoned for getting too close to the Catholics. In the Moscow Patriarchate some believed that Nikodim was a secret cardinal. One blind peasant woman known as Blessed Pelagia of Ryazan, who was revered for her prophecies, told Nikodim in 1965: 'You will die like a dog at the feet of your pope.' Or perhaps he was killed for trying to cut ties with the KGB. That is the view of the veteran TV journalist Vladimir Nevzorov, who made his name exposing corruption and is a well-known critic of the Orthodox Church.[6] Whatever the truth of these stories, Nikodim's death must have left its mark on his brightest protege.

As is now well-established, Kirill has something else in common with Putin: a KGB past. The earliest known mention of the future patriarch in publicly available KGB materials dates from February 1972, when he was a freshly ordained 25-year-old priest. Accompanied by Nikodim, Kirill, codenamed Mikhailov, flew to a meeting of the World Council of Churches in Australia.[7]

Nobody took at face value the Soviet constitution's claim that 'the church in the USSR shall be separated from the state'. All-important clerical appointments were made by the Council for Religious Affairs – a front for the fourth department of the Fifth Directorate of the KGB, which monitored the Church and other faiths. Its chairman, Konstantin Kharchev, said: 'Not a single candidate for the office of bishop or any other high-ranking office, much less a member of Holy Synod, went through without confirmation by the Central Committee of the Communist Party and the and the KGB.'[8]

One briefing paper, from 28 July 1970, is entitled: 'On the use by the organs of the KGB of the resources of the Russian Orthodox Church in counter-espionage measures within the country and abroad'. The KGB meticulously noted the performance of the clerics it had recruited and assessed their work. In 1982, the Fifth Directorate triumphantly noted that through 'leading agents, the ROC, Georgian and Armenian Churches hold firmly to positions of loyalty to the Soviet state'.[9] Priests were also useful to the S Directorate, which recruited and handled 'illegals' who worked undercover in foreign countries. The clerics had access to church registers and biographical details of parishioners, including those who died young. The KGB mined these parish lists to devise fake identities for their spies. In the early 1970s, two KGB agents in the Patriarchate were sent to carry out detailed research on parish registers in Canada. Ivan Borcha, codename Fyodor, who served in Ukrainian and Romanian communities on Canada's prairies, studied registers in Alberta and Saskatchewan. Viktor Petlyuchenko, aka Patriot, was a priest for Orthodox parishes in Edmonton and was also told to examine parish lists in Alberta.[10] One choir director in the small town of Nisku said that it was difficult for parishes in remote areas to attract priests, so her church of St Mary's had long relied upon missionary fathers who came from Russia.[11]

Apologists insist the choice was between collaboration or annihilation. By cooperating with state power, they say, Nikodim saved the episcopate from dying out. While he loyally promoted the USSR's foreign policy goals, so the argument goes, he also persuaded his KGB minders that the international prestige of the Church depended on a fresh crop of competent bishops. Nikodim was candid with young priests about the rules of the game, according to Yevgeny Komarov, editor-in-chief of the Publishing House of the Moscow Patriarchate. 'Are they asking you to write a report?' he would ask them. 'Well, write it then! By working with them [the KGB], you will be able to do more useful things for the Church.'[12]

According to Konstantin Preobrazhensky, a lieutenant colonel in the KGB who fled to the US in 1993, party officials used to enjoy teasing hierarchs from the Moscow Patriarchate: 'Seeing a person in vestments at a Kremlin party or at a conference for peace fighters, they would clap him on the shoulder and inquire loudly: "Tell us, Father, which pocket of your cassock holds your party membership ID card?" The bishop would smile a bit sheepishly, but he never objected, since everyone at that gathering shared the same background.'[13]

For a tantalisingly brief period in the early 1990s, it looked as if the Church would be forced to confront its shadowy past. A parliamentary commission was launched to investigate the 1991 failed coup. Chaired by the lawmaker and civil rights activist Lev Ponomaryov, part of its work was also to look into the Patriarchate's collaboration with the KGB. Piece by piece, a picture emerged of a church doing the bidding of the security services. For example, at the 1983 General Assembly of the World Council of Churches in Vancouver, Kirill managed to torpedo an amendment criticising the Soviet invasion of Afghanistan and urged the Assembly against making changes 'that would only be used for propaganda purposes'. What mattered, he said, was 'resolving the conflict for the sake of the people of Afghanistan'.[14] The Soviet delegation contained 47 KGB agents, mostly clergy, along with sundry translators, journalists and other personnel.[15] They spied on each other and reported back to Moscow.

The cache of documents, made public by the parliamentary deputies, revealed that most of the Orthodox hierarchy had been penetrated. Three of the most senior bishops were referred to in the

KGB materials by the codenames Antonov, Adamant and Abbat. An investigative journalist, Alexander Nezhny, worked out their identities by comparing reports in church bulletins with KGB accounts of the agents' activities. He named the trio as metropolitans Filaret, Yuvenaly and Pitirim, the cleric who sought to ingratiate himself with coup plotters in 1991. Many years later Filaret admitted 'there was not a single bishop who did not have contact' with the KGB: 'If he had no contacts, then he was not a bishop. Therefore, if one of those bishops says that he had no contacts (with the KGB), it means that he is lying.'[16] The parliamentary commission also learned that Patriarch Alexei himself had been an agent. His *klichka*, or codename, was Drozdov. The word derives from the Russian word for thrush; some thought he was called that because he sang so well for his KGB masters, but it was actually the secular surname of a nineteenth-century bishop who was the subject of Alexei's dissertation. According to the archives, in February 1988, the head of the KGB rewarded Alexei with a Certificate of Honour for his 30 years of work. Church insiders were not surprised. A few years earlier, the Gorbachev-era magazine *Glasnost* had published an article describing how Alexei had helped the authorities to collect compromising material on the private life of his predecessor, Metropolitan Pimen, in the 1960s.[17]

Members of the parliamentary commission told Alexei they would not name him as an agent if he came clean about the extent of past cooperation between the church and the KGB. The Patriarch appeared to agree. The topic was chewed over in factory canteens and fancy restaurants, in embassies and army barracks. Everybody was curious to learn more, including the then-British ambassador, who sought a meeting with the patriarch. Alexei told Sir Rodric Braithwaite that he had set up a separate commission of young bishops to investigate the collaborators, known as the 'Chekists in cassocks'.[18] It was headed by Bishop Alexander (Mogilev) of Kostroma, who warned journalists not to start a witch hunt. It was irresponsible, he said, to target alleged agents based on a handful of random documents from KGB archives. 'The Holy Church will have its say about everything. Let's just wait a little bit,' he said. More than three decades later, his commission has yet to produce a report. The speaker of parliament, Ruslan Khasbulatov, was persuaded by both Alexei and the head of the KGB, Yevgeny Primakov, to dissolve the whole inquiry. In one important specific area, however, it was too late. The archives had shown that Alexei and Kirill had been agents.

Father Yakunin, one of the commission's members, was accused of betraying state secrets. He stood his ground and wrote to Alexei in 1994: 'If the Church is not cleansed of the taint of acting as the spy and informer, it cannot be reborn.' The Patriarch had already defrocked Yakunin, having decided in 1993 that clergymen should not be allowed to run for parliament. Four years later, the priest, who called himself 'a little Luther of the Orthodox Church', was ex-communicated. He compared himself to Tolstoy, who was thrown out of the Church for heresy a century earlier. 'I have the honour to be somewhere near this great genius who was not only a great novelist, but also a great fighter for the freedom of conscience,' Yakunin said.

Zoya Krakhmalnikova, the Christian dissident only recently back from exile in Siberia, described the lies surrounding the issue as a 'national moral catastrophe'. The Church talked a great deal about coming to terms with its painful Soviet history. Yet at that time, only one senior cleric, Archbishop Chrysostom of Vilnius and Lithuania, admitted to supplying the KGB with regular reports, although he insisted that he was 'not a stool pigeon'.[19] He told *Ogonyok* magazine that some senior figures were, in spite of their notional job descriptions, fully fledged agents. He cited one example, Mefody, Metropolitan of Voronezh: 'There are in our church real KGB men who have pursued meteoric careers. The synod was unanimously against consecrating such a man as a bishop, but we were forced to take this sin upon ourselves and then what a rapid career he had. He became a metropolitan and for nearly 10 years he controlled the church money and he never liked independent honest priests, he failed to defend them – he just persecuted them.'[20]

Mefody did not directly address the claim that he was a KGB officer planted inside the Church, rather than a cleric who cooperated – willingly or unwillingly – with the security services. 'I have nothing to hide here and nothing to fear,' he said in an interview in 2002. 'I would be ashamed if I were suspected of collaborating with the CIA or having connections with organisations that worked against the state in which we were born and live, in which the people feed and support us. That is what I would call ingratitude towards the people.'[21] That same year he received an award from Putin 'for many years of conscientious labour'.

Alexei referred to his own KGB ties only obliquely. In a 1991 interview just before the coup, he acknowledged that the Patriarchate had cooperated with the Soviet authorities, while insisting that other organisations had acted the same way: 'Before those people, however, to whom the compromises, silence, forced passivity or expressions of loyalty permitted by the leaders of the church in those years caused pain, before these people, and not only before God, I ask forgiveness, understanding and prayers.'[22] The repentance seemed insincere. Oleg Kalugin, a former KGB general who left for the United States in 1995, was invited to lunch by the Patriarch and was hectored for exaggerating the Church's role. 'Yes, we collaborated with the KGB, even I did,' Alexei told him. 'But it was a struggle for peace, for disarmament. There's nothing wrong with that.' Kalugin told this story to another ex-KGB officer, Lieutenant Colonel Konstantin Preobrazhensky, who also took up US citizenship.

Further proof of Alexei's collaboration came to light in 1999 thanks to an Estonian historian. Indrek Jürjo was combing through KGB material in the State Archives in a drab Soviet-era building on the outskirts of the capital Tallinn when he stumbled on a secret document. All the Estonian security police files up until 1960 are available for scrutiny; later material was taken to Moscow's Lubyanka during the death throes of communism. But Alexei had been recruited two years earlier: 28 February 1958, although not under that name. Just like Alexei, agent Drozdov was born in 1929, spoke fluent Russian and Estonian, was a doctor of theology and was serving as an Orthodox priest in Estonia. The yellowing document was signed by a Colonel I.P. Karpov, head of the KGB in the republic, who seemed more than satisfied: 'During the period of collaboration with the organs of the KGB "Drozdov" made a positive impression. During secret rendezvous he was punctilious, energetic and convivial. He is well-orientated in theological theory and the international situation. He has a willing attitude to fulfilling tasks and has already provided materials that deserve our attention.' Jürjo said Alexei/Drozdov was an agent – not a mere informer. He would have written reports and been interrogated by a dedicated KGB officer with whom he would have met regularly in clandestine locations.[23]

The current patriarch has made public his view that assisting the security services should be a source of pride. Before the reunification of the Patriarchate with the Russian Church Outside Russia, Kirill was asked if he believed that Putin was a true Orthodox believer. He replied in the affirmative, adding: 'the fact that he was a KGB officer, well, everyone chose their own path in life and defending one's motherland was never a bad thing – first and foremost from a religious point of view'.[24]

☦ ☦ ☦

Vladimir Mikhailovich Gundyaev, to give Kirill his secular name, underwent the initiation ceremony of being tonsured as a monk in 1969. His monastic name was inspired by Saint Cyril, known as the enlightener of the Slavs who brought Russia its Cyrillic alphabet. It was a fitting name for a young man with academic ambition. At the Leningrad Theological Academy, Kirill taught dogma to students who were older than him, acting as the rector's assistant.

In 1971, when Putin was a second-year law student and had just joined the Communist Party, Kirill was elevated to the rank of archimandrite. He was sent to Geneva as the Moscow Patriarchate's representative to the World Council of Churches (WCC), a rare privilege. Grigory Skobelev, the secretary who accompanied him to Switzerland, was interviewed years later for a Russian TV documentary and said that the job was lucrative – they were paid in hard currency – and straightforward. Kirill had to deny any problem with religious freedom back home and 'not allow any anti-Soviet provocations'. When asked who gave the orders, Skobelev snapped back: 'Nobody had to tell us anything. We were all conscious of our duty as citizens and knew what a patriot should do for the motherland.'[25]

In October 2022, the Church of the Nativity of the Most Holy Theotokos, where Kirill once served in the quiet neighbourhood of Chêne-Bougeries, was splattered with red paint in a protest against the invasion of Ukraine. The church is now run by Kirill's nephew, Mikhail Gundyaev, the Russian representative at the WCC in Geneva. He told Swiss media that his uncle 'was not an agent, although he had been subjected to "strict controls" by the KGB'. A green card in a Swiss police file noted that 'Goundiaev [sic] alias Monsignor Kirill', as they called him, did work for the Soviet security services – next to the abbreviation *Funkt.* (function), KGB is underlined in red pencil. Over two decades, there are 37 entries in his file, mostly standard visa applications and a log of his entries into Switzerland. He appears twice in a list of Soviet officials 'against whom (unspecified) measures were taken' in 1979 and 1985, but there are no further details.[26]

During his posting in the early 1970s in Geneva, Kirill became close friends with the Soviet consul, Vadim Melnikov, who was also a KGB officer. Years later, when the former consul was a pensioner and Kirill became patriarch, Melnikov reminisced about their glory days in Geneva. The two men went hiking, fishing and mushroom-picking together. They went on road trips to meet the Catholic monks who trained St Bernard dogs and followed in the tracks of Alexander Suvorov, the Russian field marshal who fought the French army in the Alps. Most of all, the Archimandrite loved whizzing down the slopes at high speed. 'Of course, he was trusted by the KGB – he was skiing in the Alps long before the current political elite ever set foot outside Russia,' remarked one priest many years later. Melnikov remembered that Kirill was passionate about the sport and 'almost flew off the mountain tops'.[27]

Kirill enjoyed his life in Switzerland and has visited the country 43 times since his initial posting in 1971, despite his tirades against Western values. Back in the 1970s, the tall, bearded and perennially cheerful priest was a big hit with the Russian émigré community, especially the ladies. Melnikov said the future patriarch jokingly referred to his female parishioners as 'assets'. The consul's wife, Tamara, remembered asking the handsome cleric whether it was difficult to live without sex and he told her he contained his natural urges by taking 'contrast showers' of hot and cold water. In a documentary made by the independent TV Rain, Tamara said Kirill was a frequent guest at their Geneva home; she made dumplings and pancakes while he brought copious amounts of red and black caviar.

Around the dinner table the talk was of politics, life, sport and literature – everything but God.[28]

In 1974, both men were recalled home. Kirill was made rector of the Leningrad Theological Academy and, only half in jest, invited Melnikov to join him there and teach Marxist–Leninist theory to the students. Vadim demurred – after all, Kirill was a far greater authority on the topic: 'he knew all the subtleties, but I just learned the quotations by rote'. Nevertheless, the friendship continued. When he went on foreign trips, Kirill would bring back Marlboro Red cigarettes for Vadim, cosmetics for Tamara and fashionable sneakers for the couple's son Igor. He invited the family to his dacha for Tamara's birthday and frightened them by disappearing underwater in a pond for several minutes wearing his scuba diving kit.

Over the years, the two men drifted apart. As Kirill's career blossomed, Melnikov's nosedived. He was transferred to a job in Vladimir, three hours' drive from the capital. The friends met for the last time in 1998 in a Moscow church where Kirill, now a metropolitan, was serving. After the liturgy, Kirill invited his old friend to a banquet, crowded with officials. Once everyone had left, Melnikov poured some vodka but Kirill refused the toast on health grounds. Then the ex-consul and militant atheist asked if his friend would hear his confession. Kirill looked into his eyes, smiled and begged forgiveness. He had another meeting in half an hour. 'Maybe some other time,' he said. There would be no other time. Tamara is particularly hurt that when she wrote to Kirill to inform him of Vadim's death in 2019, she received no reply. In his last few months, her husband had been very keen to talk to his friend, but all his messages, phone calls and letters went unanswered. She understood that Kirill was a busy man who mixed with the likes of Putin, but she called his behaviour 'insulting and indecent'. Sitting in her small kitchen as her son Igor chain-smoked, she told the filmmaker Sergei Erzhenkov from the independent channel TV Dozhd that the Church was losing parishioners because many people were disappointed in the way it had developed since the end of Communism.[29]

On his way to the top, Kirill suffered a significant reversal. In 1984 he was removed from his job as head of the Theological Academy and sent to the rundown diocese of Smolensk, near the border with Belarus. It was a far cry from Geneva. Forty years later Kirill recalled that when he first arrived, he had no place to stay apart from a hut belonging to the parish watchman: 'The next morning, he asked me if I'd had a good night's sleep. "It was OK," I said. "But early in the morning a cat started running over the blanket to wake me up." The man said: "We don't have any cats here, Your Holiness. It must have been a rat."'[30]

Kirill faced many hurdles in his new job. The local commissioner from the Council for Religious Affairs reported that most parish priests lacked enthusiasm. Some had been dismissed for 'systematic drunkenness'. Almost every church needed major repairs, but Smolensk was one of the poorest dioceses in the Soviet Union. Kirill's response was to reach outwards. He expanded his empire by annexing the enclave of Kaliningrad on the Baltic coast. He brought in some energetic, young priests from Moscow and Leningrad, and threw himself into fundraising, persuading local businesses to contribute to the revival of Orthodoxy in Russia's heartland. A theological school was opened; by the mid-1990s, it had become a fully-fledged seminary.

The standard of teaching was high, and Smolensk became a hotbed of intellectual activity. Irina Ladizhenkova, who trained female choir directors, took her pupils to Orthodox competitions in Eastern Europe: 'We believed that we should show the quality of our work and our Vladyka (our bishop) gave us his blessing – he was very open to the world back then.'[31] The Smolensk seminarians were encouraged to befriend their Catholic counterparts in Poland. His experience in Geneva and elsewhere with the World Council of Churches taught Kirill how to win the support of Christians abroad. In the first few years, he hosted a string of delegations from Western Europe.

Michael Bourdeaux, the Anglican priest and scourge of the KGB, also visited the diocese. It was not easy to pull the wool over his eyes, but he was impressed by Kirill's achievements in Smolensk. He had come to present an edition of BBC Radio 4's *Sunday Worship* programme to mark Advent in December 1999. After the bell ringing and the liturgy, Kirill invited Bourdeaux to supper at his residence. 'It was a lavish meal, and the Metropolitan was charming and relaxed,' recalled Canon Stephen Shipley, the programme's producer.[32] 'Afterwards we returned to the cathedral for vespers and he anointed me with holy oil. I felt very honoured by that.' Kirill spoke about the long battle he fought with the local authorities over the theological school and how relieved he was by Gorbachev's reforms. 'During the last ten years, we have passed through darkness into light,' Kirill said, adding that he was 'especially emotional' about the college he had established for young women.

Kirill's feminist leanings only went so far. In his last year in Geneva, he was horrified when a group of Protestants put forward the possibility of admitting women into priesthood during an All-Christian congress. In a TV documentary marking his seventieth birthday, he said the idea of bringing women into Church ranks alerted him to the moral degradation of the West. 'I witnessed a deepening crisis,' he said. 'We did everything to stop it.' Although standards were high at the women's college, it was more of a wife factory. Ladizhenkova, who still teaches female choir directors, told me how important it was to help the seminarians to find suitable wives, or *matushkas*, little mothers, as Russian priests' spouses are called. 'One of Kirill's ideas was for boys to choose girls in their circle during their studies, so that they could form a strong couple,' she said. 'He told them that they should support each other as they travel the same path, serving God.' According to Orthodox tradition, priests cannot get married but married men can become priests. That means a priest must get hitched before he is ordained, and there is sometimes an unseemly scramble by seminarians to find 'the right one' in the nick of time.

It is not clear why Kirill was banished to Smolensk, but he told Bourdeaux it was punishment for criticising Brezhnev's war in Afghanistan. He later expanded on the theme with a journalist. It was just 'common sense' that sending troops into Afghanistan was 'a tremendous historical mistake' and he was 'pretty certain that it should have never been done'. He added that he had co-authored the draft of a resolution by the World Council of Churches condemning the 1979 invasion, so that he could tone the language down and avoid what he called 'excessive politicisation'.

Vadim Melnikov believed his friend had been packed off to a provincial see for getting on the wrong side of another powerful cleric who was also a known KGB agent.[33] Metropolitan Filaret, code-name Antonov, headed the Ukrainian part of the Orthodox Church during the Soviet era. The strong personal enmity between Kirill and Filaret would later help to fuel the conflict between the Russian and Ukrainian churches. After Filaret set up a rival Ukrainian church in 1992, he was excommunicated by Moscow.

Whatever actually transpired in Leningrad in the early 1980s, after the death of his protector, Metropolitan Nikodim, Kirill felt vulnerable. He was hauled in front of the Council for Religious Affairs for a dressing down. He told a reporter the memory of that day still rankles: 'I was told something like this: "You should always remember that you are the last in line, the worst bishop of the Russian Orthodox Church. And you will remain so. Your task will be to stay quiet in Smolensk, to follow in the others' footsteps and to master the skill of building relations with the authorities in a society that does not pin its future on religious faith." That's the sort of instruction I heard then.'[34]

That was his low point; it did not take long for his star to rise again. Kirill constructed a new power base in western Russia. He did not stay in the rat-infested hut – he soon built himself a comfortable house and later repossessed Smolensk's episcopal palace. In Soviet times, it had been the headquarters of the regional KGB. Starting in the Gorbachev period, Kirill established close relations with the Smolensk civic authorities, which gave him a head start in his rebuilding programme. He was the first bishop to reclaim a substantial swathe of ecclesiastical buildings, including the episcopal palace and administrative buildings adjacent to the cathedral. His ability and energy did not go unnoticed. In 1989, five years into his exile, he was recalled to the capital and, following in the footsteps of his mentor Nikodim, put in charge of the Department of External Relations (DECR). That job made him a leading figure in international Church affairs.

Nowadays, he likes to tell people that his provincial exile was the making of him. 'Walking those dirt roads to parishes that had opened after World War Two only to lead a squalid existence in semi-ruined buildings' and hearing about the everyday struggles of penniless villagers helped him to realise that 'Russia is much wider than Moscow and Leningrad'.[35]

Ladizhenkova, the choir director, said Smolensk was a test which he passed with flying colours. 'To rise so high, he needed to toughen up somehow,' she told me. 'And I know how hard he worked on himself because the Kirill who first came to us was not the same person who became Patriarch 24 years later. He was a completely different man'.

☦ ☦ ☦

When Kirill entertained guests at his dinner table in Smolensk he often boasted that they were eating the best bread in Russia. He explained to Bourdeaux in painstaking detail all about the grain, the milling process and the finances. Kirill not only sensed which way the political winds were blowing, he also had a wily instinct for profit.

Once he was made the Church's equivalent of foreign minister, Kirill spent more time in Moscow to nurture what eventually turned into a formidable business empire. As Patriarch, Alexei had around 40 members of staff; Kirill's Department for External Church Relations (DECR), housed in a turquoise building in the Danilovsky Monastery, had a 300-strong workforce. Taking advantage of tax incentives provided for businesses established by religious organisations, the DECR founded the Peresvet commercial bank, the Nika charitable foundation, a media outlet called Free People's Television (SNT) and other structures.

In the early 1990s, the Church was exempted from paying customs duties on some items, which seemed uncontroversial at the time. People largely sympathised with an institution which had suffered seven decades of persecution and needed help to rebuild. The Church enjoyed an immense level of trust and legitimacy. But a few years later, Russians were amazed to learn that the Patriarchate had become Russia's largest supplier of foreign cigarettes. Most Russian clerics see smoking as a sin, according to an Orthodox website edited by Putin's favourite bishop, Tikhon Shevkunov.[36] Yet the Moscow Patriarchate had imported vast quantities of cigarettes, especially Camel and Winston, under the guise of 'humanitarian aid'. Kirill's Nika Foundation was the main link. The charity's vice president was an archpriest, Vladimir Veriga, who also happened to be the commercial director of the DECR. Nika imported billions of cigarettes and netted hundreds of millions of US dollars in profit. In 1996 alone, Nika imported about 8 billion cigarettes into the country. Every tenth cigarette smoked at the time was brought into Russia by the Church. Because they were imported free of duty, the government missed out on about $40 million in tax.[37] Other importers, who were forced to pay customs duties, lost market share and began leaking details of the scheme to the media.[38]

At first Kirill denied that such a business was taking place, then he denied the Church was selling the cigarettes directly. He said they were distributed by secular or special government organisations, such as the Russian army in Chechnya. He later told a BBC interviewer that 'unfortunately some journalists present this picture from the wrong side'.[39] When the story could no longer be contained, Kirill tried to shift the responsibility onto the government. At a press conference in the Danilovsky Hotel in February 1997, he said much of the humanitarian aid sent was of no use to the Church, 'for example hundreds of motors for refrigerators, window frames and finally cigarettes from Philip Morris Products Inc in Basel Switzerland. "Should we burn these cigarettes or send them back?" he asked. "We turned to the government, and it made a decision: recognise them as humanitarian cargo."'[40] Journalists were told that the money from the cigarettes was being used for social programmes and to restore ruined churches. No detailed financial reports were made public.

The investigative journalist Sergei Bychkov, who broke the story and dubbed Kirill the 'Tobacco Metropolitan', was astonished by the sums of money involved.[41] He showed me a letter dated 4 November 1996 and signed by the First Deputy Finance Minister Andrei Vavilov. It says the State Customs Committee calculated that up until 15 October 1996, the Church imported 18 billion cigarettes duty free, netting 830 billion roubles – roughly $476 million at the time. Over the same two-and-a-half-year period, the duty on 21 million litres of wine it imported was also exempted, the equivalent of 242 billion roubles or $179 million. The average monthly salary in Russia in the mid-1990s was less than $100. According to Bychkov, more than $50 million worth of Church cigarettes then ended up stuck in customs warehouses. 'Russia is going through difficult times,' he wrote. 'There are hundreds of thousands of kids living on the street in our country. The liquidators of Chernobyl [people who helped clean up after the 1986 nuclear disaster] are penniless and starving. Old people are forced to beg. Why not clear customs of the tobacco and give the proceeds to orphans or liquidators?'[42]

Yeltsin eventually put a stop to charitable exemptions in 1997; the loss of tax income was increasing Russia's budget deficit. Other charitable organisations which relied on receiving tax-free humanitarian aid from abroad suffered as a result. Reflecting on the affair two decades later, the academician Sergei Komkov wrote: 'Being the president of the All-Russian Education Fund in those hard times and having the relief from customs duties, I did not even think about importing alcohol or tobacco to help children in Russia. We brought children's clothing, shoes and food from Southeast Asia.' Some goods were sold to raise money for schools and some donated to children in orphanages.[43] Andrei Kuraev described Yeltsin's ban on tax exemptions as indiscriminate and unfair. He wrote that the heads of charities went to Kirill with a request: 'Could you, in a Christian way, ask the president not to punish other people because of your activities?' To which they received a response to the effect that 'we must be united: we worked together, we will stop together'.[44]

In 2009, the eve of the elections for the new patriarch, the tobacco scandal resurfaced. Hilarion, one of Kirill's proteges, leapt to the defence of his boss: 'In the nineties, I repeatedly asked the Metropolitan: "Why don't you respond to these attacks? If you didn't sign the documents, why don't you name the names of those who did sign them?" His answer was always the same: "I can't and don't want to 'frame' anyone." By naming names, we will strike a blow at the Church.'[45]

In the mid-1990s, the Patriarchate was also involved in an even more lucrative business – oil exports via the International Economic Partnership (MES in Russian), in which it had a 20 per cent stake. If Kirill's subordinates at the Department of External Church Relations kept quiet about the deal, Yuri Tavrovsky, MES's press secretary, was open about the Church's financial interest. He said that between 1992 and 1996, the group exported more than 20 million tons of oil and oil products. Its total profit in 1996 was $2 billion. But in July

1997, regulations on oil exports were tightened up and the Church stopped trading.

Officially, Kirill does not own any palaces, yachts, limousines, jets, vestments, watches or other luxury items. Some are gifts from well-wishers. On paper most assets belong to the Church.[46] According to one investigation by Russian journalists, Patriarch Kirill owns three apartments under his secular name, Vladimir Gundyaev, in Moscow and St Petersburg, including a penthouse near the Kremlin.[47] These are separate from the twenty-odd grace and favour residences at his disposal, including the former home of Russia's imperial family, south of St Petersburg in Tsarskoe Selo. The Kremlin's property management department financed renovations there to the tune of 2.8 billion roubles. On the government procurement website only the client and the cost were indicated. Any contractors bidding for the job needed an FSB licence clearing them for work related to state secrets.[48] A Church spokesman dismissed press reports that the complex was a private residence for Kirill as 'total absurdity'. He said the Patriarch might stay there from time to time but it was also for visiting government officials, foreign delegations to St Petersburg and visiting parishioners.[49]

Kirill often rails against consumerism. At a student rally in Moscow in 2009, he warned that an economic system 'built solely on the pursuit of profit, on indifference to the fate of people, on disregard for moral norms' could collapse at any moment, 'burying ordinary people under its rubble'. When a billionaire was arrested in 2007 in connection with an alleged prostitution ring in the French ski resort of Courchevel, Kirill told a state-run TV channel: 'We all know what happens when our fat cats start throwing money around abroad, they bring shame on Russia.' He added that conflict between rich and poor was responsible for the overthrow of the tsarist regime, which led to the tragedy of revolution and civil war.

Yet the Patriarch acknowledged that questions about his wealth had become all-pervasive during a sermon to celebrate the Feast of St Elijah.[50] He cited the example of an elderly bishop he met on a flight when he was still Metropolitan Kirill, in charge of the DECR. The bishop complained that his diocese was in dire straits and asked for money. Kirill replied that the Patriarchate would send funds, but the old man shook his head. He wanted some of the Metropolitan's own money, since he had read that Kirill had six billion dollars at his personal disposal. 'I looked at this bishop,' Kirill told the congregation, 'and I asked if he was joking and he said no, not really. So, you see, this nonsense got into the bishop's head and he believed it.' Media stories about his property, Kirill told them, were designed 'to discredit those who proclaim the truth of God, so that the people stop listening to us'.

☦ ☦ ☦

When Patriarch Alexei died in December 2008, his body was taken to Christ the Saviour and displayed for three days in an open casket surrounded by candles and flowers. Tens of thousands of people queued in the rain outside to catch a last glimpse of him, although his face, like that of Orthodox saints in catacombs, was covered by a white and gold embroidered cloth. Both Prime Minister Putin and his stand-in president, Medvedev, bent down to kiss him.

Once the six-hour funeral service and private burial rites were over, the race was on to elect Alexei's successor. As acting head of the Church, Kirill was the clear front runner. However, the government, nervous about the financial crash and possible social unrest, was thought to prefer the more conservative Metropolitan Kliment of Kaluga and Borovsk. One aide worried that Kirill was a 'difficult customer' and 'too complicated'.[51] Some officials had not forgotten his role in drawing up the Church's Social Doctrine in 2000, which decreed that the state's authority was not absolute. It included red-button issues for Orthodox conservatives like abortion while also addressing social inequality and poverty. At a Christmas service attended by Medvedev, Kirill suggested the government had a moral duty to address the financial crisis. The expert Sergei Filatov captured the wariness. 'Among the bishops, he's the only real politician. If I were president, I'd be afraid of such a man,' he said.[52]

Inside the Church, traditionalists distrusted him as a *zapadnik*, a Westerniser, who had been involved in the ecumenical movement and favoured closer ties with Rome. Ever the strategist, Kirill sought to appease the conservatives just before the crucial vote was cast.

Addressing the church council, he echoed Alexei's hostility towards missionaries. 'We have noted with bitterness that members of the Catholic clergy and monastic orders are among the newly formed enlighteners of Rus,' he told them. The electorate was varied. Among lay delegates were government officials and well-connected businessmen. Even a circus director from the southern city of Astrakhan had a vote.[53] Celebrity magazines ran profiles of the 'charismatic' Metropolitan and praised his oratory skills.

When reports about the alcohol and tobacco imports resurfaced, a former tax minister, Alexander Pochinok, went on the radio insisting that Kirill had nothing to do with the deals.[54] He said Alexei had been cash-strapped and had asked the government to help. In one interview, Pochinok blamed Metropolitan Kliment, who also worked in the DECR in the 1990s – and a decade later happened to be Kirill's rival for the top job in the Church. 'Through this tax-free corridor, almost everything was imported into Russia,' said Pochinok, 'from tobacco to six hundred Mercedes saloons. At the same time, in official documents vodka was listed as wine, and a Mercedes car as an ambulance.' Pochinok added that Alexei 'realised the hole he was being dragged into' and abandoned the scheme with Kirill's full support.[55]

Four days after the interview appeared, Kirill emerged the victor. He won 508 of the votes cast by the 702-member Church Council at a secret ballot at Christ the Saviour. The following Sunday, as he was enthroned, the cathedral's mightiest bell tolled sixteen times, denoting his position as the sixteenth patriarch of the world's largest Orthodox Church. He was dressed in a green mantle symbolising eternal life and wore the patriarch's white koukoulion. The headdress with long side flaps like the ears of a bloodhound was originally worn by Egyptian monks. It was supposed to look like the caps worn by babies to remind holy men of children's purity. To the cry of *Axios!*, Worthy in Greek, the metropolitans of Kyiv and St Petersburg lifted Patriarch Kirill and seated him three times on the throne in the altar of the cathedral.

Western reporters hailed Kirill as a 'trailblazer' and a 'moderniser' who was not afraid of wading into politics. The Russian media focused more on his pledge to preserve the unity of the Church.

The patriarch's task, he said in his first address, was to prevent schisms and false teachings. Dissent, he stressed, 'should not weaken the common efforts to build the house of God'. He signalled that he would build relations in line with the constitution, according to which the church is separated from the state. It was every Christian's duty to care for orphans and the poor, invalids, the elderly, the imprisoned and homeless. 'The voice of the church must also become the voice of the weak and the powerless, of those seeking justice,' he added. He pledged to make young people the recipients of his 'special care'.

Kirill announced a plan to rejuvenate the clergy and expand the Church. In a series of reforms, he increased the number of dioceses by slicing up existing ones into several parts. Just before he took over at the end of 2008, Russia had 159 dioceses and 203 bishops. A decade later these numbers had doubled. Over the same period nearly 10,000 new parishes and 9,844 extra clergymen were created. Dividing the metropolises and dioceses into smaller structures, the Patriarch nurtured a team of young, loyal bishops who owed their meteoric careers to him.

Media was also central to his strategy. Kirill was already well known to Russian TV audiences through his sermons on his *Word of the Shepherd* programme, regularly aired on Channel One since 1994. He wanted to address a wider cross-section of society. He delivered sermons in football stadiums; he addressed crowds from the stage of a rock concert in Kyiv during festivities to mark the 1,020th anniversary of the baptism of Rus. Sergei Chapnin, then editor of the *Journal of the Moscow Patriarchate*, was initially excited by this outreach work. He called the new Primate's open-air preaching 'one of his brightest and most impressive initiatives'.[56] Wherever he went, Kirill made a point of meeting teenagers and students in front of TV cameras. Paraphrasing Dostoevsky, who called the hearts of men a battlefield, Kirill once said that the media sphere was 'exactly where the devil fights with God'. Two months after he was enthroned, he created a Synodal Information Department to raise the profile of the Church and ensure it spoke with one voice. Instead of choosing a cleric to run it, Kirill picked the chairman of the department of international journalism from Moscow's prestigious Institute for International Relations, a training ground for diplomats.

In a sea of black cassocks, Vladimir Legoyda stands out in his polo-neck sweaters and smart jackets. Disarmingly suave, he has a slight American twang in his voice when he speaks English, a hangover from his time as an overseas exchange student. Although he sometimes went to church in Moscow, he first got excited about Orthodoxy in northern California. While living there he met a rock guitarist, Justin Marler, who ditched a lucrative record contract as a punk rock musician to join the St Herman of Alaska Monastery, established by American Orthodox missionaries. Legoyda helped him and some other monks to put out a self-published magazine called *Death to the World*, which blended Orthodox asceticism with punk subculture. The cover of the first issue featured a monk holding a skull and the words 'The Last True Rebellion'.[57] On his return to Russia, Legoyda saw a gap in the market and began 'an Orthodox magazine for doubters'. *Foma* is named after Doubting Thomas, the apostle who needed to touch Jesus' ribs before believing in his resurrection. The glossy monthly aims to be intellectually provocative, focusing on culture, philosophy and theology.

Kirill appointed this apparent liberal as deputy editor of the Church's official publication, the *Journal of the Moscow Patriarchate*, alongside an arch conservative, Vsevolod Chaplin, as his spokesman on social affairs. Chaplin suggested discotheques and bars should be replaced by 'Orthodox nightclubs', where young people would gather for late-night readings and discussion.

As a secular professional and Orthodox believer, Legoyda understood his boss needed new strategies to reach his unchurched flock. Given the lack of functioning churches in some parts of the country, Kirill prioritised the development of online Orthodoxy. By 2015 there were around 10,000 websites, including many individual blogs by priests or online representations of parishes and monasteries. In a country as vast as Russia, many people use these sites to help them create their own religious communities. Some priests living in small villages with no more than a dozen parishioners have tens of thousands of followers online, in Russia and abroad. Andrei Kuraev, who was defrocked for disobedience and for publicising various Church scandals, had the comparatively low rank of deacon but is Orthodoxy's best-known independent voice. I was walking through a flea market in Vienna with him when two middle-aged Georgian women came rushing up, timid smiles on their faces. 'Father Andrei, is it really you?' one of them asked, clutching his arm. 'Please look after yourself. We all need you so badly!' they said.

As Ksenia Luchenko, author of a guidebook to the Orthodox Internet, points out, 'the converse case is also true: many clerics in high offices and positions remain almost unknown to the internet users, their online authority is merely formal, and their opinion is insignificant'.[58] In 2010, the Church launched its own YouTube channel and in the opening address Kirill hoped that it would 'bring proactive, especially young, people closer to the word of God, God's wisdom, the law of God that is the law of life'. The new patriarch also created personal pages on Facebook and its Russian equivalent VKontakte, and an Instagram account. The medium may be modern but not so much the message. Ordinary clergy and the laity feature little except to provide backdrops in photo opportunities featuring senior clerics. Church platforms appear to stimulate dialogue between users, but often any real debate is quickly stifled. On Kirill's personal page on VKontakte, the comment function is strictly moderated. Most of the time it is not available.[59]

In the first few years of his leadership, the new Patriarch was seen as a liberal ecumenist with a broad understanding of foreign affairs. Many took at face value his pledges to strengthen the Church and make it independent of political and economic interests. Although the Patriarchate had canonised hundreds of victims of the Communists and had become a veritable factory of twentieth-century saints, Kirill had shown little personal interest in confronting the perpetrators of Soviet-era crimes. Yet some dared to hope that under him the Church would become a strong moral force and would address the twenty-first century problems plaguing Russia – poverty, lawlessness and corruption.

Archimandrite Cyril Hovorun put his faith in the new Patriarch. Born and brought up in Ukraine, Hovorun first excelled in theoretical physics before focusing on theology. He was ordained by Kirill and advised him in different capacities from 2002 to 2012, before and after he became patriarch. Hovorun was spokesman for the Moscow Patriarchate in Kyiv and was also given the brief to shake up religious education. Kirill initially seemed like the 'most open-minded hierarch in the Orthodox world'. Hovorun remembers an encouraging boss who was good company, filled with creative ideas and 'completely different to most other bishops'. He admired the Patriarch's erudition and oratory skills. He told me that Kirill was curious about religious education and culture around the globe. 'But then instead of importing ideas and seeing how they might apply to Russia, he began exporting them,' Hovorun said. 'His concept of *Russky Mir* (Russian World) became ever more nationalistic and belligerent.'

A hundred days into his leadership, the Patriarch was asked about his Social Concept for the Orthodox Church that described freedom as above all else, freedom from sin. A journalist from the daily *Izvestia* asked whether a religious person needed freedom of speech, assembly and elections. Kirill replied that political freedoms were important – within the right moral guidelines. He explained his understanding of 'symphony', the concept inherited from Orthodox Byzantium defining the relations between church and state. He said it 'meant specifically the independence of the secular and spiritual authorities from one another and their cooperation, but in no event their merger'.

Kirill was not always in lockstep with the authorities. Shortly after taking power in 2000, Putin decided to restore the Soviet national anthem, ditching the Yeltsin-era 'Patriotic Song' originally composed by Mikhail Glinka in 1833. The President preferred the stirring Second World War melody written by the composer Alexander Alexandrov which started with the words: 'Unbreakable union of free republics/Welded forever by the mighty Rus". Yeltsin, and many from the outgoing government, were appalled. Russia's veteran human rights groups, Memorial and the Moscow Helsinki Group, said that the Soviet hymn, even with new lyrics, 'evoked the spirit of the Stalinist empire, built on the bones of millions'. The world-famous cellist Mstislav Rostropovich vowed not to stand when it was played. Kirill described the decision as 'wrong from the start' and said the Glinka version was more suitable for a modern hymn, adding that it was 'a great mistake to see a country's anthem as a mindless combination of music and words, where components can be replaced at random'. They were all ignored.

On occasion, Kirill seemed to take the side of impoverished Russians against the government. In March 2011, he called soaring utilities tariffs 'an outrage' and urged ordinary people to defend their rights. 'A real civil society cannot exist unless people want to make life around them better, to make a personal contribution to the effort to change the social situation,' he said. He was even more outspoken in December that year amidst widespread anger at ballot rigging in parliamentary elections.

✝ ✝ ✝

A young Orthodox priest, Father Dmitry Sverdlov, volunteering as an observer at a Moscow polling station was shocked by the fraud taking place in front of his eyes. In a blog on the Orthodox website Pravmir, he described seeing two equally sized stacks of ballot papers, yet 690 votes were recorded for Putin's United Russia against 202 for the Communists. His request for a recount was turned down. 'What are you doing?' Sverdlov asked the schoolteachers turned polling clerks. 'We all saw what happened here. Your job is to teach children and now you are participating in a lie; you are destroying our country with your own hands!'[60]

Similar outrage brought thousands onto the streets after polling day. On the second night of the protests, hundreds were arrested, including the former deputy prime minister, Boris Nemtsov. Riot police armed with batons drove people out of the city's Triumph Square. With each passing day, the crowds grew bigger and the Church more vocal. A popular Moscow priest, Father Andrei Zuevsky, posted a sermon on his Facebook page attacking the arrogance of those in power. 'They refuse anyone but themselves the right to decide what is good and what is bad,' he wrote. Even a conservative archpriest who headed the Church department overseeing relations with the army and law enforcement defended believers' rights to join the protest. 'What's Orthodoxy got to do with it?' he said. 'Can the Orthodox go to the baker's? Of course – the Constitution is for everyone.'

When no fewer than 100,000 people marched along Sakharov Avenue on 24 December, Kirill called for 'real civic dialogue'. A week later he surprised many by describing the protests as a 'legitimate negative reaction' to falsified results and the actions of government bureaucracy. He could no longer ignore the largest demonstrations in Moscow since the early 1990s. This was the moment when the anti-corruption blogger Alexei Navalny shot to prominence with his pithy description of Putin's United Russia as 'the party of crooks and thieves'.

In a televised sermon on Orthodox Christmas Day, 7 January 2012, Kirill reinforced the message, saying it would be a 'very bad sign' if the authorities ignored the protesters. Although the Church could not take sides, Kirill said that everyone has 'the right to freedom of expression, even if they view things differently from the state'.

At this point, Russia's leading music journalist, Artemy Troitsky, had an idea: he wanted to forge links between Navalny, an Orthodox believer, and the Church. Together with other well-known intellectuals and opposition figures, Troitsky had made speeches at the demonstrations against election fraud. All wore white ribbons, symbols of the so-called Winter Revolution. A rattled Putin ridiculed them for 'looking like condoms'. Troitsky's gleeful response was to address the crowds dressed in a white, furry sheath and a Santa Claus hat. Offstage, Troitsky engaged in some quiet diplomacy and asked a friend at the Patriarchate to introduce him to Kirill's media manager, Legoyda. He suggested a partnership between the protest movement and progressive forces inside the Church. They talked about the Orthodox saint Nil Sorsky, a fifteenth-century anti-corruption campaigner who led the *nestyazhateli*, the non-possessors' movement, which opposed land ownership by the Church. Legoyda was cautiously enthusiastic. 'He thought it would be a positive step – to emphasise solidarity with the people and refocus on spiritual rather than material things,' said Troitsky. 'But then, at our second meeting, he told me that he had spoken with somebody and there was no interest in such an alliance.' That person, he indicated, was Kirill.

The democracy movement was gearing up for its first big protest of 2012, seen as a major test of the protesters' resolve. If the turnout was large, many believed the authorities would have to make some concessions to the opposition. There were signs of nervousness in the Kremlin. The previous October, Medvedev had stunned Russians and foreign governments by meekly announcing he would not run for a second term as president; he would step aside for Putin.

Two days before a rally scheduled for 4 February, Kirill made a U-turn. At a liturgy to celebrate his third anniversary as patriarch, he made no mention of the protest. Orthodox believers, he said, 'do not know how to join demonstrations, their voices are not heard. They pray in the silence of monastic cells and at home.' Raising the spectre of the Bolshevik Revolution and the chaos of the 1990s, he warned that Russians had been seduced before with disastrous results. 'Remember that the loudest yells, the most piercing words, aren't always the genuine, true and honest ones,' he said.

Did somebody lean on the Patriarch to change his tune? Or perhaps, sensing that Putin was not going to budge, Kirill swiftly changed tack. It was a tactic his predecessors had used at previous times of strife.

Four days later, at a meeting on 8 February with religious leaders at the Danilovsky Monastery, Kirill told Putin his presidency had been 'a miracle from God' and that his restoration to his rightful position would be a cause for celebration: 'You once said you toil like a slave in the galleys, with the only difference that no slave showed such dedication.' Putin replied that the separation of church and state had always been a 'primitive notion'. From now on both men should devote themselves to 'a totally different idea of cooperation'.

☦ ☦ ☦

It was this sycophancy that prompted Pussy Riot's performance in the Cathedral of Christ the Saviour a fortnight later, begging the Mother of God to banish Putin and castigating his lackey Kirill. The young women used the Patriarch's secular surname to drive home their contempt: '*Patriarch Gundy believes in Putin / Better believe in God, you vermin!*' With its description of a priest in black robes with golden epaulettes, their 'punk prayer' condemned a Church infiltrated by the secret police, its misogyny and homophobia, corruption, the penetration of religion into secular schools, superstition and above all its craven attitude to power.

> *Congregations genuflect*
> *Black robes brag gilt epaulettes,*
> *Freedom's phantom's gone to heaven,*
> *Gay Pride's chained and in detention.*

KGB's chief saint descends
To guide the punks to prison vans
Don't upset His Saintliness, ladies
Stick to making love and babies.[61]

Those who complained that the cathedral was the wrong venue to stage a political protest were missing the point. In her court statement, one band member, Yekaterina Samutsevich, who had trained in computer programming, said they chose Christ the Saviour as their platform precisely because it had been 'used openly as a flashy backdrop for the politics of the security forces'. Another of the jailed band members, Maria Alyokhina, later pointed out in her prison diary that the cathedral that the women were accused of maligning was itself tainted by corruption: 'Government officials and other higher-ups' were able to bypass day-long queues to view the holy belt of the Mother of God, from the Vatopedi Monastery on Mount Athos. Christ the Saviour made a fortune from hosting corporate events and selling 'fine porcelain eggs and custom-made replicas of imperial medals for 500 bucks' in its gift shops.[62] An Orthodox believer, Alyokhina was involved in a number of religious charities and argued passionately that the Church belonged to the people, not the authorities in hock to Putin.

Nadezhda Tolokonnikova, the youngest in the group and a philosophy student, explained that the performance was prompted by Kirill's calls for voters to back Putin in March. 'We, like many of our fellow citizens, wrestle against treachery, deceit, bribery, hypocrisy, greed and lawlessness peculiar to the current authorities and rulers,' she wrote on her blog just before their trial. 'That is why we were upset by this political initiative of the Patriarch and we could not fail to express that.'

I had a foretaste of Pussy Riot's tactics two years before, when I met members of an art collective to which Tolokonnikova once belonged. Despite its name *Voina*, which means War, its weapons were satire and showmanship. Voina's members caused a stir in 2008 when they staged an orgy at Moscow's State Biological Museum. Five couples, including a heavily pregnant Tolokonnikova and her then husband Pyotr Verzilov, walked into one of the exhibition halls, stripped off and started having sex. The performance, which was filmed and posted online, was called 'Fuck for the Little Bear Cub Successor'. It referred to Medvedev, whose last name derives from *medved*, the word for bear. He often talked about boosting Russia's birth rate. When people complained the stunt was pornographic, the artists said they were reflecting the obscenity of fake elections. Putin, they argued, had presented the country with a fait accompli by picking 'a politician whom no one knew at the time' to be the next president. 'At that moment, they truly did screw the country,' said Tolokonnikova. 'We portrayed this as best we could, using the traditions of modern art.'[63]

I wanted to meet the collective and had been emailing someone called Sandra. She would not give me a phone number but arranged a late-night rendezvous outside a Moscow metro station. As I stood stamping my feet in the cold, I realised I had no idea what she looked like. To make matters worse, a guy in a hooded blue jacket kept eye-balling me. I avoided his gaze and walked a few paces away. Then it emerged that he was 'Sandra', otherwise known as Oleg Vorotnikov, one of Voina's founders. As we roamed the dark streets, he told me about entering a supermarket dressed in an Orthodox cassock, gold cross and a policeman's peaked cap. It is a freakish image, prefig-uring the punk prayer, and seemed to belong to the mismatched heads, bodies and legs of a children's card game. Calmly, Vorotnikov strolled down the aisles, helped himself to five large bags of food and pushed his trolley past the cashier, without paying. Nobody chal-lenged him. The stunt, he explained, was a protest against the fact that priests and police officers in Russia seem to be above the law. 'A cop in the priest's robe is like Satan,' Vorotnikov said. 'He can do whatever he likes.'

Pussy Riot initially believed that their Christ the Saviour action had been a washout. Hardly anyone was in the cathedral at the time apart from a few security personnel, a sacristan and a woman trim-ming candles. One member of the group was chased away by guards and the flash-mob-like performance of the four others lasted less than a minute before they too were escorted off the premises. It was the video later posted online, which combined footage from Christ the Saviour with clips shot in another Moscow cathedral, that attracted attention and led to the group's arrest a few weeks later. The soundtrack was a potent combination of punk-style screaming with the opening melody and refrain from Sergei Rachmaninov's 'All-Night Vigil' – *Bogoroditse Devo, Raduisya* – an Orthodox version of 'Ave Maria'.

Pussy Riot's critique of church–state relations did not go down well with traditionalists. Many in the anti-Putin intelligentsia regarded it as disrespectful and in poor taste. Navalny, the leading opposition figure, called it 'idiotic'. A survey by the All-Russian Centre for Public Opinion Research showed that only 13 per cent of people believed it was a political protest; the overwhelming majority saw it as delinquency or blasphemy. As it turned out, Pussy Riot's act was extremely useful for Putin. As church historian Geraldine Fagan later observed: 'It allowed him to drive a wedge between the Church and the Russian opposition; a relationship which, had it been left to foster, could have been devastating to him.'[64]

Many Russians went online to express their anger against the women. One television presenter headlined his blog post *Voina Bliadei*, the War of the Whores. Scenting blood, the Church went on the attack. In a post entitled 'Blasphemy Before the Holy Gates', Vsevolod Chaplin, the Church spokesman, demanded a fitting punishment for the women. 'We cannot and we will not live in a state where such actions are possible,' he wrote. Under existing legislation, offending religious feelings or desecrating sacred objects only carried a penalty of up to 1,000 roubles, which, in his opinion, was 'far too mild'.[65]

Sergei Rybko, a Moscow priest and a Soviet-era hippy, came to Orthodoxy through rock music. He was so enamoured of Deep Purple that he once presented its lead vocalist, Ian Gillan, with an icon of Our Lady of Vladimir. He was an effective missionary and delivered punchy sermons at open-air concerts. He told crowds they belonged to Sgt Pepper's Lonely Hearts Club, but that they would never feel isolated if they reached out to God. Given his dissident past, some assumed he would defend Pussy Riot. Not a bit of it. 'They should be given forced labour,' he declared. 'Anyway, they are not real punk musicians. They were paid to perform.'[66]

In the absence of a tougher law, prosecutors charged three of the women with 'hooliganism motivated by religious hatred', an offence that carried a jail sentence of up to seven years. In March, 46 per cent of people polled by the respected Levada Centre wanted the women locked up, though the percentage dropped to 33 per cent by July.[67] Even though they had no prior criminal record, they were deemed too dangerous to be granted bail and appeared in a tightly guarded glass box at Moscow's Khamovnichesky District Court. The language used in a secular courtroom recalled the Salem witch trials. The judge castigated the women for their tight-fitting mini-dresses, their 'demonic twitching' near the altar, and the improper way in which they crossed themselves. Such behaviour, she ruled, 'offended the sensibilities of Orthodox believers'. Most people called as witnesses by the prosecution had not seen the alleged crime – except online or in TV reports. One told the court he was so alarmed by the 'black energy' emanating from the video he called the police. The trial was described as an inquisition and an exorcism by one of Pussy Riot's lawyers. Vladimir Zhiyanov, Alyokhina's father, looked bewildered when the verdict was read out: two years in a penal colony for each of the women. 'I guess Putin is trying to tell us how it's going to be while he's in power,' he said. 'He will make the rules up as he sees fit. If that's the case, God help us.'[68]

The women had already spent five months in custody, away from their families and young children. Tolokonnikova's daughter, Gera, was four years old, while Alyokhina had a six-year-old son, Filipp. Even before the trial opened, people who initially took the side of the Church were starting to sympathise with Pussy Riot instead. Lidia Monavia, a Christian charity worker running a Moscow children's hospice, appealed directly to the Patriarch, urging him to ask the authorities to close the criminal case. 'We, the authors of this letter, are believers,' she wrote. 'Most of us consider such behaviour in church intolerable. Yet we consider the reaction towards this event even more intolerable.' Her petition was signed by 5,000 lay members of the Church.

Kirill was in no mood to turn the other cheek. In his first public statement a month after the punk prayer, he said: 'the devil has laughed at all of us. We have no future if we allow mockery in front of sacred shrines.' He was most annoyed by the approach of Deacon Kuraev, one of his subordinates, who suggested the Church's reaction flew in the face of Orthodox tradition. In his blog, Kuraev reminded the Patriarch that the performance had taken place during the February carnival, or *Maslenitsa*, 'a time of buffoonery'. Under Peter the Great, nobody would have been shocked by Pussy Riot's swearing and brightly coloured costumes – subversive acts were part of Church life.

Intrigued by Kuraev's interpretation, I went to see him in his Moscow flat a few months later. For hours, I sat in his kitchen drinking tea with his father, Vyacheslav, who told me he was an atheist and had been secretary to a leading Communist Party ideologist. Eventually, Kuraev turned up on his trademark motor scooter, his black robe flapping behind him. By now it was late at night, but our interview was constantly interrupted by phone calls. I noticed the icon screensaver on his mobile and the incongruous ringtone – Bob Marley's 'Get Up, Stand Up'. Instead of punishing the Christ the Saviour performers, he told me, true Orthodox clerics should have served them pancakes and mead in keeping with the spirit of the season. Human rights activists from the Moscow Helsinki Group agreed. In a protest letter, they invoked the ancient Russian tradition of the *Yurodivy*, or Holy Fool, who was able, with impunity, to criticise the tsar. Instead, 'the well-educated and courageous followers of Saint Basil' were behind bars. Kuraev said the punks should have been encouraged to repent in the cathedral on the Day of Forgiveness, at the start of Lent, 40 days before Easter.

In the fourth week of Lent, with the three women already in pre-trial detention for twenty days, the Patriarch presented their actions as an affront to the Church and an attack on the Russian state. Addressing a congregation after the liturgy of St John Chrysostom, he said Russia owed its existence to Orthodoxy. Faith had moved people to 'the greatest feats', including the defence of the Fatherland against Napoleon. He reminded them that Christ the Saviour, desecrated by Pussy Riot, was originally built to honour that 1812 victory. Although he did not mention Kuraev by name, he said 'there are people who justify this blasphemy, downplay it and seek to interpret it as some funny joke. That is sad and I'm feeling profoundly appalled that amongst these people, there are those who call themselves Orthodox.' A circular letter was sent to all churches in Moscow, to be read out after the liturgy. Addressed to the chief prosecutor, it demanded that the women be investigated for extremism and requested the maximum sentence for hooliganism and aggravated blasphemy. In some churches, it was pinned onto a noticeboard, with space for supporters to sign their names underneath.

A month later, the Patriarch called on believers to attend a *molitvennoe stoyanie*, a standing prayer in defence of the faith. Tens of thousands gathered outside Christ the Saviour, where he addressed them from a specially built stage. Crammed inside metal barriers, many people held imperial flags, icons and banners. The Cossacks were out in force, along with members of the pro-Kremlin Night Wolves biker club. The Patriarch compared modern 'defilers' with the foes of Christ and told the crowds that the Church had once again come under attack from 'enemy forces'. Then he conducted a service in which twenty bishops in full red and gold regalia lined up to purge the blasphemy. Priests carried recently vandalised crosses and icons from churches outside Moscow alongside a pockmarked icon which the Bolsheviks had sprayed with bullets back in the 1920s. The message was clear: oppression of clerics and believers remains an ever-present threat. Some cities set up armed Orthodox militias to defend churches from 'vandalism'.

Legoyda, Kirill's supposedly more liberal spokesman, claimed the punks had gone further than the Bolsheviks in attacking the church. 'The God fighters of Soviet times would at least lead the believers out of the church before attempting to destroy it, to desecrate it. This recent "protest action" took place in a functioning church, right in front of the faithful.'[69] For all his bluster, Legoyda admitted he personally did not see a reason to keep the women in custody. On the other hand, Vitaly Milonov, a United Russia deputy from St Petersburg, known for his campaign against LGBT+ rights and for posing in an 'Orthodoxy or Death' T-shirt, was delighted they were being punished. He warned they would not be safe once they got out of prison. 'They're not accepted as human by most of society; they are mad Valkyries,' he told me.

The justice minister, Alexander Konovalov, said that as a practising Christian he found the protest in the country's main church 'unpleasant'. But speaking 'soberly and rationally' as a lawyer, he doubted the women deserved a prison sentence.[70] Putin, meanwhile, remained studiously neutral. He apologised before all the believers and the clergy for Pussy Riot 'if they violated the law'.[71] Later, on a visit to London, he said he hoped they would 'not be judged too harshly'.

One retired priest, Father Vyacheslav Vinnikov, likened the baying of the mob against the women, led by the Patriarch, to those who wanted to crucify Christ. Kuraev spoke of his sadness that 'today many people consider the church to be a generator of hatred and vindictiveness while the women of this feminist band are already donning the Martyr's Crown in place of those ski masks they wore on February 21st'.[72] He was referring to the brightly coloured balaclavas the women wore for their short-lived performance, face coverings which inspired activists all over the world.

If the masks gained iconic status so did another widely viewed item that year – Kirill's Swiss watch. Photographers in Ukraine first noticed the $30,000 Breguet timepiece on the prelate's wrist during a prayer service in St Volodymyr's Cathedral in 2009. Journalists and bloggers noted the white gold case and crocodile-leather strap. On that same trip, he warned against the dangers of Western capitalism. 'If the whole of society embarks on the path of unbridled consumption, then our land will not withstand it,' he told Ukraine's Inter TV channel. 'It is very important to learn Christian asceticism. This is the ability to regulate one's appetite. This is the victory of a person over lust, passions and instinct.'

The watch was largely forgotten until April 2012, when a picture emerged of Kirill wearing it in a meeting with Konovalov, the justice minister. The Church's PR team made matters worse by using Photoshop to remove it but neglecting to erase its reflection on a shiny table.[73] People joked that the disappearing watch was truly a miracle. At first Kirill denied wearing it; then he claimed it was a gift from a wealthy parishioner. The affair was a spectacular case of media mismanagement. But some believed it was stage-managed by the security services to bring the Patriarch to heel.

Another curious story surfaced around the same time about a property in the House of the Embankment, the famous block opposite the Kremlin built for the Soviet elite. One of its residents, Lidiya Leonova, fell out with her neighbour, a retired cardiologist and former health minister, Yury Shevchenko. She claimed building work in his apartment had caused 26 million roubles' ($900,000) worth of damage to her five-bedroom property. Although she lived in the flat, it belonged to the head of the Church. Leonova was upset to find that 'all of the property, including the library, was covered in a thick layer of dust'. She told the court that hazardous 'nanoparticles' from the renovation of Shevchenko's home on the floor below had drifted upstairs and ruined the Patriarch's precious furniture and books. Instead of getting out the vacuum cleaner, she decided to sue Shevchenko, who was seriously ill at the time. When the court ruled in her favour, bailiffs seized his bank cards and banned him from travelling abroad for cancer treatment. To pay Leonova her compensation, he was also forced to sell the apartment, which he had bequeathed to his children.

Shevchenko's son, also named Yuri, said he and his family, all Orthodox believers, were initially relieved to learn the flat upstairs was owned by the Patriarch. They never imagined he would allow the case to go to court. 'What disturbs me is that this case has driven my parents mad,' he said. 'My father is sick, my mother has been working on these legal issues for about three years; such aggressive lobbying has elements of sadism.'[74] When asked about the affair on the radio by a Kremlin-friendly journalist, the Patriarch said it would be 'incorrect' to forgive Shevchenko. Having insisted the case had nothing to do with him, he added magnanimously: 'I did my best: instead of deep cleaning the books, I agreed to an ordinary clean, which saved a substantial amount of money.' Any leftover funds, he pledged, would go to charity.[75]

The dust scandal, as journalists called it, inevitably led to questions about the litigious Leonova and why she was living in the Patriarch's flat. *Ogonyok*, a weekly magazine popular in the perestroika era, identified her in 2004 as the daughter of a cook who once prepared banquets for Communist bigwigs in Leningrad. It suggested Kirill had met her while he was at the seminary there and alleged that they had 'shared the warmest relations' for more than three decades.[76] The Church says Leonova is one of the Patriarch's second cousins. Despite being a layperson, she is said to live in the world like a nun and moved with Kirill from Leningrad to Smolensk to assist with his work in the diocese. A spokesman for the Moscow Patriarchate called questions about Kirill's private life 'unethical'.

The Patriarchate complained an information war was being fought against the prelate and his church. Some believe this was the result of Kirill initially siding with people protesting against rigged elections. 'I think he was made to understand that there's plenty of *kompromat* [dirt] on him and he should keep his mouth shut,' said journalist Artemy Troitsky. Others said it was his handling of the punk prayer that led to the negative publicity. Kuraev said his 'strange hysterical reaction' to the women was used by the Kremlin political strategists to drive a wedge between the Patriarch and the people. 'He lost credibility in the eyes of many believers and that made him hostage to state power,' Kuraev told me. The *Vedomosti* business newspaper said the Church had just committed its 'biggest error since 1901', the year when it excommunicated Tolstoy.

In the wake of the Pussy Riot affair, the government passed legislation against insulting the religious feelings of believers. It is now routinely employed to crack down on any form of dissent. Scores of people have been charged or convicted under the law, including a man from Stavropol, in southern Russia, whose home was raided by armed police after he wrote 'There is no God' in an online chat. He spent a month in a psychiatric ward on the orders of a judge who said: 'No one in their right mind would write anything against Orthodox Christianity.' It recalls Soviet times when dissidents were locked up in psychiatric wards.

Lev Lur'e, a St Petersburg historian, argues that the Church has replaced the Communist Party as a way of forcing obedience in an authoritarian regime. Its unforgiving position towards Pussy Riot suited Putin as he prepared for his third term as president. Those who demonstrated against him and sympathised with the punks were, conveniently, also critical of Orthodoxy. 'He says his political enemies are not just against him and his government but against the traditional values of Holy Russia,' says Lur'e. 'And those on the side of these female hooligans – they are just godless traitors.' From her prison cell, Alyokhina wrote: 'I thought the church loves all its children, but it seems it only loves those who vote for Putin.'

The affair marked a watershed in church–state relations. Never again would Kirill do or say anything which contradicted or questioned the authorities. Tracing the career of Russia's sixteenth patriarch, the filmmaker Sergei Erzhenkov notes that like Putin, Kirill came to power as a Westerniser and a modernist but will be remembered as an arch reactionary. In Soviet times, taking the lead from his spiritual father Nikodim, Kirill swore allegiance to atheists in the KGB and they swiftly promoted him. In the 1990s he welcomed money changers to the temple, and in the 2000s he turned the Church into an ideological department of the state.

11. HOLY LAND GRAB

Honour Goes to God; the priest gets the bacon.

RUSSIAN PROVERB

The waves were choppy, and the wind stung my face as we approached the island. At first, it was a blur of rocks and pine trees, but as we got closer, the sun bounced off white walls and golden crosses. Emerging from the dark waters of Ladoga, Europe's largest freshwater lake, stood the fairytale apparition of a monastery.

I was leaning over the ship's railing with Mikhail Shishkov, press officer for Bishop Pankraty, who is in charge of Valaam, one of the jewels in the crown of Russian Orthodoxy. 'It's beautiful now but twenty years ago it was in ruins,' said Shishkov. 'When it was returned to the Church in 1989, only six monks came here to pray, but today we have nearly two hundred brothers and Valaam is flourishing.' The monastery, thought to be the oldest in Russia, has been through many cycles of destruction and renewal. Built sometime between the tenth and fourteenth centuries, it was a northern outpost of Eastern Orthodoxy against the heathens and it defended Russia against the Protestant Swedes. During its golden age in the late-eighteenth century, monks from Valaam travelled to Alaska as missionaries.

Despite its remote location, a hundred miles north of St Petersburg, it attracts tens of thousands of tourists and pilgrims every year. Putin has dropped by with the likes of Italy's Silvio Berlusconi and the

Belarusian dictator Aleksandr Lukashenko in tow. With a smile, Shishkov said the President suffered from *Valaamka*, a mysterious condition which affects everyone who spends time on the island. 'I bet you will catch it too,' he said. 'Once you leave here you can't stop dreaming about the place and longing to come back.'

On arrival, I was introduced to Father Iosif, a poster boy for the resurgent Church. He looked like one of Chekhov's eternal students, but when he spoke English, it was with a New York twang. At the age of sixteen, he decided he wanted to become a monk. His father, who ran a St Petersburg furniture company, was horrified and packed him off to business school in the US, hoping to knock some sense into him. 'As you can see,' Father Iosif said, 'that didn't work. Instead, I persuaded my parents to come to church and now they are practising Orthodox Christians.'

As we walked around the five-domed Cathedral of the Transfiguration, I wondered if Iosif was devoted to more than just the Church. He proudly showed me a small copy of the red-robed Mother of God of Valaam, the monastery's most famous icon. An inscription underneath explained that it was sent into space and orbited the earth 488 times. 'Whose idea was that?' I asked. Iosif suggested the decision was taken at the highest level and mentioned that Putin is a frequent visitor. 'He is our benefactor, a person who provides aid in all possible ways to our monastery.'

'Is the President a holy man?' I wondered.

'Only God knows that,' he replied.

The President and the Patriarch have had residences built on the island. Kirill's place is on a pine-clad promontory next to the newly constructed Church of St Vladimir. With the Kremlin's help, Kirill wanted to restore the grandeur and spiritual seclusion of the monastery. Unfortunately for him, 500 secular people also lived on Valaam and felt it was their home too.

Before the Revolution, Valaam had more than 2,000 monks living by the cathedral and in sketes, small communities scattered over a group of surrounding islands covering almost 15 square miles. For much of the twentieth century, the monks disappeared. After 1917, Valaam suddenly found itself on the Finnish side of the border, with contact with Russia cut off. Two decades later, at the start of the Winter War between the USSR and Finland, Soviet planes bombed the island and the monks fled. They founded a new community, which exists to this day, on a lake in northern Finland. At the end of the Second World War, the border shifted again. Valaam was part of the Soviet Union and the monastery was turned into a naval base and rest home for war invalids. Part of the island was declared a nature reserve.

After celebrations for the millennium of Orthodoxy under Gorbachev, the government handed the monastery and the rest of the island's property back to the Church. The following year, Filipp Muskevich was offered a job by the regional government in Karelia to run the forestry department. He moved to Valaam from Estonia with his wife Lyudmila and their two small daughters. The Muskevichs were delighted with their new home and their neighbours, the black-robed clerics with their hauntingly beautiful style of choral singing. They shared potatoes and milk with the monks and taught them how to light stoves. Lyudmila told me she vividly remembered their first Christmas when they walked across the ice to a half-built church and attended the liturgy in the semi-darkness: 'The atmosphere was very special, and we were so happy. We felt everything was right with the world.'

As time went by, life on the island became less idyllic. The monastery used new legal powers to monopolise the growing tourism industry on Valaam. Long-term residents, unconnected to the Church, were encouraged to resettle on the mainland. Those who resisted increasingly found themselves in court. The Muskevichs were among the first to be targeted.

When I met Lyudmila and Filipp in the autumn of 2012, they were camping out in a cramped room in the Winter Hotel in the centre of the island. Once a grand mid-nineteenth century residence with wide stone staircases, the hotel had been a hospital and a school for navy cadets. Now it was rundown, with broken masonry and paint peeling off the walls. Still, it was home for about a hundred residents who wanted to stay on the island. Some of the apartments offered to laypeople in the town of Sortavala, 40 kilometres away, were in a renovated slaughterhouse on the edge of an industrial estate. The street was called *Fanerniy Tupik*, Plywood Dead End.

The Muskevichs were not tempted to move there from their cosy home in the refectory of the Resurrection Skete – a skete is a smaller commune within the monastery for one or just a few monks. But the monastery said it needed the family's apartment for its tourism operation. The family went to court and won four times but were eventually evicted after their home was reclassified as unfit for habitation.

Filipp told me how local bailiffs arrived on a ship and broke down the door. His neighbour in the Winter Hotel, Irina Smirnova, said she and others tried to stop the eviction by shouting 'shame, shame' at the bailiffs, but to no avail. Irina moved to the island in the 1980s as a museum guide and for many years worked happily with the pilgrimage service of the monastery. She and her ex-husband, a historian, have written books and academic studies about Valaam. 'My daughter was born here, my heart and soul belong to this place,' she said. 'How can I move?' Like other locals, she tried pointing out that the resettlement programme was supposed to be voluntary and that there was no work for her in the nearest towns on the mainland, which were plagued by unemployment.

Filipp told me that he did not blame the Church for protecting its turf, although he no longer attended the monks' services. 'What disappoints me,' he said, 'is the state, which provided rights for its citizens then took them away and didn't give us any protection. Our state is becoming more theocratic. I think what happened to us on Valaam was the start of a process that is obvious to everyone now.'

On the monastery's website, I read about Alexei's impressions of Valaam when he first visited as a nine-year-old boy before the Second World War. He recalled 'a spiritual archipelago' in which 'every inch of land was hallowed by deeds, prayers, and labour'. In 2005, as patriarch, he asked the regional authorities to control unregulated tourism to Valaam, which he said was disturbing the monks and damaging the pristine environment. He also insisted that the monastery should help the laypeople who chose to stay on the island. He called the locals 'the flock'. After Kirill succeeded him, the policy hardened.

On the boat back, the monastery's press officer insisted that nobody had been thrown onto the street. If the Muskevich family didn't want to accept the accommodation provided on the mainland, that was their hard luck. 'Russia is becoming a state governed by the rule of law, laws that must be obeyed whether you like them or not,' he told me.

In 2015, the Winter Hotel was declared unfit for habitation, and a year later, the building caught fire in the early hours of the morning when most people were asleep. It took a long time to put out because the fire brigade was understaffed. State TV reported blandly that 'an old unused hotel building' in Valaam was damaged by fire and 70 people were evacuated. Many islanders, including an ex-firefighter who was the last secular mayor on Valaam, believed it was an arson attack organised by the monastery. Water and electricity supplies were cut off to any parts of the building which survived the flames. The monastery did not want to provide alternative accommodation, even mattresses, to the victims of the fire. Only the Lutheran Church of Sortavala came to the rescue, sailing over from the mainland with emergency supplies. Meanwhile, the monastery's website was flooded with offensive comments about the locals, saying that all the 'normal people' had left long ago and those who remained were 'all drunkards'. Comments which sympathised with the fire victims were immediately deleted.[1] Soon afterwards, the state allocated 322 million roubles to rebuild the hotel and create a spiritual and educational centre on the site. Valaam's only public school and hospital were closed.

Filipp Muskevich left the island with his family after the fire and moved abroad. Speaking in late 2023 from his new home in northern Israel, he said he was sick of lawsuits and had grown disillusioned with Russia. 'We've had rockets flying over us from Gaza and Lebanon,' he said. 'This place obviously has many problems. But I feel safer than I did on the "peaceful" island of Valaam. Here at least I have some rights as a citizen.'

Kirill called the secular islanders' problems 'microscopic'. The previous year he ordered the dismantling of food and souvenir outlets run by the locals because he felt a monastery was 'no place for trade' and that it interfered with pilgrims' prayers. He complained that the entrepreneurs sold goods 'often of a non-Orthodox nature'. A grocery store which once belonged to a resident was closed after monks complained about being next to a place selling alcohol.

However, when Russian journalists visited in 2017, they found that the monastery had opened its own shop in the same building which sells, among other things, vodka, beer and cigarettes – only the prices were higher.[2]

When I returned to Valaam in October 2021, nearly a decade after my first visit, the Winter Hotel was unrecognisable. It was gleaming white, like a wedding cake, with carpeted corridors, flatscreen TVs in each room, and moody black and white portraits of the monks along the walls. The flower beds and vegetable patches were immaculately tended by an ever-changing army of volunteers who stayed in a hostel and had no permanent residency status. The same was true of employees on the island's many construction sites. Vera Skobeleva, the director of the monastery's real-estate firm, maintained it was impossible to build replacement housing for the locals on the island. 'New construction cannot happen anywhere on the archipelago,' she said. 'We are building only monasteries and chapels. These are not the premises in which ordinary citizens are supposed to live.'

Kirill is no ordinary citizen. Seemingly dissatisfied with his predecessor's residence, he had himself a new one built on an outlying island where locals liked to go fishing. Now anyone who tries to approach is met by heavily armed guards.[3] The Patriarch and his guests whizz around the archipelago in *Pallada,* a $4-million yacht. One entrepreneur, who sold upmarket souvenirs and had a 'good relationship' with Bishop Pankraty, proudly told me how she had tried out its white leather seats. Shishkov, the press officer, told me the luxury vessel did not belong to Kirill and was certainly not, as rumoured, a present from the President. It had instead, he said, been gifted to the monastery by the energy company Lukoil in 2005.[4]

Gavril Frolov's story is intriguing and instructive. A monk who had been ordained as a deacon, Frolov was a steward who acted like Valaam's Mr Fixit. The monastery's website described him in 2014 as 'a sociable person' who holds many 'meetings with builders, contractors, officials, solving restoration issues'. He had made the usual vows of chastity, poverty and obedience, but then he had a change of heart. By 2020, he had become a powerful property developer in St Petersburg, building shopping malls and sports arenas. He also married the daughter of a billionaire.

A Radio Liberty investigation[5] identified the ex-monk as the son-in-law of Gennady Timchenko, the man known as 'Putin's oil trader'. Timchenko made his $22 billion fortune mainly through his Switzerland-based commodity trading company Gunvor. He wisely sold his shares to his Swedish partner the day before he was hit with US sanctions for Russia's seizure of Crimea in 2014. Timchenko and his wife Elena are among Valaam's biggest philanthropists. Their daughter Natalia founded a company, Akanthus Atelier, specialising in religious artefacts. Frolov was the general director and later owner when Natalia left the company after giving birth to a daughter. Akanthus' clients include the Valaam Monastery. The company's Instagram account features the St Sergius of Radonezh wooden chapel which was completely destroyed in the post-war era. Akanthus Atelier craftsmen worked on the interior decoration and iconostasis, and 'now you can see it in all its former historical glory'.[6]

The Church does not rely solely on donations from the state and its flock. Back in 2000, 30 out of 80 dioceses claimed that they were too cash-strapped to send the required 10 per cent of their income to Moscow, to the Patriarchate. The remaining 50 donated between 3 and 4 per cent.

Two decades ago, the official income of the dioceses was 500 million roubles.[7] Experts tell me it is now most likely ten times higher. 'No one seems to know how much it costs to support a bishop?' wrote Sergei Chapnin, a former Church insider who edited the Patriarchate's *Journal*. 'How much does it cost to maintain a metropolitan? Finally, what does it cost the Church to support its patriarch? No one has ever presented those numbers. Sadly, that provides grounds for assuming that the current church administrative system is profoundly corrupt. More than once have I heard it said that the bishops treat the funds obtained from the churches as their personal money.'[8]

One bishop told me that he handed the equivalent of £1,500 every two or three months to the Patriarch's chief of staff. 'That was a way of ensuring he told Kirill good things about you,' the bishop said. 'I would hand him the money in an envelope and ask him to pray for me.' Churches are not required to install cash registers and tax officials avoid looking into parish accounts. The church boasts industrial assets, a granite quarry, building companies, a computer firm and several hotels. The Sofrino factory, just north of the capital, is a major source of income. An Orthodox megastore, it produces ecclesiastical goods from candles to furniture, and from icons to gold utensils that can fetch up to £15,000 each.

After the financial crisis of the 1990s, the Church began pushing for its own bank with low-interest loans. But its forays into finance have not gone well. In its first incarnation, Sofrino was the 'Old Bank', run by a group close to the former patriarch Alexei and to Kirill. It handled the Church's property and money given by the state and other sources for the restoration of churches. It also dabbled in loans and investments. But the Old Bank's licence was revoked in 2014 because it had almost four times more debt than assets.

Another bank, Peresvet, which had a blue and white onion dome logo and was half-owned by the Church, had the official title of the Joint Stock Commercial Bank for Charity and Spiritual Development of Fatherland. For more than two decades, big state companies stashed their cash with the bank. But the international credit ratings agency Fitch downgraded Peresvet on the grounds that almost a tenth of its loans were to companies seemingly without real businesses. Soon afterwards, in October 2016, Aleksandr Shvets, its chief executive officer, left Russia and is thought to be living under another name. Investigators concluded that the management of a related company, Peresvet-Invest, received loans of up to 770 million roubles, which were converted into dollars and ended up in accounts in an offshore firm registered in Cyprus. An FSB officer, Oleg Pronin, co-owner and general director of the Peresvet-Invest, was found guilty of embezzling 1.1 billion roubles ($18 million) from the 'Church's bank' and received a four-year prison sentence in May 2021. Two years earlier, Peresvet had to be bailed out by the Russian state amid mounting bad loans.[9]

Back in 2000, Moscow University researchers investigating Church finances called the Church 'a grandiose offshore zone' with its own independent financial and manufacturing activity and 'huge potential for money-laundering by the economy's shadow and criminal sectors'. Few cases have been successfully prosecuted. The Church has become such an important pillar of national ideology that the authorities absolve it of any economic sins. In the past few decades, the Church has exploited its privileged status to develop huge business interests with an annual turnover of millions and possibly billions of pounds, but priests in rural parishes are still languishing in poverty.

☦ ☦ ☦

In 2017, one journalist calculated that over a decade, 43 million roubles – roughly $700,000 or £550,000 – of taxpayers' money had been lavished on each Valaam monk and novice.[10] The state also invested 2.3 billion roubles supplying electricity to the island – nearly a third of the total amount the government spent on upgrading power networks in eleven cities for the 2018 football World Cup. An employee of the Federal Grid Company admitted the power cable laid under Lake Ladoga to Valaam would be enough to supply a small European country with electricity. He was at a loss to explain why a small island mainly inhabited by monks accustomed to praying by candlelight needed quite so much power.[11]

The property rights of the Church have ballooned over the past two decades. Ever since Peter the Great turned the Church into a government institution, clerics served in churches and chapels built and maintained by nobles, merchants and civilian communities. In the 1990s, Yeltsin ordered the government to gradually transfer churches and associated territory from the central state to religious organisations. But no deadline was set, and his 1993 decree did not cover municipal or privatised property.

As soon as Putin became president, a battle began for the second wave of restitution. Demands for the authorities to hand over property grew more persistent as land prices shot up. In 2004, the Duma passed a law on returning property confiscated by the Bolsheviks. Putin said he was deeply convinced that the expropriation of the Church had been 'not simply immoral, but illegal' and vowed that the historical injustice would be put right.

The law also applied to Muslim, Catholic, Buddhist and Jewish assets, but the Orthodox Church benefitted the most, greatly expanding its real-estate empire. If in the 1990s, restitution mainly covered churches, it now included any building that had once belonged to the church. Thousands of museums, concert halls, colleges, schools and residential blocks were affected. Six years later, in 2010, parliament further strengthened the Church's claim on lands seized under Communism. The new law gave authorities just two years to return property if a court found in the Church's favour. Horrified museum directors argued that the Church could not possibly restore and maintain so many old buildings and that precious artworks could be damaged. In Ryazan, south of Moscow, 26,000 local people signed a petition opposing the takeover of the mediaeval city centre and national park. They said the Church struggled to fill the two cathedrals they already had. The real goal, they claimed, was to evict five museums on the site and turn the hilltop palace into a luxury residence for the head of the local diocese.

Some of the most unlikely buildings were affected by the law, including the All-Russian Research Institute of Fisheries and Oceanography. Staff were told that they had to vacate their five-storey building in Moscow which had been purpose-built for marine biologists in the 1930s. But lawyers said it stood on the foundations of a nineteenth-century convent and the Church wanted it back. Sophisticated aquariums for endangered salmon species had to be hurriedly dismantled and moved to a new site along with 500 employees.

After taking back a huge number of properties, the Church used only some for religious purposes. The rest would be put to commercial use. The Patriarch set up a business investment programme, which announced in 2007 that it would build hotels and business centres in several cities.

I was given an insight into how the system works from Maksim Mitrofanov, one of the young bishops appointed by Kirill. Mitrofanov was born in Saratov into an observant family; the children were baptised, and church holidays were celebrated even though this was the Soviet era. By the time he was an altar boy, Gorbachev's perestroika reforms had started. His father, a research physicist, was destitute in the 1990s and his parents decided to emigrate to the US.

Mitrofanov studied history at university in Moscow while doing night courses in theology. When he was ordained in 1997, his sharp intelligence did not go unnoticed. Barely into his twenties, he was appointed director of academic programmes at the Saratov seminary where he taught church history to middle-aged priests and deacons. A high-flyer, in 2007 he was sent to London, the year that canonical communion was restored between the Orthodox Church and the Church outside Russia. After a seven-year stint as an archpriest at the cathedral in Kensington, he was promoted to a diocese in the north of Russia. The bishop of Vologda had just been elevated to a metropolitan and his sprawling diocese of 150,000 square kilometres, three times the size of Belgium, was split into three parts. Mitrofanov became Flavian, Bishop of Cherepovets and Belozersk in north-western Russia. As soon as he arrived, the Patriarchate gave him 'very clear orders' to increase the number of parishes by at least ten each year. They also told him to open monasteries. During the golden age of monasticism, from the fourteenth to the sixteenth century, the Russian north had been renowned for them. By 2014, in Mitrofanov's new diocese, there were none.

I asked Mitrofanov how much the Patriarchate gave him for such an ambitious programme. He smiled: 'Actually, it's the other way around. The more parishes I established, the more money I had to send to them. It's a financial pyramid.' In other words, around 38,000 parishes support Russia's 314 dioceses, and diocesan bishops like Mitrofanov send money to Moscow. The money moves in one direction – upwards.

His task was not easy. Cherepovets, the main industrial city, has the biggest steel smelter in Europe but few other claims to fame. Many churches had been decrepit for decades and contained no miraculous icons or holy relics to attract pilgrims. Mitrofanov was advised to look for 'sponsors'. He tried his best but admitted he felt disorientated. In London he had rubbed shoulders with the globalised Russian elite; from there he had been parachuted into a hard-scrabble, hard-drinking town. In the Soviet era, Cherepovets was surrounded by corrective labour camps. Prisoners were used to build the city's factories and its huge blast furnace. Few of their descendants found well-paid jobs or gained access to higher education. Married priests in the diocese's towns and villages would not allow their wives to appear with them in public.

Mitrofanov described the place as provincial and backward-looking. But within five years he had got three monasteries up and running. The support came from a most unlikely source. One February evening, just after dusk, he was working on some papers in his study when a monk and a priest banged on his door. 'They were both very excited,' he recalled. 'They said, Vladyka, Your Grace, we were passing by and saw the abandoned Holy Trinity Filippo-Irapsky monastery – please let us restore it for you!' Only one wall was still intact, the rest of the building was in ruins. But the monk swore he would find construction materials and sponsors as long as the new bishop gave his blessing. 'I thought he was a fantasist at the very least, but I had no money to rebuild it,' he said. 'It wasn't considered an architectural monument so there were no government grants. I thought, *What have I got to lose?*'

The excited monk, a character with beady brown eyes, a round face and wispy white beard, was Gerontiy Chudnevich, a reformed criminal. He had done fifteen years behind bars for aggravated robbery. Born in a prison in eastern Siberia, Chudnevich told me he remembers little about his mother. Early on, he was sent to an orphanage. From there he went to a boarding school in the Ukrainian city of Kharkiv. He had a series of odd jobs as a child, mending shoes, herding cows, selling watermelons in the market. He was later apprenticed to a military plant which made bridges. Before long he wound up in juvenile detention, before graduating to adult prisons. When in jail in the Urals, a priest began making regular visits to the inmates. Inspired, Chudnevich decided to repent and turn his life around. He built a chapel inside the prison and, once he got out, he travelled to Optina Pustyn, the famous monastery south of Moscow which became a spiritual retreat for Tolstoy and Dostoevsky. One of the elders there, Schema-Archimandrite Iliy (secular name Alexei Nozdrin), Kirill's confessor, blessed him to travel beyond the Arctic Circle to build churches. Never one to shirk a challenge, Chudnevich began with the reconstruction of a monastery called Holy Trinity Trifonov-Pechengsky on the shores of the Barents Sea. For many centuries it was the northernmost monastery in the world. Fittingly, it was founded in 1533 by Saint Trifon of Pechenga, himself a repentant robber.

When Chudnevich arrived, he found that the spot where the monastery once stood had become a graveyard for old cars and a rubbish dump. Undeterred, he bought two abandoned barracks nearby for his workers and built a wooden farmstead before starting on the monastery itself, which was consecrated at the end of 2012: quite a feat for a man who was semi-literate and had no formal architectural training. Svetlana Stasenko, a filmmaker, tracked the rebuilding process in a documentary called *Once There Were Twelve Thieves*.[12] The film cuts from drone shots of a striking and desolate landscape to close-ups of men as they haul timber and saw logs in sub-zero temperatures. Most have deeply lined faces, mournful eyes and very few teeth. The workforce was almost entirely made up of homeless men, just out of prison, with nowhere to go. He provided them with food, clothes and a place to sleep. In exchange they worked long hours for no pay. Their free time was mainly spent in church, praying, ringing bells and learning liturgical chants. Chudnevich became abbot at the *metochion*, a church in the closest city, Murmansk, nearly 100 miles to the south. Since he was shuttling between the city and the monastery, he appointed Vyacheslav, another man recently released from prison, to supervise the construction.

The Bishop of Murmansk and Monchegorsk, a former naval officer and the head of the Church on the Kola Peninsula, said local journalists flocked to the site to find out what was going on. They quizzed him on why so many of the monks and their helpers had tattoos. Was this some kind of monastic tradition? The bishop explained that the monastery was named after Trifon, the outlaw who was later canonised. 'We're practically at the end of the earth,' he said. 'It's freezing cold and dark for most of the year. This is no place for romantics. People who come here have a past – they are running away from something. Back in the sixteenth century, they ran here to save their heads from the chopping block.'

Monks and parishioners called the restored monastery a miracle. They were impressed not just because the builders had mastered time-honoured carpentry techniques of erecting large structures without using a single nail, but because Chudnevich had brought dozens of former prisoners to God. But when Kirill visited the monastery to sanctify it in the summer of 2016, he thought otherwise. TV news reports show him flanked by army officers, clerics and a security guard; there is no sign of the master builder, Father Gerontiy. Nor did Kirill make any reference to him when he thanked the bishops, monks, benefactors and local authorities. He asked the monastery's abbot, David, if any of the ex-cons were still on the premises. Not at the moment, Your Holiness, came the reply. 'Thank God for that!' snapped Kirill. He instructed the abbot not to accept any former prisoners in the future.

So, this was the pyramid: the Patriarchate requires money to be sent upwards, by whatever means. It requires local priests to build churches, by whatever means. Yet when a former criminal repents, constructs something extraordinary and guides ex-prisoners towards the path of God, he is shunned.

By the time of Kirill's visit, Chudnevich had already been supplanted as abbot by his once-trusted foreman, Vyacheslav. Although Father Vyacheslav had done time for murder and once was a leader of the *Solntsevskaya Bratva* crime syndicate, the Patriarchate found him easier to control.

By contrast, Chudnevich was fiercely independent. He owned some small businesses in Murmansk, including a car-wash, a hotel and a sand quarry, which helped to raise funds for the monastery and a nineteen-domed cathedral he was planning to build in the middle of the city. It emerged later that all the money and materials collected for the new cathedral disappeared. When the authorities laid the blame on him, he had a heart attack and left the region. As a result, he never got the chance to build the cathedral nor to finish his work at the Trifonov-Pechenga monastery. Wooden towers constructed as workshops and living quarters for the monks remain uninhabitable more than a decade later. The bakery which produced the prosphora, unleavened bread for the Eucharist, stopped working and half the monastery stands empty. After he was banished from Murmansk, many parishioners stopped coming to services. After all, the charismatic ex-robber had been one of the main attractions.

Chudnevich spent six months in solitary prayer before he turned up on Bishop Flavian's doorstep in Cherepovets. He began by restoring the cells and living quarters of the monks at nearby Filippo Irapsky Monastery. Originally a small hermitage, then a larger monastery, in Soviet times it was a psycho-neurological boarding school – basically a prison for people with learning difficulties – before it fell into ruin. Chudnevich and his team of workers rebuilt the Church of the Mother of God of Kazan and a chapel on the bank of the Andoga

River where an angel appeared to Monk Filipp in the early sixteenth century. Three years later, on 24 July 2019, the monastery's Kazan Church was consecrated. Bishop Flavian of Cherepovets (Maksim Mitrofanov), resplendent in a white and gold surplice, led the Divine Liturgy as Chudnevich looked on.

'Looking back, I am amazed by this project,' said Mitrofanov. 'Thanks to Father Gerontiy we managed to save some of the original structure. I didn't breathe down his neck. He had full freedom to work however he wanted.' Despite the restoration work, it is not easy to fill the church on Sundays. The nearest village is six kilometres away. The resident cleric in charge, Abbot Iov, says some staunch older women walk there and back at least once a week. But most Sundays there are only fifteen parishioners for the liturgy, and for major church celebrations, such as Christmas and Easter, the church is barely a third full.

When I spoke to Chudnevich in 2023, he was still recovering from a stroke which followed his heart attack, but he still seemed to revel in his tough guy reputation. He recalled with pride breaking one man's jaw and another's nose when he was an army conscript. Both, he explained, were older recruits from Chechnya and they tried to bully him into making their beds. He made no attempt to gloss over his criminal past but was vague on the specifics of his fundraising. 'The Lord arranged everything,' he kept telling me.

Stasenko, the filmmaker who got to know him well, agreed that he may still have ties to the criminal underworld. However, she remained in awe of his untutored talent as a builder, comparing him to the teenage hero in Andrei Tarkovsky's film *Andrei Rublev,* who manages to cast a huge bronze bell even though his father never told him how to do it. 'He is a man of God,' she told me, somewhat grandiloquently. 'I am sure that one day he will be canonised for everything he has achieved.' Listening to her, I was reminded of one of the most popular Orthodox hymns, *Pesnya o blagorazumnom Razboinike*, or Hymn of the Penitent Thief, sung during the candle-lit matins of Good Friday. It evokes the image of the thief, crucified beside Christ, who repents and discovers paradise 'in a single moment'.

Russia's enormous size creates a formidable challenge for the revival of religious life. Before the Bolshevik Revolution, weekly services were attended by the whole parish, usually consisting of hundreds of people. Now most rural priests count themselves lucky to have five to ten faithful parishioners. The problem is not just a lack of interest but a demographic crisis. Russia is haunted by ghost villages and small towns. In the 1990s, 15,000 communities ceased to exist. Almost half of the country's agricultural land has fallen into disuse. The Patriarch's determination to replace places of worship destroyed under Communism runs up against demographics. According to a 2018 study, each year around 200,000 Russians abandon rural areas for the cities, and yet it is in these villages that half the total parishes are based.[13] These small churches have to pay market rates for electricity, heating and water, and they struggle to survive.

In some places, urban and rural, there was a real shortage of churches. A Duma deputy in the 1990s complained that in his constituency of Dzerzhinsk, an overnight train journey east of Moscow and one of the country's most polluted cities, 'there are 300,000 inhabitants but not a single church; priests have to perform services inside an abandoned railway wagon'. In all, more than 23,000 churches that had been demolished or fallen into disuse were rebuilt in the first two decades of the post-Soviet era. A year after he became patriarch, Kirill announced 200 new churches for the capital alone. He insisted that his aim was modest given that the city would need nearly 600 to reach the nationwide average of one church per 11,200 Russians. A decade later, he said that three new churches were being built somewhere in Russia every day, although it later emerged that figure included parishes abroad. In December 2022, in an address to the diocesan assembly of Moscow, Kirill proudly announced that 134 of the 200 planned new churches for the capital had already been built or were in the process of being constructed.[14]

Nikolai Mitrokhin, an expert on contemporary Orthodoxy, argues that Kirill decided 'to sell the church's political support to the regime' and was duly rewarded with money for his construction programme. After the pandemic, he received 2.2 billion roubles ($30 million) for the completion of the capital's churches, roughly half the total he had sought for the whole of the previous four years.[15] Kirill's building frenzy was far from universally popular. Indeed, it sparked protests in dozens of cities.[16] In Moscow, St Petersburg, Krasnoyarsk, Chelyabinsk, Ulyanovsk and Nizhny Novgorod, crowds rallied in parks and green spaces holding banners which read 'Stop the Church!' Even some clergy privately admit that today the number of parishioners does not remotely match the number of new churches. The larger a church, the more obvious it is when it is half-empty.

Statistics gleaned from the Interior Ministry suggest that only one in a hundred Russians attend Christmas services and three in a hundred attend the Easter Service, the most important celebration in the Orthodox calendar. In 2009, the year Kirill was enthroned, it was estimated that only 0.5 per cent of the population went to church services once a month or more.[17]

In Moscow, plans for at least 27 planned churches were stopped after meeting fierce resistance. Some of the most violent confrontations took place in 2015 in the north-east of the capital. In the Torfyanka Park there were clashes between local residents, the authorities and Orthodox activists from a group called *Sorok Sorokov*, Forty Times Forty. The name refers to the supposed 1,600 churches which graced Moscow before the Revolution. Supported by the Patriarchate, the militia group claims to have 200 active members and 10,000 supporters. A hotchpotch of businessmen, wrestlers, skinheads and former neo-Nazis, the group is one of the unofficial enforcers of Kirill's 200 Churches programme, organising muscular prayer vigils at proposed sites. Andrei Kormukhin, the group's leader, called opponents of the new church 'enemies of Russia'. An elderly couple who spoke against it received death threats. One night their front door was smashed in by cross-wearing vigilantes.

Loketski, a street artist who hides his identity like Banksy, has targeted the glut of new, unwanted churches. One work, *Set'* (Chain), compares them to fried-chicken franchises, depicting Kirill as a smiling Colonel Sanders. The letters KFC are replaced by RPC (the Russian acronym for Russian Orthodox Church in Latin letters). The image appeared at a construction site in one neighbourhood of St Petersburg.[18]

In 2019, weeks before the Patriarch's 'three-churches-a-day' boast, thousands demonstrated against a new church in another park more than a thousand miles away in Yekaterinburg. Matters got so out of hand that Putin felt required to intervene. In this city, on the border of Europe and Asia, two local oligarchs had been thwarted when they tried to ingratiate themselves with the Patriarchate and the Kremlin. Energy firms and other large enterprises had long been pressured into contributing to church building. The results are sometimes garish. Igor Altushkin, a scrap-metal merchant turned copper tycoon, and Andrei Kozitsyn, Russia's leading zinc miner, wanted to build a new Church of St Catherine in a city centre park in honour of the city's patron saint. The scheme, on the edge of a pond which dates back to Peter the Great, included a skyscraper with offices, a car park and a gym.

To the fury of the oligarchs, the Patriarchate and the diocese, the locals made clear they preferred to keep their green space. The Yekaterinburg Diocese, which includes the city and surrounding towns, already had 312 churches and chapels, they argued. Alyona Smishlyaeva, a resident in her thirties, was surprised one morning to be confronted by a metal construction fence when out for her pre-breakfast jog. 'My immediate response was to climb over it because I think of this space as public land,' she said. When the security men tried to stop her, she escaped them by climbing a tree. Police in helmets carrying automatic rifles threatened to drag her down by force. 'I wasn't afraid, but I decided to scream my head off because that is what girls are told to do if attacked and my voice filled the whole square,' she said. 'I am not against a new church but not one built in an atmosphere of such hostility and with such arrogance.' She was interrogated at the police station for six hours and fined for trespassing. After coordinated attacks in the local media, she was no longer able to find freelance work as an events organiser to pay her mortgage, so she was evicted from her flat. She now lives abroad.

A rapper who goes by the name of Naum Bleek told me he considered himself Orthodox but had stopped attending services because of the Church's greed. It angered him that in one Yekaterinburg convent, the cheapest candle cost 40 roubles – almost twice the price of a bus ticket – when the actual value of the candle was around 20 kopecks. 'I don't like to see our grannies ripped off when some bishops are living in luxury,' he said. For him, the central square was 'a little island of freedom in the city where you can breathe a bit of fresh air'. He wrote a song called 'The Square Must Stay', which became the anthem of the protest. I tried to capture the spirit of it in my translation:

> *Mr Kozitskin, Mr Altyushkin*
> *The Church on the Shore ain't your plaything*
> *A crowd of People have given you their views*
> *Read all about it in Yekaterinburg's News*
> *The Square is our own Church of the People*
> *Gifted by nature – a tree not a steeple*
> *We don't give a damn about cash from copper metals*
> *We'll breathe the scent of freedom, of grass and flower petals.*

Protesters formed a human chain around the building site despite the presence of the riot police. On the fourth day the entire park was fenced off as Interior Ministry troops were deployed in gas masks. Alexei Mosin, head of the local branch of Memorial, worried people might be seriously hurt. He opposed the new church even though his own great grandfather had been killed for his faith. Mosin wanted the diocese to focus on restoring the old churches which previous generations had prayed in. 'We shouldn't aim to build as many churches as possible,' he said. 'It's not an Olympic competition in which we have to be "Stronger. Higher. Faster".' He added: 'The Church should come to people and ask them: "Brothers and sisters, do you need a church?" Because when there's a need, people will support it and donate their last few kopecks. But often the Church doesn't ask – it just declares: "We are going to build one here".'

At first Putin acted as if he was stunned by the demonstrations. 'Are these people atheists?' he asked, in one of his trademark rhetorical questions. But when protesters began tearing down the fence, he stepped in. 'A church should unite people, not divide them,' he declared. Construction was suspended. It was a rare victory for civil society. Despite the intimidation and more than 30 arrests, the protesters had prevailed.

Father Maksim Menyailo is head priest at Yekaterinburg's Church on the Blood, built just over a mile away on the execution site of the

Romanovs. When I went to see him a few months after the protests, he was still smarting from losing the battle over St Catherine's.
I asked if the city needed more churches, pointing out statistics
I had been given showing that barely 2 per cent of the city's residents attended the Christmas and Easter liturgies. Father Maksim
answered my question with his own figures: 'Today in Yekaterinburg
we have one church for 40–50,000 people. One church! And we
have one alcohol shop for every 600 people. So, as you can see, the
numbers are not in our favour.'

In his opinion, the overwhelming majority of people in the city
were Orthodox – even if they did not know it themselves. To my
bemusement, he began talking about a teenage conscript and pris-
oner of war who was brutally murdered in the breakaway republic
of Chechnya in the mid-1990s. The nineteen-year-old in question,
called Yevgeny Rodionov, was not a local lad, so at first I didn't
understand why the archpriest had mentioned him. Later, I understood that a cult had grown up around this unfortunate young border
guard. He is routinely portrayed as a modern Christian crusader
who made the ultimate sacrifice for his country when confronted
by Muslim separatist rebels. 'Rodionov was an ordinary guy, who
liked sports,' Maksim said. 'But he was beheaded because he didn't
want to take off his baptismal cross. Tell me, is he a Christian or
not? He didn't go to church much, but he had religious culture in
his DNA; he inherited it through literature, through films, through
talking with his relatives, so we can't say that only those who go to
church on Sundays are Orthodox Christians.' When I asked whether
the money spent on new churches was a priority given the economic
difficulties, he was affronted: 'If we don't build churches, we will
stop being Russians. Then why should we even live on the earth at
all? This is our contribution to the civilisation of the world.'

It is hard to imagine a Russian church without candles, but in one
new Orthodox structure there are none to be found. A year after
Russia illegally annexed Crimea in 2014, the authorities announced
they would build the world's first underwater church off the coast

of Sevastopol, home of the Black Sea fleet. A cross weighing three tonnes was erected on the seafloor. The construction team said a stone altar and waterproof icons would follow. It was the brainchild of Tikhon Shevkunov, the cleric reputed to be Putin's confessor. He had just been sent to head the metropolis of Simferopol and Crimea, where he helped to design a theme park at Chersonesos, the site of Prince Vladimir's (Volodymyr's) baptism. Like Kirill, Tikhon is, or at least was, an enthusiastic scuba diver. The sea-floor church is as much a land grab as a testimony of religious faith, reminiscent of a stunt in 2007 when submarines planted the Russian flag underneath the North Pole to stake a claim to the Arctic's oil and gas deposits.

Of all the structures that blend religion and militant nationalism, none beats the Main Cathedral of the Russian Armed Forces, west of Moscow, variously described as sacrilegious and grotesque. One cleric called it 'a pagan temple to the God of war'. It encapsulates the Putin era. The President opened it alongside his defence minister, Sergei Shoigu, and the Patriarch in June 2020, on the anniversary of the Nazi attack on the Soviet Union in 1941.

Although billboards across Moscow urged people to visit, the cathedral, 30 miles west of Moscow, is hard to reach without a car. As I approached, the looming structure clad in khaki with ice-blue windows resembled the castle of an evil wizard in a Disney film. Towering green streetlamps resembled oversized cacti. As soon as I got out of the taxi, I was yelled at by a security guard for failing to go through the metal detector. The crisp autumn air was filled with booms and thuds, and I wondered if some kind of battle was being re-enacted, but it was just the sound of a construction crew building a winter ice rink.

Inside, immense glittering mosaics commemorate different battles in Russian history, from medieval times to Napoleon to the present day. Special emphasis is laid on the Great Patriotic War, and symbolic numbers are integrated into the design: the bell tower is 75 metres tall to mark the 75th anniversary of the end of the war; the diameter of the main dome is 19.45 metres. The place seemed tailor-made for selfies. I watched visitors posing in front of mosaics and filming their feet as they walked up metal steps and across floors made of melted-down trophy weapons and German tanks.

An interactive display called 1418 Steps to Victory – one step for each day of the Soviet war effort – is housed in two exhibition halls flanking the cathedral. The opening depicts Soviet life before Hitler's invasion – a 1930s paradise filled with happy girls with ribbons in their hair, blue skies, heroic workers and brightly coloured trams. Stalin's purges are nowhere to be seen. If you stand with your back to the iconostasis on the right-hand side above the archway, one particular mosaic can be discerned. These are the little green men, as they came to be known, armed with machine guns as they seized Crimea. The faces of Putin and his defence minister Sergei Shoigu were supposed to be there too, along with senior figures from the security forces, until a news outlet leaked the pictures. They were hurriedly edited out.[19] Putin's spokesman Dmitri Peskov said that when the President heard about it 'he smiled and said: "someday grateful descendants will appreciate our services but now it is too early to do this".'

Another mosaic depicted Stalin's head on a Red Army banner, but it was also removed at the last minute. Sergei Chapnin, former editor of the *Journal of the Patriarchate*, wrote that he could imagine the image of Stalin in an Orthodox church, 'but in a radically different context, in one of the cauldrons with boiling tar' in a fresco depicting the Last Judgement. Chapnin saw the cathedral as a 'giant propaganda project' and a temple to a 'new post-Soviet civil religion'.[20] He said the artists and priests involved would one day be ashamed of what they had done, something that for the moment seems unlikely given the extent of Stalin's official rehabilitation.

Some of the angels have that socialist-realist faraway glint in their eyes. There is also a profusion of red stars and a stained-glass hammer and sickle. Alongside 'the return of Crimea', other military interventions listed under floating archangels include the crushing of uprisings in Hungary in 1956 and in Czechoslovakia in 1968, the invasion of Afghanistan in 1979, two wars in Chechnya, 'forcing peace on Georgia' in 2008, and the 'fight against international terrorism' in Syria.

In the crypt stands a large mosaic of Vladimir and Olga, the founders of Orthodoxy a millennium ago, baptising people in the River Dnipro. This overlooks a walk-in turquoise and gold baptismal font which seems to belong more to a luxury spa. The army cathedral, which cost 6 billion roubles (about $86 million), was supposed to be funded entirely from donations. In reality, the bulk of the money came from the Moscow mayor's office and the regional government. Some private gifts raised eyebrows, and not all the donations were voluntary. On the first anniversary of the building's consecration, Shoigu gave a speech praising citizens and military personnel for their patriotic generosity. But conscripts from Khabarovsk on the Pacific Coast and paratroopers from Pskov, on the other side of the country, complained that their wages and bonuses had been cut to beef up the fund-raising drive. Alexander, a signals officer sent to southern Ukraine at the beginning of the 2022 invasion, deserted while on leave in Russia and fled abroad. He took off his uniform, doused it with petrol, set it alight in protest at the war and encouraged other servicemen to do likewise.[21] He told me that in 2018 and 2019 senior officers demanded that he and his comrades hand over part of their salary to the army cathedral, and the sums were large. Officers were required to hand over 35–40,000 roubles in a one off payment, around $500 at the time.[22]

On the way out I spotted the inscription on the cornerstone of the cathedral:

In the name of the Father and the Son and the Holy Spirit, this main shrine of the armed forces of the Russian Federation was constructed in honour of Christ's resurrection by the Patriarch of Moscow and all-Russia Kirill, Russian Federation President V.V. Putin, and Russian Defence Minister S.K. Shoigu on September 19, 2018.

Two trinities rolled into one.

☨ ☨ ☨

There is another story, a story of good people striving to preserve archaic churches and reinvigorate rural communities. Many of the famous cathedrals and churches are inspired by European architecture. But the wooden chapels scattered around the north of the country belong to a uniquely Russian tradition. In Soviet times, a large number were destroyed, taken apart to repurpose their logs or turned into warehouses. In the years immediately after, they were left to rot. The race is now on to save those that remain.

For the past two decades, Father Alexei Yakovlev, a priest from Moscow, and his wife Tatyana, who is a landscape painter, have spent their summers in the village of Vorzogory on a promontory on the White Sea. Founded at the time of Ivan the Terrible, the village was famous for its carpenters who built wooden ships for the monks of the Arctic Solovetsky Monastery. On their first visit in the early 2000s, the priest and his wife met a pensioner, Sasha, who was busy splitting a tree trunk with an axe. He was not preparing firewood. He told them that for years he had been singlehandedly trying to repair the wooden bell tower of the church because he feared one day it would collapse before his eyes. 'We were so inspired by his example that we started helping him,' said Father Alexei.

The priest spread the word among his Moscow parishioners, who included some skilled craftsmen and joiners. Over a few summers, they rescued two churches from the seventeenth and eighteenth centuries, alongside the rickety bell tower. Emboldened by his success, in 2006 Father Alexei founded a group called *Obscheye Delo*, Common Cause.[23] Every summer hundreds of volunteers set off with tents and enough food to last a fortnight to camp in parts of Karelia, Arkhangelsk, Komi and the Vologda regions. They patch leaky roofs, fix broken windows, prop up walls, replace rotten crowns in foundations and dig trenches to act as firebreaks. They launched a charm offensive to recruit local people to act as caretakers. In just a few years, *Obscheye Delo* has turned into a popular grassroots movement with a network of members from all walks of life. It has carried out 360 expeditions and restored 187 churches.

Yulia Pyrenkova, a shy sales executive from Moscow, told me she joined because she felt something was missing in her life. Now a seasoned volunteer, she recalled her first trip, during which she helped restore a nineteenth-century church in a Karelian village called Kubovskaya: 'In the morning before the Liturgy we read the Akathist of the Mother of God before the Smolensk icon. Then the service began. At the end, Father Lazar told us that it was the first Liturgy served in the Smolensk church since it was closed by the Bolsheviks. We received Holy Communion. It was quiet and dignified.' Yulia picked up many skills from a local woman who organised the carpentry festival. She went to concerts, performed traditional dances, baked traditional Karelian pies and sang folk songs around a campfire. It may sound like a glorified holiday camp but, apart from the spiritual benefits, the group has helped to forge ties between city dwellers and the neglected countryside.

Yuliana Nikitina, an Orthodox youth worker, believes the Russian landscape has transformational powers. Most summers she sets off in three cars packed with delinquent adolescent boys on a road trip around the Murmansk region in the north, near the Norwegian border. They sleep under canvas and visit a succession of monasteries. 'The scenery in the north is bleak but also stunningly beautiful,' she told me. 'Sometimes the kids complain and ask why we can't hang out with normal people instead of monks. I say to them: "Listen, guys, apart from the monks, nobody is that keen to see us."' Most of the time, the boys live in a special facility sponsored by the Church. The St Basil the Great Adaptation Centre on St Petersburg's Vasilevskiy Island is a residential centre for teenagers on probation. Unusually well-funded, it has a team of counsellors and therapists. On my first visit in 2012, some of the boys were learning the urban acrobatic sport of parkour to improve their fitness and stamina. Many had been weakened by years of drug and alcohol abuse. On my next visit, they had opened a small cafe and were training to be baristas.

Hardliners have criticised the project for mollycoddling the teenagers. They thought they should be behind bars, not making cappuccinos. Nikitina, who founded the centre in 2004, rolls her eyes at such comments. 'I tell such people, "Okay, well in that case, let's just poison these kids or lock them up for life! Is that really what you want?" If not, we have to work with them to reintegrate them into society.' Having visited Denmark and other parts of Europe to look at different youth justice policies, Nikitina is convinced that small residential groups produce the best results and cut reoffending rates. Her brisk, no-nonsense approach has allowed her to create an island of tolerance in Russia's second city with the support of a few influential clerics.

'When the boys arrive, most say the Church is just for old grannies or losers, but they usually change their minds,' she says.

'The goal of our organisation is not to promote the Orthodox faith, but to help teenagers in difficult life situations.' The boys arrive via a court order and most are from atheist backgrounds; a few are Muslims. Visits to rural parishes and monasteries often awaken their curiosity about religion. 'They realise that no one is forcing them to go to church, no one is forcing them to participate in sacraments or be baptised. But they see a very different life, and at first it seems strange and wild to them and then they grow to accept it.' Planting and digging up potatoes or collecting firewood can be therapeutic for damaged souls. Nikitina added that campsites and youth hostels are reluctant to allow young offenders to stay: 'They have stereotyped ideas about the boys and imagine they will steal or smash things up. But in a small parish, I know we will always be welcome because there are never enough hands on deck.'

Too often impoverished priests in remote places are expected to perform a variety of miracles with no help whatsoever. Take the case of Father Mikhail Goncharov, who for twelve years has been trying to renovate a dilapidated eighteenth-century church in the Siberian village of Antsiferovo, on the banks of the Yenisei River. 'To inspire someone's first steps toward God, a church needs to have splendour,' he said. 'Aesthetics are important to people. And here there is nothing but disorder and cold.' Unable to attract parishioners, Father Mikhail raised some funds by acting as the village taxi driver, but the muddy roads often proved too much for his minivan. When he appealed through the media for spare parts to fix his vehicle, some locals accused him of 'airing their dirty laundry in public' and stopped speaking to him. Nor was the diocese sympathetic. 'To serve is to struggle,' said one of its deacons. 'If there is a parish, there will be a salary. No parish, no salary. The diocese can donate wine for the service, and that's it. That's how it is everywhere, all over the country.'[24]

Wherever they serve, the Church expects its priests to behave like salesmen. They charge for services like weddings, baptisms and funerals, and also for special prayers, such as for soldiers serving on the front, or for the sick. In affluent parishes, many earn money from blessing cars, apartments, businesses, helicopters, even personal computers. Like senior managers, bishops husband their resources, passing money up the pyramid to the Patriarchate. Impoverished village priests might get 10,000 roubles (£85) a month while their counterparts in large churches and monasteries in big cities receive 30 to 40 times more. The Moscow Patriarchate does little to mitigate the income disparity.[25]

Some clerics are more enterprising than others. Mother Superior Feofaniya is an abbess with Oprah Winfrey-like business skills. She unearthed a little-known Stalin-era miracle worker and got her turned into a saint. Within a few years she had built a thriving cult around the peasant woman and transformed her monastery into one of the wealthiest in the country. The saint, Blessed Matrona Nikonova, was born in 1881 without eyeballs in a small village near Tula. By the time the girl was seven, local people credited her with divine vision and healing powers. Stalin supposedly paid her a secret visit in 1941 when the Germans were advancing on the capital. She prophesied that if he remained in Moscow and restored the Church to its glory, the motherland would be saved.

When Patriarch Alexei made Feofaniya abbess of Moscow's Pokrovsky (Intercession) Convent in 1995, restoring the place seemed an impossible job. There were no crosses or domes on the churches, many religious buildings had been turned into offices and the Ministry of Fuel Energy had taken over the church. Feofaniya decided she needed a patron saint to help reverse the fortunes of the place. She was determined to get Matrona canonised. Although the blind peasant woman had been revered by some as a miracle worker during her lifetime, in 1997 the Synodal Commission for Canonisation found no grounds to elevate her. Religious scholars said her story was riddled with inconsistencies. One accused her of promoting paganism and folk religiosity, 'practised by ignorant, superstitious people'.[26] The head of the Moscow regional diocese, Metropolitan Yuvenaly, threw letters proposing Matrona's canonisation into the bin. But when he received an order signed by the Patriarch, he stopped scoffing. Feofaniya prevailed upon the Patriarch to override the Synodal Commission. By 1999, Matrona was canonised as a Moscow saint, and in 2004 her 'church-wide glorification' took place.

Now thousands of believers pour through the gates of the Intercession Convent every day. Clutching flowers, they queue for at least two hours to get into the Church of the Protecting Veil to catch a glimpse of Matrona's holy remains. It is widely believed that the saint can help women to get married and bring back straying husbands. A policeman stands next to a crowd-control barrier. Some women join another long queue, past more collection boxes, to mount a few steps and kiss the icon of Matrona encased in glass on the church wall. When I visited towards the end of the pandemic, every few minutes a masked nun wiped the lipstick marks off the glass with disinfectant.

The convent does not make the scale of donations public, but it is estimated to rake in half a million dollars a month – a fifth of which goes to the Patriarchate. One newspaper claimed that even the beggars at the entrance to the convent are the richest in the country.[27] Perhaps Matrona is popular because she seems so familiar. Her life as an ordinary, marginalised Soviet woman was close to that of the grandmothers and great grandmothers of her current devotees. Her family was deprived of their meagre land and farm animals under Stalin's collectivisation drive. Like many people living in the capital, she was an illegal migrant. In 1932, the Soviet government introduced an internal passport system to limit the size of urban populations. It was especially hard to get a *propiska*, or residency stamp, for the most desirable cities – Moscow, St Petersburg and Kyiv. Some resorted to fake marriage or paid hefty bribes to get the required stamp on page 14 of their internal passports.

Abbess Feofaniya also came from humble origins far from Moscow and began her monastic life working in a cowshed. She has come a long way since then. After renovating the convent, she built a five-star hotel nearby where guests can get married and skip the queue to view the saint's relics. In 2018, Kirill gave her a new asset to manage, the Danilovsky Hotel, next to one of his official residences. To the fury of many Muscovites, she tried to annex the local park, which has existed since the 1930s but was once the convent's cemetery. Feofaniya also created a sprawling retail empire with some of her brothers. It produces church literature and souvenirs as well as secular goods under the 'Pokrovsky Convent' brand, such as chocolates and anti-cellulite soaps. Members of her family also own several country residences and hotel complexes near the Trinity Lavra of St Sergius in Sergiyev Posad.

Feofaniya's commercial acumen has made her one of the most powerful women in Orthodoxy. Much as the Patriarch appreciates the income she generates, he had to rein her in after journalists reported that she was whizzing around town in a $190,000 Mercedes-Benz S-Class. After days of silence, Kirill 'blessed' the abbess to sell the car and advised her to use donations at the convent for 'social and philanthropic aims'. Church insiders say she is not known for her charity. A young priest serving at the convent who had a sick baby son in need of a liver transplant did not dare ask the abbess for help because he felt that she was no more approachable than the Patriarch himself.[28]

Ever since the early sixteenth century, the Church has been torn between two opposing forces – the *stiazhateli*, or possessors, and the *nestiazhateli*, non-possessors. The latter were led by Nil Sorsky, a monk from a remote hermitage in the forests beyond the Volga. He argued that monasteries had too much land for their own good. The Church, he insisted, should be separate from the state and renounce worldly wealth. Monks should stick to their vows of poverty and focus on life beyond the grave. Elaborate liturgy mattered less to God than a simple prayer filled with contrition. The *nestiazhateli* might be seen as the Protestants of the Orthodox Church with their focus on an individual's relation to God. The possessors, on the other hand, also known as Josephites after their leader Joseph of Volokolamsk, wanted rich, powerful churches with extensive land-holdings. They glorify God through impressive rituals and splendid icons. For them, harmonious relations between Church and ruler are paramount.

It is clear which of these forces has the upper hand in Russia today. In 2021, a young priest, Roman Stepanov, from Cheboksary, a small city on the Volga in central Russia, irritated his seniors by calling on Kirill and other clerics to declare their income and property. He also demanded that they acknowledge the earnings and real estate of 'their closest relatives and cronies'.[29] He was sacked and defrocked for his insolence, although, in the official version, his bishop said he was being punished for taking drugs and cohabiting with another woman after his marriage broke down. Comparing himself to the *nestiazhateli* of the Volga region, Stepanov said: 'In ancient times, princes first supported the elders from the non-possessors' movement but later they backed those who wanted a rich church. Then the clerics-turned-landowners said whatever they were told to say. In other words, property guaranteed political loyalty – and it is just the same today.'[30]

Five centuries ago, Sorsky imposed harsh rules on himself as an ascetic but advocated religious freedom for others. He opposed punishing those deemed to have strayed from the true path of Orthodoxy. One of his disciples, a monk called Vassian, urged clemency towards heretics at a Church council in 1503: 'Where in the tradition of the Gospels, Apostles, and Fathers are monks ordered to acquire populous villages and enslave peasants to the brotherhood? We petition the rich, fawn slavishly, flatter them to get out of them some little village. We wrong and rob and sell Christians, our brothers. We torture them with scourges like wild beasts.'

After the fall of Communism, as Russia plunged headlong into materialism, many felt a deep spiritual hunger and yearned for something to help them make sense of their lives. When the Church grew ever-more acquisitive, few were surprised. Artemy Troitsky, the leading cultural journalist of his time, said that if many priests under Gorbachev were seen as dissidents, under Yeltsin they had become 'Orthodox yuppies'. Taking the cloth was a standard career move for those who wanted to make money. 'I don't care if priests become very fat or very wealthy,' said Troitsky, 'this is none of my business.' But, he added, to protect its wealth the Church became more reliant on the state and lost what independence it had. Putin used the Church to reinforce his power and to mobilise it on the frontline in his culture war against the West.

12. CULTURE WARS

Unlimited power in the hands of limited people
always leads to cruelty.
ALEKSANDR SOLZHENITSYN, *THE GULAG ARCHIPELAGO*

Andrei Tkachev, a married archpriest and father of four, is not a man to mince his words. He once told a group of Orthodox young men how to avoid being henpecked by their future wives: 'You need to break the woman over your knee, knock off her horns, bend her over, rub her face and stuff her into a washing machine.' Do not allow her to wear makeup – it is the 'pornographic paint' of modern civilisation. Any man who cannot break a woman's will is not a real man; he should avoid marriage and become a monk instead. 'Women are arrogant, nasty creatures,' he added, his voice rising to a crescendo. 'If a woman doesn't get whacked in the face at least once in her life, she won't understand anything.'

One of the young men present secretly recorded this 'spiritual conversation' and shared it on Orthodox websites. Tkachev was unabashed. He compared his directness to a coach addressing a football team but denied he was promoting domestic abuse.[1] Surprisingly, though, a female member of the upper house of the Russian parliament appeared to do just that. Elena Mizulina told a group of reporters that wives were usually to blame for the 'rudeness, absence of tenderness and respect' in families. 'We women are weak creatures and do not take offence even when we are hit,' she said. 'A man beating his wife is less offensive than when a man is humiliated.'

Mizulina and Tkachev made these remarks in 2016, but they seemed inspired by a famous text written five centuries earlier. *Domostroi*, Domestic Order, is a set of guidelines for a harmonious household compiled by Silvestr, a priest who took Ivan the Terrible's confession. Filled with quotations from the Bible, it portrays a world in which women lead subservient and secluded lives. Alongside advice about how to knead dough or pickle cabbage, the book advocates hitting children 'to save their souls'. It adds: 'If women do not fear men or do not do what their husbands or fathers tell them, then whip them with a lash commensurate with their guilt, though do so privately, not in the public eye.' As for servants, they can be flogged publicly, but 'with pregnant women or children', the *Domostroi* explains, 'damage to the stomach could result, so beat them in a careful and controlled way, albeit painfully and fearsomely'.

Today, many women fear Russia is sliding backwards – not all the way back to those days, but not too far off, either. And with the blessing of the Church, whose own commission on family, motherhood and childhood values insisted that the Bible tolerates 'intelligent and loving use of physical punishment as an essential part of the rights given to parents by God himself'. In 2015, state-funded antenatal clinics began handing out booklets to pregnant women with 'Useful Tips for Strengthening Family Relationships'. Women are advised to always put themselves second and 'not to awaken the "beast" in a man' because 'every husband wants to be the head of the family; this is his God-ordained destiny'. A (male) columnist from the business newspaper *Kommersant* called it 'offensive' and a testament 'to the new mediaeval epoch'.

In the early part of the twentieth century, the young Soviet Union liberalised divorce and abortion, permitted cohabitation, and ushered in a host of reforms that instigated a sexual revolution. The beatniks of California may be credited with inventing free love in the 1960s, but it could be said that the real precursors were women like Lenin's lover Inessa Armand and the revolutionary feminist Alexandra Kollontai, who argued that in a Communist society sexual satisfaction should be as straightforward as drinking a glass of water. Not all these things worked out so well in practice, but the revolution led women to challenge patriarchal structures that had existed for centuries.

For many years Putin made an implicit pact with his people – stay out of politics and your living standards will improve. But in his third term, as the economy slowed and his popularity slumped, his priorities changed. He sought to distract attention from corruption and economic hardship at home by seeking enemies abroad – the degenerate West. To fight this 'battle', he forged alliances with hardcore nationalists and the most conservative elements in the Church. This mission was made easier by the growth of authoritarian populism elsewhere. Some experts point to similarities between right-wing evangelicals in the US and Islamic conservatives, the so-called 'Baptist–burqa' coalition.[2] Europe too has been sucked into the culture wars. In Hungary, Italy, Germany, the Netherlands, France, Britain and elsewhere, a war against 'woke' raged. The populist right claimed for itself the mantle of champions of ordinary hardworking families. Putin saw an opportunity. President and patriarch have, for a decade and more, made clear they sided with this other Europe. They portrayed Russia as a refuge for social conservatives and pure Christians who abhor abortion, same-sex marriage and other Western depravities.

A wife's obedience to her husband has become a central tenet of 'modern' Russian Orthodoxy. Bishop Panteleimon, head of the Patriarchate's department for charity, advised Russian women not to nag their husbands during the Covid lockdown to avoid rows. If they failed, he said, they should punish themselves by doing 'ten bows' of repentance or by 'giving up chocolate or surfing the internet for a day'. Reported cases of domestic violence more than doubled in the first month of the pandemic. Later on, the return of traumatised and brutalised men from fighting on the front in Ukraine was another factor. Reliable statistics are hard to come by, but in one independent study, the murders of more than 18,500 women from 2011 to 2019 were analysed.[3] Nearly two thirds of them died at the hands of a partner or relative. In Western Europe, 29 per cent of murdered women are killed at the hands of their partners, a still terrible proportion but significantly lower. As many as 36,000 Russian women face daily abuse at home, according to a 2017 Human Rights Watch report. Countries around the world are plagued by domestic violence. What makes Russia different is the extraordinary level of resistance to attempts to protect the victims.

Margarita Gracheva and her husband Dmitri, from the town of Serpukhov outside Moscow, were childhood sweethearts. But their relationship soured when she began working in the advertising section of the local newspaper. Despite having a degree, Dmitri could only find work driving a forklift truck, and he became resentful of her career and jealous of her male colleagues. One night in December 2017, he beat her up in front of their children, and the following day threatened her with a knife. Terrified, she went to the police. The desk officer told her to write a statement and said they would get back to her in twenty days. Five days after the case was dropped for lack of evidence, Dmitri offered to drive her to work. On the way, he parked the car, dragged her from her seat, took an axe from the boot and chopped off both her hands. Then he dumped her in the emergency department of their local hospital before driving to the police station and confessing to his crime.

Margarita's mutilated left hand was retrieved from the forest and sewn back on in a nine-hour operation. A crowdfunding campaign raised 6 million roubles (just over $90,000) for a prosthetic right hand, which was fitted in Germany. Although Margarita published a book about her recovery, she did not relish the publicity. She told me she felt she had to go on TV and tell her story to ensure her ex-husband would not be let out of prison too quickly. He was eventually given a fourteen-year sentence.

In Moscow, parliament had been toying with the idea of clamping down a little on domestic violence, putting it on the same level of serious crime as 'hooliganism' and hate crimes. Conservatives were appalled. Their poster woman, Mizulina, introduced a bill downgrading battery in the home from a criminal to an administrative offence; it was passed by an overwhelming majority and signed into law in February 2017. The fine for wife-beating was set at 5,000 roubles (£60), not much more than a parking ticket. The victim was now made responsible for collecting evidence and bringing the case.

Oksana Pushkina did not vote with her fellow MPs. A former rhythmic gymnast and a well-known TV journalist, she had been elected the previous year as a member of the pro-Kremlin party, United Russia. Her constituency west of Moscow included the elite Rublyovka suburb where Putin has his official residence. But her anger over the treatment of women turned her into a rebel. When five female reporters and producers, including a BBC colleague, accused the chairman of the parliament's foreign affairs committee, Leonid Slutsky, of attempting to grope and kiss them during interviews, their complaints were laughed off. Many Russians, including high-profile women, treat the #MeToo movement as ridiculously woke. Pushkina, however, supported the journalists and said politicians convicted of sexual harassment should be sacked.

I met her in her office in the Duma two years after the article for battery was removed from the Russian Criminal Code. She was conducting a lonely campaign to get the law overturned. 'From the grandstand of parliament, we've basically said you can beat up your whole family,' she told me. 'This is a very bad law. Domestic violence has nothing to do with traditional values. It is a crime that deserves punishment.' Over the past ten years, individual bills on the prevention of domestic violence have been introduced to the Duma more than forty times, but none has passed a single reading. Undaunted, Pushkina planned to bring in restraining orders, which have never existed in Russia, to keep abusers away from their victims, along with anti-sexual-harassment measures and steps to promote gender equality. She received a torrent of hate mail. More than 180 church and family groups addressed an open letter to Putin asking him to block such measures, describing them as the work of 'foreign agents' and supporters of 'radical feminist ideology'. An enlarged photograph of Pushkina decorated with the American flag was attached to hot air balloons and released outside the Duma.

Andrei Kormukhin, the leader of the group *Sorok Soroka* which advocates church building, described the restraining measures she proposed as 'monstrous'. Giving testimony to a parliamentary committee, the hulking figure stood at the lectern, warning that Pushkina's initiative would lead to 'the genocide of the family'. He later convened a rally in Moscow's Sokolniki Park at which protesters held posters of coffins decorated with skulls. Their message was that laws to protect women in their homes would kill men who would be unjustly banished from their families.

Pushkina's campaign was blocked by Kirill and by Shevkunov, Putin's confessor. According to sources in the Duma, the Patriarch personally asked Putin to remove the 'dangerous' issue from the parliamentary agenda.[4] In December 2019, he delivered a sermon in the Assumption Cathedral of the Kremlin, in which he condemned violence in the home but warned 'we must not allow strangers with unclear goals and thoughts to invade the family space'. Laurie Bristow, the British ambassador, had gone to see one of Kirill's most senior clerics, Metropolitan Hilarion, on 3 February 2017, just before the Duma decided to decriminalise domestic violence. 'He took an absolutely hard-line approach,' says Bristow. 'He said it was up to the government to decide such matters and seemed to find it awkward that I was asking about the Church's view.'[5]

Around this time, another story of abuse caused an outcry, at least among some. Mikhail Khachaturyan was a minor mafia boss and an ostentatious believer who went on regular pilgrimages. On social media he liked to be known as Michael of Jerusalem. He posted pictures of himself bathing at holy sites and hobnobbing with prominent Orthodox clerics and public figures. In July 2018 he was found dead in the corridor outside his Moscow apartment. His three teenage daughters confessed to attacking him while he was asleep with pepper spray, a hunting knife and a hammer. They faced up to twenty years in prison for murder. Investigators found evidence that Kristina, Angelina and Maria had been physically and sexually abused by Khachaturyan for years. He had driven their mother, Aurelia Dunduk, out of the family home at gunpoint in 2015. When she reported that her husband had beaten her after her first daughter was born, the police called him to the station. As he arrived, they ripped up her statement in front of him. She never dared to seek help again. He forbade his daughters from contacting their mother and focused his aggression on them instead. 'They were protecting themselves – they actually had no choice,' the mother told me. 'If they hadn't killed him, we'd have found the bodies of the three girls in that flat.'

Thousands of people, horrified by the sisters' ordeal, took to the streets and signed petitions calling for their release. Their lawyers had hoped that charges of premeditated murder would be downgraded to self-defence or that they might be exonerated. At that point, Metropolitan Hilarion, head of the Synodal Department for External Church Relations, waded in. 'If this trial leads to an acquittal, it will not send a good signal to society,' he said. 'People will think that there is no need to turn to law enforcement agencies, you can simply lynch a person and you will be acquitted.' He would not want his words to in any way influence the course of the investigation, he added.[6]

A few months later, the Deputy Prosecutor General, announced he would uphold the murder charges and the case would go to trial. Not all priests shared the Metropolitan's views. The sisters had 'committed a terrible crime', said Archpriest Alexei Uminsky, rector of Moscow's Holy Trinity Khokhly Church, but they needed 'understanding, sympathy, compassion as victims'. He added that the case highlighted the problem of domestic violence, 'which very often is not just hushed up, but completely negated'.[7]

In the midst of these high-profile cases, Pushkina's draft legislation was attacked on the Patriarchate's media outlets and on Tsargrad TV, the conservative religious channel. In a calculated move, the Kremlin leaked an unfinished, watered-down bill that had not been agreed upon by the co-authors, two lawyers and a human rights activist, who had been working with Pushkina. This led to infighting which helped discredit the initiative. The speaker of the upper chamber, Valentina Matvienko, whose career blossomed under Putin, responded by saying there was 'no need to rush' and effectively buried it. 'Ultra-conservatism, fundamentalism and totalitarianism have triumphed in my homeland,' Pushkina told me a few years later. Looking back, she felt her campaign against violence was 'almost naive' when preparations were already underway for the assault on Ukraine. 'In the early days, I found allies for the bill within the President's administration, but as my tenure in the Duma drew close, they vanished into thin air,' she said.[8]

In 2021, United Russia did not invite Pushkina to run for a second term. Her replacement is a pop star who wrote a song praising an intercontinental ballistic missile.[9] Some suspect the Church was protecting its own. Religious expert Nikolai Mitrokhin says that each year a small handful of priests are imprisoned for violent behaviour. He cited the case of a priest from Orenburg, in south-west Russia, who received a 21-year sentence for rape and other crimes against young children 'The Church understands that if there are stricter controls, then not just individual priests, but dozens of them will be locked up,' he said.[10]

Pushkina is convinced that the Church opposed her bill to pre-serve the status quo. 'If we pass a law, their centuries-old structure breaks down,' she said. 'The male state does not want to lose its strength and its leverage over us women.' Although she assured me that she remained a party loyalist and felt 'Russia is too big to function without a strongman leader like Putin', she rolled her eyes when I asked about pressure from the Church. Intriguingly, she draws on her experience of working in the United States in the 1990s, report-ing for an American news channel on attacks on abortion clinics by far-right radicals. 'All the worst things I saw in America, I see in Russia now,' she said.[11]

Opinion polls point in the opposite direction, indicating that two thirds of the country is opposed to a ban on abortion.[12] One priest from Tula, south of Moscow, recently lamented that only a minor-ity of his regular parishioners are pro-life: 'They read morning and evening prayers, call on God's blessing for every undertaking, do not eat, do not drink, and some even do not brush their teeth after midnight before Communion, but at the same time they consider it possible to kill their own child.'[13] The Soviet Union was the first modern state to formally legalise abortion in 1920. However, wor-ried about the falling birth rate, Stalin made it illegal in 1936. That ban was repealed only after his death in 1953.

'As a member of the clergy, I testify that an abortion is a disaster and a tragedy for the woman and those close to her,' the Patriarch has declared. He insists that Russia's demographic crisis could be solved, 'as if by the wave of a magic wand', if the country learned 'to dissuade women from having abortions'. The number of abortions has dropped, but not for the reasons the Patriarch might approve of. In the late Soviet era, the average woman had six terminations in her lifetime, because of the absence of other kinds of birth control. Once contraceptives became more accessible, the number of abor-tions plummeted. According to one prominent demographer who worked for Rosstat, the government statistics agency, the number of abortions for non-emergency reasons has fallen fourteen-fold since the 1990s.[14] In those days, women could end their pregnancies with-out condition until 12 weeks or until 22 weeks for a wide range of 'social reasons', such as divorce, unemployment or money problems.

The list of reasons has been whittled down under Putin's leadership and since 2012 later-stage abortions are permitted only in the case of rape and danger to a mother's life.

For years, Orthodox clerics have played on fears of a shrinking population to lobby for a clampdown. Russia, like much of the developed world, is saddled with an ageing population and a falling birth rate, which has slid to 1.5 children per woman. Russia's population has fallen to 144 million, 2 million fewer than in 2000 when Putin came to power.

The notion that motherhood is a sacred and a patriotic duty is hammered home by pro-Kremlin youth groups, nationalist organisations and many of the country's 40,000 priests. At Moscow's Peter and Fevronia Club, named after the two patron saints of marriage, Father Alexei Gomonov runs a speed-dating night for Orthodox singles every Sunday after Vespers. The church also organises pilgrimages, charity visits and ballroom dancing. He tells the men and women shyly flirting over cups of tea that their duty is to 'go forth and multiply'. Anyone who abstains, he intones, is 'violating God's law, and that is not good'.[15]

Having vilified women's right to choose, some politicians have moved onto attacking their right to work and to higher education. Mikhail Murashko, Minister of Health, denounced 'women's perverse desire to prioritise their careers over having children'. Margarita Pavlova, a member of the upper house, said 'young women should be steered away from studying' and give birth instead. One Duma deputy called for childless people to pay higher taxes. Another suggested, in an echo of the dystopian novel *The Handmaid's Tale*, that thousands of female prisoners be temporarily released from custody to get pregnant and sent back to prison if they fail.[16]

In October 2023, a year and a half into his invasion of Ukraine, Putin urged women to have as many as seven or eight children. Russia needed large families to preserve its traditions and its population. He is desperately worried about the demographics, but he has also worsened them. At least 100,000 Russians have been killed since February 2022. The war in Ukraine has also triggered waves of emigration, and many of those who fled are of child-bearing age. Every opportunity is used to blame women, linking the population crisis back to abortion. One poster even suggests it will be their fault if Russia loses the war: a picture of an embryo is displayed next to a camouflaged soldier. The text reads: 'Protect Me Today So I Can Protect You Tomorrow'.[17]

Anna Kuznetsova, a psychologist married to an Orthodox priest, has promoted a discredited genetic phenomenon known as telegony. The idea is that a woman's previous sexual partner may influence the characteristics of her child sired by another man. Kuznetsova saw abortion as 'an evolutionary catastrophe', arguing that uterine cells have 'an information-wave memory' and can remember everything that happened to them.[18] Kuznetsova, who works in pre-abortion counselling in Penza, south-east of Moscow, is no provincial crank; she has served as Russia's Children's Rights Commissioner and deputy chair of the Duma.

The Moscow archpriest Maksim Obukhov, who founded an organisation called Pro-Life, says he and his fellow campaigners once felt like 'rebels on the edge of society' but now feel they have real influence on policy makers. He welcomed a 2011 law which obliges state-run clinics to show women an ultrasound if they are considering terminating their pregnancy. 'When the woman hears the heartbeat,' he said, 'this is when we get real success.' Another initiative proposed by Kirill and already implemented in parts of Russia is a ban on what is called 'incitement to abortion'. The western region of Mordovia, for example, has introduced fines of up to 200,000 roubles (£1,800) for trying to persuade a pregnant woman to have an abortion. The Patriarch has called for these measures to be introduced nationwide.

As in the United States, the right to a safe legal abortion has turned into a postcode lottery. The conservative Belgorod region could be seen as Russia's Bible Belt, a Slav Oklahoma. Its governor, a former agronomist who worked on collective farms and then found God, has adopted the only law on 'spiritual safety' in the country. Schools and universities are banned from celebrating non-Orthodox holidays like Valentine's Day and Halloween. Certain rappers and heavy metal bands are prohibited. Alcohol sales are restricted. Women seeking an abortion have to get a document signed by a priest as well as a psychologist. Father Nikolai Dubinin, a priest from the town of Stary

Oskol, said the counselling scheme had saved dozens of lives and many of the rescued babies had been baptised in his church.

Children's campaigners and policy makers have expressed concern about the impact an abortion ban would have on the country's overcrowded and poorly resourced orphanages.[19] The plight of abandoned children was exacerbated by a veto on adoptions by foreigners. American families were excluded in 2012 in retaliation for the US Congress' Magnitsky Act, which froze the assets of Russian officials accused of corruption. Then a bill passed in 2022 extended the adoption ban to citizens of other countries 'that commit unfriendly actions' against Russia – nations supportive of Ukraine. Archpriest Vsevolod Chaplin, a spokesman for the Patriarchate, had already suggested the path to heaven would be closed to children adopted by foreigners because 'they won't get a truly Christian upbringing'.[20]

Despite the reverence for motherhood, the Orthodox Church has a curious approach to childbirth. Bishop Niphont of Novgorod once explained that if a woman happened to give birth to a child inside a church, the building had to be sealed for three days, then reconsecrated.[21] That was back in the twelfth century, but even today a special prayer is read on the first day after a birth, which petitions God to 'cleanse the mother of all defilement'. Another set of prayers is read 40 days later, when the mother is allowed to come back to church and the priest asks God to 'wash away her bodily defilement and spiritual defilement' and make her worthy of partaking in the communion.

I turn to Sister Vassa Larin, the Russian-American nun whose research helped to reunite the Orthodox Church abroad (ROCOR) with the Patriarchate. She is scathing about the notion of women's 'unclean' blood contaminating the Eucharist. A nun and a professor of liturgy now living in Vienna, she points out that opinions about female so-called 'ritual impurity' have been diverse across the centuries and different Orthodox jurisdictions. She told me about a conversation with a Moscow priest who agreed it was ridiculous to describe women as 'impure' for giving birth. But he added that the Church was sticking to the old rules 'for the women's own good' because some were so devout that they would come to services when they ought to be resting at home with their baby.

When, at nineteen, Sister Vassa left her liberal arts college in the US to join a convent of the Russian Orthodox Church Abroad in France, she had a rude awakening, despite her strict religious upbringing. During her monthly periods, she, like her fellow nuns, was banned from Communion; she also could not kiss icons, help to bake the altar bread, drink holy water or clean the church. She was not even allowed to light the lamp that hung before the icons in her own cell. Now Vassa tells anyone who will listen that stigmatising menstruation reflects pagan and Old Testament fears of the material world and has nothing to do with Christian anthropology or the doctrine of salvation. 'Jesus Christ says explicitly that sin is the only thing that defiles us,' she says. Now in her early fifties, Sister Vassa is an unusually free-spirited voice in the Church. Until the war in Ukraine, she sat on two of its commissions – one on Canon Law, the other on the Liturgy and Church art. The author of many scholarly articles and books, she left her teaching job at Vienna University to present a podcast and YouTube channel, Coffee with Sister Vassa, with 20,000 subscribers around the world.

Although she has helped to spread the word about her church and its traditions, some clerics and laity were furious that an Orthodox nun had the temerity to appear online. Female bloggers, specifically priests' wives, known as *matushki*, Little Mothers, are tolerated on social media so long as they stick to conservative agendas. Many parrot patriarchal ideas about the inherent sinfulness of women. One popular blogger, Matushka Yekaterina, suggested women are to blame for getting raped. 'In most cases, the girl herself triggers violence,' she wrote. 'I have an acquaintance who drank alcohol, wore makeup, put a short skirt on and went for a walk to a park where she met a boy. It all ended sadly. She suffered severe psychological trauma, but with God's help and confession, she accepted her blame and she could find the strength to forgive her abuser.'[22]

Russian nuns, like Victorian children, are supposed to be seen but not heard and to be unquestioningly obedient. This attitude is clearly portrayed in a book by a young photographer and artist which caused a stir when it was published in 2016. Maria Kikot's *Confessions of a Former Novice*[23] provides a terrifying glimpse into life behind the walls of the St Nicholas Cherno-Ostrovsky convent, south of Moscow. Kikot fled the secular world in search of spiritual growth but found herself in an authoritarian hell. She described nuns being worked to the bone, denied food and suffering psychological abuse from a despotic abbess.

Kikot's story may have inspired a video game about a rebellious nun who is expelled from her convent in the nineteenth century and embarks on a journey of self-discovery in a moody, snow-covered landscape. Dmitry Svetlov, the game's developer, received a great deal of attention on social media, not just for the twists and turns of the adventure called *Indika,* but for his views on the invasion of Ukraine. On the website of his Warsaw-based publisher, he announced: 'This war is a consequence of the political infantilism of Russians, which comes from an Orthodox culture where obedience and patience are the greatest virtues.' Furious gamers accused Svetlov of Russophobia. He and most of his employees have since relocated to Kazakhstan.[24]

Sister Vassa's first video was innocuous enough, the story of a third-century teenage saint. It initially appeared on the ROCOR's New York-based website but was removed after several clergymen complained. ROCOR stopped posting her material but she continued to self-publish. Her audio podcasts, video courses and online shop selling books, prayer calendars and Coffee with Sister Vassa mugs have become popular. The income covers her rent, pays for technical assistance with her online ministry and gives her a licence to speak her mind. 'I think it's healthy for me to take personal responsibility for whatever I say without anybody worrying about me speaking for "the Church",' she says.

When she received a letter from the devout mother of a gay teenager, she replied as she saw fit. The fourteen-year-old boy's parents were supportive when he came out to them, but they worried about the reaction of their parish priest. They feared their son, who was an altar boy and loved going to church, could be ostracised once he started dating. So, they sought the nun's advice. Sister Vassa replied by praising the family's 'unconditional love' for their child. She acknowledged that leading an active sexual life as a gay person is a sin in the eyes of the Church. But, she added, sexuality, whatever the orientation, is 'rather a messy business' and double-standards should not be applied to gay people simply because they are the minority. She ended with a dose of common sense: 'let him date in the daylight, with your knowledge, so he's not chased into some kind of underground, of illicit hook-ups'. The nun's 2017 post enraged both clergy and laity, who accused her of 'encouraging children to have gay sex in their parents' homes'. The Holy Synod of the ROCOR put out a statement telling its flock to disregard her advice 'as contrary to the teachings of the Gospel and pastorally harmful'.

As in the US and elsewhere, homosexuality has become a political acid test. Kirill's intolerance of any form of LGBT+ rights has been a godsend for Putin. When he began his third presidential term in 2012, in the wake of massive protests about the doctored elections, he needed some kind of ideology to justify his staying in power. He seized on 'traditional values' rooted in history, which supposedly encompassed patriotism, reverence for the mysterious Russian soul, respect for authority – and heteronormative ideals of family and gender. In the rhetoric of Kirill and the Kremlin, rights for sexual minorities, alongside feminism, multiculturalism and atheism, are not just foreign to Russia's belief system; they are existential threats to the nation.

The invasion of Ukraine in 2022 was depicted in these terms – the great fightback of decent, traditionalist, God-fearing Russians against a non-existent state governed by Nazis that had fallen under the West's decadent spell.

Two weeks after the Russian troops rolled in, the Patriarch delivered a sermon in Christ the Saviour on Forgiveness Sunday. This is the day on which the faithful prepare for the penitential season of Great Lent, the 40-day fast, an opportunity to reflect on sins and ask forgiveness of each other. It was on Forgiveness Sunday in 1861 that Metropolitan Philaret of Moscow announced that serfdom had been abolished.[25] Many wondered if Kirill might choose this date to finally condemn Putin's unprovoked 'special military operation'. By the second weekend of the invasion, Russian troops were carpet-bombing Mariupol. A young boy playing football in the besieged port city had just died after his legs were blown off. Hundreds of civilians had already been killed. But instead of offering any words of regret, the Patriarch embarked on a denunciation of homosexuality and other social ills. In a barely coherent passage, he argued: 'Those who claim world power allow countries into their realm of excessive consumption and apparent freedom only if they agree to a straightforward and horrifying test – organising a gay-parade is a test of loyalty to this powerful world.'

The battle for Ukraine, he insisted, was about more than politics; it was a question of 'human salvation'. Just as NATO was encroaching on Russia's sphere of influence militarily, gay-rights campaigners were invading its spiritual space. 'We have entered into a struggle that has not a physical, but a metaphysical significance,' he said.

Weeks before the invasion Kirill made a surprising announcement: Russia's Church was expanding into Africa. It would establish an exarchate, an outpost, on the continent and set up hundreds of parishes in more than 25 African countries. The move was a blatant challenge to Patriarch Theodore of Alexandria, since Sub-Saharan Africa has long been under his jurisdiction. It looked like an act of revenge. Kirill had told the Orthodox world to cold shoulder the newly independent Ukrainian Church, but Theodore had recognised it (along with Bartholomew in Constantinople and the patriarchs of Greece and Cyprus). Russian clerics argued they had no choice but to protect African believers who didn't accept a split in the global Orthodox community. Furious, the Alexandrian patriarch called the priests from Moscow 'false shepherds' who 'sow Africa with dirty money'.

Impoverished African clerics were receptive to Russia's advances. I spoke to Dean Father Philip Chasia from a remote part of western Kenya who had opened a new kindergarten with Russian cash. The children were taught to sing *Gospodi Pomilui* ... 'Lord Have Mercy on Us' in Church Slavonic. Their school was named St Alexander Nevsky, after the medieval warrior prince – on instructions from Chasia's superior in Moscow, more than 9,000 kilometres away. The dean told me of the seventeen priests under his authority, fourteen had left the Alexandrian Patriarchate for the Russian Church. One priest said his monthly stipend had doubled under the Russians. Others have received scholarships for their children to study in Moscow, funded by businesses such as the state-owned nuclear energy company Rosatom.[26] Cyril Hovorun, the Ukrainian-born theologian who once worked closely with Kirill, said the Church's move masked a new scramble for Africa. In the Soviet era, Russia had a strong presence in some parts of the continent, but it has recently expanded – especially in unstable countries such as the Central African Republic and Mali. These have become strongholds of the Wagner Group, the Russian mercenaries accused of propping up dictators and committing human rights abuses. 'The Kremlin now has two arms in Africa,' he said. 'One is the hard one, Wagner, and the other is the soft power of the Church. That was the real reason for the new Exarchate. The recognition of Ukraine by the Patriarchate of Alexandria is just a pretext.'

Beyond hard-edged geopolitics and mineral extraction, there is another reason for Kirill's Africa crusade. Russia is battling for influence in the global south. It cannot compete with the Chinese when it comes to building new roads and railways. It is exporting weapons and culture wars instead. Same-sex relations are illegal in more than 30 countries on the continent. Uganda, where the Patriarch is building a spiritual hub for East Africa opposite the presidential palace,[27] recently introduced one of the world's toughest anti-LGBT+ laws. It includes the death penalty for 'serial offenders'. At a summit in St Petersburg last July – with Putin at his side – Kirill welcomed African leaders and dignitaries. He told them Western values lead to cultural and spiritual degradation. 'Most African countries categorically reject legalising same-sex unions, euthanasia and other sinful phenomena,' he said. 'We are always happy to meet like-minded people.'[28]

☦ ☦ ☦

German Sterligov founded a commodities exchange in the Gorbachev era, becoming one of Russia's first legal millionaires since the Revolution. When I first met him in 1991, Sterligov was a cocky 24-year-old who thought making money was ridiculously easy. He named his building materials exchange Alisa, after his dog, and preferred discussing philosophy to business. As his fortune grew, he was feted in the West as the archetypal New Russian businessman, partying with the likes of Bill Gates and Ted Turner.

In the intervening years he has undergone a transformation, largely propelled, he says, by his Orthodox faith. After unsuccessful attempts to enter politics, Sterligov gave up his luxury apartments and his yacht for an Amish-type retreat in the woods where he forced his family to live like nineteenth-century peasants. He drove a horse and cart, home-schooled his children and took up organic farming. His wife and daughter wore headscarves and ankle-length skirts. He told visiting TV crews he was defending traditional values. He then opened a grocery chain, which refused to serve gay customers. As a concession to the authorities worried about bad language, he changed the rustic wooden signs in the windows from 'No Faggots Allowed' to 'No Sodomites Allowed'. Homophobia became the main selling point of Bread and Salt, which offers natural food and other products made by 'Russian peasants'. After a string of complaints in Moscow and after a shop window was smashed in St Petersburg, Sterligov sold some branches of the store and removed some signs. In smaller towns and cities, the response was a collective shrug.

Few Orthodox believers share Sterligov's eccentricity or his appetite for self-publicity. Yet the Church has helped turn Russia into a dangerous place for gay men and women. Hate crime is rife. Social-media accounts are filled with videos of men and women being beaten up and humiliated. Some have been lured to a rendezvous through a dating app, only to be confronted by thugs. The violence is filmed and victims are threatened with blackmail. Across the country, Orthodox vigilantes, waving icons and wearing skull-and-crossbones, hunt down homosexuals and disrupt gay rights demonstrations. Gay people are stigmatised as being a danger to children and, like pro-choice women, blamed for Russia's demographic decline.

Homosexuality was not always taboo. Same-sex relations and cross dressing were commonplace among all social classes in the sixteenth century. Foreign visitors were often taken aback by the permissiveness. Visiting Moscow in 1568, the Elizabethan poet George Turberville was more shocked by the open homosexuality of the Russian peasants than by Ivan the Terrible's bloodthirstiness.[29] Peter the Great introduced a ban on gay sex, but only for his soldiers. It was not until Nicholas I – the tsar of the 'Autocracy, Orthodoxy, Fatherland' slogan – that a law was passed against *muzhelozhstvo*, men lying together. This stripped offenders of their rights and sent them to Siberia for five years. But it did not explicitly address lesbians, although the Church would punish girls for being 'tomboys'.[30]

The law was abolished in the wave of 'free love' philosophy that swept the country after the revolution of 1905. Stalin reintroduced the ban on sodomy in 1934, as he tightened his hold on all aspects of life, including the most intimate. His commissar of justice, Nikolai Krylenko, announced that there was no reason for anyone to be homosexual after two decades of socialism. Those who persisted in this 'bourgeois perversion' were criminals engaged in counter-revolutionary activities.

At the start of the 1990s, consensual sex between men was still punishable by up to five years in prison. I remember going to Moscow's Clinical and Diagnostic Centre for Medicine and Reproduction, which held a weekly 'club' for gays and lesbians on Monday evenings. The room was packed with people of all ages gathered around a small TV screen to watch a video about gay rights in Scandinavia. One engineering student had brought out the first LGBT newspaper, called *Tema*. The capital had little nightlife, but for gays the problem was particularly acute. There were a few well-established *pleshki*, or pick-up places; these included the rent boys' fountain opposite the Bolshoi Theatre, the dingy Cafe Sadko around the corner in Pushkin Street, the Central Baths, known as the gay banya, and a few designated metro stops like Oktyabrskaya that were popular for late-night trysts.

Many gay men, however, were afraid to go to these places. Even though sodomy was decriminalised in 1993, being gay was classed as a mental illness until 1999. Like in Victorian England, the law did not acknowledge lesbians, but they did not escape persecution. I met a young woman sent to a psychiatric hospital when she was sixteen after being caught in bed with another girl at a St Petersburg student hostel. 'The director of my school decided I was mentally unbalanced, and they pumped me full of injections. I was so miserable I tried to kill myself,' she told me, pushing back her sleeves to reveal the scars on her wrists.[31] Few politicians were prepared to openly support the *golubye* – the light blue crowd, Soviet-era slang for LGBT. In one poll in 1991, the year Communism officially ended, a third of respondents said gays should be 'liquidated', another third wanted them 'isolated', while 6 per cent said they should be 'helped'.

Gradually, as the country opened up, so did gay bars and clubs. For a brief period, the Moscow club Chance became world famous for the naked men who frolicked alongside tropical fish in a huge aquarium. Among the creative classes, camp aesthetics and fashion were the height of cool. An artist friend and pirate TV presenter, Vladik Mamyshev, better known under the pseudonym 'Vlad Mamyshev-Monroe', was thrown out of the army for dressing as Marilyn Monroe. At one opulent party thrown by a German magazine in the Metropol Hotel, an Orthodox priest was chatting Vladik up, seemingly unaware he was talking to a man in drag.

Shortly after Putin came to power, Yulia Volkova and Lena Katina rose to stardom with a song called 'I've Lost My Mind'. In a moody, rainswept video, the teenagers prance around in skimpy Britney Spears-style tartan skirts, singing *Ya soshla s uma/Mne nuzhna ona* – 'I've gone mad/I need her'. The bubblegum pop duo's name Tatu is an abbreviation of the Russian phrase *Ta lyubit Tu*, This girl loves That girl. They were hand-picked in a talent show by an advertising guru; it soon emerged that the sapphic sex was just a marketing ploy. Nevertheless, close-up shots of the girls kissing passionately created a sensation at the time. Yulia later said many gays wrote to say how grateful they were to Tatu for helping them to come out and 'feel like people'.[32]

That same year, 2000, a council of bishops met at Christ the Saviour to adopt the Church's first 'social doctrine'. Unlike Catholics, Orthodox clerics do not have a tradition of formally setting out the Church's position on how people should lead their lives. The new guidelines, developed by Kirill when he was still Metropolitan, condemned genetic engineering, approved of private property and reconfirmed the Church's close relationship with the military. They were also pro-life and stridently anti-gay. 'The Holy Bible and the Church doctrine unequivocally condemn homosexual ties as a perverse distortion of the God-given nature of the human being,' the document said. Bishops called for a ban on LGBT+ people working as teachers, senior army officers and prison governors. They strongly condemned proposals for gay marriage and transsexual operations.

The document was interpreted by some activists as a licence to attack gay people in the street. An attempt to hold Moscow's first gay rights rally in 2006 ended in 120 arrests and a German MP being hit in the face. The following year, the radical Union of Orthodox Banner Bearers ambushed a small march in support of tolerance for sexual minorities. The group, who wear black T-shirts bearing skulls and the phrase 'Orthodoxy or Death', became known for their attention-grabbing stunts such as burning 'satanic' Harry Potter books and running a stake through a toy monkey to protest the teaching of Darwinism in schools. Others punched people holding rainbow flags or pelted them with ketchup and eggs.

In the wake of Pussy Riot, I went to St Petersburg to meet Vitaly Milonov, now a Duma deputy but back then a member of the regional parliament. Sandy haired with a strawberry-blond beard, he had the aura of an art history lecturer as he gave me a tour of his church and explained the provenance of its icons. Milonov has devoted his political career to whipping up homophobia. Just that week, his assistant in the city hall had urged people to boycott a brand of milk because the cartons featured a smiling dairyman in a green field standing in front of a rainbow. The brand was a subsidiary of Pepsi-Cola, a company which is 'actively and aggressively financing and promoting homosexuality', the aide said. He had asked the prosecutor's office to investigate whether children were being put at risk.[33]

As we left the church, Milonov began talking about a recent Madonna concert in his city. During the show, the singer had handed out pink wristbands which fans were asked to wear to demonstrate their 'tolerance for the gay community'. Milonov was the author of a new law prohibiting 'homosexual propaganda' among minors in St Petersburg – a law described as 'a ridiculous atrocity' by the Queen of Pop on her website. Some people in the West see us Russians as 'wild bears', Milonov responded, 'just because we don't respect homosexual families'. In the wake of the concert, the Union of Russian Citizens, a group set up by nationalist businessmen, sued Madonna for $11 million for 'moral damage'. At their office in the centre of St Petersburg, as they discussed the lawsuit, I was shown posters of Madonna in fishnets covered in swastikas. The American singer was a 'homo-fascist', Viktor Sherenko, one of the group's leading members, told me: 'Fascism is forcing an alien point of view onto another people or culture – and it makes no difference whether you do it with tanks or by making alien sexual relations fashionable and modern. It took us 70 years to get rid of Communism but thank God we got rid of this Liberalism much faster – it has only taken two decades.'

Milonov's anti-gay initiative was signed into law by the then mayor of St Petersburg, Georgy Poltavchenko, a Putin confidant and former KGB officer who had helped fund the Russian monastery on Mount Athos. On the pretext of protecting those under eighteen, the law effectively outlawed all LGBT+ rights and awareness events. Individuals found guilty of propagating 'the false perception that traditional and non-traditional relationships are socially equal' faced stiff fines. Milonov's law was later adopted by the federal government, unleashing a fresh wave of violence.

The Russian actor Ivan Okhlobystin, who spent ten years as an Orthodox priest before his movie career took off, argued that homosexuals should be burned alive. 'I would put all the gays alive into an oven,' he told his audience during a 'spiritual meeting' in the Siberian city of Novosibirsk in 2013. 'This is Sodom and Gomorrah. As a religious person, I cannot be indifferent about it because it is a real threat to my children.'

In the run up to the Sochi Winter Olympics the following year, the law against homosexual propaganda came under a global spotlight. One British TV crew embedded itself with vigilantes from a group called Occupy Paedophilia who go on 'safaris' to track down and humiliate gay people. The victims are lured to an apartment through online messages only to be trapped inside and confronted by homophobes. The footage was harrowing, but the anti-gay crusaders were so confident that they were doing the right thing, they did not ask the filmmakers to blur their faces.[34]

Like many, the Soviet-era dissident Father Sergei Rybko conflates homosexuality with paedophilia. 'Permitted evil just gives rise to more evil,' he said. 'Paedophiles, gays and people like this are basically serving the devil.' Rybko has had a high profile, but nothing compared to Malofeev, the Orthodox billionaire who for years has been dripping petrol onto the culture wars bonfire. His Tsargrad channel offered in 2017 to pay for one-way plane tickets to the US for 'medically certified sodomites'. One of the hosts told viewers that California is 'proposing to facilitate the granting of green cards for Russian perverts. If you are homosexual, we really want you to move there, where you can openly submit to your sins.'[35]

Malofeev castigates the decadent West but courts like-minded conservatives wherever they happen to live. He has sponsored conferences on family values attended by gay-marriage opponents from the US and Europe. He set up a private school inspired by the tsarist past to educate Orthodox patriots. 'An adult can choose his own way he wants to entertain himself in the bedroom,' he says. 'But the state and taxpayers should not support teaching children different ways of sexual perversion.' The investment banker has also created and bankrolled a lobby group which helped bring about legislation to 'clean up' the internet. Human rights groups say Malofeev is acting as the country's unofficial censor. He said he was just trying to protect vulnerable Russians from child pornography and other 'dirty material'.

In 2013, as Ukraine was in the midst of a tussle over joining the European Union, Putin deployed his culture-war forces there to try to sow division. Billboards appeared showing same-sex stick figures holding hands, with the slogan: 'Association with the EU means same-sex marriage.' The group behind the posters, Ukrainian Choice, was funded by Viktor Medvedchuk, a businessman, former Ukrainian MP and a personal friend of Putin's. Russian TV channels, watched in Ukraine, came up with a rhyme: *V Evropu Cherez Zhopu*, the Way to Europe Is Through the Arse.

The Kremlin later played on homophobia to encourage Russians to back Putin's constitutional reforms which allow him to stay in power until 2036. A TV promo was made in 2020 by a media group linked to Yevgeny Prigozhin, who headed the Wagner group of mercenary fighters only to challenge Putin's hold on power (and subsequently die in a plane crash). The advert shows a young boy from an orphanage going from joy to heartbreak as he discovers he is going to be adopted by two men. 'Here's your new mum. Don't be upset,' one of the new parents tells the child as he introduces his partner, who promptly offers the boy a dress. A woman working at the orphanage spits on the floor in disgust. 'Will you choose such a Russia? Decide the future of the country – vote for amendments to the constitution,' says the voiceover.

Putin has vowed that Russia will not legalise same-sex marriage while he is in the Kremlin. Kirill has described it as 'a very dangerous apocalyptic symptom'. In 2016 he blamed increased acceptance of homosexuality for the rise of ISIS, arguing that some Muslims were flocking to the Caliphate as a way of escaping the 'godless civilization' that celebrates Gay Pride.

Yet Russia has its fair share of gay people holding influential jobs – secular and clerical. Since Orthodox priests are allowed to marry before they are ordained, Church authorities say they are less open to temptation than their Catholic counterparts. Although they are supposed to be celibate, homosexuality among clerics is commonplace, says the academic Nikolai Mitrokhin.[36] He contends that despite the official rhetoric, most priests are fairly tolerant. A young man with a 'non-standard sexual orientation', he says, 'finds a warm welcome in the Church' and can ascend the ecclesiastical career ladder like any other. A bishop's sexual proclivities are raised only if he antagonises too many people. For example, in 1990s Yekaterinburg, priests were sick of handing over icons and vestments from their parishes to their overbearing prelate, Bishop Nikon. He also forced them to buy candles from the diocese at inflated prices and charged extortionate fees for signing administrative documents. Eventually, the disgruntled priests accused Nikon of drunkenness and of flaunting his homosexuality.

In 2013, a scandal erupted in Kazan, and this time the Moscow Patriarchate could not look the other way. Roman Stepanov, the bold young priest who in 2021 asked the Patriarch to declare his income, was in 2013 a student at the city's seminary. He said some of his classmates had been sexually harassed and assaulted by staff, including the abbot. Stepanov, who had experienced sexual abuse himself as a child, felt he had to take action and drafted a complaint. The Church's education committee sent an inspector to investigate. Three quarters of the students interviewed confirmed they had heard about the abuse or had suffered from it personally. One teenager described being forced to sit on his teacher's lap while the priest grabbed his genitals; another was plied with vodka and assaulted in a sauna.

This affair might have stayed under wraps were it not for Andrei Kuraev, the deacon who supported Pussy Riot and had long been a thorn in the side of the Patriarchate. When he heard that the Church had sent an inspector to Kazan, he hoped that Kirill had finally decided to treat the problem of paedophilia and sexual harassment among the clergy seriously. So Kuraev wrote about the Kazan scandal on his popular LiveJournal blog. Before long he was inundated with stories from across the country about senior churchmen abusing their authority to prey on altar boys, young priests and seminarians.

Kuraev believed that the alleged predator from Kazan would be brought before a church court. But the abbot and the others accused were instead transferred to other dioceses. Metropolitan Anastassy of Kazan and Tatarstan rebuked the seminarians for making their official complaint in the first place. 'As Judas betrayed Christ, so you are betraying the ideals of our theological school,' he thundered after the inspectors had left. Students who had testified were expelled. When some people accused Kuraev of undermining the Church with his stream of revelations, he stressed that he was not fighting gay clerics but cover-ups: 'From a legal point of view if a superior harasses his subordinate that is a crime, regardless of the gender and the age of the victim. They may be the same age; the subordinate may even be older than his boss but using power to satisfy one's lust is a crime in any case.'[37]

Kuraev lost his teaching job at the Theological Academy where he had worked as a professor for more than a decade. He was also sacked from his post at MGIMO, the Moscow Institute for International Relations, which trains future diplomats. He was sent for 40 days to atone for his sins in the capital's Novospassky Monastery. Nobody told him what he should repent for, beyond a generalised accusation of 'making shocking statements on the internet and the media'.

Alexander Usatov, an archpriest in the southern diocese of Rostov and Novocherkassk, knew of many clerics who were regularly having sex with male superiors to secure promotions. In 2012, he confessed to the head of his diocese, Metropolitan Mercurious, that his marriage was falling apart. After a long internal struggle, he realised he was gay and felt he had to leave the Church. The bishop told him not to worry. 'Live apart from your wife and continue your service,' he reassured Usatov. 'But if you cause a scandal, I will destroy you.'[38] Apart from serving in church, Usatov headed the spiritual and educational centre of Rostov Cathedral and was in charge of education at the Don Theological Seminary. He was candid with his students about a wide range of topics and felt they valued him for that. Over time, he felt increasingly uncomfortable about hiding his sexual orientation.

Having to lead a double life, like many other clerics, had eroded his respect for the Church as an institution and even his belief in God. Yet gay clergy, from the most junior priest to the most senior prelate, are useful in another respect. The more vulnerable they are, the more frightened they are about their 'sinning' coming out into the public domain, the more susceptible they are to *kompromat*, to compromise material, otherwise known as blackmail, with the Church hierarchy and the FSB working hand in hand. One spies on the other, one or the other may be gay. Everyone is suspicious of everyone else.

In March 2020, Usatov went back to see Mercurious about his crisis of faith and asked to be defrocked. The bishop ordered him to retire on health grounds instead. 'How do you expect me to explain to the Patriarch that a priest anointed fifteen years ago, in charge of catechism at the cathedral and at the spiritual academy, doesn't believe in God?' His superior was clearly at the end of his tether. 'Go see your mum,' he told the archpriest. 'Or take your loverboy to the Canary Islands, or whatever, just get out.'[39] Usatov was secretly recording this conversation on his phone and later put it online, as he explained his true reasons for leaving the Church – but only once he was safely outside Russia. Usatov said he was determined to free people from 'shackles of lies and fear in the Church, where the "elite" clerics indulge in gay relationships, but mentally cripple homosexual and bisexual priests, monks and parishioners'.

Maxim Mitrofanov, the cleric who left his posting at the cathedral in London for a promotion to bishop in north Russia, believes he was the victim of a honey trap set by the FSB. He says agents tried to recruit him several times in several locations, without success. He had already been trusted with sensitive assignments. In 2018, he was sent to Lebanon officially to discuss humanitarian aid for refugees from the war in Syria. Unofficially, his job was to pass a message to the Syro-Jacobite Orthodox Church under Patriarch Ignatius Ephraim II Karim and the Antiochian Orthodox Church headed by Patriarch John X in Damascus. Kirill and Putin wanted to ensure that the Orthodox prelates in the region would oppose Ukraine's bid to establish a church independent of Moscow.

The Syria recruitment trip failed. Mitrofanov was also approached on a trip to the US to serve at the St Nicholas Orthodox Church in Manhattan and collaborate with Russian intelligence. He was not interested in that either. Then the authorities tried a different tack. While based in Cherepovets, he missed city life and often spent his weekends in St Petersburg, visiting the opera and seeing friends. One rainy autumn night, he ordered some takeaway chicken. The delivery guy who came to his door had shoes full of holes and was soaking wet. The bishop invited him inside for a cup of tea to warm up. The young man introduced himself as Kain Montanelli, not his real name. He said that he was the son of a priest from the Urals and that he had fallen on hard times. He had applied to enter the FSB academy in St Petersburg but had failed the physical examination and was now sometimes working as a male escort. 'I told him it was terrible that he was selling his body,' said Mitrofanov. 'I warned him that it was dangerous for his health, that he could be infected with HIV and I decided I had to help him.' The bishop hired him as an administrative assistant and rented an apartment for him and his girlfriend. 'It was more of a father–son relationship,' he told me.

After a while, he noticed that Montanelli seemed to have an alternative source of income, and in December 2019, the young man and two of his friends were arrested and charged with manufacturing drugs. They were lured into the business by a contact on the darknet, a man Mitrofanov now believes was an FSB officer. Around the same time, Mitrofanov's flat in St Petersburg was searched. Agents seized his credit cards, mobile phones and 570,000 roubles (around £5,000) in cash. The FSB lieutenant in charge told Mitrofanov the agency had been tracking him since 2007, when he began serving in London. He said it would be wise of him to cooperate. Mitrofanov replied that he would have nothing to do with a 'diabolical organisation' which was 'up to its elbows in the blood of Russian priests and the Russian people'. The FSB officers eventually left, and he heard no more until the following March, when the Russian media began publishing reports about a drug laboratory found in the bishop's apartment and hinted that he had taken a rent boy as his lover.

Metropolitan Dionisy, the Patriarchate's chief of staff, summoned Mitrofanov to Moscow and chastised him for refusing to work with the security services. 'Why do you need these problems?' he asked the bishop. 'Everyone cooperates.' Just like the archpriest from Rostov, he was instructed to sign a letter of resignation on health grounds. Then he was sent to a grim monastery in the Vologda region, east of St Petersburg, to reflect on his shortcomings. Mitrofanov did not stay there long. He returned to St Petersburg and kept a low profile until, on 2 December 2020, the FSB burst into his apartment at dawn. The officers, headed by the same FSB lieutenant, handcuffed both Mitrofanov and a cousin who was staying with him.

'They threw us on the floor and beat us until we bled – it was extremely brutal,' Mitrofanov recalled. 'They wanted to scare me into working for them. They had called in one of my priests from the Cherepovets diocese, a good friend of mine, and scared him witless. He begged me to cooperate. He said I would suffer a lot unless I agreed.' The bishop's terrified cousin also tried to persuade him to do the authorities' bidding. The investigator told him if he did not want to work with the FSB as a free man, he would do it from prison instead and told him to pack a change of clothes and a toothbrush. Eventually, the bishop was released. He was again summoned to the Patriarchate and told to return to the monastery until called to a meeting of the Supreme Church Court. Mitrofanov said he would comply, but two days later, he got on a plane to Britain.[40]

When I first met Mitrofanov in London in late 2021, he looked pale and jittery. He said he had been unwell but was now recovering. The next time we met, he told me that there had been an attempt on his life when he visited his mother at her home in the US. One day, when she was out of the house, a TV repairman came to the door and told Mitrofanov that some cables needed adjusting. He looked legitimate, armed with a standard toolbox. Just before he left, the man asked to use the bathroom. Mitrofanov thought no more of it, but a few hours later he had trouble standing. Then he fell into a coma. His mother prayed over him day and night for four days. Doctors told her there was a high chance her son would never walk or speak again. But after a month in hospital, he recovered.

He said he still did not know what kind of poison was used. He told me that he suspected the 'repairman' came from a special unit of the GRU, military intelligence, tasked with eliminating Russia's enemies abroad. He thought the assassin smeared a highly toxic substance on the toilet seat or one of the bathroom taps. 'A priest I know in Russia had told me only to open my front door with gloves on – in case the GRU tried a repeat of the Salisbury incident,' said Mitrofanov, referring to the botched 2018 attempt to murder the former military officer Sergei Skripal and his daughter Yulia with the nerve agent Novichok. 'I thought that he was being ridiculously paranoid.' Yet Mitrofanov had already been warned by high-level security officials in the US that he might be in danger. The FBI is well aware of attempts to recruit Orthodox clerics as spies.

In 2021, they stopped a senior representative of the Department for External Church Relations at the US border. According to a memo that I have seen, the FBI suspected he was a Russian intelligence officer operating under non-official cover. The FBI distributed a six-page notification to Orthodox communities across the United States titled 'Russian Intelligence Services Victimize Russian Orthodox Church and other Eastern Orthodox Churches'. On the church official's laptop they found documents from the foreign and military intelligence services outlining 'areas of cooperation' including 'the involvement of clergy in operational activities'. The file's metadata showed it was created on 20 March 2009, shortly after Kirill became patriarch. The FBI also discovered the church official had compromising material about a number of clerics and members of their families, presumably to blackmail them into collaboration. The official's publicly available WhatsApp profile depicts a cat wearing army camouflage and a collar decorated with the words 'Military Intelligence' and the bat symbol of the GRU.

Now Mitrofanov is constantly on his guard. For months, he worked as a hotel receptionist. When the full-scale invasion of Ukraine was launched, he went to Kyiv to work as a volunteer, helping engineers assess bomb damage to infrastructure. He has been told that he would be welcome to serve in Orthodox churches which come under the control of the Ecumenical Patriarch in Constantinople rather than the Moscow Patriarchate, but he regards that as too big a risk. He is keeping a low profile.

In the spring of 2020, as much of the world was frantically trying to source ventilators, oxygen and protective clothing for medics, Kirill dithered over how to handle the pandemic. His initial response was to drive around Moscow's ring road in a Mercedes van with a holy icon, blessing the Russian capital with prayer. A live broadcast on a religious TV channel showed the Patriarch's van with tinted windows escorted by other vehicles with flashing blue lights.

As infection rates climbed, the patriarch bowed to health warnings and urged worshippers to stay away from church. But he left it up to local dioceses whether or not to hold services. As a result, churches in 43 of the country's 85 regions remained open for Easter, the most important service of the year. A group of confused believers wrote an open letter to the Patriarch asking whether it was true that it was 'impossible to become infected in a church'. Across Russia, worshippers continued to kiss icons, not a face covering in sight. Several bishops criticised or even sabotaged the restrictive measures imposed by civil authorities. Such a disconnect between state and church was unprecedented in the Putin era.

In Moscow, as the choir sang, one of Kirill's favourite priests, Father Andrei Tkachev, stood in front of the iconostasis wearing a gas mask. He wanted to mock all those weaklings who had chosen to protect themselves by covering their nose and mouth. Ripping the mask off after crossing himself, Tkachev told the congregation to 'laugh at this nasty devilish thing'. He intoned: 'Switch off the television; then there will be no Coronavirus.'[41] Another bishop, Metropolitan Luka Kovalenko, told believers that Covid had been created by George Soros, the Vatican and even the Istanbul-based Ecumenical Patriarchate, home of Kirill's arch-rival Bartholomew I.

Nearly a year later, the abbot of the Solovetsky Monastery in the Russian Arctic, Bishop Porphyry Shutov, warned against vaccines which made 'human beings susceptible to external control'. He said that 'any Christian responsible for his or her salvation must stop', for fear of becoming genetically modified.[42] Monasteries around the country were soon infested with the virus; elderly clerics were dying in large numbers. But none of the Covid-denying hierarchs ever took their words back, even after they caught the virus. Some were hospitalised in elite medical centres and recovered. Other clergymen and laypeople who obediently followed their edicts were less fortunate.

The Church might have been a rallying force at a time of national trauma but instead was split apart. Kirill was forced to threaten priests who ignored public health measures with tribunals. One expert in Church affairs said 'refusal to obey government rules on the closure of churches is seen by some as a new form of martyrdom'. Some older believers and clerics likened the ban on attending church to Soviet repression.[43]

One of the best known Covid rebels, Father Sergei, is otherwise known as Nikolai Romanov. A former policeman who spent thirteen years in a prison colony for armed robbery and murder, he was upon his release allowed to become a priest and helped to establish the Sredneuralsk Convent near Yekaterinburg in the early 2000s. He has been dubbed the 'Rasputin of the Urals'. It is unclear how Romanov rose so quickly, but he is closely associated with the secretive cult of the *tsarebozhniki*, tsar worshippers. He even changed his secular Christian name to Nikolai. Like other members of the cult, he asserts that Nicholas II deliberately sacrificed himself and his family to atone for the sins of the Russian nation. Despite DNA evidence to the contrary, they insist that the royal family's bodies are still buried in a pit called Ganina Yama, less than an hour's drive from the Yekaterinburg mansion where they were executed. The area has been turned into a religious Disneyland, with shrines, shops and cafes, and a multitude of icons in honour of the tsar.

The ex-policeman's ultra-conservative brand of Orthodoxy has attracted many celebrity followers, who were drawn particularly to his 6am public exorcisms and fiery sermons. Some of his followers came to live at the convent with their families. Children from broken homes were dumped there. Some reports emerged of beatings and psychological abuse towards teenagers, but the local diocese turned a blind eye.[44] During the pandemic, Romanov described measures to prevent the spread of Covid as a plot orchestrated by Jews. He encouraged the faithful to disobey public health orders. In May 2020, the Church stripped him of his abbot's rank for breaking monastic rules and later excommunicated him. He ignored the rulings, gathering his supporters – along with some armed Cossacks and Donbass war veterans – surrounding the convent and expelling the abbess. Remarkably, Yekaterinburg's diocese did nothing. The spokeswoman, Anzhela Tambova, told journalists the priest's followers would soon desert him and the convent would return to the bosom of Mother Superior Varvara. 'The Lord will put everything in its place, as has happened repeatedly in the history of the Russian Orthodox Church,' she said.

It was not until Romanov called on Putin to step down and branded him the 'forerunner of the Antichrist' that riot police finally stormed the convent and arrested him. The charge sheet against him mentions a speech, disseminated online, in which he allegedly incited several nuns to commit suicide. A three-and-a-half-year sentence for that offence, along with offending religious beliefs and vigilantism, was on appeal extended to seven years for 'inciting hatred'. His tirade against Putin had crossed a red line.

The raid was a blow to Kirill's authority – to the Kremlin it seemed he had been unable to keep his clerics in check. Fundamentalist groups that had been marginal in the Church when Kirill was crowned in 2009 had subsequently became mainstream. Indeed, it could be said they now have the upper hand. By promoting traditional values, the Patriarchate tried to co-opt the ultra-conservatives but was often outmanoeuvred by them. The pandemic was the latest such example. Kirill and Putin had been railing against 'liberals' for years. But Russia, along with the US, India and Brazil, suffered some of the highest rates of infection and death. To fight the virus, the Patriarch and the President temporarily found themselves on the same side as liberal media and liberal priests. They were forced to agree with clerics like Father Alexander Borisov, a priest from Moscow's Church of Saints Cosmas and Damian, who early on asked his congregation to pray online. Borisov, the spiritual son of the murdered priest Aleksander Men, had previously been under fire from conservatives for reaching out to Catholics and Protestants, for holding liturgies in memory of Muscovites who had died of AIDS and for sheltering demonstrators attacked by the riot police.

By cultivating the fundamentalists, the Church created a force that is hard to control. Kirill Serebrennikov, one of Russia's most courageous directors, underscores this point with his black comedy

Uchenik, The Student, about a high-school pupil who turns into a religious zealot. Instead of engaging with his mother, friends or teachers, the teenager, Veniamin, spouts passages from Matthew, Luke and Leviticus. Like some American fundamentalists, he interprets them literally. He strips naked during a sex-education class and wears a gorilla suit in protest at being taught Darwinist theories in a biology lesson. The Church establishment, 'with its candles, old ladies and Mercedes-driving priests', arouses the boy's contempt. 'You have a comfortable position, right?' he tells the school's portly cleric, Father Vsevolod. 'You have created a convenient God who forgives everything and you have settled for that but the Lord says: "Think not that I am come to send peace on earth: I came not to send peace, but a sword".'[45]

The film grows ever darker as the headmistress progressively caves into theological bullying from her fire and brimstone pupil. She begins by acquiescing to a bikini ban in swimming lessons and ends by endorsing his strident anti-Semitism and homophobia. Predictably, the conservative TV channel Tsargrad branded the film 'a manifesto of the Antichrist' and said the director was 'trying to convince the viewers that there are no good believers'. More disturbingly, the liberal TV Dodzh alleged that Metropolitan Tikhon Shevkunov took such a dislike to the film that he encouraged the authorities to slap a court case on its director.[46] Serebrennikov was found guilty of embezzlement in 2017, spent twenty months under house arrest and was handed a suspended sentence on what most observers believe to be trumped-up charges. He has since left Russia. Shevkunov, the cleric close to Putin, denied that he had ever seen *Uchenik* and told the journalist Zoya Svetova that rumours of his complaints to Putin or the then culture minister Vladimir Medinksy were just the 'morbid imagination' of Russia's 'progressive creative society'.[47]

Recent films by another well-known director, Andrei Zvyagintsev, also depict the slide towards religious authoritarianism. *Loveless* is a 2018 drama about a couple going through a bitter divorce. The husband, Boris, is a salesman for a tech firm run by a devout businessman who expects all his employees to be married with large families. Anyone who does not fit into the company's 'Russian

Orthodox Shariah Law', as Boris's spurned wife calls it, faces the sack. Boris is desperate to conceal his divorce, along with his new and heavily pregnant girlfriend.

The best-known film of this genre is Zvyagintsev's *Leviathan*. Featuring a corrupt mayor in league with a venal bishop, it presents such a bleak picture of the Church that a spokesman for the Patriarchate said it had been 'made to please the West'.[48] In a modern take on the story of Job, a car mechanic loses his wife, his freedom and his house. In the last scene, the ramshackle structure has been bulldozed to make room for a new church. The mayor, afraid that his dealings will be exposed, hopes the church will buy him peace of mind and divine protection.

That Russia, spiritually ill at ease, politically ever darker, was the Russia that embarked on war.

13. THE WAR IN UKRAINE

Watch us, Lord, as we dive to the bottom.
Teach us to breathe underwater.
ARCHPRIEST ALEXEI UMINSKY QUOTING ROCK
MUSICIAN BORIS GREBENSCHIKOV

A dozen people turned up for the Sunday morning liturgy in a converted sauna. The pine cabin stood in a garden sloping down to the River Volga. My colleague Yaroslava and I had driven five hours north of Moscow to the village of Novy Bely Kamen in the Kostroma region to meet one of Russia's bravest priests: Father Georgy Edelstein, the boy from a Jewish-Catholic family in Ukraine who narrowly escaped the Babi Yar massacre in 1941 and converted to Orthodoxy in his teens. Now approaching 90, he is an imposing figure, very tall with a crown of white hair and a silver cross around his neck. For many believers he embodies the conscience of the Church. After he took holy orders, Communist officials grew so sick of his insistence on religious freedoms that they denied him a parish to serve in. His wife lost her teaching job and the couple had to sell their books to survive. When the regime collapsed, Edelstein loudly denounced clerics who had collaborated with the KGB. *Po-koh-ya-ni-yeh* (Repentance), he kept telling me, enunciating every syllable, is missing from Russian society. If the authorities had stopped persecuting the priest by the time of our visit in October 2021, it was because he lived in such a remote spot, his church was tiny and he had retired from his parish in Karabanovo, the nearest town.

I stood at the back of the congregation admiring the simple white iconostasis as the air filled with incense and Edelstein sang in a quavering voice. Communion wine was distributed in little paper cups rather than the traditional spoon because of the pandemic. His sermon was brief but clear: using force is wrong and a Christian should not raise his sword against a fellow human being. At the end of the service, one of the choir singers, an angular woman in her forties, confronted the priest. 'How would we Russians have fought off the Mongols with that approach?' she asked. Edelstein began to reason with her in gentle but urgent tones. By the time we got back to his house, he looked tired. We turned down an invitation for lunch and began the long drive back to Moscow.

Four months later, Russia invaded Ukraine.

Putin's Special Military Operation was the culmination of his imperialistic world view. For months satellite imagery showed movements of armour, missiles and heavy weaponry massing around Ukraine. Kremlin officials repeatedly denied that Russia had plans to invade. Despite mounting evidence and warnings from US intelligence, the military build-up was dismissed as sabre rattling. It was not until Russian university students were asked to donate blood and plasma supplies were moved to field hospitals near Ukraine's borders that many feared this was no training exercise. Yet Ukrainians – and millions around the world – were horrified by the scale of the onslaught in the early hours of 24 February 2022.

As dawn broke, tanks bearing the white Z symbol rumbled across the Belarusian border in the north and across the Russian border in the east and from occupied Crimea in the south. Cities were shelled and missiles struck targets across the country. Russia's assault marked the first territorial invasion of a sovereign state in Europe in 80 years.

According to one Ukrainian official, speaking nine months later, the invasion date was planned far in advance. Early that morning,

Ukraine was scheduled to disconnect its energy system from the Russian and Belarusian grid, to reorient it towards the European power system. The technical preparations were completed at 1am on 24 February, four hours before the attack began. With blackouts and phone lines down, Russia's military thought seizing Kyiv would be a pushover.[1]

As it happened, Ukraine managed to decouple from the Russian grid in record time. But 24 February may have been chosen for another reason. The date had an occult-like significance for Putin, as it was the birthday of one of his role models, Admiral Fyodor Ushakov.[2] The eighteenth-century naval commander who defeated the Ottomans and won Crimea for Catherine the Great spent the last decade of his life in a monastery thanking God for his victories at sea. When Putin came to power, Ushakov became the patron saint of the Russian navy. The President mentioned him in an address to 100,000 people in Moscow's Luzhniki stadium, a month after sending his troops into Ukraine. Against a backdrop of red, white and blue flags, he declared: 'The beginning of the operation coincided, quite by chance, with the birthday of one of our outstanding military leaders ... who did not lose a single battle.' He recalled Ushakov's words that 'the storms of war would glorify Russia'. As bombs rained down on Ukrainian civilians, Putin claimed that the main reason for invading his neighbour was 'to spare people suffering, and to prevent genocide'.

Back in the Kostroma region more than 200 miles away, Edelstein and a fellow priest, Father Ioann Burdin, were the first Russian clerics to publicly condemn the war. Edelstein posted a letter of protest on the parish website, the day after the invasion, saying Christians should not stand aside when atrocities are carried out. 'We will not repeat the crimes of those who hailed Hitler's actions on 1 September 1939. We cannot close our eyes and call black white, evil good, and say that Abel was probably wrong and provoked his older brother,' he wrote. A couple of weeks later, Burdin delivered a sermon at his Resurrection Church in Karabanovo. He spoke about Russian troops shelling Kyiv, Odesa and Kharkiv and 'killing citizens of Ukraine, brothers and sisters in Christ'. Someone denounced him to the police. The priest was charged with discrediting Russia's armed forces, under the new military censorship law that carries a prison sentence for repeat offences. He got away with a 35,000 rouble fine (roughly £300). Although it was swiftly paid by supporters and although 292 other clerics, inside and outside of Russia, had joined him in signing an anti-war petition,[3] Burdin was shaken. He told me he was upset to see local priests wearing the ribbon of St George on their cassocks. Like the ubiquitous Z symbol, the orange and black striped ribbon, which dates back to Catherine the Great, has become a mark of support for Putin's war.

Most of Russia's 40,000 priests have been cowed into silence. They know they can be defrocked at the stroke of a pen, like Ioann Koval, a Moscow priest who swapped the word 'victory' for 'peace' in the text of the obligatory *Prayer for Holy Rus*. A few have even been jailed for opposing the war. Father Ioann Kumaryov received a three-year sentence after a St Petersburg court found him guilty of spreading 'fake news' about the army. There can be no dissent from the official line.

On the first day of the invasion, Patriarch Kirill said he was praying for 'the speedy restoration of peace'. But he failed to condemn the violence.[4] In the days that followed, he made vague statements about reducing 'the degree of confrontation' between Russians and Ukrainians, but his exhortations sounded half-hearted. By the first Sunday of the war, when it was clear there would be no instant victory parade in Kyiv, his tone changed. Echoing Putin, he said Russians and Ukrainians are 'one people', the people of 'Holy Rus', who had been propelled against each other by external 'dark evil forces'.[5] On Forgiveness Sunday, while Burdin pleaded for an end to the bombing of Ukraine, Kirill blamed the war on Europe's fixation with gay pride parades. He told the congregation in Christ the Saviour that they were witnessing 'a civilisational conflict' between the 'sinful' and 'devilish' West versus the 'holy' and 'spiritual' people of Russia and Ukraine. The disconnect between his words from the pulpit and facts on the ground grew ever-more glaring. During a sermon at the Cathedral of the Russian Armed Forces, Kirill declared that Russians are 'very peace-loving and long-suffering people' who have no 'aspirations for war'.[6]

That same day, 3 April, pictures of corpses lying in the streets of Bucha were beamed around the world. More than 1,400 civilians in the commuter town near Kyiv were massacred during the month-long Russian occupation.

The following month, Pope Francis, who had been calling for a ceasefire, spoke to Kirill on a video call. He was surprised to see the Orthodox prelate constantly stealing glances at a sheet of paper and mechanically reeling off justifications for the war, such as NATO expansion in Eastern Europe. 'Brother, we are not state clerics,' Francis said, after listening patiently for several minutes. 'We cannot use the language of politics but that of Jesus.' More pointedly, he warned Kirill not to blindly follow the Russian President. 'The Patriarch cannot lower himself to become Putin's altar boy,' he said.[7] Kirill may have been privately irritated and humiliated by the Pope's remark, but he continued to echo his political master's voice.

As casualties mounted, his sermons grew darker. 'Malicious forces' and even a 'civilisation of death' was trying to 'erase Orthodox Russia from the face of the earth', he told his flock.[8] When the Kremlin announced a partial mobilisation in September 2022, the head of the Church turned himself into a recruiting officer for the army, telling newly drafted men that dying for the fatherland 'washes away all sins'.

According to many scholars, Kirill's embrace of the Russian World ideology amounted to 'ethnophyletism' – a church term for religion fuelled by nationalism. The practice was condemned as heresy back in 1872 when the Ecumenical Patriarchate in Constantinople ruled that Orthodoxy must never be tied to the fate of a single nation or race. More than 60 theologians from Greece, the US and elsewhere signed a letter of protest against the war. They said the slaughter inspired by 'this vile and indefensible teaching', with the connivance of the Church, was 'profoundly un-Orthodox, un-Christian and against humanity'.[9] Kirill was unmoved. Once a relatively liberal cleric who skilfully hedged his bets and reached out to other churches, he had become an active participant in war. His priests threw holy water over conscripts, over tanks, planes and weapons. Two months into the war, some blessed traditional Easter cakes iced with the Z symbol.[10]

By January 2024, some 700 priests had made more than 2,000 trips to the zone of the so-called Special Military Operation.[11]

Most were chaplains offering spiritual comfort to Russian troops, but some took up guns. Father Andrei Dorogobid, who served in the riot police before his ordination, was one example. For many years he taught marksmanship alongside his job as rector in eastern Siberia. In November 2022, Dorogobid volunteered to train front line troops and also 'repeatedly carried out combat missions and participated in assaults on fortified areas' for which he earned a medal 'for courage'. Asked whether he personally shot at the enemy, he replied 'it's better not to ask such questions'.[12]

The social-media profiles of *siloviki*, or securocrats – influential officers in Putin's army and security forces – are increasingly filled with religious icons and battlefield prayers. There is scant evidence that any of them were particularly religious before the war. Superstition, hardwired into the Russian psyche, now seems rampant, along with faith in miracles. According to the pro-Kremlin tabloid *Komsomolskaya Pravda*, 'Orthodox battalions' in Donbas sustained fewer casualties when they were renamed after medieval warrior saints. 'No more heavy losses,' blared the newspaper's headline.[13]

In the late spring of 2023, as Kyiv was gearing up for its counteroffensive, nerves were jangling in the Kremlin. The wonderworking icon of St Seraphim of Sarov, painted at the time of Tsar Nicholas II, was put on a military plane and flown over areas deemed vulnerable to drone attacks. Putin ordered that Andrei Rublev's *Trinity* icon be moved from Moscow's leading museum, the Tretyakov Gallery, to the Cathedral of Christ the Saviour. Perhaps he imagined it would make a good photo opportunity and imbue the war with metaphysical significance for Russians watching TV. Or maybe he sincerely believed moving the country's most precious icon to the cathedral would bring success to the battlefield.

Putin's superstitiousness has been widely commented on in the Russian media. Former Kremlin press pool journalists recount tales of being prohibited from stepping on Putin's shadow and how a deputy prime minister rearranged a meeting based on astrological advice.[14] Some sharp-eyed observers noticed a red thread around Putin's right wrist at a Eurasian summit in 2022 – the Kabbalah bracelet is supposed to ward off misfortune and ill health. His habit of sitting behind an absurdly long meeting table during the pandemic was partly political theatre, partly his pathological fear of infection. Accompanied by his defence minister, Sergei Shoigu, the President has often visited the Altai Mountains of southern Siberia where traditional prophets and healers commune with the spirits of nature and deceased ancestors.

One historian cum spin doctor, who boasts of close ties to the Kremlin, claimed Putin and Shoigu sought guidance from a shaman while planning the invasion of Ukraine.[15] Whether there is any truth in that, many Russians mix Orthodoxy with mysticism and a dash of the occult. They may travel to monasteries to ask advice from the *startsy,* holy elders, but hedge their bets by consulting tarot cards and sorcerers. 'Putin has absorbed this religiosity which came from the atheist void in the late Soviet years,' Archimandrite Cyril Hovorun told me. 'It is very syncretic, like a Russian salad of different religious views and traditions mixed up together. And the common denominator is a belief in magic.'[16]

As the journalist Ksenia Luchenko points out, if the intention had been to allow the faithful to pray in front of the famous icon in a holy setting, the *Trinity* could have been transferred to the Church of St Nicholas – a functioning place of worship inside the Tretyakov Gallery complex where religious artefacts are preserved in special climate-controlled environments.[17] Nobody was petitioning the Patriarchate, clamouring to venerate Rublev's angels at Christ the Saviour. But in Russia nobody can go against the express wishes of the President and expect to get away with it.

Archpriest Leonid Kalinin, who trained as a sculptor, was head of Kirill's council on Church art. For decades, he had been obsequiously loyal to the Patriarch and Putin's government, but his expertise as a restorer of old artworks was to prove his undoing. When the President wanted to move Andrei Rublev's *Trinity* to Christ the Saviour, Kalinin advised against it. The fifteenth-century masterpiece, depicting three translucent angels from the Book of Genesis, is Russia's equivalent of the *Mona Lisa*. He warned that the icon was fragile and could suffer irreparable damage without expert care in a museum. Almost instantly, Kirill defrocked him for 'obstructive' behaviour.

I texted the archpriest to express my surprise. I had spoken to him several months earlier about his role in the design of Christ the Saviour back in the 1990s and more recently in the Cathedral of the Armed Forces. He wrote back admitting his shock: 'I thought protecting the icon was my job, but I guess I made a mistake.' Later, he sent me messages on Facebook saying his wife was expecting another baby, money was tight, and he was trying to make ends meet by taking private commissions for new icons and sculptures. Kalinin's plight struck me as a microcosm of the tangled relations between church and state. This story about war, a leader's paranoia and a talismanic icon could have been told at almost any point in the last thousand years of Russian history.

☦ ☦ ☦

In those dramatic first hours and days, Ukrainians did all they could to stop the Russian advance. People threw up makeshift barricades of car tyres, bricks and scrap metal; they faced down tanks armed with hammers and hunting rifles. President Volodymyr Zelensky, a former comedian, posted regular video updates from the streets of Kyiv. He refused offers to evacuate him from the country. 'I need ammunition, not a ride,' he told US officials. Writers and sports stars got into khaki and joined the defence. Army volunteers included around 40,000 women, serving as soldiers and combat medics. Ukraine now has the most feminised army in Europe. Tens of thousands more sewed camouflage netting in subways and church basements, mixed batches of petrol for Molotov cocktails, cooked food for troops and sent supplies to the front.

The resistance turned into a national awakening – Ukraine under fire became a truly independent nation. But there was one area where solidarity was conspicuously absent – the Orthodox Church.

Although the Orthodox Church of Ukraine, the country's self-governing church, had been granted official status in 2019, at the time of the invasion most believers still belonged to the Ukrainian Orthodox Church under the Moscow Patriarchate. On 24 February, its head, Onufriy (Berezovsky) Metropolitan of Kyiv and All Ukraine, pleaded with Putin to 'immediately stop the fratricidal war'. Conflict between two nations of Orthodox Christians was, he said, 'a repetition of the sin of Cain who treacherously killed his brother out of envy'. Onufriy praised the Ukrainian army, 'defending our land and our people.' But during the liturgy, he and most of his clerics continued to commemorate Kirill, as head of their church. Some parishioners refused to go to services in which the name of the Moscow Patriarch was mentioned.

I met Father Andriy Golovin in Bucha. The atrocities committed here by Russian troops galvanised many countries into sending weapons to Ukraine. On 10 March, a week into the occupation, the Bucha authorities began digging a mass grave on the grassy patch behind Golovin's Church of St Andrew. They had no choice: the cemetery on the outskirts of town was too close to the frontline. Picking up the dead from the street was risky because of snipers but some corpses were being eaten by dogs. Townspeople collected as many bodies as possible in supermarket trolleys and wheeled them along shell-scarred pavements to the church. Some were wrapped in black body bags, others in sheets. When I arrived in September 2022, Golovin said forensic teams had only just finished identifying the remains. He was conducting services in a chapel in the basement of his church. Not just through fear of renewed attacks, but because in the main church, icons had given way to an exhibition of gruesome photographs. We stopped in front of a picture of a corpse lying face down in a puddle. The dead man had a strip of white cloth tied around his elbow and he was clutching a packet of spaghetti. 'He was a pensioner who had just left his house to collect some humanitarian aid,' said the priest.

Golovin had never served in the Moscow-linked Ukrainian Orthodox Church. He belonged to a different splinter group, the Kyiv Patriarchate, before joining the independent Orthodox Church of Ukraine. He acknowledged that most priests in Ukraine were still tied to the Moscow Patriarchate but predicted that would soon change. 'Pardon me if this doesn't sound very church-like,' he told me. 'But imagine somebody thinks they're watching a romantic movie and they get hardcore porn instead.'

Ukraine is the Moscow Patriarchate's second-largest canonical territory. It has a much higher rate of churchgoing than Russia, as

Viktor Yelenskiy, head of the national Service for Ethnic Policy and Freedom of Conscience was keen to tell me when we met in Kyiv. 'So called "Holy Russia" has among the highest rates for crime, alcoholism, abandoned children and suicide, but when it comes to attending religious services, it is near the bottom, roughly on par with the Netherlands,' he said. The UOC may still have more parishes than its independent rival, but its future is uncertain, said Yelenskiy, 'because the wave of fury in society is very strong'. Many will never willingly return to a church which has any affiliation with Moscow. The trauma will endure for years to come. Father Serhiy Chudynovych, abducted from his OCU church when Russian troops occupied Kherson, was accused of being a member of Ukraine's territorial defence force. His captors beat him, stripped off his clothes and threatened to rape him with a police baton. Now, whenever he hears the Russian language, his blood pressure shoots up and he feels as if he cannot breathe.[18]

Even those churches under Moscow's jurisdiction have not escaped Russian aggression. In August 2022, Russian soldiers burst into the Church of St Olha in the Kherson region of southern Ukraine. They handcuffed the priest, Father Ihor Novosilskiy, and put a bag over his head. Then they threw him on the floor of their car 'like a dog' and took him to a series of detention centres where he was almost starved to death. He was tortured with electrodes for speaking Ukrainian and failing to memorise the words of the Russian anthem. 'I told the guards that I have my own country,' he said when he was finally released 262 days later. 'I know its anthem by heart so why should I learn another one?' By the end of 2023, fourteen priests from the UOC had been killed, twenty wounded, and five had disappeared.

Many UOC priests rebelled against their church's hierarchy and left to join the rival Orthodox Church of Ukraine (OCU) either in protest or because their parishioners had forced them to. Mounting grassroots pressure obliged Metropolitan Onufriy to convene a meeting of all the dioceses in late May 2022. At the end he announced that the UOC was a separate entity and had removed all references to Moscow from the Church's founding documents. But in Moscow the Patriarchate paid no attention and continued to include UOC clerics and officials in various commissions or working groups. A few months later, in November, Onufriy's Synod not only failed to condemn the collaborationism of some bishops in the Russian-occupied territories, but even described them as 'heroes'.

In the summer of 2022, in the north of Kyiv, I met a priest who gave me an insight into how the UOC had collaborated with the authorities in the past. Serhiy Berezhnoy, an army chaplain, was based in a small wooden chapel not far from the spot where Grand Prince Volodymyr ordered mass baptisms in 988. As a teenager, Berezhnoy served as an altar boy in the Donetsk region of eastern Ukraine at the time of the 2004 presidential elections and was asked to distribute some leaflets to the parishioners. On one side there was an icon and on the other a prayer for the election victory of Viktor Yanukovych, the Kremlin-friendly local governor and prime minister. He lost to the pro-European Viktor Yushchenko who became president after the Orange Revolution. Berezhnoy remembered how he felt handing out the prayer sheets. 'I truly feared that if Yanukovych lost the election, the evil West would destroy our Holy Trinity of Russia, Ukraine and Belarus.' When Berezhnoy opted to leave the UOC for the self-governing OCU in 2018, his decision cost him his parish and his marriage. His father-in-law was a priest in the Moscow-affiliated church and his wife could not forgive him.

Many Orthodox believers in Ukraine have been told that the self-governing OCU is an impostor church, and they are reluctant to join it. In July 2023, I accompanied a group of pilgrims on a weekend trip from Kyiv to the Pochaiv Monastery in western Ukraine. Next to me in the minibus sat a woman and her eight-year-old daughter. They were from Bucha and had endured three terrifying weeks cowering in their cellar. But the mother, who spent much of the journey reciting feverishly from a pocket-sized prayer book, told me she feared losing divine grace if she left the Moscow-linked church. She had heard that people in the OCU were 'schismatics', more interested in politics than God.

In all, only two Ukrainian bishops have switched sides – Metropolitan Oleksandr Drabynko in Kyiv and Metropolitan Symeon Shostatskyi from Vinnytsia, west of the capital. At the beginning of 2024, Kirill released an official calendar, featuring portraits of all the bishops of the Moscow Patriarchate, including 52 from Ukraine. One of these, Bishop Agafangel of Odesa, saw the city's Transfiguration Cathedral devastated by a Russian missile strike. During the first 21 months of the full-scale invasion, Russian troops looted or wrecked at least 630 religious buildings in Ukraine.

Ironically, the churches under Kirill's jurisdiction suffered the most – more than 80 were destroyed and 200 damaged at the last count. The late-eighteenth century baroque cathedral in Odesa, torn down by Stalin in 1936, had been painstakingly rebuilt and was consecrated by the Patriarch in 2010. 'Whatever the goal of this so-called shameful special military operation,' the bishop wrote to Kirill, 'it cannot justify killing and violence, destruction, and forced displacement. We still don't understand: who and what do they want to liberate us from? Life itself?' Despite this public expression of outrage, neither Agafangel nor the other 51 bishops have formally denied their affiliation with the Moscow Patriarchate.

Georgiy Kovalenko was once the official spokesman for the UOC and ran its information department. Now he is part of the rival OCU. Sitting with him in the autumn sunshine on a bench outside Saint Sophia's Cathedral in September 2022, I admitted I was confused. Why, eight months into the full-scale invasion, were so few bishops on the side of Ukraine's self-governing church? His answer: money. Russia's Church, he said, was like the gas and oil giants Gazprom and Rosneft, 'a department of state'. 'When we were granted the *tomos* (independent status), several clerics told me that they would have liked to join the Orthodox Church of Ukraine,' he said, 'but unfortunately their "sponsor" was against it.' Kovalenko was talking about businessmen such as Vadim Novinsky, a Russian oligarch granted Ukrainian citizenship in May 2012 by the Kremlin-friendly Ukrainian president Viktor Yanukovych. Yanukovych also helped Novinsky to get a seat in the Ukrainian parliament as a member of his Party of Regions. Novinsky was so active in championing pro-Russian legislation that fellow parliamentarians called him 'Putin's Whip'. The oligarch was ordained a protodeacon of the UOC by Onufriy in 2020. He is currently under sanctions and wanted by the Ukrainian authorities for collaboration with the Russian occupier – an accusation he has denied. In April 2023, Swiss journalists spotted Novinsky in red and gold vestments officiating at the Easter service at the Russian Orthodox Church of the Resurrection of Christ in Zurich.[19] Six months later, Maryan Zablotsky, a Ukrainian MP from Zelensky's Servant of the People Party, alleged the UOC had engaged one of America's highest paid lobbyists and Novinsky had footed the bill.

Zablotsky, born in western Ukraine, had dreamed of erecting a statue of Ronald Reagan in Kyiv. He venerated the US president's libertarian ideas and attacks on the evils of communism. But when Russia invaded, he was horrified that some members of the US Republican party he had once so admired were blocking aid to his country. On his Facebook page he claimed that the 'FSB in cassocks' had been paying the lobbyist Robert Amsterdam $1,400 per hour 'to throw dirt on Ukraine'.[20] He insisted that one of the aims was to spread false narratives among members of Congress and staff that the Ukrainian authorities were persecuting the Ukrainian Orthodox Church linked to the Moscow Patriarchate – more often called by its acronym UOC-MP.

The PR exercise resonated with some on Capitol Hill. Marjorie Taylor Greene, the far-right representative from Georgia, accused Kyiv of waging 'a war against Christianity'. She echoed Kremlin newspeak on Steve Bannon's *War Room* podcast,[21] stating as fact that Ukraine's government was 'attacking Christians' and 'executing priests'. 'Russia is not doing that,' she added. 'They are not attacking Christianity. As a matter of fact, they seem to be protecting it.' A grotesque claim given that two years into the full-scale invasion, 39 priests from different churches across Ukraine had died from Russian shelling or were killed execution-style by Russian troops. Even her fellow Republicans started calling Taylor Greene 'Moscow Marjorie', while a Florida Democrat submitted an amendment appointing her as 'Putin's Special Envoy to the United States Congress'.

Such propaganda is hardly limited to the US. A recent investigation by *Der Spiegel* and Bellingcat (which specialises in open-source intelligence gathering) revealed that a political strategist working as a research assistant for a German MP was also employed by Russian intelligence.[22] Acting on instructions from his FSB handler, the assistant, who was of Ukrainian origin, persuaded the MP from the far-right AfD (Alternative for Germany) party to protest against a delivery of tanks to Ukraine. The assistant also instructed the MP to tell the Bundestag about the 'persecutions' suffered by Ukraine's Moscow-affiliated church. He told him to complain to Pope Francis about a parliamentary bill that would outlaw the UOC.

However, in Ukraine, the continued loyalty of some to the UOC is not just about money or disinformation. There are some patriotic UOC priests who support the Ukrainian army and do what they can to help refugees and people in need because of the war. Karen Nikoforov, a theologian who runs a project called Religion on Fire, documenting war crimes against all religious communities in Ukraine, belongs to the UOC but is not pro-Kremlin. He told me religion is now in a state of flux. 'Many Orthodox believers want to stay in the church in which they were baptised and with the priests they love and trust,' Nikoforov said. 'They also prefer to hear Church Slavonic they are familiar with during services – it's a question of tradition.' The OCU has formally adopted Ukrainian as its liturgical language, and also ditched the Julian calendar in favour of the Gregorian calendar introduced by Pope Gregory XII in the sixteenth century. In 2023, for the first time, millions of Ukrainians celebrated Christmas with the Western world on 25 December, instead of 7 January when Russian and other Eastern Orthodox churches mark Christ's birth.

Zelensky, a secular Jew (accused of being a Nazi by Russian propagandists), is not aligned with any of the churches. Yet he spoke of Moscow-backed Orthodoxy 'weakening Ukraine from within'. In November 2022, the country's security agency, the SBU, began searching UOC monasteries and churches across the country. In some raids they unearthed weapons, Russian passports, stacks of banknotes and pro-Kremlin propaganda. Zelensky vowed he would 'never allow anyone to build an empire inside the Ukrainian soul'. Around 100 UOC priests have so far been accused of collaboration and espionage-related crimes, according to the security services, and nearly twenty senior clerics have been stripped of their Ukrainian citizenship. One priest from Luhansk received a twelve-year sentence for informing the enemy about Ukrainian troop movements, while an abbot from Sumy near the Belarusian border was given fifteen years for working for the FSB. 'It's shameful to admit, I took pictures of the places where Ukrainian soldiers were billeted,' he told a Ukrainian TV journalist. 'The devil led me astray.'[23]

The SBU raids were prompted by mobile phone footage of people praying for Russia during a church service at the Kyiv Pechersk Lavra – the Monastery of the Caves. Perched high above the Dnipro River and ringed by stone walls, it is a sprawling complex of churches, housing for monks and a labyrinth of subterranean passages dug deep into the hillside. In September 2022, clutching a beeswax candle, I joined the constant stream of pilgrims and tourists stumbling through the almost pitch-black catacombs. These narrow underground tunnels are lined with mummified monks who have lain there for centuries. Here, in glass coffins covered with embroidered cloth, are the remains of Nestor the Chronicler, credited with writing the first history of Kievan Rus', *The Tale of Bygone Years*, and Ilya Muromets, the paralysed son of a peasant who was miraculously cured. He arose from his bed on top of the wood stove in his parents' hut to become a legendary warrior.

To many, this monastery is the holiest site in the Slavic world. It was founded by a monk from Mount Athos, about half a century after Prince Volodymyr converted his people to Christianity. Together with the Cathedral of St Sophia, it is both the cradle of Ukrainian identity and the place where the Russians believe their state began. It has become a battleground for the soul of Orthodoxy in Ukraine. Until last year, its abbot was Metropolitan Pavel Lebed, also known as Pasha Mercedes because of his taste for pricey cars. I first came across him in 2013 while making a film about HIV. The bishop succeeded in closing Ukraine's only specialist AIDS clinic at that time, which was in a former tuberculosis hospital in the monastery's grounds. 'I find it unpleasant to be living next to people who have lived a dissolute life and got infected with all sorts of diseases while I spend my life in prayer and ask God for forgiveness,' he said on TV. A decade later, in April 2023, Pavel was put under house arrest for preventing a government commission from entering the Lavra. Later, he was charged with denying the existence of Ukraine as a sovereign state, following an SBU wiretap. To the fury of his supporters in Kyiv and Moscow, the abbot was forced to wear an ankle bracelet for several weeks, then jailed. He was released a month later, in August 2023, after posting nearly a million dollars' bail. According to his lawyer, the money was collected by parishioners.

For months, the clerics from the Lavra have been defying eviction orders. Black-robed monks and their supporters have been involved in scuffles with police and officials from Ukraine's culture ministry. In December 2022, the UOC was warned that the state was terminating its lease for two churches on the territory of the Upper Lavra, including the Holy Dormition Cathedral where Christmas services were held by the rival OCU for the first time on 25 December. Three months later, the government ordered the UOC to vacate the lower Lavra as well, which was home to 200 monks, various churches and the caves filled with saintly relics. It also contained shops, cafes and small hotels. The monks were furious. From Moscow, Kirill's spokesman Vladimir Legoyda denounced the Ukrainian authorities as being motivated by 'a wild, monstrous desire to exterminate'. Maksym Ostapenko, who took over the site as director of National Kyiv-Pechersk Historic-Cultural Preserve, said the monks would be allowed to stay if they could 'prove they have no ties with the aggressor state and work out a new transparent way of working with our government'. At the time of writing, the matter was still in the Court of Appeal.

When I met Ostapenko in London, he told me about his inspection of the Lavra after most of the monks had decamped. He showed me a picture of an eighteenth-century door which he said had been used as target practice for knife throwing. He found images of Nicholas II and Patriarch Kirill, a badge from the Russian Ground Forces and leaflets about Ukrainian heretics. In one building, the clergy left behind dozens of machines for counting banknotes. 'Business in the Lavra was super profitable,' Ostapenko told me, adding that at least a third of the hundred monks who protested about being made homeless had their own flats in Kyiv.[24] A few monks with disabilities or no other place to go have stayed put. Some went to Europe or to the Middle East. A church insider told me that a handful turned up in Dubai. There are no Orthodox monasteries there – yet – but apparently some are living in villas or on yachts owned by oligarchs.

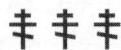

304

Early one morning in July 2023, with some trepidation, I caught a train going east. The final stop was Kramatorsk, where two weeks earlier a Russian ballistic missile had smashed into a pizza restaurant much frequented by journalists and aid workers. Thirteen people were killed, including Viktoria Amelina, a young poet and novelist. My train was packed with subdued-looking soldiers who had been on leave and were returning to the battlefield. The carriage was quiet – most people were trying to catch up on sleep. At the penultimate stop, Slovyansk, I got out and drove for 30 kilometres along deserted, rutted roads. I had been tipped off about a frontline monastery with a murky recent past.

Monks first settled on a spot above the Siverskiy Donets River in the fifteenth century, burrowing into the chalk cliff to create chapels and cells. Their Svyatohirsk Lavra, or Holy Mountain Cave Monastery, suffered under both Catherine the Great and the Communists. In the 1990s, it was restored by the Moscow-friendly local governor, Yanukovych. Surrounded by thickly forested hills, it played an intriguing role in the early stages of Russia's war against Ukraine. Tetyana Derkach, a Kyiv journalist specialising in religion, described the Svyatohirsk Lavra as 'the most prominent centre of *Russkiy Mir* ideology' in the Donbas.[25] It was, she wrote, the spiritual power base of the so-called 'Donetsk clan', a group that included Yanukovych, his prime minister and a group of oligarchs who made their fortune in Ukraine's industrial heartland.

On the morning of 12 April 2014, armed men in balaclavas and camouflage surrounded the police department of the town of Slovyansk, half an hour's drive from the monastery. It later emerged that they were supported by Russia's leading Orthodox oligarch, Konstantin Malofeev, whose Tsargrad media group promotes conservative Christianity and Putin. They built barricades from mounds of tyres and sandbags topped with barbed wire. Then they hung the Russian tricolour on the building. The men said they were locals from the self-proclaimed Donetsk People's Republic, but in fact they were Russian army 'volunteers' led by a former FSB officer, Igor Girkin, known by his *nom de guerre* Strelkov, or 'Shooter'. In November that year, when 4,300 people had already been killed in the conflict, Girkin was interviewed by *Zavtra*, a conservative Russian daily.

'I was the one who pulled the trigger of this war,' he boasted, adding that 'nobody there wanted to fight' until his unit seized Slovyansk.[26] Girkin also bragged that he was under holy protection. 'All of my personal bodyguards were the clergy, monks and hieromonks of the Svyatohirsk Lavra. All of them. To the last man,' he told Archpriest Vsevolod Chaplin, another of Kirill's spokesmen. 'One novice monk was the commander of one of the units in the Slovyansk brigade. He held quite a senior post in the Lavra, he was responsible for economic affairs.'[27]

In Slovyansk, people said that the Lavra was used as a clandestine barracks for Russian agents disguised as monks. These rumours were endorsed by the former mayor, Nelya Shtepa. Once the town had been retaken by Ukraine in July 2014, she was arrested for allegedly colluding with the separatists – a charge she denied. In a Ukrainian court two years later, she testified that at one point in 2014 the Svyatohirsk Lavra had housed 250 Cossacks, all preparing to fight against Ukraine.[28] The abbot of the monastery, Archbishop Arseniy (Yakovenko), ridiculed her claim. 'Female nature is mysterious, and fantasy is unpredictable,' he said. Besides, he added, the Lavra fed and housed hundreds of tourists and pilgrims every day, and it would be impossible for a large group of saboteurs to go unnoticed.[29]

Eight years later, during the full-scale invasion, the pilgrims stopped coming to Svyatohirsk. The monastery became a shelter for hundreds of displaced local people and some nuns whose nearby convent had been reduced to rubble. They arrived in a column protected by Ukrainian troops. Many of them were still living there when I visited and told me how grateful they were to find a haven as well as free meals. The monastery's golden domes gleamed in the sunlight, but its whitewashed walls were scarred with shrapnel marks. Outside the main church, an elderly refugee showed me the fresh flowers on the graves of three monks and a nun killed by artillery and rocket strikes on 30 May and 1 June 2022. Despite this, the Svyatohirsk monks commemorated Kirill during the service.

Afterwards, I was hoping to meet the abbot, Metropolitan Arseniy, but was told he was indisposed. Perhaps he was feeling vulnerable because Zelensky had issued a decree in December 2022 suspending his Ukrainian citizenship – nine months later, he was arrested for allegedly sharing information with the Russians about Ukrainian army checkpoints in the Kramatorsk district of the Donetsk region and was facing eight years behind bars. I was invited to lunch instead by Archimandrite Feofan, the treasurer of the monastery. He brushed aside a question about influence from Moscow and told me the monks 'do not listen to Kirill'. Yet he repeated familiar Kremlin rhetoric justifying the invasion. This 'terrible trial' was caused by an 'artificial divide' between ethnic Ukrainians and Russians in the Donbas, whom he called 'one people'. God had allowed the violence to happen 'to repair a nation'. Stroking his beard, he leaned back in his chair and challenged me like a quizmaster. 'Do you know what is causing the highest number of deaths in Ukraine nowadays?' he asked. 'Abortions. They kill more people than the ongoing war.'

His tone was cordial, if wary, until I asked whether the former FSB officer Igor Girkin had received a blessing at the monastery. In an icy voice, Feofan said: 'I don't know anything about that.' He did not want to be associated with a man convicted of helping to shoot down a Malaysian passenger plane and killing all 298 people on board over eastern Ukraine in July 2014. The militia commander was found guilty in absentia by the International Criminal Court (ICC) in The Hague and sentenced to life imprisonment. Girkin ignored the verdict and remained at liberty in Russia until he criticised Putin's handling of the war and called the President 'a cowardly waste of space'. In January 2024, he was handed a four-year sentence for extremism.

☦ ☦ ☦

Putin himself is wanted by The Hague for one of the most emotive issues in this war – accusations that Russia has stolen Ukrainian children. In March 2023, the ICC issued arrest warrants for the President and his commissioner for children's rights, Maria Lvova-Belova, for the forced deportations of more than 16,000 Ukrainian children across the border to Russia. Lvova-Belova and her husband, a computer programmer turned Orthodox priest, have five biological and eighteen adopted children, most recently a fifteen-year-old boy from the destroyed city of Mariupol. Children were promised desperately needed respite in holiday camps in Crimea, only to find they were not allowed to return home. Many were sent to Russian foster families and some were adopted. Russia offers its citizens up to $2,000 in government aid per child. On TV, dazed children are filmed receiving teddy bears, gifts and hugs from strangers. Their own parents or legal representatives have often spent months looking for them across the vast Russian Federation. Kateryna Rashevska, a legal expert who has been helping to return children to Ukraine, said under Russian law adoptive parents can change a child's name, place of birth and date of birth within six months. 'That makes it extremely difficult to find such children, especially the youngest ones,' she told me.

The Church's role in this affair is significant. Just days after the ICC had issued an arrest warrant for Lvova-Belova, Kirill received her in Moscow, praised her work and discussed measures to 'protect orphans'. A Centre for Family Placement of Children and Church Care of Children was created in the first year of the invasion by the Patriarchate's charity department. There is no mention of Ukraine on its website, but some believe the centre was set up to respond to and facilitate the deportation of Ukrainian children. Kirill has addressed groups of school-aged Ukrainians at least three times since the war began. In July 2022, in Moscow, he met children from the occupied Donetsk and Luhansk regions, from Kharkiv and from Kyiv. The children, wearing white T-shirts decorated with doves and crosses, took part in a procession to celebrate the anniversary of the Baptism of Rus'. They walked from Christ the Saviour Cathedral in the summer heat under leaden skies; when they reached the statue of Prince Vladimir outside the Kremlin, the Patriarch warned them that sometimes people break away from their spiritual roots and reject their true identity for a false one because they are seduced by an ideology which on the surface seems more attractive and successful. 'All the children listened very attentively,' said Oleg Yanovsky, an official from the Patriarchate, shepherding the group. 'While we stood there, a thunderstorm started but the patriarch continued talking. With every sentence came a clap of thunder, almost in time with his speech, and at some point, many of the children started to sob. I was alarmed until I realised it was a kind of catharsis for them.'[30]

One Church-linked organisation called *Vnuki* (Grandchildren), which describes itself as a 'patriotic movement', brought children to Moscow from Ukraine to meet Kirill and other senior clerics, including Putin's alleged confessor, Metropolitan Tikhon Shevkunov. Its website says it aims to 'integrate children from the liberated territories, who have lived for a long time under the influence of Ukrainian propaganda, into the Russian mental space'.[31]

Some of the deported children who managed to return to Ukraine have described their experiences in this 'Russian mental space'. Serhii, an orphaned sixteen-year-old from Mariupol, was taken to Donetsk by local officials. According to charities and the government in Kyiv, these officials helped the authorities in occupied Ukraine to send children to Russia. While he was being treated for his injuries in a hospital, Serhii's Ukrainian birth certificate was confiscated and then 'lost'. He was sent to the southern Russian town of Rostov on Don and then to a string of orphanages in the Moscow region, even though he said he wanted to go back home and live with his older sister. Instead, he was given a Russian passport and sent to a devout Russian family in Sergiyev Posad, home of the St Sergius Holy Trinity Monastery. The Zaitsevs, who had three biological and two adopted children, were regular churchgoers. They put a tracking device on Serhii's phone and monitored his calls. 'The most annoying thing was that they kept talking about Ukrainian Nazis all the time,' Serhii later recalled. 'I asked them to stop but they ignored me. So, I kept quiet.'[32] One local TV channel filmed Serhii picking berries and sitting around the dinner table with his new family. He was also shown at an army museum learning how to mend tanks.[33] The caption under the film read: 'Despite all the difficulties that he has had to endure, this boy feels great in his foster family and is optimistic about the future.' But Serhii secretly sent appeals for help to lawyers and human rights defenders in Ukraine. They eventually managed to smuggle him out of Russia. When he was back in Ukraine, his Russian adoptive parents begged him to return, offering to pay for his travel. 'Come back, otherwise we will have problems,' they wrote.

Despairing of the dilemmas they are forced to confront, many clerics are demoralised and afraid. The defrocking of Alexei Uminsky, a priest beloved by the Moscow intelligentsia, was a seminal moment. The church court said the archpriest had broken his oath by refusing to read the *Prayer for Holy Rus*. Since the partial mobilisation was announced in September 2022, the prayer has been compulsory at all church services. Zoya Svetova, the journalist and daughter of the Soviet era's last Christian dissidents, was one of Uminsky's parishioners. She said his dismissal felt like the last act of a play, testifying to the Church's 'gradual and steady destruction from within'. Uminksy had visited the tycoon-turned Putin opponent, Mikhail Khodorkovsky, while he was in pre-trial detention at a remote penal colony. He also urged officials to show 'Christian mercy' and allow a doctor to see the late jailed opposition leader, Alexei Navalny.

Navalny's death in an Arctic prison in February 2024 caused a global outcry. For nine days the authorities refused to allow his mother to collect his body from the morgue unless she agreed to a secret burial. His widow, Yulia Navalnaya, emphasised that the actions of the authorities offended the feelings of believers. 'We knew before that Putin's faith was fake,' she said in a video appeal, 'but now we see that more clearly than ever. Faith is not about kissing an icon. Faith is about goodness, about mercy, about salvation. And not a single true Christian could ever do what Putin is now doing to my already dead husband Alexei ... it's not even hatred – it's some kind of Satanism or paganism.' Nearly 5,000 priests, laity and Christians of other denominations urged the authorities to release Navalny's remains. 'Even Pontius Pilate, who decided to execute Christ,' read the petition, 'did not prevent the extradition of the Saviour's body and his burial. Don't be crueller than Pilate.'[34]

Thousands of mourners turned out for Navalny's Moscow funeral, defying orders to keep away. Hundreds were detained in the days that followed, after they were identified by surveillance cameras and footage posted online. Laying flowers at a makeshift Navalny memorial was enough to get you arrested. One Moscow priest, Dmitry Safronov, read prayers at Navalny's grave to mark 40 days since his death. According to Orthodox beliefs, on the fortieth day, the deceased's soul stops wandering around the earth and ascends into heaven. Kirill immediately suspended Safronov and forbade him to wear a cassock or a cross. The priest, who has four young children to support, was instructed to do three years of penance, working as a low-paid psalm reader.

At the church of the Life-Giving Holy Trinity, Uminsky was replaced by Father Andrei Tkachev, one of Orthodoxy's most vitriolic hawks. 'A warrior's death is better than any other,' he told his congregation in April 2023. 'People die like pigs, drowning in their vomit. It is much better to die for your motherland with a weapon in your hand like a man, like a hero ... then your soul will be in paradise.'[35]

Tkachev's fire and brimstone sermons may be disturbing, but I was more struck by a video from the Church of the Prophet Elijah in the Tver region. By now, I thought I had become inured to the Church's propensity to shock. Still, I was aghast to see Bishop Adrian (Ulyanov) of Rzhev and Toropetsky threaten Ilya Gavryshkiv, a young priest. 'With us you are Father Ilya but outside church you are just Ilyushka,' sneers the bishop using a pejorative diminutive. 'A little nobody!' Then he summons the priest to stand on the steps in front of the altar and forces him to apologise to his parishioners. Stammering, eyes down, the 28-year-old cleric blames his own 'stupidity and lack of understanding' before confessing that he signed an anti-war letter and prayed for peace instead of for victory. It is a scene reminiscent of Stalin-era show trials. The parishioner who informed on the young priest filmed it and proudly posted it online.

The Moscow Patriarchate has long tentacles and disobedience is punished wherever it is found – even outside Russia. Nobody is safe if they have got on the wrong side of the authorities, not just opposition politicians and journalists, but churchmen too. All across Europe over the last couple of years, I have met a growing band of Russian clerics who have fled their country. Some have tried setting up elsewhere, serving under a different jurisdiction. Others have left the Church for good, scarred by their experiences.

In Vilnius, the capital of Lithuania, I saw a large slogan on the city hall which read: 'Putin, The Hague is waiting for you'. The local authorities renamed the road leading to the Russian embassy 'Ukrainian Heroes Street'. Lithuania prides itself on standing up to tyranny and was the first country to break free from the Soviet Union. Most Lithuanians are Catholics. But since the end of the eighteenth century, when the tsarist empire took over the Grand Duchy of Lithuania, Orthodox churches have fallen under Moscow's control. Metropolitan Innokentiy, the head of the Lithuanian Orthodox Church, at first condemned the invasion of Ukraine. 'Patriarch Kirill and I have different political views,' he wrote on 18 March 2022. 'We live in a free, democratic country. Lithuania is not Russia.' Most of his clerics were relieved. They did not want to be forced to commemorate Kirill, and they put out a statement saying 'since he supports the war, we cannot celebrate him as a great leader and our father'.

But Innokentiy's independent stance was short-lived. By June he had sacked five of his anti-war clerics, accusing them of attempting to provoke a 'schism' in the Church. One of them, Vitalijus Mockus, was his private secretary and the second-most important cleric in the diocese. Mockus was trained in a Russian seminary but served at the St Paraskevi Church in Vilnius, where services were held in Lithuanian. When we met in a Vilnius café, to my surprise he whistled a few bars of a song by The Scorpions, a German rock band. 'Wind of Change', an anthem for the end of the Cold War, embodied his hopes that religious life would blossom and the Moscow Patriarchate would be cleansed of its KGB heritage. 'That hope has melted, and we are facing a catastrophe,' he said, adding he was still shocked at the manner of his dismissal. 'I was called into Metropolitan Innokentiy's study and told I had two hours to transfer all my files and documents to my successor,' he said. 'When I read the statement calling us schismatics my hands started trembling. I felt afraid to be in the building.' Mockus told me he was driving a Bolt taxi to feed his family – the other clerics were also doing odd jobs to get by.

In September 2022, I visited Andrei Kordochkin, the dean of the newly built cathedral of St Mary Magdalene, in the north of Madrid. A bear-like man in his forties, Kordochkin co-authored an open letter to the Russian government a few days after the invasion, calling for peace and an end to the war, which was signed by nearly 300 of his fellow priests, scholars and preachers both inside and outside Russia. 'We would hope that for our brothers and sisters in Ukraine this will be an expression of our solidarity,' he wrote, 'because, in the words of the Apostle Paul, when one part of the body feels pain, the whole body of the church suffers.'[36]

Kordochkin made no secret of his antipathy to Kirill and his sanctification of the war. He said that the Z symbol daubed on Russian tanks stood for 'zombies' and likened the Patriarch's approach to Orthodoxy to the regime in a maximum-security prison. When Kordochkin came to Spain as a young priest in 2004, he led services in a former greengrocer's cum mobile phone shop. The Patriarchate forced him to abandon the parish in Spain he had nurtured for almost two decades. In November 2023, he moved to a small town on the German–Dutch border where he is working as an academic and part-time priest, serving under the Ecumenical Patriarchate of Constantinople. Together with a fellow Russian cleric based in Germany, a musician and a journalist, he has set up a group called *Mir Vsem,* Peace for All.[37] It supports priests inside Russia who have lost their livelihoods for criticising the war in their sermons, signing anti-war appeals, refusing to pray for 'victory' or to collect money for the army. He told me many priests are horrified by the direction their Church has taken but they cannot afford to lose their jobs, especially if they lack transferable skills, and have large families.

Even pro-regime clerics can be punished if they put a foot wrong – and this extends to the very top of the Church. Metropolitan Hilarion, Kirill's de facto foreign minister, was widely tipped to be the next patriarch. Born Grigory Alfeyev, he was a musical prodigy as a child and studied at Tchaikovsky Moscow State Conservatory before he left to become a monk in (then-Soviet) Lithuania, where he took the name Hilarion. He has composed choral works, including a St Matthew Passion, and has written a slew of theological books as well as a flattering biography of his boss.[38] Father Christopher Hill, the Mancunian who has served as a Moscow priest for the past three decades, befriended Hilarion and helped him to prepare for postgraduate studies at Oxford. He recalls that the late Metropolitan Kallistos (Timothy Ware), the UK's leading authority on Orthodoxy, thought very highly of the young Russian.

But on 7 June 2022, at a meeting of the Holy Synod, Kirill suddenly turned against his heir apparent. Hilarion was dismissed from all his positions and appointed metropolitan of Budapest – a job he had held two decades earlier at the start of his Church career. Less than half a percentage of the Hungarian population are Orthodox Christians. The Budapest diocese has barely a dozen priests and four deacons. It was a humiliating demotion. Unusually, in the official minutes, not even perfunctory thanks were recorded for his services over the years. According to Church insiders, the only remark the Patriarch made was succinct: '*Tak Nado*' – This had to be done. Several Church insiders have told me that his dismissal was a direct order from Putin.

Hilarion was no rebel, nor could he be described as an anti-war cleric. The University of Fribourg in Switzerland had withdrawn his professorship, disappointed that the Metropolitan had failed to use 'his ecclesiastical and political influence, to publicly and unequivocally condemn Russia's military invasion of Ukraine'.[39] But if Hilarion did not criticise the war, he did not condone it either. Just before he packed his bags, Hilarion served his last liturgy in Moscow at the Mother of God 'Joy of All Who Sorrow' Church where he was appointed rector in 2009. He hid his fears of assassination behind bureaucratic language and cryptic allusions. The Synod's decision was 'required by the current socio-political situation', he told his parishioners, and had nothing to do with any professional shortcomings on his part. 'The road took a very sharp turn, I didn't keep my eye on it and ended up on the hard shoulder,' he added. 'But it's better this way – otherwise my car might have rolled over, careered into a ditch and exploded.'

When I saw Hilarion in Budapest nearly a year later, he was more explicit. He told me he was extremely upset by Kirill's behaviour and had not spoken to him for nine months, but suggested his boss had spared him from a worse fate. 'Like being sent as an army chaplain to the frontline?' I asked. 'Or simply exterminated,' he replied.

It is hard to know if Hilarion really believed Putin might have had him killed for failing to show sufficient enthusiasm for the war. But the climate of fear inside the Church should not be underestimated. The former bishop Flavian believes he was poisoned for refusing to collaborate with the FSB. Clerics live in terror of their superiors, who in turn fear their political masters in the Kremlin.

Many bishops still have a KGB mindset and are also convinced that dark external forces are bent on their destruction. One anecdote is revealing: in 2018, Kirill went to meet his counterpart Bartholomew in Istanbul. It was a last-ditch attempt to dissuade the Ecumenical Patriarch from blessing Ukraine's declaration of religious independence. They sat at a table laden with snacks and drinks. When Kirill reached for some mineral water, his bodyguard whipped the glass from his hand before he could take a sip and handed him a bottle of water from his bag instead. One of Bartholomew's senior clerics later ridiculed the Russians' paranoia. 'As if we would try and poison the patriarch of Moscow!' he said.[40]

After our chat in a side room, Hilarion invited me to admire his Cathedral of the Assumption of the Blessed Virgin Mary, a richly decorated baroque structure in which crystal chandeliers dangle from high ceilings. Overlooking the River Danube, it looks far more Catholic than Orthodox. I walked through the city to my hotel past streets closed to traffic and a temporary stage in Kossuth Square draped in white cloth. The Pope would celebrate Mass there in two days' time. As I left, Hilarion mentioned that he was to have an audience with him. They had already met several times during Francis' pontificate. Hilarion had organised a historic meeting between Francis and Kirill in Cuba in 2016 – the first between a pope and a patriarch of Moscow since the schism of 1054. When Hilarion was demoted, some in the Vatican worried Rome had lost a key contact in the Russian Orthodox world. But on 29 April 2023, the day after I met Hilarion, I saw pictures of Francis kissing Hilarion's pectoral cross. Far from being ostracised, Hilarion still appeared to be acting as Kirill's right-hand man. The Pope has noticeably toned down his criticism of the Patriarch since he scolded him for being 'Putin's altar boy' at the beginning of the war. Francis' suggestion in March 2024 that Ukraine should have the courage 'to raise the white flag' and negotiate a settlement with the invaders was met with consternation in Kyiv and its Western allies.

Hilarion may also be running errands for the Kremlin. Even if Hungary is a backwater in Orthodox terms, politically it is a staunch Putin ally. The populist right-wing president, Viktor Orbán, has dragged his heels on EU sanctions against Russia and blocked

European and US-led efforts to support Ukraine. In September 2022, Hungary's deputy prime minister, Zsolt Semjén, received a Patriarchal Order of Glory and Honour, 2nd class, on a royal blue ribbon. This award came a few months after Kirill was taken off the EU sanctions list, at Hungary's insistence.

☦ ☦ ☦

On initial reflection, it might seem that the Patriarch has flourished under Putin; he has political power at the right hand of the country's leader, alongside spiritual hegemony for the resurgent Orthodox faith. He prides himself on combining modern technology with old-fashioned values. He portrays his close relations with the Kremlin as a twenty-first century version of the ancient Byzantine doctrine of *symphonia*, in which church and state work together for the good of the nation. Apart from the military and the FSB, no other organisation has enjoyed such prominence and protection in post-Soviet Russia. With more than 100 million believers, he leads by far the largest national church in global Orthodoxy. He has enormous resources at his fingertips, including generous funds for church building. He leads a luxurious lifestyle with fleets of cars and mansions at his disposal.

But there is another way to read this: Kirill has earned that power by debasing his church and its liturgy. Once he became an active combatant in the war, he tied his personal fate to Putin's and that of his clique and lost his spiritual authority. He quotes the Bible not to teach Christian values and illuminate his flock, but to support the Kremlin's military and political goals. Instead of recruiting souls, he has become an army recruiter. As casualties mount, he promotes a death cult, urging Russians to lay down their lives in Putin's unprovoked war against Ukraine to 'wash away their sins'. Hovorun, his former advisor, suggests Kirill has replaced the Christian concept of martyrdom with a brand of religious terrorism. 'Martyrs sacrifice their own lives, whereas religiously motivated terrorists sacrifice their lives *and* the lives of others,' he said.[41]

A document approved by the Church at the end of March 2024, *The Present and Future of the Russian World*, goes even further.

It states that Russia is fighting 'a Holy War' to save humanity 'from the onslaught of globalism and the victory of the West, which has fallen into Satanism'. Such Manichean rhetoric has long punctuated Kirill's wartime sermons. But the document also states that 'the entire territory of modern Ukraine should enter the zone of exclusive influence of Russia' and that the possibility of any regime hostile to Russia there 'must be completely excluded'.[42] The last two words imply that any Ukrainian who does not want to live in this 'zone' must somehow be eliminated. One Ukrainian theologian says the document endorses genocide.[43] He compares it to tracts of the *Deutsche Glaubensbewegung*, the pro-Nazi church movement of 1930s Germany which supported the doctrine of the Third Reich, sacralising xenophobia, sanctioning the unification of church and state, along with the synthesis of Christianity and German National Socialism.

The Patriarch's pitiless aggression towards Ukraine flouts Christ's second-most important commandment – after loving God, to love thy neighbour as thyself. As a result, he has lost some of his best clerics to his arch-rival in the Orthodox world. Bartholomew has taken many anti-war priests defrocked by the Moscow Patriarchate under his wing. The clerical 'refugees' include the popular Archpriest Alexei Uminsky, now serving in France, and Father Ioann Koval, who was sacked after praying for peace instead of victory and is now in a parish in Antalya, Turkey. The five defrocked Lithuanians are back in the pulpit; instead of driving taxis, now they serve the Ecumenical Patriarch. The outspoken Protodeacon Andrei Kuraev was also restored to his rank by Constantinople.

Kirill's unwavering support for the war has alienated millions of Ukrainian believers and severed relations with Kyiv after three centuries of domination from Moscow. Perhaps he sees this as unavoidable collateral damage in the service of a greater cause. But he stands to lose more than Ukraine. His approach has splintered a faith with 300 million believers around the world. Orthodox communities across Africa are in turmoil after Kirill bribed hundreds of priests to side with Moscow. One Kenyan bishop I spoke to complained of 'an invasion creating confusion, division and chaos'.[44] For many, these tensions evoke the Great Schism, a millennium ago, which separated the Orthodox East from the Catholic West. Bartholomew has tried for decades to bring all the Eastern Orthodox churches together but has been continually rebuffed by Moscow. Russian clerics have long resented Bartholomew's title of 'First among Equals' and his status as the most senior figure in the Orthodox world. Archimandrite Feofan, the monk who invited me to lunch in the frontline monastery of Svyatohirsk, called the *tomos* Bartholomew granted Ukraine 'uncanonical' and dismissed the OCU as 'a Turkish church'. Clerics like him distrust Bartholomew's more tolerant and cosmopolitan approach to Orthodoxy.

In many ways, Bartholomew is diametrically opposed to his Russian counterpart, according to Archbishop Nikitas Loulias, the most senior cleric of the Ecumenical Patriarchate in the UK. Nikitas has known both Kirill and Bartholomew for decades. He told me that Bartholomew, the son of a barber who ran a coffee shop, has never forgotten his roots. He often visits the island of Imbros, now known by its Turkish name, Gökçeada, in the Aegean Sea. 'Bartholomew is one of these people who does not live in his own world,' said Nikitas. 'He lives in the reality of the world around him, that is why he is so involved in issues like modern slavery, human trafficking and climate change.' Bartholomew is known as the 'Green Patriarch' for his focus on the environment. Back in 1997, he was the first global religious leader to call harm to the natural world a sin against God.

Nikitas himself was born in Florida to an ethnic Greek family but studied at the spiritual academy in St Petersburg. He said Kirill treated him well when they met but there was a certain distance: 'He was not exactly standoffish, but in the Moscow Patriarchate you always felt there was a wall between them and everyone else. A false formality.' In contrast, whenever Nikitas dines with Bartholomew, the Patriarch often gets up from the table to serve his guests the dishes himself. Like Pope Francis, Bartholomew strives, in a low-key fashion, to be more inclusive on social issues, including gay rights. Nikitas assured me that disaffected Slav believers are flocking to the services of the Ecumenical Patriarchate across Europe. 'If the Church in Russia is doing such a great job,' he said, 'why do so few of their people go to church?' It is hard to predict which vision of Orthodoxy will prevail – one which is interested in adapting to the modern world or one inspired by imperial conquest and inquisitions which hark back to medieval times.

In repressing any clerics who oppose his brand of Orthodoxy, Kirill has become an accomplice of Putin's security state. But the disease has spread right through the Church. The problem is not just that there is one person at the top who has become authoritarian. There is an infrastructure below him staffed by people who have no conscience and blindly carry out orders. Dismissing priests for opposing the war shows the hierarchy's contempt for its subordinates and spits in the face of Russia's believers.

In my travels across Russia and Ukraine, I have been struck by the bravery of some remarkable individuals. But the relationship between the Church hierarchy and political might has barely changed over the centuries. Regardless of what transpires on the battlefield, or what happens to Russia's economy or what sort of intrigues unfold inside the Kremlin, the Church will try to exploit the growing conflict between East and West to cement its authority. For more than a millennium, it has shown astonishing survival skills. From the Mongol yoke, to tsarist demagoguery and enlightenment, Soviet atheism, the chaotic 1990s and an increasingly dictatorial Vladimir Putin, it has demonstrated an uncanny ability to ingratiate itself with power.

ACKNOWLEDGEMENTS

Many people in Russia, Ukraine and beyond have given me invaluable support to navigate the complexities of Orthodoxy, particularly at a time of war. Some of them are mentioned in this book, others have preferred to remain anonymous.

Yaroslava Kiryukhina, a BBC colleague, greatly assisted with research and contacts among the clergy, including her father, Archpriest Alexander Kiryukhin. He welcomed me into his church in Aprelevka on the outskirts of Moscow and introduced me to fellow priests, choir singers and parishioners. London-based journalist Anna Pivovarchuk also helped me to conduct interviews online at a time when many Russians were reluctant to speak to foreigners, and her assistance has proved invaluable.

Among the Orthodox clergy I would like to thank Archpriest Kirill Kaleda, rector of the Church of the New Martyrs in Butovo; Father Georgy Edelstein, who served at the Church of the Resurrection of Christ in the village of Karabanovo, Kostroma region; Father Ioann Burdin, who replaced him but was banned from ministry for opposing the war; Archpriest Andrei Kordochkin, whom I first met at the Cathedral of Saint Mary Magdalene in Madrid; Sister Vassa Larin, for her insights into Orthodox rituals and politics; Archimandrite Cyril Hovorun, who helped with introductions across the Orthodox world; Vladimir Seliavko, Gintaras Sungaila and Vitalijus Mockus, now serving in Vilnius under the Patriarchate of Archpriest Vladimir Sorokin, of the Prince Vladimir Cathedral in St Petersburg;

Archpriest Konstantin Kobelev, who visits prisons in the Moscow region; monks Brother Feofil and Father David, who demonstrated a unique style of liturgical singing known on Valaam; Hieromonk Geronty Chudnevich, who built northern monasteries; Archpriest Maxim Minyailo of the Church on the Blood in Yekaterinburg; Viktor Norkin, a former seminary teacher; Maxim Mitrofanov, former bishop of Cherepovets; Archpriest Stephen Platt of the Oxford church of St Nicholas the Wonderworker; and Father Christopher Hill of St Catherine's Church in Moscow, who inspired me with his passion for the Orthodox liturgy when we first met in 2000.

I owe a special debt to Misha Glenny, rector of the Institute for Human Sciences (IWM), where I spent an enjoyable and highly stimulating three months in spring 2023. I had many lively conversations with many of the other fellows at IWM on a variety of topics. Apart from Misha, I am particularly grateful to Ivan Krastev, Kirill Rogov, Katherine Younger, Mischa Gabowitsch, Mariia Shynkarenko and Clemena Antonova for their many suggestions and advice. Maria Derntl and Franz Graf made me feel at home, while Katharina Gratz and Zsófia Koós procured books from Vienna's university libraries to aid my research. Aleksandr Verkhovsky, director of the SOVA Centre, which monitors religion and nationalism in Russia, made time for me during my last visit to Moscow.

In the UK I would like to thank: Richard Davies for his hauntingly beautiful photographic work documenting the churches of northern Russia; Richard Temple and Ivan Samarine for sharing their expertise on icons; Geraldine Norman, an authority on Russian art and advisor to the State Hermitage Museum; Professor Simon Franklin, Emeritus Professor of Slavonic Studies at Cambridge; Dr Serhii Shumylo, director of the International Institute of the Athonite Legacy, who sent me many useful pieces of research; Alan McCormack, dean of Goodenough College in London, connecting me to the Ecumenical Patriarch's clergy; the Rev Canon Malcolm Rogers, former chaplain at St Andrews Anglican Church in Moscow; Orlando Figes, one of the most respected writers on Russian history, who provided wise counsel; Bruce Clark for his perspectives on Russia's leading religious thinkers; Victoria Clark for her original take on Orthodoxy across Eastern Europe and the

Balkans; Dr Robert Collins of Birkbeck University, who investigated the split in Britain's Orthodox community; Elisabeth Schimpfössl of Aston University, for her work on well-heeled Russians; Sir Rodric Braithwaite, author and ambassador when the Soviet Union fell apart; Sir Laurie Bristow, who served as the UK's ambassador to Moscow nearly two decades later; Xenia Dennen, a Russian specialist and chairman of the Keston Institute, Oxford, and her colleague in Texas, Larisa Seago, who curates the archives of this organisation dedicated to the religious diversity of Russia and the defence of believers' rights.

Rock critic, concert promoter and all-round cultural guru Artemy Troitsky has helped me in countless ways over the years and generously put me up in Moscow when I started researching this book. More recently, he read a draft and made several suggestions. Francis Fitzgibbon cast a fresh eye on the text, while Jan Butler also read the manuscript and enhanced many of my translations from the Russian.

A number of journalists and filmmakers have also shared their ideas and experiences with me, including Zoya Svetova, Andrei Soldatov, Irina Borogan, Albina Kovalyova, Oleksandr Soldatov, Sergei Bychkov, Tetyana Derkach, Nikolai Mitrokhin, Tatyana Movshevich, Svetlana Stasenko, Andrei Zolotov, Ilya Arkhipov, Sergei Khazov Cassia, Felix Corley, Michael Simkin, Anđela Milivojević, Kirsty Lang, Bernhardt Odehnal, Tessa Szyszkowitz, Elisalex Henckel, Irina Varskaya, Mike Lanchin, Kristine Pommert, Mike Gallagher, Bridget Harney, Penny Murphy, Nick Sturdee, Tim Whewell, Arseniy Sokolov, Emily Buchanan, Helen Grady, Lionel Barber, Juliet Butler and the art historian Catherine Phillips. Sergei Erzhenkov's films for TV Dozhd deserve a special mention. Ksenia Luchenko's articles and Telegram channel 'Orthodoxy and zombies' are among the best sources for what is happening inside the Church. I was happy to be joined by Aleksander Palikot and Andre Luis Alves in eastern Ukraine. Kenneth Perry and his colleagues at Cosain run an excellent hostile environments course for freelancers and distribute regular security briefings for which I am grateful.

This book owes much to the people I got to know on my first visits to Russia and Ukraine. Galina Novikova and her parents Viktor and Larisa Vzyatyshev invited me to stay in their two-room apartment in the Shchyolkovskaya district of Moscow and ignited my lifelong fascination with Russia. Later, I was introduced to the poet Yevgeny Yevtushenko and his family, and spent memorable days with them at their home in the writers' colony of Peredelkino. Vira Nanivska, whom I first met when she was a psychology professor at Moscow State University, left for her native Ukraine to run a foreign policy and governance think tank after the collapse of the USSR. More recently, she threw open her home in the Carpathians to refugees from the war. Tatiana Yurkova hosted me in Kyiv, her colleague Stepan Davidyuk drove me to many places in Ukraine and her next-door neighbour, an Orthodox priest, calmed my nerves when the bomb sirens went off. I am also indebted to my friends the novelist Andrei Kurkov and his wife Elisabeth for their insights, wit and hospitality over the years.

I was delighted to have been engaged by my agent Catherine Clarke at Felicity Bryan. She was extremely constructive and supportive at the outset and set me on the path of writing this book. I am also grateful to Duncan Heath, the former publisher and editorial director of Icon Books, who commissioned *The Baton and the Cross*. Since then, throughout the writing process, my editor Connor Stait has been an excellent guiding hand. Thanks also to copy editor Steve Burdett and Rhiannon Morris, publicist at Icon Books.

Sadly, my parents Clare and Eric are no longer with us, but I hope they would have approved. My sisters have been a source of great comfort over the last two years. Alex and Constance, my amazing daughters, have cheered me on. I owe the biggest debt to my husband John Kampfner. Without his love, expertise and tireless support, I would never have attempted, let alone finished, this book.

ENDNOTES

Prologue

1. Evgenia Kirichenko, *Moscow's Cathedral of Christ the Savior: Its Creation, Destruction, and Rebirth, 1813–1997*. Translated by. Thomas H. Hoisington.
2. Letter 1609 to Nadezhda von Meck, 8/20–10/22 October 1880.
3. Igor Grabar, *Peterburgskaia Arkhitektura*, pp. 283–84.
4. Konstantin Akinsha and Grigorij Kozlov with Sylvia Hochfield, *The Holy Place: Architecture, Ideology, and History in Russia*, p. 88.
5. Evgenia Kirichenko, *Moscow's Cathedral of Christ the Savior*, p. 238.
6. Ibid., p. 352.
7. Extract from Pasternak's memoirs, reproduced in I. Ilovaiskaya-Alberti's book *Razrushenie* (Destruction), pp. 34–35.
8. Konstantin Akinsha and Grigorij Kozlov with Sylvia Hochfield, *The Holy Place*, p. 122.
9. Karl Schlégel, in *Naum Gabo and the Competition for the Palace of Soviets*, Moscow, 1931–1933 (Berlin: Berlinische Galerie, 1993), p. 178.
10. Gleb Sobolev, 'Istoriya odnogo mesta', *Proekt Rossiya*, No. 2, 1996, p. 63.
11. V. P. Mokrousov, 'Blagoye delo', and Vladimir Potapov, 'Narodnaya svyatynya', in Khram Khrista Spasitelya: Sozdaniye-razrusheniye-vozrozhdeniye (a special edition of *Pravda*), April 1992, p. 1.
12. Vladimir Soloukhin, *Searching for Icons in Russia*, Harvill Press London 1971, p. 18.
13. http://obchina-xxc.ru/news/100_letie_velikogo_georgija_sviridova/2015-12-13-291
14. 'Obrashcheniye prezidenta Rossiiskoi Federatsii k chlenam obshchestvennogo nablyudatel'nogo soveta po vossozdaniyu Khrama Khrista Spasitelya' (8 September 1994), in ibid., p. 214.

Introduction

1. Jean-François Colosimo Albin Michel, *La Crucifixion de l'Ukraine*, October 2022.
2. Spas TV channel 'War and the Bible', 21 November 2022: https://rutube.ru/video/0f225bbb5fa998d009d6e17448b0fc22/?playlist=233429&playlistPage=1
3. Alexander Solzhenitsyn from *Stories and Prose Poems*, translated by Michael Glenny, 1970, pp. 214–16.

Chapter 1

1. Особенности национального пиара [Peculiarities of National PR], OLMA Media Group, pp. 85–86. Vladimir Medinsky tells about the art of managing society – from Vladimir Monomakh to Joseph Stalin.
2. Yaroslav Hrytsak, *Ukraine, The Forging of a Nation*, Sphere, p. 47.
3. V.N. Tatishchev, *Istoriia rossiiskaia*, 7 volumes (Moscow-Leningrad: 1962–1968), vol. 2, pp. 61 & 227.
4. https://www.pravmir.ru/vtoroe-kreshhenie-rusi-film-mitropolita-volokolamsko-go-ilariona-video/
5. Anna Smolchenko, 'Disney Looks to Reanimate Russia's Cartoon Sector', *The St Petersburg Times*, 2 May 2006: https://tinyurl.com/6dmzef55
6. https://www.rbc.ru/politics/21/05/2015/555c4c609a79476fc40b2037
7. Victoria Clark, *Why Angels Fall*, Picador 2000, p. 23.
8. Author conversation with Michael Binyon, February 2024.

Chapter 2

1. Sir Rodric Braithwaite, 'A Tale of Two Ivans', *The Invention of ...*, BBC Radio 4, 9 January 2023: https://www.bbc.co.uk/programmes/m001gx4h
2. Quoted by Berthold Spuhler, *The Golden Horde. Mongols in Rus' (1223–1502)*.
3. https://pravoslavie.ru/6866.html 27 October 2006, Hieromonk Job (Gumerov). This is the website edited by Tikhon Shevkunov, the powerful cleric seen as Putin's personal confessor.
4. *New York Times*, 3 August 2014: https://www.nytimes.com/2014/08/03/world/europe/from-pilgrims-putin-seeks-political-profit.html
5. *Gazeta Ru*, 20 July 2014: https://rg.ru/2014/07/21/putin.html
6. https://www.newsru.com/russia/24sep2010/putin.html 24 September 2010. The Pskov diocese refuted the 'utter nonsense' that Putin's wife became the abbess of the monastery.
7. *The Fall of an Empire: The Lesson of Byzantium*, 2008: https://www.youtube.com/watch?v=FdZz7pmWdF0

Chapter 3

1. T. Hunczak, *Russian Imperialism from Ivan the Great to the Revolution*, New Brunswick 74, p. ix (quoted by Orlando Figes).
2. Oleg Gordievsky and Christopher Andrew, *KGB: The Inside Story of Its Intelligence Operations from Lenin to Gorbachev*, 1999.
3. Benson Bobrick, *Fearful Majesty – The Life and Reign of Ivan the Terrible*, p. 84 quoting the Russian historian Solovyov.
4. John Malov from the St Elizabeth convent in Minsk: https://catalog.obitel-minsk.com/blog/2022/08/ivan-the-terrible-how-could-faith-and-violence-coexist-in-one-person
5. Lies about Ivan the Terrible: https://vse.kz/blog/1432/entry-31896-lozh-ob-ivane-groznom/
6. https://youtu.be/hRAgSGhHP5w Archpriest Chaplin: God sanctioned the destruction of people, Ekho Moskvy Radio, 15 August 2016.

7. Radio Liberty, 16 August 2016: https://www.svoboda.org/a/27926421.html
8. MoskovskyKonsomolets,16October2016:https://www.mk.ru/social/2016/10/16/pozor-i-neschaste-rossii.html
9. Isaiah Gruber, *Orthodox Russia in Crisis*, Northern Illinois University Press, 2012, p. 8.
10. A.N. Mouravieff, *A History of the Church of Russia*, 1842 (reprinted 2004), p. 166.
11. https://www.upi.com/News_Photos/view/upi/40b791fcc335f6283f63b-5b181e94bc8/President-Putin-Attends-the-National-Unity-Day/
12. Georgy Fedotov, *Sviatiy Filip Paris*, YMCA press, 1928.
13. Philip Longworth Alexis, *Tsar of all the Russias*, page 96.
14. Orlando Figes, *The Story of Russia*, 2022.
15. Sainte Russie. *Souvenirs et Réflexions Grasset*, 1956.
16. Russian Welcomes Back Old Believers, 18 October 2019: https://www2.stetson.edu/religious-news/191018a.html

Chapter 4

1. Geoffrey Hosking, *Russia: People and Empire*, Harvard, 1997, p. 226.
2. Captain John Perry, *The State of Russia, Under the present Czar*, 1716.
3. Lindsey Hughes, *Russia in the Age of Peter the Great*, Yale University Press, April 2000.
4. Boris Uspenskij and Victor Zhivov, *'Tsar and God' and Other Essays in Russian Cultural Semiotics*, Boston, 2012, p. 231.
5. Robert K. Massie, *Peter the Great: His Life and World*, 1980.
6. Jovan E. Howe, 'Traditional Culture and the Old Ritualists', *Journal of Eastern Christian Studies* Volume 50, Issue: 3–4, 1998.
7. Evgeny Anisimov Lenizdat, *Vremya Petrovskih Reform*, 1999, p. 333.
8. A Lenten Letter, *New York Times*, 9 April 1972: https://www.nytimes.com/1972/04/09/archives/a-lenten-letter.html

Chapter 5

1. Richard Pipes, *Russian Under the Old Regime*, page 242
2. Isabel de Madariaga, *Russia in the Age of Catherine the Great*, Weidenfeld & Nicolson, 1981, pp. 114–18.
3. Portrait by the Danish court painter Vigilius Eriksen, 1778.
4. H. Rogger, *National Consciousness in 18th Century Russia*, Cambridge Mass, 1960, page 37.
5. Konstantin Netuzhilov, *Water of Life*, Journal of the St Petersburg Diocese, 2016.
6. Andrei V. Ivanov, *A Spiritual Revolution: The Impact of Reformation and Enlightenment in Orthodox Russia*, University of Wisconsin Press, 2020.
7. *Antony Lentin Voltaire and Catherine the Great: Selected correspondence*, Cambridge 1974, p. 49.
8. Geoffrey Hosking, *Russia: People and Empire*, p. 231.
9. How Putin Blundered into Ukraine, *Financial Times*, 23 February 2023: https://www.ft.com/content/80002564-33e8-48fb-b734-44810afb7a49

Chapter 6

1. *Kommersant*, 9 December 2013: https://www.kommersant.ru/doc/2359275
2. Lesley Chamberlain, *Ministry of Darkness: How Sergei Uvarov Created Conservative Modern Russia*, Bloomsbury Academic, p. 13.
3. Orlando Figes, *The Story of Russia*, Bloomsbury, p. 135.
4. https://philhist.spbu.ru/11-biblioteka/istochniki/138-radishchev-a-n-pute shestvie-iz-peterburga-v-moskvu.html
5. *The Siberian Times*, 24 July 2015: https://siberiantimes.com/other/others/news/n0326-new-handwriting-analysis-suggests-russia-tsar-did-not-die-as-history-books-said/
6. Lesley Chamberlain, *Ministry of Darkness*, p. 128.
7. Letter II, pp. 35–36: http://az.lib.ru/c/chaadaew_p_j/text_0010.shtml
8. Lesley Chamberlain, *Ministry of Darkness*, p. 128.
9. Ibid., p. 158.
10. Simon Sebag Montefiore, *The Romanovs*, Weidenfeld & Nicolson, 2016, p. 383.
11. Orlando Figes, *Natasha's Dance*, p. 331.
12. Alexander Herzen, My Past and Thoughts, Moscow 1958, p. 221.
13. David W. Edwards, 'The System of Nicholas I in Church–State Relations' in Robert L. Nichols and Theofanis George Stavrou, eds., *Russian Orthodoxy under the Old Regime*, University of Minneapolis Press, 1978, pp. 154–69.
14. Geoffrey Hosking, *Russia: People and Empire*, p. 234 quoting Igor Smolitsch, *Geschichte der russischen Kirche 1700–1917*.
15. https://www.encyclopedia.com/history/encyclopedias-almanacs-transcripts-and-maps/russian-orthodox-clergy
16. I.S. Belliustin, *Description of the Clergy in Rural Russia*, The Russia Reader Duke University Press, p. 123.
17. Revolt From Below, Gregory L Freeze from *Russian Orthodoxy Under the Old Regime*, p. 107.
18. Ibid.; Gregory L. Freeze, 'P.A. Valuyev and the Politics of Church Reform (1861–62)', *The Slavonic and East European Review*, Vol. 56, No. 1 (Jan 1978), pp. 68–87.
19. Gregory L. Freeze, *The Russian Levites: Parish Clergy in the Eighteenth Century*, Harvard University Press, 1977, pp. 194–210.
20. Letter of 8 July 1879 to Catherine Tiutcheva.
21. General Hans von Schweinitz, *Briefwechsel des Botschafters General v. Schweinitz*, Berlin, 1928, pp. 362–63; Louise Creighton, *Life and Letters of Mandell Creighton* (London, 1904), pp. ii, 150, 155.
22. Mikhail Zygar, *The Empire Must Die : Russia's Revolutionary Collapse 1900–1917*, New York Public Affairs, 2017.
23. Robert F. Byrnes, *Pobedonostsev: His Life and Thought*, Indiana University Press, pp. 358–68.
24. Mikhail Zygar, *The Empire Must* Die, chapter 1.
25. Marc Raeff, Review of *Pobedonostsev: His Life and Thought* by Robert F. Byrnes, *Political Science Quarterly*, 85(1970):3:528.
26. Translation by Nicholas Kotar: https://nicholaskotar.com/2017/11/17/constantine-great-russias-secret-tsar/

27. From an interview with Metropolitan Nizhny Novgorod, Nikolai Kutepov, Nezavisimaya Gazeta, Section Figures and Faces, 26.4.2001: http://krotov. info/spravki/1_history_bio/20_bio/1924kute.html

28. See for full statement of the Commission: https://encyclopaedia-russia.ru/article/ kanonizaciya-carskoj-semi/

29. Geoffrey Hosking, *Russia: People and Empire*, p. 244.

30. Douglas Smith, *Rasputin: Faith, Power, and the Twilight of the Romanovs*, p. 70.

31. Ibid.

Chapter 7

1. http://xn----dtbiacgg5bk6aido5c2d.xn--p1ai/museums/muzej_uralmashzavoda_ (g.ekaterinburg)/

2. Lyrics by Lev Oshanin, 1955: https://rupoem.ru/oshanin/den-za-dnem.aspx

3. Helen Rappaport, *Ekaterinburg: The Last Days of the Romanovs*, Windmill Books 2008, p. 1.

4. Comment of Yuri Andropov, chairman of the KGB, cited in *Rosisskaya Gazeta*: https://rg.ru/2013/05/29/reg-urfo/xram.html

5. Helen Rappaport, *Ekaterinburg*.

6. Yuri Slezkine, *The House of Government: A Saga of the Russian Revolution*, p. 164.

7. James Thrower, *God's Commissar*, University of Virginia, p. 39.

8. Dimitry Pospielovsky, *Soviet Antireligious Campaigns and Persecutions: Volume 2 of a History of Soviet Atheism in Theory and Practice and the Believer*, London: Macmillan, 1988, p. v.

9. Harvard historian Richard Pipes estimates that '300,000 clergymen' alone were killed by the Soviet regime. *Alexander Yakovlev: The Man Whose Ideas Delivered Russia from* Communism, DeKalb: Northern Illinois University Press, 2015, p. 67.

10. *The Red and the White*, BBC World Service, November 2017: https://www.bbc. co.uk/programmes/w3csvsjq

11. https://www.fragrantica.com/news/Smolny-Institution-for-Nobl e-Maidens-founded-by-Catherine-the-Great-16184.html

12. Richard Pipes (ed.), *The Unknown Lenin: From the Secret Archive* (1996), pp. 152–54.

13. Celebrations in honour of the Shuya new martyrs in the Resurrection Cathedral in Shuya, 11 May 2022: https://shuya-eparhia.ru/2022/05/11/post_43083/ 2

14. Ivan M. Andreev, *A Brief Overview of the History of the Church of Russia from the Revolution to Our Days*, Jordanville, 1952.

15. Marx [1848], 1967.

16. A. L. Beglov, The concept of 'catacomb church': myths and reality, Menevskie Readings, 2006, Scientific Conference.

17. Wallace L. Daniel (translator), *Women of the Catacombs: Memoirs of the Underground Orthodox Church in Stalin's Russia*, Cornell University, 2021, p. 12.

18. Ibid., p. 110.

19. Radio Vokreseniye: https://pravradio.ru/audioarchive/ct10/yr2015/mn7/dy30# a10021

20. Interview with author, 4 Feb 2024.
21. Quoted in Robert H. McNeal, *Stalin: Man and Ruler*, Macmillan Press, p. 241.
22. Stephen Kotkin, *Stalin, Volume One: Paradoxes of Power 1878–1928*, New York Penguin.
23. Simon Sebag Montefiore, *Young Stalin*, Weidenfeld & Nicolson, London, 2007, p. 46.
24. Ibid., p. 62.
25. Ronald Grigor Suny, 'Beyond Psychohistory: The Young Stalin in Georgia', *Slavic Review* 50: 48–58, 1991.
26. Archpriest Sergius (Gakkel), 'How does Western theology after Auschwitz relate to the thinking and liturgical life of the Russian Orthodox Church?' St Petersburg, 26–28 January 1998, 1999, p. 94.
27. Pravda o religii v Rossii 1942 Moskovskaya patriarkhiya (Moscow Patriarchate).
28. Steven Merritt Miner, *Stalin's Holy War*, University of Carolina Press, 2003, pp. 264–70.
29. https://www.episcopalarchives.org/e-archives/the_witness/pdf/1944_Watermarked/Witness_19440203.pdf
30. Ann Shukman, *Metropolitan Sergi Stragorodsky: The Case of the Representative Individual*.
31. *Journal of the Moscow Patriarchate*, No. 1, January 1944.
32. Charles Ashleigh, 'Radio in Russia', *Radio Times*, 6 January 1924.
33. https://pravoslavie.ru/7170.html
34. Michael Bourdeaux, *Opium of the People*, p 60.
35. Mikhail Danilushkin, *History of the Orthodox Church*, Chapter 16: Church life in the post-war period (1945–58): https://azbyka.ru/otechnik/Istorija_Tserkvi/istorija-russkoj-pravoslavnoj-tserkvi-ot-vosstanovlenija-patriarshestva-do-nashih-dnej-tom-1-1917-1970/16
36. Edward M. Bennett, 'The Russian Orthodox Church and the Soviet State, 1946–56: A Decade of the New Orthodoxy', *Journal of Church and State*, Vol. 7, No. 3, Autumn 1965, pp. 425–39.
37. Author email exchange with Nina Khrushcheva, November 2023.
38. *Bakinski Rabochi* [Baku worker], 19 June 1963, quoted in Michael Bourdeaux, *Patriarch and Prophets: Persecution of the Russian Orthodox Church Today*, London: Macmillan, 1969, p. 23.
39. *Izvestia*, 23 May 1961.
40. Icons in Space, *Foma*, 11 October 2019 https://foma.ru/aleksej-leonov-ikonyi-v-kosmose.html
41. https://twitter.com/letopisi_rus/status/1237334925361233921
42. Quoted from *Izvestiia* in Donald A. Lowrie and William C. Fletcher, 'Khrushchev's Religious Policy, 1959-1964' in *Aspects of Religion in the Soviet Union, 1917–1967*, ed. Richard H. Marshall (Chicago: University of Chicago Press, 1971), p. 145.
43. Xenia Dennen, Michael Bourdeaux obituary, *Guardian* 16 March 2021: https://www.theguardian.com/world/2021/apr/16/michael-bourdeaux-obituary
44. Michael Bourdeaux, *Opium of the People*, p. 210.
45. Ibid., p. 212

46. Dmitry Pospielovsky, *The Orthodox Church in the History of Russia*, St Vladimir's Seminary Press, 1998, p. 325.

47. Victoria Smolkin, *A Sacred Space Is Never Empty*, p. 58.

48. *Combating God and Grandma – The Soviet Antireligious Campaigns and the Battle for Childhood*, Julie de Graffenried talking about the poster V.A.Travin 'You cannot see God's light'(1975). Image courtesy of Keston Center for Religion, Politics, and Society, Baylor University.

49. *Clouds Over Borsk*, directed by Vasili Ordynsky, 1960: https://www.youtube.com/watch?v=2tAvcEqsLaQ

50. Anna Sokolova, 'Soviet Funeral Services: From Moral Economy to Social Welfare and Back', *Revolutionary Russia* 32(4):1–21, November 2019.

51. Email exchange between author and Anna Sokolova, University of Helsinki, Feb 2024.

52. Nina Khrushcheva, *The Lost Khrushchev: A Journey into the Gulag of the Russian Mind*, Tate Publishing, 2014.

53. Peter H. Juviler, 'The Family in the Soviet System,' The Carl Beck Papers in Russian and East European Studies, no. 306 (1984): 13.

54. Eshliman and Yakunin, 'Open Letter to His Holiness', 203, 211.

55. Michael Bourdeaux, *Patriarch and Prophets*, p. 199.

56. Thirty-five nations, including the Soviet Union, signed the Helsinki Accords. 'Helsinki Accords, Article 7,' 1 August 1975: https://berkleycenter. georgetown.edu/qkuotes/helsinki-accords-article-7.

57. Archpriest Victor Potapov, *A Light Shining in* Darkness. Shortened and translated from 'Possev', May 1986; a lecture originally delivered November 1985 in Nyack, NY: https://roca.org/oa/volume-vi/issue-59-60/a-light-shining-in-darkness/

58. Zoya Krakhmalnikova, *Listen, Prison!: Lefortovo Notes, Letters from Exile*, Redding, California: Nikodemos Orthodox Publication Society, 1993.

59. Ibid.

60. https://lib.misto.kiev.ua/POLITOLOG/yakowlewnn.txt

61. Zoya Krakhmalnikova, *Listen, Prison! Lefortovo Notes, Letters from Exile*.

62. https://topreading.ru/book-188676-feliks-svetov-otverzi-mi-dveri (published YMCA).

Chapter 8

1. *Komsomolskaya Pravda* – Volgograd, 30 December 2004 interview with Vladimir Baglaysky.

2. For the 20th anniversary of the Cathedral of Christ the Savior: what role did Soloukhin play in its restoration? https://youfrom.ru/en/2020/08/20/k-20-letiyu-hrama-hrista-spasitelya-kakuyu-rol-solouhin-syigral-v-ego-vosstanovlenii/

3. Michael Dobbs, 'Soviet Leader, Wife Reveal Being Baptised', *Washington Post*, 6 July 1989.

4. B.A. Filippov, The impact of the Soviet-American negotiations of 1985–89 on changes in Soviet faith policy: historical and political contexts of Gorbachev's visit to the Vatican: https://periodical.pstgu.ru/en/pdf/article/7801

5. Ibid.

6. Alexander Soldatov, 'Patriarch of the Entire USSR', *Novaya Gazeta*, 3 June 2021: https://novayagazeta.ru/articles/2021/06/03/patriarkh-vsego-sssr (the article quotes historian Maxim Mastykin, a former employee of the Publishing Department of the Moscow Patriarchate about Pimen recruitment by the security services)

7. Soviet Religious Propaganda Apparatus and Operations, February 1987: https://www.cia.gov/readingroom/docs/DOC_0000761608.pdf

8. Lessons Learned from Gorbachev's anti Alcohol Campaign, *Sputnik News*, 6 May 2020. The viniculturist was Dr Pavel Gologriga: https://sputnikglobe.com/20200506/lessons-learned-from-gorbachevs-anti-alcohol-campaign-1079221047.html

9. Bill Keller, *The New York Times*, 8 June 1987.

10. Wallace L. Daniel, *Russia's Uncommon Prophet: Father Aleksandr Men and His Times*, 2016.

11. Savely Yamschikov, *The Art Newspaper*, June 1993: https://www.theartnewspaper.com/1993/06/01/conservator-on-conflict-with-russian-orthodox-church-we-saved-church-art

12. Author's interview with Sorokin, autumn 2022.

13. Steve Raymer, 'Clergymen serve prisoners in Russia', *National Geographic*, 25 March 1992.

14. Gleb Kaleda, 'Stop on your ways – Notes From a Prison Priest': https://azbyka.ru/otechnik/Gleb_Kaleda/ostanovites-na-putjah-vashih-zapiski-tyuremnogo-svjashhennika/

15. Rodric Braithwaite, *Across Moscow River – The World turned Upside Down*, Yale University Press, p. 101.

16. Jane Ellis, *The Russian Orthodox Church: Triumphalism and Defensiveness*, Palgrave MacMillan, 1996

17. John Kampfner Cassell, *Inside Yeltsin's Russia*, 1994, p. 44.

18. Elena Alekseeva Vadim Kantor, Interview with Alexander Borisov about the 1991 coup. *Pravmir*, 26 August 2016: https://www.pravmir.ru/protoierey-aleksandr-borisov-ya-prosil-soldat-ne-podnimat-oruzhiya/

19. John Burgess, *Holy Rus': The Rebirth of Orthodoxy in the New Russia*, Yale University Press, 21 February 2017.

20. Flore Martinant de Preneuf, *The Historical and Political Significance of the Reconstruction of the Cathedral of Christ the Saviour in Moscow*, 1997, p. 49.

21. Author interview, March 2023.

22. M Ardov, 'We Have More Important Tasks than Building Christ the Saviour', *Izvestia*, 13 July 1994. The priest left the Moscow Patriarchate soon afterwards and joined a noncanonical church in Suzdal, north of the capital.

23. VTSIOM poll institute, survey conducted on 12–13 September 1994: 'Do you agree with the Moscow authorities' decision to rebuild the cathedral of Christ the Saviour?'

24. Author interview by phone, April 2023.

25. Nikolai Zyat'kov, 'Kto stroit nash domT', *Argumenty ifakty*, no. 34, 24 August 1995, p. 3.

26. 'Khram-Spasitelia stanovitsia simvolom rossiiskogo kapitalizma,' *Finansovye izvestiia,* 29 August 1995.

27. Interview with Thomas Calice Kalmar Lighting, Vienna, March 2023.

28. 'Presidents, Patriarchs and Profits', BBC *TimeWatch* presented by art historian Gerladine Norman: https://www.youtube.com/watch?v=eCTZr84duls

29. Valeriy V Chervyakov a, Vladimir M Shkolnikov b, William Alex Pridemore c, Martin McKee d, 'The changing nature of murder in Russia', *Social Science & Medicine*, Volume 55, Issue 10, November 2002.

30. Olga Matich, *'Whacked but Not Forgotten': Burying the Mob*, Stanford University, 2001.

31. *Pravmir*, 12 June 2005: https://www.pravmir.ru/ya-starayus-ne-prileplyatsy a-k-zemnym-veshham/

32. Elisabeth Schimpfossl, *Rich Russians*, Oxford University Press, 2018.

33. Author interview, December 2023.

34. Donald Jensen, *The Boss: How Luzhkov runs Moscow*, Nov 1999: https://demokratizatsiya.pub/archives/08-1_Jensen.PDF

35. Kirichenko, in L. Polinovskaya(ed.), *Khram Khrista Spasitelya*, p. 27.

36. Flore de Preneuf, 'Facade of glory: a Potemkin cathedral for the new Russia', *Wall Street Journal*, 24 November 1996.

37. Konstantin Akinsha, *The Holy Place Architecture, Ideology and History in Russia – The Concrete Cathedral*, Yale University Press, 2007.

38. http://rusbaptist.stunda.org/dop/jakunin.htm

39. Flore de Preneuf, *Facade of Glory.*

40. https://radonezh.ru/2021/07/09/vladimir-resin-za-desyat-let-v-moskve-post roili-pravoslavnye-hramy-obshchey-vmestimostyu

41. Author interview with Richard Temple, June 2023.

42. 'Presidents, Patriarchs and Profits', BBC *TimeWatch.*

Chapter 9

1. 'How the Russian Government Fell in Love with Mysticism', *Proekt Media*, 29 May 2019: https://www.proekt.media/en/article-en/kremlins-elder-elijah/he Kremlin's Elder

2. 'Divorce of the Putin couple has no religious aspect', TASS news agency, 11 June 2013: https://tass.com/archive/694795

3. Anna Politkovskaya, *Putin's Russia*, Harvill, 2007, p. 280.

4. Vladimir Putin, *First Person: An Astonishingly Frank Self-Portrait by Russia's President Vladimir Putin*, Publicaffairs Reports, April 2000.

5. George W. Bush, *Decision Points*, Crown, 9 Nov 2010.

6. No soul? Who? Me?, NBC News, 15 June 2021: https://youtu.be/tIkTrYg4AdE

7. BBC *Breakfast with Frost*, 5 March 2000: http://news.bbc.co.uk/hi/english/static/audio_video/programmes/breakfast_with_frost/transcripts/putin5.mar.txt

8. John Kampfner, 'A president craves understanding: Vladimir Putin gives our political editor a homily, over tea and fruit cake', *New Statesman*, 13 September 2004.

9. Choosing Order Before Freedom, 19 December 2007: https://content.time.com/time/specials/2007/personoftheyear/article/0,28804,1690753_1690757,00.html

10. J. Hemment, 'Nashi, Youth Voluntarism, and Potemkin NGOs: Making Sense of Civil Society in Post-Soviet Russia', *Slavic Review*, 71(2), 2012, pp 234–60.

11. Filipp Bobkov and Eduard Makarevich, *The KGB and Power*, Rodina, Moscow, 2019.

12. https://tvrain.tv/teleshow/reportazh/putin_ne_verujuschij_chelovek_eks_bankir-450387/

13. Sovietskaya Rossiya, *Church and State*, 1990.

14. Quoted by Bruce Clark in The Tablet, 14 April 2022 https://www.thetablet.co.uk/features/2/21764/how-putin-s-faith-in-philosophy-is-underpinning-the-use-of-force-in-ukraine

15. Quoted by Robert E Berls Jnr in Nuclear Threat Inititiative, June 2021: https://www.nti.org/analysis/articles/strengthening-russias-influence-in-international-affairs-part-ii-russia-and-its-neighbors-a-sphere-of-influence-or-a-declining-relationship/

16. Anna Akhmatova, 'Courage', 23 February 1942, Translation by D.M. Thomas.

17. Kirill Metropolitan of Smolensk and Kaliningrad. Transcript of council hearings Russian World Assembly 1996, 12 November – quoted by Dmitry Adamsky, *Russian Nuclear Orthodoxy*, Stanford, p. 75.

18. Ruslan Kadrmatov, 'Priests Will Eradicate Hazing', *Nezavisimaya Gazeta*, 11/19/2003.

19. Putin visits the Panteleimon Monastery on Mount Athos, the official YouTube channel of the Moscow Patriarchate, 31 May 2016: https://youtu.be/arbrYjFV8l4

20. Alexander Dugin interviewed by the Dutch Protestant newspaper *Reformatorisch Dagblad*, 7 March 2018: https://www.rd.nl/artikel/747208-stem-van-een-patriot-echt-de-russische-wereld-bestaat

21. Author interview with Cyril Hovorun, November 2023.

22. William J. Burns, *The Back Channel: A Memoir of American Diplomacy and the Case for Its Renewal*, 2020.

23. Quoting an interview in the now defunct Televisoon suisse Romande, 9 October 2015: https://english.alarabiya.net/News/middle-east/2015/10/09/Archbishop-of-Syria-s-Aleppo-welcomes-Russia-strikes-

24. Marat Gabidullin, *Moi, Marat, ex-commandant de l'armée Wagner – Les dessous de l'armée secrète de Poutine enfin révélés: Au coeur de l'armée de Vladimir Poutine*, Michel Lafon, 12 May 2022.

25. *Jerusalem Post*, 7 July 2008: https://www.inopressa.ru/article/07jul2008/jpost/jerus.html

26. Andrei Soldatov and Irina Borogan, *The Compatriots*, Public Affairs, 2019, p. 204.

27. Sophia Kishkovsky, *The New York Times*, '2 Russian Churches, Split by War, Reuniting', 17 May 2007: the author is the daughter of a priest and grew up in Sea Cliff, the same Long Island emigre community as Jordan.

28. Author interview by phone with Peter Holodny, February 2024,

29. Andrei Soldatov and Irina Borogan, *The Compatriots*, p. 218.

30. Sarah Riccardi Swarz, *Between Heaven and Russia: Religious Conversion and Political Apostasy in Appalachia*.

31. Putin's Christian Russia as a Model for America – *The Revealer* Podcast, 7 April 2022: https://therevealer.org/putins-christian-russia-as-a-model-for-america/

32. Sarah Riccardi Swarz, *Between Heaven and Russia*.
33. 'Putin's Reunited Russian Church', *Time* magazine, 17 May 2007: https://content. time.com/time/world/article/0,8599,1622544,00.html
34. Rodric Braithwaite, *Across the Moscow River – The World turned Upside Down*, p. 36.
35. Bid to Ban Missionaries Fails in Russia, press-telegram, 28 August 1993.
36. Metropolitan Kirill, 'Tserkov bolshinstva v usloviiakh religiozni svobody', Tserkov i Vremya 1 (8) 85–100, 1999.
37. 'Russia's Persecuted Jehovah's Witnesses', *Heart and Soul*, BBC World Service, 18 October 2020: https://www.bbc.co.uk/programmes/w3ct1659
38. Yaroslav Sivulskiy: https://www.independent.co.uk/news/world/europe/russia-jehovahs-witness-crackdown-surgut-religion-discrimination-a8790761.html
39. Svetlana Solodovnik, Nikolai Pavlovich, 'What Are They Teaching Our Kids?', East–West Church Report 2005: https://www.eastwestreport.org/?view=article &id=511:2013-12-02-07-33-18&catid=86:1-r-13-1
40. Tobias Köllner, 'Patriotism, Orthodox religion and education: empirical findings from contemporary Russia', *Religion, State and Society*, Vol. 44, No. 4: http:// dx.doi.org/10.1080/09637494.2016.1246852
41. 30 August 2005: https://www.forum18.org/archive.php?article_id=639&pdf=Y
42. Ilia Peresedov, 'General Education or Parish Church Schools?' *New Times*, 3 September 2007: https://newtimes.ru/articles/detail/10464
43. 18 October 2023 interview on the Business Online website: https://m. business-gazeta.ru/amp/610809
44. *My Duty Not to Stay Silent*, a film by Vladimir Kara Murza: https://www.you-tube.com/watch?v=7LBJU6TLGoQ
45. Interview with author and in Georgiy Edelstien's book *Prava na Pravdu* (The Right to Truth).
46. Robert Weinberg, *Blood Libel in Late Imperial Russia: The Ritual Murder Trial of Mendel Beilis*, Bloomington: Indiana University Press, 2013.
47. *Haaretz*, 8 February 2008: https://www.haaretz.com/2008-02-08/ty-articl e/a-grave-with-a-particularly-sad-story/0000017f-db14-d856-a37f-ff-d449a40000
48. Irina Papkova, 'Contentious Conversation: Framing the "Fundamentals of Ortho-dox Culture" in Russia', *Religion, State and Society*, vol. 37, no. 3, September 2009, 300.
49. Exorcising demons (Orel-Zheleznogorsk), filmed by Dmitry Myznikov, Nov 2013: https://www.youtube.com/watch?v=bSOFYjNQPQ0
50. Mikhail Rubin, Roman Badanin, with Yulia Lukyanova and Maria Zholobova, 'The Elder of the Kremlin', *Proekt*, May 2019.

Chapter 10

1. *Patriarkh 2016 dir Saida Medvedeva* documentary, State channel Rossiya 1: https://www.youtube.com/watch?v=lrgIFFeWWcM
2. https://smolensk-i.ru/society/patriarh-kirill-potom-ya-ponyal-chto-sovsem-ne -sluchajno-gospod-privel-menya-v-gorod-smolensk_413489

3. Interview by Andrei Vandenko, *Pravmir,* March 2015: https://www.pravmir.com/patriarch-kirill-by-denying-god-s-truth-we-ruin-the-world/

4. Christopher Andrew, *The Sword and the Shield: The Mitrokhin Archive and the Secret History of the KGB,* 'The Penetration and Persecution of the Soviet Churches', Basic Books.

5. Felix Corley, 'The Svyatoslav Files: Metropolitan Nikodim and the KGB', 2018: https://www.academia.edu/37223006/The_Svyatoslav_Files_Metropolitan_Nikodim_and_the_KGB

6. Nevzorov interview with Yuri Dud, 2018: https://www.youtube.com/watch?v=zcjKJ7FHDL

7. FSB Central Archive, f. 5, op. 19, por. No. 273, d. E62, p. 90, quoted by Felix Corley, *The Mikhailov Files: Patriarch Kirill and the KGB,* 2018: https://www.academia.edu/37152767/The_Mikhailov_Files_Patriarch_Kirill_and_the_KGB?hb-g-sw=37256947

8. Yevgenia Albats, *The State Within a State: The KGB and Its Hold on Russia – Past, Present, and Future.* 1994, p. 46.

9. Felix Corley, 'The Svyatoslav Files: Metropolitan Nikodim and the KGB', 2018.

10. Email exchange with church historian Felix Corley regarding his research into the Mitrokhin archive.

11. 'Spy charges rock world of tiny church', *Calgary Herald,* 7 October 1999 – story triggered by publication of Christopher Andrew's book *The Sword and the Shield* on the Mitrokhin archive.

12. Yevgeny Komarov, 21 Feb 2020: https://ahilla.ru/nikodim-rotov-kirill-gundyaev-gosha-shevkunov-o-filme-papa-russkij-i-ne-tolko/

13. Konstantin Preobrazhensky, *Putin's Espionage Church,* the Centre of Counter Intelligence and Security Studies, 2008: https://web.archive.org/web/20081209002520/http://cicentre.com/Documents/putin_espionage_church.html

14. David Gill (ed.), *Gathered for Life: Official Report of the Sixth Assembly of the World Council of Churches,* p. 161: https://ia903105.us.archive.org/18/items/wcca20/wcca20.pdf

15. Felix Corley, *Religion in the Soviet Union: An Archival Reader,* p. 370.

16. Radio Liberty, 23 December 2018 – Yuvenaly and his KGB codename 'Adamant' is mentioned in Felix Corley's *The Mikhailov Files: Patriarch Kirill and the KGB,* 2018: https://www.radiosvoboda.org/a/29671187.html

17. KGB agent 'Drozdov' is identified as head of Russian Orthodox faith by Fen Montaigne, 10 May 1992.

18. Sir Rodric Braithwaite, *Across the Moscow River,* p. 36.

19. Interview in *Rossijskaia Gazeta,* 1992, No. 52, p. 7.

20. Mikhail Pozdnyayev, '"I Cooperated with the KGB ... but I Was Not an Informer": an Interview with Archbishop Khrizostom of Vilnius and Lithuania', *Religion, State & Society,* vol. 21, no. 3 & 4, 1993.

21. 'I Never Even Thought About Becoming a Senior Cleric', *Nezavisimaya Gazeta,* 2 October 2002: https://www.ng.ru/ng_religii/2002-10-02/1_mefodiy.html

22. 'Patriarch Alexei II: I Take upon Myself Responsibility for All that Happened', *Izvestia* No 137, 10 June 1991.

23. Quoted in Russian Patriarch 'was KGB spy' James Meek, *Guardian*, 12 February 1999.

24. Patriarch Kirill interview on NTV Metropolitan; Kirill: Putin, as a deeply religious person, sincerely contributed to the reunification of the Russian Church, 21 May 2007. Подробнее: https://www.newsru.com/religy/21may2007/putin.html

25. Russian Pope Sergei Erzhenkov, TV Dozhd, 2020: https://www.youtube.com/watch?v=tjDiDDVWQlA

26. Sylvain Besson, Bernhard Odehnal, 'With Putin's Pope in the Mountains', *Tages-Anzeiger*, 4 February 2023. Federal Police records, Switzerland, which go up to 1989 and then stop.

27. 'For Me He is Just Kirill', *Moskovskiy Komsomolets*, 29 January 2009: https://www.mk.ru/social/news/2009/01/29/2244-dlya-menya-on-prosto-kirill.html

28. Interview with Tamara Melnikova in *Russian Pope* – film on TV Dozhd presented by Sergei Erzhenkov.

29. *Russian Pope*, 40.33, Tamara Melnikova: https://www.youtube.com/watch?v=tjDiDDVWQlA

30. Andrei Vandenko, 'Patriarch Kirill, of Moscow and All Russia', in TASS special project Top Officials, 10 March 2015: https://tass.com/top-officials/781767

31. Interview with author, March 2023.

32. Interview with author, November 2023.

33. https://www.mk.ru/social/news/2009/01/29/2244-dlya-menya-on-prosto-kirill.html

34. Andrei Vandenko, 'Patriarch Kirill, of Moscow and All Russia'.

35. Interview with Kirill conducted by Andrei Vandenko for the news agency TASS, 2015: https://tass.com/top-officials/781767

36. Is Smoking a Sin, Pravoslavie website, Sretensky Monastery, 8 June 2016: https://pravoslavie.ru/94052.html

37. Andrei Zolotov, 'Orthodoxy, Oil, Tobacco, and Wine: Do They Mix?', East–West Church and Ministry Report, 1997: https://www.eastwestreport.org/articles/ew05108.htm

38. Alexander Soldatov, *Novaya Gazeta*, 4 August 2020: https://novayagazeta.ru/articles/2020/08/04/86520-sovsem-arhierei Also government letters reproduced in Kuraev's livejournal blog authorising the tax cuts: https://diak-kuraev.livejournal.com/1390222.html

39. *Presidents, Patriarchs and Profits*, BBC Two, 13 March 1999.

40. *Novaya Gazeta*, 4 August 2020: https://novayagazeta.ru/articles/2020/08/04/86520-sovsem-arhierei

41. Sergei Bychkov, 'Business-Tobacco; "To Smoke or Not to Smoke?"', *Moskovski Komsomolets*, 3 Oct 1996; and 'They [the Holy Synod] Removed Metropolitan Kirill from the Cigarette Trade', *Moskovski Komsomolets*, 5 January 1997.

42. Sergei Bychkov, 'Tabachniy Metropolit', *Moskovkiy Komsomolets*, 18 February 1997.

43. http://www.portal-credo.ru/site/?act=news&id=122775 Sergei Komkov

44. 11 May 2016: https://diak-kuraev.livejournal.com/1390222.html

45. Metropolitan Hilarion interviewed on 23 January 2009 by Interfax: https://web.archive.org/web/20120802191551/http://www.interfax-religion.ru/?act=interview&div=209

46. Aleksander Soldatov, *Novaya Gazeta*: https://novayagazeta.ru/articles/2012/02/14/48244-za-chto-rabu-bozhiemu-kirillu-blagodarit-171-raba-na-galerah-187

47. *Meduza*, 28 October 2020: https://meduza.io/en/feature/2020/10/28/new-proekt-investigation-uncovers-millions-of-dollars-in-real-estate-belonging-to-patriarch-kirill-and-his-family-members

48. Irina Pankratova, '"Smart home" for the patriarch: a residence worth 2.8 billion rubles is being built for the head of the Russian Orthodox Church near St. Petersburg', 21 May 2019: https://thebell.io/umnyj-dom-dlya-patriarha-dlya-glavy-rpts-stroyat-rezidentsiyu-stoimostyu-2-8-mlrd-rublej-pod-peterburgom

49. Remarks by head of the press service of the Patriarch of Moscow and All Russia Kirill Alexander Volkov, 21 May 2019: https://www.gazeta.ru/social/2019/05/21/12368533.shtml?updated

50. Press service of the Patriarch of Moscow and All Rus, 2 August 2020: http://www.patriarchia.ru/db/text/5672310.html

51. Geraldine Fagan, 'Moscow is braced for an Orthodox election shock', Forum 18, New Service, 24 January 2009.

52. Agence France Press, 29 January 2009.

53. Sophia Kishkovsky, 'Russian Orthodox Church Elects Outspoken Patriarch', *The New York Times*, 27 January 2009.

54. http://echo.msk.ru/programs/razvorot/567410-echo/

55. *Izvestia*, 23 January 2009: https://iz.ru/news/344739

56. Chapnin, *Journal of the Moscow Patriarchate*, issue 2, 2010, p. 48.

57. http://www.desertwisdom.org/dttw/links/dttw-zine01.pdf

58. *Digital Icons: Studies in Russian, Eurasian and Central European New Media*, No 14 (2015): 123–32.

59. Hanna Stahle, *Russian Church in the Digital Era – Mediatisation of Orthodoxy*, p. 77.

60. Father Dmitry Sverdlov's blog on *Pravmir* about his experience as an election observer: https://www.pravmir.ru/vybory-kak-eto-bylo-na-samom-dele-chast-2/

61. Translation by Carol Rumens, 20 August 2012: https://www.theguardian.com/books/2012/aug/20/pussy-riot-punk-prayer-lyrics

62. Maria Alyokhina, *Riot Days*, Penguin, 2017.

63. Radio Svoboda, 27 December 2013: https://www.svoboda.org/a/25214238.html

64. Geraldine Fagan, 16 November 2013: https://www.opendemocracy.net/en/odr/russias-spinning-moral-compass/

65. Archpriest Chaplin, 22 February 2012: https://pravoslav-pol.livejournal.com/8714.html?page=2

66. Tom Esslemont, BBC News, 11 August 2012:https://www.bbc.co.uk/news/world-europe-19207439

67. Levada Centre, The Pussy Riot Case, 31 July 2012: https://www.levada.ru/2012/07/31/rossiyane-o-dele-pussy-riot/

68. Simon Shuster, *TIME*, 2 August 2012: https://world.time.com/2012/08/02/russias-pussy-riot-trial-a-kangaroo-court-goes-on-a-witch-hunt/

69. Vladimir Legoyda, 'The reaction to Pussy Riot's prank is a test of the maturity of civil society', *Pravmir*, 7 March 2012: www.pravmir.ru/vladimir-legojda-reakciya-na-vyxodku-pussy-riot-eto-test-na-zrelost-grazhdanskogo-obshhestva/

70. 'Minister of Justice on Pussy Riot: as a "practising Christian" I am outraged, but they did not deserve prison', *Gazeta Ru*, 4 April 2012:https://www.gazeta.ru/politics/news/2012/04/04/n_2276125.shtml

71. V. Putin apologised to believers for the 'punk prayer' of Pussy Riot, 7 March 2012: https://www.rbc.ru/society/07/03/2012/5703f46f9a7947ac81a65a03

72. ExoMoskvy,8March2012:https://www.pravmir.ru/protodiakon-andrej-kuraev-situaciya-vokrug-gruppy-pussy-riot/

73. 'The Russian Orthodox Church is deceitfully "excusing" Patriarch Kirill', Glavnoe (Ukrainian website), 4 April 2012: https://glavnoe.in.ua/news/n98494

74. Courtney Weaver, 'UnOrthodox Behaviour Rattles Church', *FT*, 13 April 2012: https://www.ft.com/content/8da92478-8573-11e1-a75a-00144feab49a

75. Vladimir Solovyov, Shafran Anna, 'The Church has gone into dialogue with society' – reported by Vesti FM, 2 April 2012 https://webcitation.org/68in9wCZ-m?url=http://radiovesti.ru/articles/2012-04-02/fm/39919#

76. http://www.ogoniok.com/archive/2004/4831/04-20-23/

Chapter 11

1. Marina Bocharova, 'Closed Island', Takie Dela, 30 May 2017: https://takiedela.ru/2017/05/zakrytyi-ostrov/

2. 'Valaam's Billions', 7x7, 7 February 2017: https://semnasem.ru/valaam-mlrd/

3. 'Valaam Battle for the Cells', BBC News, 11 November 2015: https://www.bbc.com/russian/russia/2015/11/151111_valaam_residents

4. The Valaam Monastery explained the origin of the yacht allegedly donated by Putin, 12 July 2017: https://www.interfax.ru/russia/570325

5. https://www.rferl.org/a/russia-monk-oligarch-exclusive-frolov-timchenko/31557238.html

6. 26 April 2019 Instagram post from Acanthus Atelier: https://www.instagram.com/p/Bwt86L2n_0d/?utm_source=ig_embed&ig_rid=3be96309-68a0-4474-99c0-2f72eb0fde09

7. Anna Kuchma, 'Where does the Russian Orthodox Church get its money from?', Russia Beyond the Headlines, 9 March 2016: https://russialist.org/where-does-the-russian-orthodox-church-get-its-money-from/

8. Sergei Chapnin, *Financial Situation of the Russian Orthodox Church and Its Clergy*, George Fox University, 2020: https://digitalcommons.georgefox.edu/cgi/viewcontent.cgi?article=2219&context=ree

9. *Kommersant*businessnewspaper,25October2019:https://www.kommersant.ru/doc/4135504

10. 'Render Unto Caesar what Belongs to Caesar – How 43 Million Roubles of State Money Were Spent on Each Valaam Monk', 7x7, 20 October 2017: https://newizv.ru/news/2017-10-20/kesaryu-kesarevo-na-kazhdogo-valaamskogo-monaha-potracheno-43-mln-rubley-gosudarstvennyh-investitsiy-252741

11. Gleb Yarovoy, 'Valaam's billions', *Meduza*, 2017: https://meduza.io/feature/2017/02/10/valaamskie-milliardy

12. https://www.stalkerfest.org/programma/film/kray-zemli-ili-zhili-12-razboynikov

13. Higher School of Economics, Moscow: https://publications.hse.ru/articles/211425956
14. Report of His Holiness Patriarch Kirill at the Diocesan Assembly of Moscow, 22 December 2022: http://www.patriarchia.ru/db/text/5985883.html
15. Ibid.
16. *Vedemosti* based on research by M13, a media monitoring and cyber security company, 21 May 2019: https://www.vedomosti.ru/politics/articles/2019/05/21/802088-protiv-stroitelstva-hramov
17. Niklolay Mitrokhin and Aziza Nuritova, 'The Russian Orthodox Church in Contemporary Russia: Structural Problems and Contradictory Relations with the Government, 2000–2008', *Russia Today*, Vol. 76, No. 1 (Spring 2009), pp. 289–320.
18. 19 February 2020: https://interesnoe.me/view/content/upd/25694407
19. MBK, 24 April 2020: https://mbk-news.appspot.com/news/mozaika/
20. Sergei Chapnin, 'Armed Iconostasis', *Forbes*, 5 May 2020: https://www.forbes.ru/obshchestvo/399735-vooruzhennyy-ikonostas-kak-rpc-udivila-rossiyu-put inym-i-stalinym
21. Goodbye Weapons!: https://www.youtube.com/watch?v=q3r5zM3YnvE
22. Interview with author, October 2023.
23. https://obsheedelo.ru/
24. Evgeniya Volunkova 2023: https://takiedela.live/en/post/to-serve-is-to-struggle/
25. Sergei Chapnin, 'Financial Situation of the Russian Orthodox Church and Its Clergy', George Fox University, 2020: https://digitalcommons.georgefox.edu/cgi/viewcontent.cgi?article=2219&context=ree
26. JeanneKormina:https://www.academia.edu/5244322/Canonizing_Soviet_Pasts_in_Contemporary_Russia_The_Case_of_Saint_Matrona_of_Moscow
27. https://www.mk.ru/moscow/2015/05/27/nishhie-sobirayut-40-tysyach-rubley-v-den-blagodarya-matrone-moskovskoy.html
28. Andrei Kuraev, LiveJournal, February 2020: https://diak-kuraev.livejournal.com/2733414.html
29. The Manifesto of Father Roman Stepanov, 4 September 2021: https://www.youtube.com/watch?v=8tNzEUe305k
30. *Confession of a Priest* film by Sergei Erzhenkov, TV Rain, 15 October 2021: https://youtu.be/LwyezolOqIo

Chapter 12
1. *Pravmir*, 2 March 2016. https://www.pravmir.ru/nuzhno-zhenshhinu-lomat-ob-koleno-protoierey-andrey-tkachev-obyasnil-svoyu-skandalnuyu-rech/
2. Clifford Bob, *The Global Right Wing and the Clash of World Politics*, 17 May 2012.
3. https://readymag.website/algorithmsveta/algoritmsveta/
4. 'Why Was the Domestic Violence Law Not Passed', Verstka Media: https://verstka.media/pochemu-ne-prin
ili-zakon-o-domashnem-nasilii
5. Author interview, February 2024 – Sir Laurie Bristow was Moscow ambassador 2016–20.

6. 'The possibility that the Khachaturyan sisters might be acquitted worries the Orthodox Church', 22 February 2020: https://news.ru/society/vozmozhnost-opravdaniya-sestyor-hachaturyan-obespokoila-rpc/

7. 'The priests who support the sisters', *Pravmir*, 17 August 2020: https://www.pravmir.ru/czerkov-za-sester-svyashhenniki-aleksej-uminskij-i-pavel-ostrovskij-o-dele-hachaturyan/

8. Text exchange with author, February 2024.

9. Denis Maidanov, 'Sarmatushka': https://youtu.be/hB8oGY2_gVM

10. Ibid. https://verstka.media/pochemu-ne-priniali-zakon-o-domashnem-nasilii

11. Felix Light, 'A Feminist Pro-Kremlin Lawmaker Who Supports LGBT Rights,' *Moscow Times*, 21 December 2020.

12. https://fom.ru/Obraz-zhizni/14951Data source: FOMnibus – a weekly all-Russian door-to-door survey; 17–19 November 2023, 53 constituent entities of the Russian Federation, 104 settlements, 1,500 respondents: https://www.rbc.ru/politics/19/12/2023/658072299a794723bd030b4c

13. Andrei Gorbachev, Family Matters Abortions, January 2020: https://pravoslavie.ru/127534.html

14. RIA Novosti, 23 November 2023: https://ria.ru/20231123/abort-1911135078.html

15. Matthew Luxmoore, 'Inside the Immaculate World of Russian Orthodox Dating', 14 February 2019: https://www.rferl.org/a/inside-the-immaculate-world-of-russian-orthodox-dating/29770034.html

16. https://lenta.ru/news/2023/11/17/v-gosdume-predlozhili-osvobozhdat-zhenschin-za-klyuchennyh-v-obmen-na-rozhdenie-detey/

17. https://www.currenttime.tv/a/reproduktivnoe-davlenie-na-zhenshin-na-fone-voiny/32401803.html

18. Medical Portal of Penza Region, 31 July 2009: http://medpnz.ru/page.php?al=abort_evoljucionnaja_katastrofa_

19. https://www.themoscowtimes.com/2016/09/29/russias-abortion-debate-is-back-a55545

20. Archpriest Vsevolod Chaplin: The adoption of Russian children abroad most often means for them a falling away from the Church, 24 Dec 2012: https://klikovo.ru/news/12493.html

21. *Voprosy Kirika*, in Russkaja Istoricheskaya Biblioteka VI (St. Petersburg 1908), cited by Sister Vassa Larin, 15 July 2010: https://theinnerkingdom.wordpress.com/2010/07/15/on-ritual-impurity-by-nun-vassa-larin/

22. Nadia D. Zasanska, 'New Producers of Patriarchal Ideology: Matushki in Digital Media of Russian Orthodox Church', Ukrainian Catholic University, p. 18: https://www.essachess.com/index.php/jcs/article/view/466/491

23. https://www.labirint.ru/reviews/goods/594964/ Also see this report on Dozhd TV: https://youtu.be/SqcY4rVImlo?list=PLOmHLYf-nMJztoe5CN8ZM5-IK0jLt02-E

24. INDIKA – a short overview of the game and the political background around it, Russian video game news website, 4 May 2024: https://dtf.ru/games/2656096-indika-nebolshoi-obzor-igry-i-politicheskogo-fona-vokrug-nee

25. Katherine Kelaidis, *Holy Russia, Holy War*, SPCK, 2023, p. 77.

26. Ksenia Luchenko, 'Propaganda in Holy Orders: Africa, Ukraine and the Russian Orthodox Church', European Council on Foreign Relations, 20 September: https://ecfr.eu/article/propaganda-in-holy-orders-africa-ukraine-and-the-russian-orthodox-church/

27. A model of the grandiose Orthodox complex in Uganda will be presented at the Russia–Africa summit, *Komsomolskaya Pravda*, 23 July 2023: https://www.spb.kp.ru/daily/27534/4799542/

28. Address by His Holiness Patriarch Kirill at the 2nd Russia–Africa Summit, 27 July 2023: https://mospat.ru/en/news/90568/

29. Rictor Norton, *The Myth of the Modern Homosexual: Queer History and the Search for Cultural Unity*, London, 1997. p. 253.

30. Martin Duberman, Martha Vicinus, and George Chauncey, Jr. Duberman, Martin B. (editors), *Hidden from History: Reclaiming the Gay and Lesbian Past*.

31. Blue People in a State, *Guardian*, Lucy Ash, 15 December 1992

32. Shaun Walker, *Independent*, September 2008: https://www.independent.co.uk/arts-entertainment/music/features/tatu-from-russia-with-lust-943444.html

33. *Fontanka* Newspaper, 28 September 2012: https://www.fontanka.ru/2012/09/28/136/

34. Ben Steele, *Hunted*, Channel Four, 2014: https://www.steelefilms.net/watch-films/2017/5/12/hunted

35. Tsargrad TV, *Afisha* magazine, 14 July 2017: https://daily.afisha.ru/relationship/6105-chto-v-golove-u-veduschego-cargrad-tv-kotoryy-goto v-otpravlyat-geev-v-ssha/

36. Interview with author in Bremen, March 2022.

37. *Moskovsky Komsomolets*, 18 May 2017: https://www.mk.ru/social/2017/05/18/andrey-kuraev-raskryl-golubye-tayny-rpc-videozapisi-lyudey-pokhozhikh-na-episkopov.html

38. Author interview with Alexander Usatov, January 2023.

39. https://www.youtube.com/watch?v=9b_t6lo5uKU

40. Sergei Khazov Cassia, 16 December 2020: https://www.rferl.org/a/whats-behind-fsb-case-against-a-russian-orthodox-bishop/31004285.html

41. 22 March 2020: https://youtu.be/WoD6EFYSpq0

42. The video recording of the sermon was deleted from the YouTube but is still available at: https:// expertmus.livejournal.com/video/album/459/?-mode=view&id=15845

43. Ksenia Luchenko: https://carnegiemoscow.org/commentary/82036

44. 20 July 2020: https://www.bbc.com/russian/features-53250902

45. King James Bible Matthew 10 verses 34 to 39.

46. Tikhon Shevkunov complained to Putin about Serebrennikov before the searches at the Gogol Center, 15 November 2017: https://tvrain.tv/news/shevkunov_pozhalovalsja_putinu_na_serebrennikova-450327/

47. https://orthochristian.com/108470.html

48. *Moscow* Times, 21 January 2015: https://www.themoscowtimes.com/2015/01/21/russian-orthodox-church-says-leviathan-panders-to-western-prejudice-a43098

Chapter 13

1. 'Power play: How Russia missed its window to crash Ukraine's electrical grid by stealth', CBC News, 3 November 2022: https://www.cbc.ca/news/politics/russia-ukraine-kyiv-electricity-grid-1.6638410

2. Luke Harding, *Invasion: Russia's Bloody War and Ukraine's Fight for Survival*, Guardian Faber, November 2022.

3. Orthodox priests' petition calling for ceasefire the war, 6 March 2022: https://docs.google.com/forms/d/1yOGuXjdFQ1A3BQaEEQr744cwDzmSQ1qePaaBi4z6q3w/viewform ?edit_requested=true

4. Patriarch Kirill's address to the hierarchs, clergy, monastics, and faithful of the Russian Orthodox Church, 24 Feb 2022: http://www.patriarchia.ru/en/db/text/5903803.html

5. Patriarchal Message on 27 February 2022: http://www.patriarchia.ru/db/text/5904390.html

6. Patriarchal Sermon in the Cathedral of Christ the Saviour on 6 March 2022: http://www.patriarchia.ru/db/text/5906442.html

7. Luciano Fontana, *Corriere Della Sera*, 3 May 2022: https://www.corriere.it/cronache/22_maggio_03/pope-francis-putin-e713a1de-cad0-11ec-84d1-341c28840c78.shtml

8. Patriarchal Sermon at the Seraphim-Diveyevo monastery on 23 October 2022. Official website of the Moscow Patriarchate: http://www.patriarchia.ru/db/text/5970578.html

9. A Declaration of Orthodox Theologians on the "Russian World" (Russkii Mir) Teaching, March 2022: https://faithineurope.org.uk/wp-content/uploads/2022/03/220313-Volos-Academy-Declaration.pdf

10. Sister Vassa Larin, 'The Role of the ROC in the War Against Ukraine', first presented at the University of Exeter on 17 Jan 2024: https://www.youtube.com/watch?v=fw-04ps894A

11. 25 January: t.me/voennyotdel/3713

12. Karina Pronina, 'If a Priest Picked up a Weapon, It Doesn't Mean Anything', 10 September 2023: https://baikal-journal.ru/2023/09/10/esli-svyashhennik-vzyal-v-ruki-oruzhie-eto-ni-o-chyom-ne-govorit/

13. Dmitry Steshin, 'Faith and miracles on the front line: "Our battalion was named in honor of the saints - and there are no more heavy losses"', *Komsomolskaya Pravda*, 7 February 2023: https://www.kp.ru/daily/27462/4717455/

14. Ibid.

15. Valery Solovey, 'Shamanic ritual before a military operation: how magic influences the leadership of Russia', *Moscow Times*, 4 June 2022.

16. Conversation with author, October 2023.

17. Ksenia Luchenko, 'Sacrificing Art for War: The Handover of Russia's Trinity Icon Carnegie Endowment', 9 June 2023: https://carnegieendowment.org/politika/89928

18. Kherson Priest Shares Story of Captivity and Torture by Russian Forces, Ukrinform, 24 April 2022: https://www.ukrinform.net/rubric-ato/3465939-kherson-priest-shares-story-of-captivity-torture-by-russian-forces.html

19. 'From Oligarch to man of God. Vadym Novynsky, known as "Putin's Whip", has become a priest in Switzerland', *Le Matin de Dimanche*, 23 April 2023: https://www.tdg.ch/vadim-novinsky-dit-le-fouet-de-poutine-est-devenu-pretre-en-suisse-966941151850

20. Marayn Zablotsky, Facebook post, 9 November 2023: https://www.facebook.com/maryan.zablotskiy/posts/pfbid02wsXMUSBAQTDquSAUCqVHZy-sWSV9G2VQ3feyUiWfJHtobdYrpGvbL1KDKwtX5TDUcl

21. https://twitter.com/i/status/1777363785142964668

22. Roman Dobrokhotov, Michael Weiss, Christo Grozev, 'The far-right Bundestag aide and his rapping FSB case officer', 1 February 2024: https://theins.ru/en/politics/268805

23. Report by Oksana Radionova, TCN channel, 25 March 2024: https://www.youtube.com/watch?v=L0NHlHomSUc

24. Interview with author, 1 February 2024.

25. Tetyana Derkach, *Russia's Church in a Hybrid War Against Ukraine*, Cerkvarium, 2019.

26. Who Are You Shooter?, Zavtra, 20 November 2014: https://zavtra.ru/blogs/kto-tyi-strelok

27. Interview with Archpriest Vsevolod Chaplin, 11 October 2018: https://www.youtube.com/watch?v=ztTh-MAKWnA

28. The former mayor of Slavyansk told the court about the deployment of militants in the Svyatohirsk Lavra, Religion in Ukraine, 25 March 2016: https://tinyurl.com/4xpxxv3x

29. Bishops of the UOC reacted with irritation to the statement of the mayor of Slovyansk about the participation of local clergy in armed actions, Religion in Ukraine, 16 April 2014: https://www.religion.in.ua/news/ukrainian_news/25561-episkopy-upc-razdrazhenno-otreagirovali-na-zayavlenie-myera-slavyanska-ob-uchastii-v-vooruzhennyx-akciyax-mestnogo-duxovenstva.html

30. *Journal of the Moscow Patriarchate*, September 2022: http://www.e-vestnik.ru/files/12373/jmp_09_2022_v_gosti_k_patriahu.pdf

31. Project *With What Does the Fatherland Begin*: https://www.vnuki.info/nashi_proekty/

32. Serhii quoted by Kateryna Rashevska following author interview in March 2024.

33. 28 November 2022: https://vk.com/video-197866814_456239714

34. 21 February 2024: https://www.mir-vsem.info/post/navalny

35. Andre Tkachev, People Are Dying Like Pigs, Telegram Channel, 27 April 2023: https://www.youtube.com/watch?v=lr9L9FMRO80

36. 1 Corinthians 12

37. https://www.mir-vsem.info/en

38. Patriarch Kirill, *Lives of Remarkable People*, Young Guard publishing house, Moscow, 2019: https://gvardiya.ru/books/zhizn-zamechatelnyh-lyudey/patriarh-kirill

39. Statement by the head of the Theology faculty of Fribourg University, 8 March 2022: https://www.unifr.ch/theo/fr/actus/news/26815/declaration-publique-du-doyen-prof-mariano-delgado

40. Archbishop Elpidophorus quoted in Robert F. Worth, 'Clash of the Patriarchs', *The Atlantic*, 10 April 2024: https://www.theatlantic.com/magazine/archive/2024/05/russia-ukraine-orthodox-christian-church-bartholomew-kirill/677837/

41. Cyril Hovorun speaking to AP, 27 September 2022: https://apnews.com/article/russia-ukraine-putin-religion-moscow-0d2382ff296b7e253cd30c6bbadeed1d

42. Speech of Patriarch Kirill at the Extraordinary Congress of the World Russian People's Council, 27.03.2024. Official website of ROC-MP: http://www.patriarchia.ru/db/text/6116021.html

43. Serhii Shumylo, '"Ordinary Fascism," or The Russian World of Patriarch Kirill': https://www.wheeljournal.com/blog/2024/4/10/serhii-shumylo-ordinary-fascism-or-the-russian-world-of-patriarch-kirill

44. *Russia's Africa Crusade*, BBC World Service, January 2024: https://www.bbc.co.uk/programmes/w3ct4pkp

INDEX